AF291264

# NO UNCERTAIN SOUND

The Life and Times of

## Admiral Sir Jock Slater

Admiral Sir Jock Slater took HMS *Illustrious*' ship's motto
'Non Vox Incerta' as his own.

**1 Corinthians 14:8 For if the trumpet give uncertain sound,
who shall prepare himself for battle.**

# NO UNCERTAIN SOUND

The Life and Times of
## Admiral Sir Jock Slater

Foreword by
## HRH The Princess Royal

By
## Peter Hore

Whittles Publishing, an imprint of Porto Press
3 Connaught Road
St Albans AL3 5RX, UK

www.whittlespublishing.com




ISBN 9781849956130

# Contents

BUCKINGHAM PALACE

I know Jock as a Naval Officer, Equerry to Her late Majesty and friend, and I am delighted there is a book attempting to bring together his talent, commitment and service over longer than either of us might be prepared to admit.

He is a musician, a thinker and always an interesting and entertaining companion. His contribution to Her Majesty's Royal Navy, and every organisation he took an interest in, is hard to summarise. You could rely on him for an honest opinion and a challenging debate.

It has been a pleasure to keep in touch over his long and distinguished career and at social events since. I'm sure this book will reflect the respect and affection that I and many others have for him, and for me that included a lot of fun.

*Anne*

# Author's Preface

This is a history of the Royal Navy and of British defence policy at the end of the Cold War, seen through the prism of the career of Admiral Sir Jock Slater.

It is not an official history, has not benefitted from any official support, and I have had no privileged access to any sources. No classified papers have been accessed, only open sources. Indeed, many of the official papers written in the period under review are not yet available. Some requests, under time-consuming and cumbersome freedom of information legislation to the National Archives at Kew, have been refused after long waits.

Nor is it an authorised biography. Yes, Sir Jock has generously given me access to his diaries and other papers, to his scrapbooks and reflections on those scrapbooks. He has also patiently submitted himself to hours of fireside chats while I asked impertinent questions and recorded his answers. As necessary, I have also deferred to Jock for facts and especially dates, but he has had no editorial control over the inclusion or exclusion of events, and their narration. Their interpretation is mine and mine alone.

I have also drawn upon my own knowledge and experience of those events while I served for nearly four decades in the Navy and in the Ministry of Defence. After more than two decades as a freelance obituarist at the *Daily Telegraph* I am also able to draw upon my archive of memoirs, diaries, and other unpublished works of some 2,000 subjects whose lives have paralleled Jock's and whose careers help to tell the story of the Royal Navy in the Cold War.

Further, I have taken cross-bearings from more than one hundred actors in and eyewitnesses to the events described, including interviews with politicians, officers of the three services, and many civilians. It has been a sweet moment so to do, when papers have not yet reached – and might not ever reach – Kew but while memories are still alive and interviewees feel able to speak freely and to put their recollections into perspective. Everything is supported by emails and recordings and there are endnotes, a record of contributors, and a bibliography. Where contributors have spoken off the record or under Chatham House rules, these confidences have been respected. Quotations from Jock's papers are, I hope, obvious.

Every successful senior officer enjoys a two-for-one career. In the early years a young officer's tests and functions are practical ones concerning tactics and leadership, but, with increasing seniority, at some point between attending a staff course and the Royal College of Defence Studies, the skills needed become more political and strategic: 'platform' and 'business' skills, as the Officers Study Group inelegantly called these. So, in portraying Jock's career at the end of the Cold War and in the immediate post-Cold War period, it is inevitable that the narrative changes from the sequential to the thematic, though I have tried to keep it in chronological order. Jock served mainly at sea until midcareer before spending fourteen years as a flag officer, when he helped to shape the world we knew until the Russian invasion of Ukraine.

His thoughts are recorded here in extracts from the speeches he made, culminating in the 'Maritime Contribution to Joint Operations', which is reproduced in full. It is not my role to pass judgement, except to say that many things Jock said about the post-Cold War era were prescient.

It was LP Hartley who wrote that "the past is a foreign country; they do things differently there". As I researched and wrote about the life and times of Jock I became increasingly aware that this catchphrase applies to the Royal Navy too, a navy that has shrunk and changed since I wrote *Habit of Victory* in 2005 and edited *From Dreadnought to Daring* in 2013. Indeed, some features of the Navy in the late 20th century will be a mystery to the current generation and I hope that I have dwelt satisfactorily on and explained sufficiently how things used to be.

I am hugely grateful to Sir Jock and Lady Slater for their time and hospitality.

Also, my thanks go to the contributors who have trusted me with their confidences and who are listed in alphabetic order on the following pages. I apologise if I have omitted your name. No historian's or biographer's work is done without the skilled and enthusiastic support of archivists and librarians, and I am especially grateful to those at the Britannia Museum at Dartmouth, the British Library, the British Newspaper Archives, Churchill Archives Centre at Cambridge, Liddell Hart Centre for Military Archives at Kings College London, the National Museum of the Royal Navy in Portsmouth, and Navy List Research.

My warm thanks go to the home team, the anonymous subject experts who have kindly reviewed chapters, Peter Turner for his skilled copyediting, Rob Powell for many of the images, everyone at Whittles Publishing, Cath Harris at Words for Keeps, and Di Page at Porto Press.

Above all I wish to express my thanks to Penelope Small, who has tolerated my absences in mind and body.

All errors and omissions are mine.

PGH

# Acknowledgements

James Arbuthnot Lord Arbuthnot of Edrom, NJB Atkinson, the late Robert Avery, Adm Sir Jonathon Band, the late AF Sir Ben Bathurst, LtGen Sir Henry Beverley, VAdm Sir Jeremy Blackham, the late Admiral of the Fleet Lord Boyce, Dr E Buckley, Adm Sir James Burnell-Nugent, Capt B Burns, Julian Cazalet, RAdm RAG Clare, Capt CM Coates, Capt NCR Cooke-Priest, LtCdr IMP Coombes, Sir Robert Crawford, the late Capt AM Croxford, RAdm Sir Jeremy de Halpert, John Denholm, Brig RE Dillon, the late VAdm PA Dunt, Hon Capt JE Dykes, Cdr PM Egerton, Adm Sir Nigel Essenhigh, Dame Mary Fagan, Alistair Farley, RAdm PM Franklyn, Cdr SC Fraser, Brig A Freemantle, LtGen Sir Robert Fry, LtGen Sir Robert Fulton, LtCol GA Gelder, Cdre BAL Goldman, ACM Sir Michael Graydon, VAdm MP Gretton, the late FM Lord Guthrie, Capt EM Hackett, Lt WDA Hacking, VAdm Sir Paul Haddacks, Prof R Harding, Robert Hardman, Dr Jane Harrold, Capt JJ Hart, Capt D Hart-Dyke, Sir Max Hastings, Prof J Hattendorf, Cdre RC Hawkins, RAdm IR Henderson, RAdm RIT Hogg, LtCdr RJ Hoole, the Rt Hon Earl Howe, Cdr LSG Hulme, Cdr RD Hunter, Lady Susan Hussey, AM Sir Timothy Jenner, ACM Sir Richard Johns, VAdm Sir Adrian Johns, Adm JL Johnson USN, VAdm Sir Tony Johnstone-Burt, LtCdr CA Jones, Mrs Gillian Kerslake, Prof A Lambert, RAdm TM Karsten, Peter Keith Levene, Baron Levene of Portsoken, RAdm RJ Lippiett, RAdm RG Lockwood, RAdm TW Loughran, LtCdr D Lustig-Prean, Cdr M C Mackey, Alex J Marsh, LtCdr LE May, VAdm JHS McAnally, Capt AG McEwen, Cdre PJ Melson, Mrs JA Melson, Franklin Miller (hon KBE), Cdre J Miller, RAdm S Moore, Cdre AJC Morrow, Cdr PJ Mosse, Hon Cdre A Munns, VAdm Sir Roy Newman, Capt CLW Page, Sir Michael Pakenham, Sir John Parker, LtCdr ME Pearson, MajGen DAS Pennefather, Michael DX Portillo, Cdr JLL Prichard, Capt AGMA Provest,

Capt MJF Rawlinson, Brendan Reicheter, AB J Renshaw, Paul W Ridgway, Sir Malcolm Rifkind, RAdm AJ Rix, George Robertson Baron Robertson of Port Ellen, Prof NAM Rodger, Mrs F Rowlands, Cdr RD Sanderson, Mrs Allson Saunders, LtCol S Segrave, GpCapt Kathleen Sherit, Simon Sherrard, Gen Sir Richard Shirreff, RAdm DG Snelson, Nicholas Soames Baron Soames of Fletching, Hon Cdre AJD Somerville, Adm Sir Peter Spencer, Adm Sir Mark Stanhope, Cdr AP Sullivan, RAdm JG Tolhurst, RAdm JA Trewby, Prof G Till, Cdre PJ Tribe, Capt GM Tullis, Michael Vlasto, Cdr DA Wakefield, James Waller, the late Cdr ND MacCartan-Ward, Adm Lord West of Spithead, Cdre MW Westwood, Gen Sir Roger Wheeler, RAdm NJ Wilkinson, Hon Capt GASC Wilson, ACM Sir Andrew Wilson, Cdr DA Wines, Robert Woods, Capt Sir Nicholas Wright, Capt AJ Wright, and many others who are mentioned in the text.

# Abbreviations

ABM: anti-ballistic missile
ACDS: Assistant Chief of Defence Staff
AOSNI: Air Officer Scotland and Northern Ireland
BMD: ballistic missile defence or British Maritime Doctrine
BAOR: British Army of the Rhine
CAS: Chief of the Air Staff
CFS: Chief of Fleet Support
CGRM: Commandant General Royal Marines
CGS: Chief of the General Staff
Chiefs: collective name for CDS, CNS, CGS, CAS, and VCDS
CINCEASTLANT: Commander-in-Chief Eastern Atlantic Area
CINCHAN: Commander-in-Chief Allied Command Channel
CNS: Chief of the Naval Staff, also First Sea Lord
CNH: Commander-in-Chief, Naval Home Command
COMNORLANT: Commander Northern Sub Area North Atlantic
CORY: Commodore Royal Yachts
DMS: Defence Medical Services
DNOT: Director(ate) of Naval Operations and Trade
DNSD: Director(ate) of the Naval Staff Division
DNW: Director(ate) of Naval Warfare
FOCAS: Flag Officer Carriers and Amphibious Ships
FOF2: Flag Officer Second Flotilla
FORY: Flag Officer Royal Yachts
FOSNI: Flag Officer Scotland and Northern Ireland
FOST: Flag Officer Sea Training
FOTIs: Fleet Operational and Tactical Instructions

FXTIs: Fleet Exercise and Training Instructions
HCSC: Higher Command and Staff Course
HLG: High Level Group
ICBMs: Intercontinental ballistic missiles
JSF: Joint Strike Fighter
LSL: Landing Ship Logistics
MoD: Ministry of Defence
NMA: Naval Manpower Agency
OSG: Officers Study Group
PJHQ: Permanent Joint Head Quarters
PSA: Polaris Sales Agreement
RCDS: Royal College of Defence Studies
RFA: Royal Fleet Auxiliary
RFN: Russian Federation Navy
RNA: Royal Naval Association
RNR: Royal Naval Reserve
RUKUS: Russia UK US naval talks
SACEUR: Supreme Allied Commander, Europe
SACLANT: Supreme Allied Commander Atlantic
SDI: Strategic Defence Initiative
SDR: Strategic Defence Review
TLAM: Tomahawk land attack missiles

# Chapter 1: Uncle Ned

As the funeral cortege escorting the body of Admiral of the Fleet Andrew Browne Cunningham, 1st Viscount Cunningham of Hyndhope, slowly processed through Portsmouth, on Tuesday, 18 June 1963, few people would have recognised the young lieutenant who followed the gun carriage

In the entourage besides the First Lord of the Admiralty and four sea lords were more than a dozen admirals, including four admirals of the fleet. Rear-Admiral Royer Dick,[1] Cunningham's former Chief of Staff, and Captain Hugh Lee,[2] his flag lieutenant in the Mediterranean, bore Cunningham's insignia as the procession left the naval barracks and passed along Queen Street and through the main gate of Portsmouth dockyard, where it embarked in the destroyer HMS *Hampshire*. She would carry the body into the Channel, south of the Nab Tower, for burial at sea.

**ABC's Legacy**

Cunningham, known from his initials as 'ABC', had published his autobiography, written with the help of his friend and fellow destroyer officer Captain Taprell Dorling, in 1951.[3] Others had analysed Cunningham's career and Michael Simpson later edited Cunningham's papers for the Navy Records Society.[4] But it was John Winton who gave Cunningham the epithet of the greatest admiral since Nelson.[5] John Cunningham Kirkwood Slater, Cunningham's great nephew who became known as Sir Jock, was the young lieutenant in the procession and wrote in the foreword to Winton's book:

> There was a gale force wind, clouds raced across the sky and the sea was rough as I stood with members of my family and the Board of Admiralty on the flightdeck of HMS *Hampshire*. The ship was hove

to and we'd come to bury at sea one of Britain's most distinguished admirals, ABC to the Navy, Andrew to his friends, and Uncle Ned to his relations. As the Chaplain of the Fleet concluded the service, a bright shaft of sunlight illuminated the ship, and the coffin was committed to the deep. I stood there thinking about the great uncle who'd inspired me to join the Royal Navy and wondering about those qualities of leadership that he had so successfully brought to bear during a remarkable career in which he'd seen active service in the Boer War and two World Wars.

The funeral procession in 1963 of Admiral of the Fleet Viscount Cunningham of Hyndhope. From left to right, RAdm Royer Dick, Capt Hugh Lee, Cdr Gordon McKendrick, General Sir Alan Cunningham, Wing Commander By Bramwell, and Lieutenant JCK Slater. Source: Slater archive.

Jock was amazed to see how many people lined the route to bid farewell to their wartime leader. He thought, too, about the many happy weekends he had spent with the Cunninghams at their home, the Palace House in Bishops Waltham, Hampshire, during the last years of his great uncle's life. Postwar, ABC had mellowed, but he'd still had an air of purpose, and little escaped his penetrating eye, though his racy humour and a mischievous streak were not far below the surface. Those weekends had given Jock a unique opportunity to study and understand the character of a man who, from young cadet to First Sea Lord, had devoted his action-packed life to his country and had been single-minded in his determination to ensure that the Royal Navy played a key role in its future. ABC was the epitome of destroyer captains at a time when fine seamanship and iron discipline, dashing ship-handling, aggressive tactical manoeuvring and a fighting spirit inspired great confidence in the fleet. ABC was a man of uncanny foresight, exceptional stamina, supreme courage, and sometimes ruthless action. He was vigorous, decisive, and resolute in the face of adversity. In the dark days of the 1940s, no one could have been better placed to command the Mediterranean fleet: bringing all his experience and ability to bear, he could well have been described as an admiral of destiny.

ABC was born in 1883 in Dublin, to Scot DJ Cunningham (1850–1909), physician, zoologist, and anatomist, later professor of anatomy at Edinburgh university and author of *Cunningham's Anatomy*, which is still in print today. The professor died in Edinburgh aged 59, his obituary noting that "the world of science lost a distinguished ornament [who] many of us valued as a friend". The obituarist also recorded what was surely a family attribute: "Slip-shod work was foreign to his nature; thoroughness and efficiency were his ideals."[6] ABC was educated first at the Edinburgh Academy and then at a highly successful crammer, Stubbington House, known as the 'cradle of the Navy'.[7] Though he went into the Navy aged 15 and lost his Scottish accent, he always saw Scotland as his spiritual home and was very proud to be made one of the sixteen knights of the Order of Thistle in 1945.

Among ABC's contemporaries in HMS *Britannia*, moored on the Dart, were several future admirals, but he stood out as a man who was resolute in what he wanted to do. Very soon afterwards, while serving in the light cruiser HMS *Doris*, he had his first experience of war, ashore with the naval brigade during the Second Boer War.[8] In 1908, his first command was Motor Torpedo Boat no 8, and from 1911–18 he commanded the destroyer HMS *Scorpion* in the Mediterranean and at the Dardanelles, where he earned the first of his distinguished service orders. Later he earned another DSO while commanding the destroyer HMS *Termagant* in the Channel, and a third DSO in command of the destroyer HMS *Seafire* in the Baltic in 1920.

ABC drove his destroyers with enormous professional ability and was an inspiration to all who served with him. He would stand on the engaged side of the bridge, pacing up and down like a caged tiger and be highly critical of any officer who ducked when shells were being fired. He would say, "What on earth's the point of ducking? If the shells are close enough, you're going to be killed anyway." It was not surprising that he became Rear-Admiral Destroyers in the mid-1930s in the Mediterranean, a sea he had learned to know well.

On board HMS *Hampshire*, Jock noted the conspicuous absence from the funeral party of the Chief of the Defence Staff, Admiral of the Fleet the Earl Mountbatten of Burma. Perhaps it was not surprising: Uncle Ned had been very critical of Mountbatten, deploring the way he used his royal connections and, more, he had rated Mountbatten, when in command of HMS *Kelly*, a "poor destroyer captain".[9] Many years later Jock would be astonished to read in Andrew Robert's *Masters and Commanders* that, apparently, Mountbatten had been present with Churchill in 1943 when the question of the new First Sea Lord was discussed after Sir Dudley Pound died. Jock wrote: "I think if Uncle Ned had known that he would have had a cardiac arrest!"[10]

## Palace House, Bishops Waltham

In 1936, when ABC returned from the Mediterranean having been told he would be on half pay (that there was no prospect of another job) for two years, the Cunninghams stayed in a hotel in Botley while looking for a house. Money was tight after they found the Palace House in Bishops Waltham, but they never regretted taking a long lease. Being on half pay was very depressing, though, for a man who was devoted to a life of action in the Royal Navy.

The impending Second World War rescued ABC from oblivion: in 1937 he was appointed as Vice-Admiral Commanding Battle Cruiser Squadron & Second-in-Command Mediterranean, flying his flag in the battlecruiser HMS *Hood*, and briefly he was Deputy Chief of the Naval Staff in the Admiralty 1938–39. The latter appointment was long enough for him to learn that he was not good in the cut and thrust of Whitehall battles and that paperwork drove him mad. Then, on 1 June 1939, he hoisted his flag in Malta as an acting admiral and Commander-in-Chief Mediterranean. There, he won victories at Matapan and Taranto over the Italian fleet and, after severe ship losses during the evacuation of Crete, he famously told fellow commanders-in-chief of the Army and Air Force: "It takes the Navy three years to build a ship. It will take three hundred years to build a new tradition. The evacuation will continue."[11]

Later, when the health of Admiral of the Fleet Sir Dudley Pound, the First Sea Lord, failed in 1943, Prime Minister Winston Churchill wanted Admiral Bruce Fraser as the new First Sea Lord, but the Navy made it clear that there was only one man at that stage who they wanted to be their leader, and that was ABC. Summoned back to London, the Cunninghams took Palace House back but spent weekdays living in a bedsit with Vice-Admiral Frederick

Dalrymple-Hamilton. When Churchill learned this, he insisted that rooms in Mall House, which had once been occupied by Lord 'Jacky' Fisher, should be made available. Thus, the Mall House flat became the residence for ABC and of subsequent First Sea Lords.

In Hampshire, the Allied naval commander Admiral Bertram Ramsay was living at Southwick House, where US General of the Army 'Ike' Eisenhower, Supreme Commander of the Allied Expeditionary Force, had his headquarters. This was some six miles from Palace House, whither the Cunninghams escaped at weekends. In the run-up to Operation Neptune, the Normandy landings, Ramsay and his Chief of Staff, Rear-Admiral George Creasey, spent Sundays at Palace House dining with Cunningham, who, on the night before the landings, went to Southwick House.

Despite an uneasy relationship with Churchill, ABC's offensive spirit and willingness to take risks appealed to the Prime Minister. He had a shrewd, perceptive, pragmatic intellect and his formidable reputation as a bluff, straightforward, highly accomplished fighting admiral carried him through and ensured that he wielded great influence on the direction of the war. Postwar there was a large reduction in the defence budget, which caused ABC to remark: "We very soon came to realise how much easier it was to make war than to reorganise for peace."[12]

## At Home with ABC

ABC retired in 1946, after which he attended the House of Lords irregularly, and busied himself with various appointments, including two years as Lord High Commissioner to the General Assembly of the Church of Scotland. Jock's memories of his Uncle Ned reveal a side of the character and life of the great man not told elsewhere:

> Uncle Ned and Aunt Nona as I knew them, I got to know initially in 1948 when I was taken as a 10-year-old by my uncle's elder brother John Cunningham,[13] who was a retired Indian medical service man, to visit Uncle Ned and Aunt Nona at the Palace House and his other brother General Sir Alan Cunningham,[14] who had defeated the Italians in East Africa in 1941.
>
> I remember it vividly because as a boy I knew him as the hero of Matapan and the Battle of Taranto, and what an amazing man this was. I was rather frightened of him to tell the truth but had a wonderful time because he clearly liked young people and took an enormous interest.

We played racing demon, which he was very good at providing he didn't lose. He loved playing croquet. He didn't play what I would call real croquet. He played golf croquet, and it was another game where he was extremely good at, but if a young nephew, particularly a 10-year-old nephew, played a good shot, it had to be beaten by his next shot. Otherwise, he would not be at all happy, but it was great fun … My Aunt Nona was devoted to him. As I say, they were married late. She was very presentable. She was a very shy person, and he of course was a very dominant character, but they were clearly devoted to each other, and life in that house was extremely happy … he derived enormous boyish pleasure out of simple pranks, [such as] flicking butterballs from one end of the table to the other with my aunt catching them with a side plate … Another thing he loved doing was talking backwards and you weren't really allowed to talk at breakfast unless you could talk backwards. So, marmalade was, 'edalamram', and sugar was 'ragus' … He loved pulling people's legs. Sometimes people found him impossible because he didn't realize they might be embarrassed by something or other, but he would just force on in his wonderfully destroyer-like way, but that was life at Bishops Waltham when I spent many happy weekends there.

ABC kept in touch with the Navy, not least through Jock and his burgeoning career. However intimidating his uncle could be, Jock "loved him, because I think he liked junior officers, having no son of his own, and we had great, great chats".

Jock's ship, HMS *Cassandra*, was in home waters in 1963, and not long after returning to Portsmouth in May he stayed the weekend with the Cunninghams. Uncle Ned, who had just turned 80 at the beginning of the year, "was in cracking form and longed to hear about what was going on in the Navy". A few days later, on 12 June 1963, ABC died of a heart attack in a taxi between the House of Lords and Waterloo Station. Jock went immediately to Bishops Waltham to help. Aunt Nona was remarkably calm, but worriedly she told him that Uncle Ned had that morning been to Spink's to collect his collar of the Order of the Thistle, and that this was missing. Jock rang the Metropolitan Police to enquire if they had any information, and amazingly the duty officer told him that a taxi driver had just rung in to say that in cleaning out his vehicle that evening he had found the leather box containing the collar in the back of his cab.

**A Return Alongside**

When HMS *Hampshire* returned to Portsmouth that Tuesday afternoon in 1963, after the committal, the weather had deteriorated so much that it was deemed too windy to come alongside, so her guests were taken off by a broad-beamed, paddle-driven tug in Spithead. As they entered harbour, Jock and all those present knew that they had paid homage to one of Britain's greatest fighting sailors, who had given a lifetime of sterling service to his country in the Royal Navy, which he had so loved.

# Chapter 2: The Young Jock

JCK Slater, always called 'Jock', was born in Edinburgh on 27 March 1938 into a medical family. His father, Dr James Kirkwood Slater, was a neurologist, and his mother, Margaret Claire Byrom Bramwell, known as 'Billie', was the daughter of another neurologist. Jock was the middle son of three talented brothers: his older brother, Tony, would become a general practitioner, and his younger brother, Peter, became Professor of Natural History at the University of St Andrews. His father was largely absent from home during the Second World War because he was in the Royal Army Medical Corps; the boys were brought up by Billie and by their maternal grandmother.

**Edinburgh Academy and Sedbergh School**

Billie's mother was the sister of Andrew Cunningham, the admiral known as Uncle Ned to the family. In 1942, young Jock, in the footsteps of Uncle Ned, went to the Edinburgh Academy. When Uncle Ned, now the First Sea Lord, visited Edinburgh for the VE-Day celebrations in the summer of 1945, he took Jock in his Austin Princess, driven by a naval rating, to watch the fireworks over Edinburgh Castle. Jock recalled: "I suspect that that was when I first became convinced that the Royal Navy was for me – and never changed my mind!" Jock was not close to his father and never had any serious conversation with him: "I never seemed to be able to please him. That said, I must have been a very difficult middle son and pretty bolshie! I often escaped to Granny, who always seemed to be much more encouraging. Perhaps that is why father seemed to resent the Cunningham influence."

In 1950 Jock passed the common entrance exam for Sedbergh, a boarding school, then in North Yorkshire. The headmaster and Jock's housemaster was

JH 'Rufie' Bruce-Lockhart, a Scottish international cricketer and rugby player, and a frightening man who favoured games players. Jock had a treble voice and developed a penchant for music. He loved escaping school to walk the fells, played squash and fives, but hated cricket; Rufie and Jock's father wanted him to play rugby. On his arrival Jock was asked to play the flute and agreed without knowing what it was; on reflection he would have much preferred the oboe or bassoon. There was muted praise when Jock was chosen to join the National Youth Orchestra of Great Britain in 1955, and that August he attended a fortnight's course and played in two concerts, at Watford and a prom at the Royal Albert Hall under the baton of Sir Adrian Boult. Jock also became head of his house.

The Sedbergh years were marked by a "prolonged and titanic struggle" between Jock and his father, who was concerned that "if the boy joins the Navy he will merely become a golf club secretary by the age of forty". There was some anti-Cunningham sentiment in his father's attitude, and Jock was prevented from going to Dartmouth in the sixteen-year-old entry. Despite his father's opposition ("There will be NO Royal Navy for that boy in two years' time!"), Jock, having been told that if he joined the Royal Navy Volunteer Reserves he would have a much better chance of passing the Admiralty Interview Board (AIB), joined the Reserves in Edinburgh at HMS *Claverhouse*, where he was rated as Boy Seaman. His first experience of the Royal Navy proper was a fortnight's training in the light fleet carrier HMS *Ocean* at a buoy in Portland Harbour. He was taught to sail in Orkney by Dr Derrick Johnstone.[15]

## Dartmouth

In 1956 Jock sat the Civil Service Commissioners exam and was called to the Admiralty Interview Board (AIB) at HMS *Siskin*, now part of the shore establishment HMS *Sultan* at Gosport, Hampshire. On the evening before the AIB, Jock stayed at Palace House, and Uncle Ned drove him to Gosport, dropping him off some distance from the entrance. ABC's advice was: "Be yourself and wear your kilt." The interview took place over a couple of days and followed the well-tried pattern of tests and practical leadership tasks. On 17 May 1956 Jock heard that he had passed for so-called 'special entry' of eighteen-year-olds, and even had the surprise of a congratulatory telegram from his father. A month later, after a medical in London, he received joining instructions from Dartmouth, and a japanned steel trunk from Gieves, the well-known naval tailors, containing his first uniforms, including a blazer, flannels, and a brown trilby hat. Secretly he tried everything on: "It all seemed to fit

On the ramps outside the Captain's House at Dartmouth, Jock's parents admire the Queen's sword which he was awarded as best all-round student. Slater archive.

although I was surprised the black shoes had no toe cap. Little did I appreciate that it would not be long before the toes would shine with spit and polish!"

Jock joined the Britannia Royal Naval College (BRNC) under the Committee on Officer Structure and Training (COST) scheme in a small term of 30 boys. They thought they were grown-up, while the BRNC staff, who were used to younger boys, imposed a rigorous regime and tried to dampen their aspirations. Their enthusiasm was further dented when the captain, Captain W James Munn, who had served under ABC in the Mediterranean, told them in their first week that the COST scheme had already been judged a failure.[16] However, the seven terms spent at Dartmouth and at sea in the training squadron were happy days and an admirable preparation for joining the fleet. During sea time in HMS *Roebuck*, Jock was so impressed by the cerebral Lieutenant Richard Hill's precise, meticulous, and confident ship-handling that he was inspired to become a navigator too.[17]

The captain of BRNC in Jock's final term in 1958 was Frank Hopkins.[18] Dartmouth was a success for Jock, who was appointed senior midshipman on 27 July 1958. He celebrated by signing his name on the ceiling of the gunroom.[19]

The Senior Midshipman, Dartmouth, Jock Slater contemplates his future, Winter 1958. Slater archive.

He enjoyed his first brush with royalty when Prince Philip presented a new Queen's Colour to BRNC. Then, at the December passing out parade, Acting Sub-Lieutenant Slater was awarded the Queen's Sword as the best all-round student, and a Queen's Telescope for the highest marks in exams. His parents came south for the parade, although:

> The night before, the captain invited them for a drink in his house but, much to my and Mother's embarrassment, Father refused. Indeed, he left for London as soon after the Ceremony as he could. To give him his due, he gave a generous drinks party in a private room in the Savoy Hotel a day or two later for my closest term-mates and their girlfriends before our passing out dance at the Mayfair Hotel. It was just all too sad that Father was so unenthusiastic about my chosen career and never, of course, lived to see if it flourished.

## HMS *Troubridge*

Jock's first ship, in the West Indies, was HMS *Troubridge* which in turn was the model for the radio comedy the Navy Lark featuring HMS *Troutbridge*.
Source: Wikicommons.

Jock was appointed to HMS *Troubridge*, a Second World War destroyer that had been converted into a fast anti-submarine frigate, and joined her in early January 1959 when she was lying forlorn, deep in maintenance in Portsmouth dockyard. Soon, a new ship's company was gathered, in late February she was recommissioned, and, after a work-up at Portland, she sailed for a year in the West Indies. The cast of a new BBC radio comedy called 'The Navy Lark' visited *Troubridge* and subsequently the name HMS *Troutbridge* was chosen for its fictional warship. "Judging by the hilarious end result, we gave quite the wrong impression and many of my friends at the time used to pull my leg about it!"[20]

Jock was in Edinburgh for his 21st birthday, when Granny gave him a baby statuette of Nelson, telling him, "If you keep this carefully, one day you will become First Sea Lord." He kept it on the chain that once held his father's half-hunter watch.

*Troubridge* crossed the Atlantic to become the West Indies' guardship. Showing the flag was *Troubridge*'s main role, "which meant lunch parties, dinner parties, drinks parties *ad nauseam* – activities which we became pretty good at. On the other side of the coin, we were not very effective as a fighting unit, and it was just as well we were not put to the test." From her base in Bermuda with the Senior Naval Officer West Indies embarked, *Troubridge* saluted Diamond Rock and visited the islands between British

The Nelson charm given to JCKS by his grandmother in 1959.
Source: Rob Powell.

Guiana and Saint Petersburg in Florida, Curaçao, Jamaica, and South Carolina. In the New Year of 1960 *Troubridge* was escort to Princess Mary, the Princess Royal, who was embarked in HMY *Britannia* for a two-month tour of the Caribbean. Jock also had his first experience of impromptu public speaking at the Rotary Club in Charleston, when, as the junior officer at lunch and expecting to sit at the bottom of the table, the chairman invited him to address the diners on his early life in the Royal Navy – "a baptism by fire – at least I had no time to worry about it!"

Summing up his year in *Troubridge* Jock wrote that "It was a very good overall experience although it could hardly be called stimulating professionally; that said, I learnt much of great value for the future, not least how best to handle sailors and get the best out of them."

While still in *Troubridge*, Jock was nominated for flying training. It was "the last thing that I wanted to do and I moved heaven and earth to have my name removed from the list … I even said that if I was sent for initial flying training, that I would retire North of Hadrian's Wall and not return … [However,] the dreaded medical appointment with a surgeon captain was unexpectedly remarkable: before I had even dropped my pants, he said to me 'You don't want to fly, do you?' When I said, 'No, sir', he merely replied, 'You have failed the Medical' and dismissed me."

## HMS *Yaxham*

The ex-inshore minesweeper turned trials ship, M3780, HMS *Yaxham*.
Source: Dudley Woolnough.

Instead, Jock was appointed in June 1960 as first lieutenant of HMS *Yaxham*, one of a class of nearly 100 inshore minesweepers (IMS). The Navy of the 1960s included plenty of minor war vessels in which young men could cut their teeth.[21] *Yaxham*, now a trials ship, was an archetypal junior officer's command, and her captain was the characterful Scot, Ronnie Laughton.[22] The wardroom where her two officers ate, worked, and slept was tiny, and after a week, once Laughton was confident of Jock, he would invite him to take *Yaxham* to sea and pick him up by dinghy off Ringstead in Dorset, where he had a cottage, for the day's trials and drop him off in the evening on return to Portland Harbour. There was "a healthy competitive spirit with other ships engaged in trials. I remember especially HMS *Squirrel*, another IMS, whose first lieutenant was Nick Barker,[23] and an extraordinary old ship HMS *Gossamer* … whose first lieutenant was James de Saumarez.[24] We got on very well and used to enjoy great runs ashore in Weymouth and beyond."

Jock's nine months in *Yaxham* were a character-forming experience and an excellent way to advance his seamanship, not least in the rough seas of the English Channel in midwinter.

# Chapter 3: Season Officer, 1961

Sir Jock would come to know Her Majesty's Yacht *Britannia* almost as well as anyone outside the royal family. As a teenager, he and his brother, on 16 April 1953, from high in the grandstand at John Brown's yard on the Clyde, had seen her launched by a young Queen Elizabeth II. The ship's name had been kept secret and such was the roar of the crowd that it drowned out the Queen's words. Only by mouth to mouth through the throng did the Slater brothers learn that she was called *Britannia*. The schoolboy Jock could not have known that the future of *Britannia* would be a challenge for him as First Sea Lord and come to undermine his happy relationship with the royal family.[25]

Early in 1961 the aristocratic Vice-Admiral Peter Dawnay,[26] the Flag Officer Royal Yachts (FORY), interviewed three officers with a view to appointing one of them as 'season officer' in *Britannia*. Jock never found out who the other two were but in early March 1961 he joined *Britannia* at her moorings off Whale Island as the second navigating officer and as Dawnay's flag lieutenant. The happy and close-knit wardroom was led by Commander David Roome.[27] One of Jock's fellow officers recalled that "The Royal Yacht was a superb ship with a great spirit. There was a core number of permanent sailors known as royal yachtsmen, and once a year a new lot arrived who were known as Ocean Complement and stayed one or two years … The Royal Yacht was a wonderful hotbed of excellence for all … and one of the officers who joined was a certain Lieutenant JCK Slater, who was the assistant navigator, and I think most of the time he did it all!"

## Postwar Thrift

Among *Britannia*'s officers was Lieutenant Bill Pardy,[28] the keeper and steward of the Royal Apartments, who had served in the previous royal yacht, *Victoria and Albert*, which had served the monarchy from 1901 to the fleet review of 1937. She became an accommodation ship in Portsmouth during the Second World War and was broken up in 1954.[29] A replacement was ordered by the postwar Labour government led by Clement Atlee, prompting *The Times* to tell its readers, "It was a reproach that … the monarch of the worldwide maritime empire of the British Commonwealth – born of sea power – should not be provided with the means of going afloat in state … there will be a means with which nobody could find fault on the score of waste or undue extravagance."

The Navy, explained *The Times*, needed a second hospital ship in wartime but not in peace, and that "the proposed vessel would be fitted and used as the royal yacht in peacetime but can be rapidly and easily fitted out as an up to date and efficient hospital ship in the event of war".[30] Later, an even more imaginative wartime use of *Britannia* would be mooted: a mobile shelter for the monarch in the event of a nuclear war.[31] Others knew better: *Britannia* would be another royal residence, a holiday home on the Queen's tours of the Western Islands, and a place of sanctuary during official visits abroad. As Warrant Officer 'Norrie' Norrell, who served in *Britannia* for more than three decades, told a newspaper: "It was the Queen's home. Wherever she went in the world, she could come back at night to her own staff. It was somewhere where she could kick her shoes off and relax."[32]

## Musical Debut

Auspiciously for Jock, *Britannia* sailed from Portsmouth for trials on his 23rd birthday, and then steamed out to the Mediterranean with the Queen Mother embarked for her visit to Tunisia. At sea, it was customary to invite one or two officers to 'dine aft' with the royal family, and on his first occasion Jock was relieved to find himself seated at the far end of the table. However, after dinner, Queen Elizabeth's Private Secretary, Martin Gilliat,[33] told him that the Queen Mother would like him to sit beside her on the sofa by the fireplace. Beckoned to sit down, after a few words, she said, "I gather that you were a member of the National Youth Orchestra." She was the patron.

> When I said I played the flute but was there for only for a very short time, she looked at me with her piercing eyes and said, 'We thought that it would be rather nice if you entertained us this evening.' I nearly

had a cardiac arrest and immediately said that I really did not think that I was in practice and, anyway, I needed an accompanist. She smiled in her charming way and said: 'Oh that's not a problem; Ruth plays a little.' Ruth was Lady Ruth Fermoy, her lady-in-waiting and Princess Diana of Wales's grandmother, who was in fact a concert pianist! So, I was dispatched to my cabin to get my flute, while Sir Bernard Ferguson, a guest for the trip, played the piano and sang a few songs. On my return with the music of a sonata by Alessandro Marcello, Ruth looked at it and without hesitation agreed to sight-read the piano accompaniment, which she did brilliantly. It was certainly a baptism by fire for my first of many royal encounters.

## Greek Interlude

After Tunisia, *Britannia* carried HM the Queen and Prince Philip on a state visit to Italy, and to Venice where they disembarked after a so-called private visit. Next the Duke and Duchess of Gloucester toured Commonwealth War Graves in the Eastern Mediterranean, enabling Jock to visit Mount Athos and Gallipoli. "The Australian Alan Moorehead's acclaimed 1956 book, *Gallipoli*, brought our walk ashore vividly to life. It was quite extraordinary still to see remnants of military equipment strewn about and to appreciate the remarkably short distances between the opposing forces. Looking to seaward, I thought of Uncle Ned, commanding HMS *Scorpion* throughout the campaign and how close those small ships came to the shoreline and how lucky he was to survive unscathed." The Gloucesters were joined in Heraklion, Rhodes by the Greek royal family in their yacht *Polymestis*, and the two yachts sailed in company to Suda Bay, Crete. At dinner, Jock sat next to Princess Sophia, who would become Queen of Spain.

Other royal duties took Jock to Ascot, a garden party at Buckingham Palace, dinner at the Mansion House, and to Cowes Week. On a tour of the Western Isles, picnics and expeditions were the order of the day and the junior officers in *Britannia* were kept busy. One evening they had to put on a concert party, known in the Navy as a 'sods opera',[34] which was something of a challenge for the season officers and very much a royal command performance. Jock was persuaded to impersonate his admiral, Dawnay, while singing a bowdlerised version of 'I Am the Very Model of a Modern Major General' from *The Pirates of Penzance*, with new words appropriate to his admiral. He did not think it was a good impersonation, though it seemed to go down well, but

Dawnay took his revenge. When Jock went to turn in that night he found that Dawnay's personal steward, Plato, had packed his bags and placed them at the head of the accommodation ladder. Despite Dawnay's heavy joke, Jock was still in the yacht for the royal visits to Ghana, Liberia, Sierra Leone, the Gambia, and Senegal. The Queen disembarked in Dakar and before she left she received each of the season officers in her study to present them with a signed photograph: that same day she knighted Peter Dawnay, who was in his last few weeks in command.

## Fore!

So ended a happy year away from the front line, which Jock thought was about enough, and he was delighted to be appointed as navigating officer in the destroyer HMS *Cassandra* in the Far East. This entailed a short navigation course at HMS *Dryad* and Command Team Training in early 1962, which included a visit to Portland. Jock would not forget a game of golf one weekend at Came Down, Dorset. He drove the ball off the first tee but to his horror it went much further than expected and hit another player. After rushing down the fairway to apologise he found the man unhurt but clearly incensed: "He asked me my name and then if I was in the Navy. And then asked me what ship. When I said *Cassandra*, he growled at me and said, 'That's bad luck – I am your Captain D!'" Jock's victim was Captain HA Corbett DSO, who he would see in the Far East and who would cause Jock to comment that it was a pity that he had not hit him harder!

# Chapter 4: The Navigator

The next decade of Jock's career, apart from some months on courses at Greenwich and while he was learning to become a navigational specialist, was spent at sea in ships ranging from minesweepers to aircraft carriers.

**HMS *Cassandra***

HMS *Cassandra* refueling at sea in the Far East.
Source: Wikicommons.

HMS *Cassandra* was a Ca-class destroyer, one of the first of four flotillas, each of eight ships built in wartime. Inside her 2,000 tons she somehow crammed a ship's company of nearly 200 men. Intended for operations in the North

Atlantic and Arctic oceans, after minor modernisation in the late 1950s and early 1960s, one flotilla, the 8th Destroyer Squadron, deployed to the Far East. In March 1962, Jock was officer in charge of the passengers, including some of her new crew, on a four-day trooping flight in a four-prop Britannia of British United Airways to the Far East. During a stopover in Bombay there was time for Jock to call up Hugh Byatt, nephew of Aunt Nona, who was serving at the time in the High Commission in Delhi.[35]

*Cassandra* recommissioned in Singapore on 2 April 1962. She had no air conditioning between decks and in harbour many sailors slept on the upper deck. The charthouse was air-conditioned to keep the paper charts crisp, and as navigating officer Jock slept there on an inflatable bed, much to the disappointment of the navigator's yeoman, Able Seaman Cliff Longfoot, who naturally regarded it as his privilege. Many years later, Longfoot, as chairman of the Eighth Destroyer Association, would invite Jock to become patron.

Jock was new to local waters and arranged to have time with the 104th Mine Countermeasures (MCM) Squadron to familiarise himself with the long passage out from the naval base into the South China Sea. The squadron was led by Commander William Staveley, in HMS *Houghton*, who, "ran a very taut and sharp ship and even in those days was known as 'Golden Balls'! No wonder he eventually became First Sea Lord.[36] His squadron navigator was Lieutenant Commander Jim Weatherall, who later became my course officer when I qualified as a navigator."[37]

On 24 May *Cassandra* was on her first nighttime anti-submarine exercise with a new and inexperienced ship's company. The officer of the watch on the bridge, Lieutenant Mike Adams, was supported by a safety officer, the first lieutenant, Lieutenant Commander Tom Heard. Jock was in the operations room with his captain, Commander Mike Walkey,[38] when *Cassandra* collided with her sister ship *Caprice*. Jock remembered *Cassandra* shaking violently as she went full astern, then the order "Port thirty" before she heeled over to starboard. The steam safety valves then blew "with an unforgettable noise followed by absolute silence as we all gathered our thoughts". *Cassandra* had crumpled her bows on *Caprice*'s starboard quarter. Mercifully no one was hurt but there followed a depressing six weeks under repair, a board of enquiry and the inevitable courts martial at which Jock was a witness: Walkey and Adams were reprimanded but, harshly in Jock's opinion, Heard was dismissed from the ship. Walkey never really got over the shock and became very unsure of himself, but *Cassandra*'s new first lieutenant, Lieutenant Commander Bob Gerken "soon got the ship going with an excellent spirit and thereafter we had a very busy year". [39]

After a visit to Sydney, Jock navigated *Cassandra* through the Great Barrier Reef from south to north, and on his first visit to Hong Kong fitted her into the little basin of the naval base, HMS *Tamar*. There, too, he had his first experience of Susie's side party, the Chinese girls who came on board to chip and paint the side in exchange for the ship's gash, or garbage, and who dressed in traditional costume to serve cheerfully at cocktail parties. Christmas 1962 was intended to be in Singapore, but when the British Resident in Malé reported unrest in the Maldives and requested a guardship, *Cassandra* anchored instead off the island of Dunidu over Christmas. Having navigated westwards halfway across the Indian Ocean, Jock was amazed when *Cassandra* was ordered home eastabout, across the Pacific and through the Panama Canal. During the commission she would steam 53,807 miles and visit 25 ports on five continents.

Jock took a full part in the ship's wider life, organising sports day, the squadron ball, a sods opera, and other musical concerts. He also edited a book of the ship's commission, even persuading William Connor, the diarist of the *Daily Mirror* who wrote under the pen name of 'Cassandra', to offer £200 to cover the cost. The commission ended in late 1963 when a new ship's company marched down to South Railway Jetty, Portsmouth to take over *Cassandra*, and the previous ship's company departed with many happy memories of a remarkable commission led by a wardroom that had clicked so well. Besides Bob Gerken, Jock had also become long-term friends with the ship's doctor, Surgeon Lieutenant Tony Revell.[40]

## Intermezzo

The first term of 1964 was spent on the lieutenants' course at the Royal Naval College, Greenwich. The officers lived in Sir Christopher Wren's Palace and ate in Sir James Thornhill's Painted Hall, a culture shock for many after several years at sea. Jock enjoyed learning more about the Navy and defence: the most memorable lecture of the course was delivered by young debonair Captain John Treacher, Naval Assistant to the Controller of the Navy, who delivered a brilliant address without notes.[41] Jock was surprised to receive an award of two year's subscription to *The Naval Review*, for a paper on the role of the Navy, one of the standard subjects suggested to students; unfortunately, Jock's youthful view has been lost to history.

Formally, *The Naval Review* was the quarterly journal of the Naval Society, founded just before the First World War by a group of 'Young Turks'. Its Fisherite strapline was 'Think wisely, plan boldly, act swiftly'. Its purpose was to enable officers to correspond between themselves on professional matters outside the normal hierarchy. From the beginning there was disapproval of the review. This was led during the First World War by Admiral Sir John Jellicoe, who persuaded the Admiralty to order *The Naval Review* to stop publication. However, the then editor continued to collect contributions and at war's end he published the *Review*, year by year, as it would have appeared if there had been no Admiralty embargo, and since 1919 the *Review* has been published quarterly without a break. Jock would remain a member of the Society throughout his career. His Seaford House paper, written when he was a student at the Royal College of Defence Studies (RCDS), was printed in *The Naval Review*, as was his message to the fleet after the 1998 Strategic Defence Review (SDR). He also found himself invited to lend his prestige to publications by writing forewords to books and reviews, the first of these being Bill Hewison's 1985 book on Scapa Flow, *This Great Harbour: Scapa Flow*.

After Greenwich, Jock enjoyed a break at the Outward Bound School at Burghead, Morayshire as a temporary instructor. His students were a dozen boys ranging from a Carthusian to an ex-Borstal boy; he found that "when the chips were down, the latter was far the best!" He particularly enjoyed a short cruise around the North of Scotland in the three-masted *Prince Louis*, which was skippered by Victor Clark, a retired lieutenant commander who had survived the sinking of HMS *Repulse* in the Far East and then played a sterling role in the Fall of Singapore.[42]

## HMS *Soberton*

In May 1964 Jock became first lieutenant of HMS *Soberton* based at Port Edgar, South Queensferry. *Soberton* was built as one of a large class of coastal minesweepers with names of villages all ending in –ton, she was employed on fishery protection throughout her long career. The 'Tons' weighed 400 tons, had a complement of about 35 men, and were built of wood to reduce their magnetic signatures. They were the last of the Navy's 'wooden walls'. *Soberton*'s captain was Lieutenant Commander Brian Outhwaite. He was relieved by Tom Crozier, who delegated much to Jock, including ship-handling and rare opportunities to practise minesweeping – a first-class way of learning the tough and potentially dangerous work of the sweep deck. Young Jock was already showing great qualities, and more than 50 years later he was remembered by the ship's company as "one of the best".

*Soberton*'s main duty was fishery protection and on 14 May 1964 Jock was granted a warrant by the Secretary of State for Scotland as a Superintendent of the Herring Fisheries under an act of 1860.[43] As a fishery superintendent Jock boarded fishing vessels to check their catch and their nets: one boarding was of a Soviet factory ship off Shetland, when Jock recalled being escorted to the master's cabin by two "heavies", who stood behind him while he spoke to the master: "He had a limited-English interpreter, which was just as well as the very little Russian I had learnt at Dartmouth was of absolutely no use, although the master was clearly impressed that I could say one or two words. My boat's crew clearly pleased the women manning the side of the ship and the atmosphere on departure was much friendlier than on our arrival!"

HMS *Soberton*, dressed overall, which Jock briefly commanded.
Source: Wikicommons.

Jock's first day at sea in command was on 5 May 1965 after Crozier was unexpectedly appointed to HMS *Kildarton* in the Far East during the three-year Indonesia–Malaysia confrontation known as Konfrontasi. He was determined during his short time in command to visit Orkney. However, on reaching Cape Wrath, a fierce south-westerly gale was blowing and as the seas piled up it became clear that if *Soberton* tried to turn east towards the Pentland Firth she might well broach. There followed some very uncomfortable hours as she ran before the wind past Fair Isle, eventually reaching the lee of Sumburgh Head in Shetland where she sheltered until the storm abated. "That was a character-forming experience!" Once alongside, Jock invited a large team of Orcadian friends on board, and even his father paid a visit.

Later in Ullapool, when alongside for a short stand-off on a Sunday and with some of the Sobertons kicking a football around on the jetty, Jock, relaxing in his chair on the bridge, was approached by a group of men in black jackets and black caps, who reminded him that this was the Sabbath and that it was unacceptable for sailors to play football. Jock apologised profusely, withdrew the sailors, and sailed shortly after.

After fourteen months in the Fishery Protection Squadron Jock was delighted to be appointed to HMS *Dryad* to specialise in navigation. A tough test of practical ability in HMS *Ulster* was part of the course, and one of the earlier passages he had to execute was from Stornoway to Stromness. Knowing how difficult the Hall of Clestrain was to pick out as a headmark running through Hoy Sound, the northern entrance to Scapa Flow, Jock asked his mother to park her car there and put on her headlights: the captain of *Ulster* was duly impressed, little knowing what help Jock had received. Jock won the prize for the top student of the course.

Higher matters of defence began to impact Jock's conscience and career. In the mid-1960s Britain had reached a watershed in foreign policy and the end of her major worldwide military role. By 1966, in one of a series of postwar defence reviews, Prime Minister Harold Wilson's Labour government announced that Britain "would not undertake major operations of war except in cooperation with allies". The announcement undertook to retain the UK presence in Singapore and Malaysia, but an economic crisis and the devaluation of sterling in 1967 led the Secretary of State for Defence, Denis Healey, to declare the withdrawal of British forces from East of Suez. The cancellation of CVA 01, the next in a long-planned new generation of aircraft carriers, led to the resignation of the First Sea Lord, Admiral Sir David Luce, and of the Minister of Defence for the Royal Navy, Christopher Mayhew.[44]


**HMS *Victorious***

To Jock's dismay he was sent in 1966 as second navigator in the fleet aircraft carrier HMS *Victorious.* He would rather have been appointed to a ship as the sole navigator, but the appointment turned out to be excellent experience. The navigating officer, Lieutenant Commander Bob Brook,[45] was, like many of his cloth, an able but tetchy and difficult fellow, especially with anyone who appeared on *his* bridge, and when Vice-Admiral Charles Mills embarked,[46] Brook became impossible and uncooperative with the staff, which included two excellent lieutenant-commanders, Mike Parry[47] and Robin Hogg.[48] Jock spent much time smoothing feathers.

In September, the distinguished submariner Captain Ian McIntosh took command of *Victorious.* McIntosh was a brilliant delegator who believed that his normal place was not on the bridge but in the operations room, and later, Jock was grateful to him for a fundamental lesson in command:[49]

A replenishment at sea involving four ships in the centre
of which is HMS *Victorious* when Jock was the second
navigator. RFA *Reliant*, HMS *Victorious*, RFA *Olynthus*,
and HMS *Leander* off Singapore, Christmas 1966.
Source: Wikicommons.

We were about to launch the Buccaneers for night flying not far from
the Paracel Islands en route to Hong Kong. I was on the top of the
bridge taking evening stars using an astroplot for rapid sight reduction
assisted by my navigator's yeoman in the charthouse, while *Victorious*
was working up to 30 knots to get the right wind over the deck, when it
became quickly evident from my yeoman's report that we were much
closer to the islands than I had expected and indeed were standing
into danger. I immediately ordered the captain to stop the ship to the
absolute horror of all those involved, telling him I was unhappy where
we were and rushed down to the charthouse to check the yeoman's
plotting only to discover that a simple error had been made and we
were in fact in no danger. Phew! Flying was resumed with the aviators
furious about the delay. The following morning, McIntosh asked to see
me in his cabin, and I expected the father and mother of bollockings.
Not a bit of it; Ian McIntosh said, "That is the best thing you ever did
last night and as a result I have complete confidence in you." Well – a
memorable lesson learnt.

Victorious had been launched in 1939 and had taken part in many wartime
operations, including the hunt for the German battleship Bismarck, Operation
Pedestal to relieve the Siege of Malta in 1942, and the North African landings.

While temporarily renamed USS Robin she had served in the US Navy, and at the end of the war she had been part of the British Pacific Fleet. By the late 1960s, Victorious had touched the limits of her development: fitted with 3D radar and an angled flightdeck, her displacement had grown by almost 25% from her original 29,000 tons full load. The size of aircraft she could carry had also reached its limit, and her air group consisted of some 36 aircraft – Sea Vixen all-weather fighter jets, Buccaneer low-level jet bombers, Gannet airborne early warning aircraft, and Wessex helicopters.

To launch and recover these heavy jets Jock needed to get the right wind over the deck, and the commanding officers of the air squadrons swiftly let him know if they were not satisfied. Several flying incidents showed that the Sea Vixen was operating at its limits, and it became known as an infamous widow-maker. In one incident, 50 miles south of Gan, Sea Vixen XS586 of 893 Naval Air Squadron, flown by Lieutenant Chris Hunneyball with his observer Lieutenant Bill Hart, reported loss of response to controls and Jock watched in horror as the aircraft stalled, the starboard wing dropped, the nose pitched up, and the crew ejected at 200ft with their aircraft in a nearly vertical bank. Fortunately, both men were recovered.

*Victorious*'s deployment East of Suez saw her steam almost 100,000 miles during the commission. There were visits to the American base at Subic Bay in the Philippines and a circumnavigation of Australia. In the Indian Ocean Jock took a party ashore for an exercise in beach intelligence survey (reconnaissance) on Direction Island, one of the Cocos (or Keeling) Islands.[50] He had been assured that it was uninhabited, but to his surprise a caretaker stepped out of trees to welcome Jock: "The Cable and Wireless Company had only recently evacuated the island … all the buildings were intact and gas, electricity, showers, fridges, etc., were available with running hot and cold water … so much for rugged camping. We had hoped to keep our good fortune a secret … but the admiral [Charles Mills] decided to drop in by helicopter unannounced and our secret was rudely exposed!" The actual beach reconnaissance went extremely well, accompanied by aerial photography, and two years later Jock received a letter from the Hydrographer of the Navy congratulating him on the work.

It never ceased to amaze Jock what musical and theatrical genius there was in any ship's company, and his own theatrical talent came to the fore again when he and Jeremy Black gave a rendition of 'The Green Eye of the Little Yellow God' at a sods opera.[51]

Jock hoped to take some local leave and applied to the Ministry of Defence (MoD) to travel to Vietnam, where the war was reaching its height, some twelve months before the major escalation known as the Tet Offensive. Undeterred when the request was refused, Jock applied to the Foreign Office, which readily agreed that he could visit his Orkney cousin, Bobby Cormack, who was the press officer in the embassy in Saigon. There he found it sad to see a beautiful city on the fringes of a dreadful war and to hear tanks rumbling through the streets at night. In one of the big hospitals he was taken to see, ghastly wounds, including those caused by napalm, were being treated. It was "all in all a most unusual leave".

After exercises in the South China Sea in May 1967, *Victorious* sailed for a rendezvous off Gan with HMS *Hermes*. The meeting was switched to off Aden, where the Commander-in-Chief, Middle East had requested a show of strength to support the imminent withdrawal (in November 1967), and *Victorious* and *Hermes* put on a fly-past. Next, *Victorious* transited the Suez Canal, some ten days before the Six Day War broke out. A curious rumour circulated that *Victorious*'s Buccaneers had been involved in recent bombing raids in the Middle East and, to prove this was not the case, her ship's log was requested from London, apparently for inspection in the House of Commons Library. However, in the log for the night in question, the only entry was that her captain, McIntosh, had returned on board in the early hours. Anxious not to embarrass his captain, Jock pencilled in several other innocuous entries.

Waiting for him on the jetty, when *Victorious* reached Portsmouth in June 1967, was a new, blue MGBGT, the first of many sports cars Jock would own. Some months before, he had been asked, through McIntosh, if he was prepared to navigate a Polaris boat. His response had been that if this led to submarine command, then "yes". When told it would be a one-off appointment, Jock declined. "It was the best decision I could have made as, almost by return, I received an appointment to HMS *Scarborough* as the Squadron Navigating Officer of the Dartmouth Training Squadron – right up my street!"

## HMS *Scarborough*

Jock joined the frigate HMS *Scarborough* in time for the 1967 autumn cruise of the Dartmouth Training Squadron, with Captain Ronnie Forrest in his final term as captain (D).[52] "He was an excellent boss; he allowed me to get on with my job, which was exceptionally busy, running the complex squadron programme and, at the same time, teaching the cadets on board the elements of navigation, both terrestrial and astronomical."

The other navigators in the squadron were all senior to Jock and their captains all strong, able individuals, including Mike Barrow in HMS *Torquay*, the newly promoted Robin Hogg in HMS *Tenby*, and David Eckersley-Maslin in HMS *Eastbourne*. A minor incident showed Jock's growing sense of self and propriety. When *Eastbourne* came alongside, Eckersley-Maslin found Jock's car parked in a space very close to the gangway, which was normally reserved for the captain:

> He sent for me and proceeded to tear me off a strip in front of all at the head of the gangway. I merely requested to see him in his cabin, and, when the door was shut, apologised for the inadvertent parking of my car and then firmly told him that that was no way to speak to his squadron navigator in front of his sailors! Thereafter our relations were cool; sad really as his wardroom was run beautifully by his first lieutenant, Jeremy Dreyer, and I always found it something of a relief visiting *Eastbourne* compared with the senior stuffiness of *Scarborough*. The food was better too!

Forrest was relieved in command of *Scarborough* by Captain Ian Mackay,[53] who, however, interfered in simple matters with the other captains. As in *Victorious*, Jock found himself intermediary, trying to soften Mackay's approach. For Jock, the training cruises, which included Scandinavia and the Mediterranean, were professionally stimulating, and it was rewarding to see the young officers under training develop their skill and confidence. He left *Scarborough* with a glowing confidential report.

HMS *Scarborough*
Source: Wikicommons.

## Confidential Reports

Confidential reports, or forms S206, were written on all officers, every six months if in the zone for promotion, annually if not, and also if the subject or his commanding officer was reappointed. The layout and content of the S206 changed little throughout the years of this biography. It was single-sided and contained spaces for a free-style written report on professional performance and general ability, and for remarks by senior officers. There was also a table covering ten qualities: zeal and energy, reliability, commonsense, intelligence and reasoning power, initiative and alertness, leadership, power of expression, organising ability, tact and cooperation, and social attributes, all marked on a scale of 0 to 9. A score of below 60 indicated that the subject was not good breeding stock, while a score of 75 or above probably indicated that the officer being reported on was ready for further responsibility and promotion.

It was easy to spot which reporting officers were hard markers; others were more generous and it was the job of senior officers in the reporting chain to correct this, and if the discrepancy was large, an index error might be applied to the marks. Mackay's marking on Jock's report was exceptionally high, and an ignorant and hapless junior secretary in the office of the Flag Officer Western Flotilla minuted: "No one can merit this high a mark: propose an index error of at least minus 10." The proposal was ignored.

## Lunch at White's

In January 1968, *Scarborough* was in the Mediterranean when a signal arrived stating that Jock was being considered as a possible equerry to the Queen. In March, he received an invitation to lunch at White's with the Controller of the Lord Chamberlain's Office, Sir Eric Penn, and the Deputy Master of the Household, Lord Plunket.[54] A few days later on 7 May, while back in his ship in the Western Approaches, a signal summoned Jock to St James's Palace. Three days later he was landed by helicopter for an interview with the Lord Chamberlain, Lord Cobbold, which took all of fifteen minutes: "He stood with his back to the fireplace with his hands in his pockets and was clearly at a loss about what to ask me, merely pointing out that the Queen no longer interviewed prospective equerries herself and it was his task to do so. Well, there was no indication of whether I had been chosen so off I went up to Stranraer on the night sleeper to rejoin the squadron."

Sometime later Jock was shown a copy of a minute from the Lord Chamberlain to the Queen's Private Secretary, which showed his name at the bottom of a list of royal appointments – he was indeed to be equerry to HM the Queen.

Prince Charles and Jock put on an act in a sods opera in HMY *Britannia* in Bay of Islands, New Zealand, March 1970. Source: Slater archive.

The Royal party on a visit to St Kilda, from left to right, JCKS, HRH Princess Anne, HRH Prince Philip, James Fisher, Mr Perkins. Source: Slater archive.

# Chapter 5: Equerry, 1968–71

Jock was disappointed to leave the Dartmouth Training Squadron after only a year, but excited, if also somewhat daunted, to be setting off on something completely different. He spent the summer holidays in Orkney, kitting himself out with new clothes, including uniforms, caps, a tweed suit with knickerbockers, a bowler hat, and city suits: "After the best part of ten years at sea, I certainly needed sprucing up!"

**In at the Deep End**

He relieved a soldier, a man of few words, as equerry to the Queen, and Jock had to observe his new world and learn fast. At Balmoral in late September 1968 he was taken to Loch Muick to meet the royal family at a barbeque cooked by Prince Philip. Other former equerries, who were there to shoot and stalk, volunteered words of wisdom, and Jock was glad that he had learned to shoot in Orkney. Never a great shot, he sometimes surprised even himself. The Balmoral routine was very straightforward: a big breakfast, then out on the hill either to stalk for the day or to a shoot with a picnic lunch, which the Queen and the ladies attended, followed by a big, rather late, tea. Wearing his kilt, his task before dinner was to knock up the martinis in a jug: liberal amounts of gin, a good slug of Vermouth, and bags of ice – it was wise merely to taste them.

Back in London in a flat in St James's Palace, Jock found himself alone with no one to look after him and little ability to cook, so he joined the Army and Navy Club at the other end of Pall Mall. Security was lax and tourists could walk right up to his windows; his MGBGT was parked under the arches. He was placed under the instruction of Patrick Plunket, Deputy Master of the Household, a charming and most courteous, unmarried courtier, and a personal friend of the Queen, who could not believe that anyone would not naturally pick up the dos and don'ts of royal life. Other members of the Queen's personal staff were the private secretaries Michael Adeane, Martin Charteris, and Philip Moore, who were reluctant to delegate much. However, Adeane had a house in St James's Palace and, when they had become better known, he and Jock used to walk across to Buckingham Palace in the mornings when Jock benefitted enormously from wide-ranging discussions over an excellent breakfast.

In the first two weeks there were several visits and audiences, a privy council meeting, and the state opening of Parliament. When Prime Minister Harold Wilson called he would arrive accompanied by his Private Secretary, be met by the equerry, and be escorted upstairs to wait in an anteroom. When the Queen was ready, Jock would take the Prime Minister into her presence and announce, in a clip which can be found on YouTube, "The Prime Minister, Your Majesty." What the clip does not show is that when the Queen rang a bell at the end of the audience Jock would escort Wilson's party to the equerries' room for a stiff drink.

## State Visits to Brazil and Chile

On 1 November 1968 Jock achieved eight years' seniority as a lieutenant and was automatically promoted to lieutenant commander: there was no opportunity to 'ship a half-stripe' before the Queen set out on state visits to Brazil and Chile, flying out to Recife where half a million people greeted her as she drove through the city to board the royal yacht. For Jock it was especially good to return to *Britannia*, where he was made welcome by FORY, Rear-Admiral Pat Morgan, and the members of the permanent yacht service, whom he remembered from his time as assistant navigator in 1961. It felt rather strange to have a smart cabin down aft in the royal apartments, where the royal stewards looked after him.

The Queen and Prince Philip felt very much at home on board, as did other members of the party. Jock grew acquainted with two other key members of the staff. These were Margaret 'Bobo' MacDonald, who would serve the Queen for 67 years from nursery maid to dresser. She was the daughter of a railwayman and encouraged the young Princess Elizabeth to be thrifty and frugal, and, in adulthood, the Queen enjoyed talking to a sensible Scottish countrywoman. Bobo's conservative dress sense prevailed, and she could say anything to the Queen. The second was the Queen's personal protection officer Chief Superintendent Albert Perkins, who was known only by his surname. Plunket reassured Jock that this was appropriate usage for him, too, though later Perkins suggested that he would prefer Jock to call him "*Mr* Perkins". Bobo and Perkins were two key players in the Queen's life, and Jock soon discovered that if they were happy, so was everyone else. Bobo had the Queen's ear and reported anything amiss.

Having *Britannia* in Rio was a great bonus for the Queen, who could escape home after events and not have to stay with the ambassador, however palatial his residence, or to a hotel. However, the yacht rolled in the swell inside the harbour and it fell to the young Jock to suggest that this would be eased if *Britannia* re-anchored in deeper water. The British ambassador in Brazil was Sir John Russell, an able, self-confident diplomat, who was absolutely determined to make the visit a huge success.[55] Jock recalled: "His Greek wife, Aliki, clearly thought that she was the Queen in Brazil and the arrival of the real Queen came as something of a shock to her when she was persuaded that, on the whole, she should let the Queen proceed before her!" Pre-war, Aliki had been the first Greek woman to win the Miss Europe title, and the Russell's daughter, Georgiana, had inherited her mother's beauty: "We really got quite excited about her, particularly when her dresses left little to the imagination."

On 11 November, the royal party flew across the Andes for the first ever British royal visit to Chile, where the top floors of a hotel had been specially prepared. They were being filmed by a BBC television crew led by Richard Cawston, who was directing the making of *Royal Family* (1969), which Andrew Duncan would turn into a book.[56] With Cawston's crew filming, great care needed to be exercised and, once, when a flustered Chilean admiral rushed into the hotel to ask what the situation was, Charteris replied over an open microphone: "Tense. F*****g tense." Cawston needed persuading not to use this clip.

The royal party spent a weekend at the Antumalal Hotel, Pucón, where Prince Philip and Jock went salmon fishing. All they hooked was Jock's ear, though, which required minor surgery on their return to the hotel. While they were there, a crisis began brewing in the Falklands, which Jock remembered key British figures discussing as they sat on logs around a barbeque.

While the Queen was in Chile, *Britannia* held the first of her trade or sea days on 12 and 13 November, when 80 guests were taken to sea to witness weapon firing and a flying display of the Wasp helicopter from HMS *Naiad*. Despite the perceived success of these two days it would be a further seven years before another trade day was held on board.

## Sixpence

Back in Britain, court life was a whirl of engagements, and if a guest dropped out Jock helped to make up the numbers. In February 1969 he sat next to a young, charming, up-and-coming pop singer – Cliff Richard. He also met President Richard Nixon when the president made an informal call on the Queen. At the opening of the Victoria underground line in London he carried a sixpenny bit for the Queen to pretend for the photographers that she was to buy a ticket. The sixpence went straight through the new machine and emerged in the reject compartment, twice. She was then given a ticket, which found its way into one of Jock's scrapbooks.

During the Italian state visit Andrew Duncan recorded that Jock escorted out the president of Italy's daughter, and that "Lieutenant John Slater was adept at entertaining the Queen's foreign guests at nightspots like Annabel's and other obtuberances (sic) of London's faintly chinless scene." *The Observer* chose to repeat this in its serialisation of Duncan's book: Jock was irritated but his friends in the Navy were highly amused.

The sun did not always shine: at the presentation of the Queen's Colour to 45 Commando Royal Marines, the risk of rain caused the ceremony to be moved indoors from Plymouth Hoe to the Guildhall, and when the predicted rain was replaced by sun Jock had his first experience of Prince Philip's tetchiness. The Prince clearly thought that Jock had played an unsatisfactory role in forecasting the weather.

Jock knew many of the commanding officers at the fleet review in late July in Torbay, when colours were presented to the newly formed Western Fleet. He met for the first time Dr David Owen, the impressive young Navy Minister and Labour MP for Plymouth. During the visit, the weather did turn sour and boat traffic in the bay was stopped, stranding many men ashore. Dinner was in HMS *Eagle*, followed by a sods opera, something the royal family always enjoyed, though part-way through Jock was warned that the state of the sea was such that the entertainment should be halted so that the royals could return in safety to *Britannia*. Knowing that this would not please the Queen, Jock recommended taking a risk, but that meant that the *Eagle* might have to accommodate everybody on board overnight. In the event, the show continued and the royal barge was ably handled alongside. The last to embark was the Queen, and Jock recalled, "To this day, I can see her jumping nimbly from accommodation ladder to barge; a very choppy return to HMY followed … All went into the drawing room for a nightcap and the Queen's first comment was, 'Well, that was fun, wasn't it?'"

## Summer Cruise 1969

The summer usually saw *Britannia* at Cowes Week and cruising to the Western Isles, but on 4 August 1969 there was instead a visit to Hull and one to Shetland two days later. *Britannia* then sailed to Norway to meet King Olaf and his family.

Jock undertook a recce in Shetland and stayed with the Lord Lieutenant, Robert Bruce of Sumburgh, to discuss the programme. While the two men considered a suitable picnic spot for the royal children, Jock became concerned that two maids standing by the sideboard were listening and that word might get out, but Bruce assured him that not a word would pass their lips, and it did not. The following morning, at a rehearsal of the royal route, which included an exhibition of Shetland products, an old lady, who had knitted a pair of shooting stockings for Prince Philip, asked how she would know when to make the presentation and Jock told her he would tip her the wink: in the event, she shuffled up and said in a loud voice, "Here's your socks!"

In Norway, the British royal family in *Britannia* rendezvoused with King Olav and his family who were embarked in their yacht, *Norge*. After an official banquet in Bergen, a five-day programme resembled a typical Western Isles cruise, as both families went fishing and sightseeing; even so, the visit was rather more formal than the Queen and Prince Philip might have wished.

## Windsor Castle

Court life had its own rhythm at Windsor Castle, just as it did at other palaces, under the watchful eye of the Queen herself. Jock remembered her "inviting me to accompany her round the bedrooms before the guests arrived on the Monday evening; she had an incredibly good eye for detail and clearly a pretty good knowledge of each of the guests". One of Jock's tasks was to make the guests feel at home, though his own bedroom was about as far away from the royal apartments as it could be, so getting there and back in no time and changing at speed was something of a challenge.

Jock's first Christmas-in-waiting was at Windsor, when presents were laid out on tables in the drawing room on Christmas Eve, each one marked with names from the Queen down to Jock: he kept the cuttings from the labels on some of his presents, including the Queen's present, which came from the Lord High Admiral, but later he could not remember what the various items were. His present to the Queen was a metal wastepaper basket from Carnaby Street for the beach hut in Norfolk, with the famous Kitchener meme over the words 'Keep Your Country Tidy'.

## Second Year

Back at Balmoral at the start of his second season as equerry, Jock enjoyed escaping to play golf on the little nine-hole course that was beautifully looked after but of no interest to any member of the royal family until Prince Andrew was older and took up the game. "It was a good way of entertaining Harold Wilson, the Prime Minister, who always played with a pipe in his mouth; furthermore, his protection officer was particularly good at finding his balls and not those of the opposition."

Jock also became more aware of the battalion which provided soldiers as beaters and ponymen to assist the stalkers and ghillies. There were two ghillies' balls each year, to which several soldiers were invited, after which they were expected to write a letter of thanks to the Queen. At one point, it was obvious that their sergeant major had stood in front of the blackboard at Ballater barracks and dictated to them what to write. The Queen asked Jock to tell their commanding officer that they should write their own letters of thanks, and that he should select a few to submit to her: one letter started, "Dear Queen – you were the Bell of the Ball (except for Princess Anne) …."

At Sandringham, life, as witnessed by Basil Boothroyd, was more relaxed.[57] There was shooting in the day and films were popular after dinner. It was Jock's task to order suitable films. He could have gone to see them in advance as his predecessors had, but his ordering strategy was riskier and sometimes he was embarrassed by "writhing sheets". On one occasion he fell asleep during a film and the royal family and guests tiptoed out at the end so as not to disturb him. "I was not allowed to forget that in a hurry." The Althorp children were sometimes home from school and among them Jock remembered a vivacious eight-year-old: little did he think that eleven years later she would marry Prince Charles.

## Fiji, Tonga, New Zealand, and Australia

During the royal tour down under in March and April 1970, *Britannia* again showed her worth. The royal party, including Prince Charles and Princess Anne, arrived in Fiji after a very long flight and, using the yacht as a mobile palace and home-from-home, were quickly into action for a full two days, before *Britannia*'s short passage to Tonga and four-and-a-half day passage to New Zealand and Australia. There was a disaster in the rough waters of the Cook Strait when three sailors were washed overboard from the frigate HMNZS *Waikato*. One drowned. Jock watched the rescue attempt from the bridge of *Britannia*. The pilot of *Waikato*'s Wasp was Nigel Burbury, a term-mate at Dartmouth to whom he had been best man in London in 1961.

At a concert in Dunedin Jock's host urged him to listen to the next singer because she would become famous: she was 20-odd-year soprano Kiri Te Kanawa. On passage to Australia the Queen requested a sods opera, enabling Jock to dust off *Musical Fairy Tale*, which he had written in the Far East some years before and which he and Prince Charles performed.

Each bay where Captain Cook had allegedly landed held its own ceremony and Jock particularly remembered the welcome at Townsville, where a covered stage was erected on the beach for the royal party. From his vantage point by the steps he noticed a movement under the stage, peered down, and found a young Aboriginal boy who smiled conspiratorially at him. Jock kept a close eye on him during the speeches, and, towards the end, the Queen was invited to unveil a plaque. To do this she had to press a button and by some miracle the curtain opened; in fact, the button lit up a light below the stage and the boy hauled on a rope to open the curtain above. Job completed, he turned to Jock with a beaming smile and held his thumbs up.

## Scotland 1970

That summer in Scotland not everything went to plan. After a busy day in Glasgow and Kilmarnock with the Queen, Jock accompanied Prince Charles to dine with the Royal Company of Merchants of the City of Edinburgh, but failed to check the dress for the evening. As they drove down the Mound towards Merchants' Hall the Prince and Jock noticed that the hosts were all in white tie and tails. Prince Charles immediately wanted to turn round and change, but Jock encouraged him to bluff it out. Nevertheless, the Merchants were unhappy and Jock was in no doubt that he had given the wrong advice, and the next morning he sent a dispatch rider with a letter of apology to the Master. Then, after the Commonwealth Games in Edinburgh, the royal family took their traditional cruise of the Western Isles. *Britannia* anchored in Thurso Bay so that everyone could drive up for lunch with the Queen Mother. It was the first of Jock's many visits to the Castle of Mey.

Later, Jock took passage in *Britannia* for the short trip to Portsmouth and then went straight into the Royal Naval Hospital, Haslar to have his nose repaired – it had been broken while boxing at school. He convalesced in Bishops Waltham with Aunt Nona, took a summer break in Orkney, and was on duty in late September at Balmoral. There, Prince Philip came into the equerries' room and said he had read that the poet, novelist, and travel writer Eric Linklater, when a student at the University of Aberdeen, had come to Balmoral to beat during the grouse shooting season and he wondered if Linklater would like to come as a guest. Jock volunteered that he knew the Linklaters but did not let on that Eric had a booze problem:[58]

> It was therefore with some unease that I greeted the Linklaters a few days later. The first thing that Eric said was: 'Jock, I will try not to let you down' and for most part Eric was pretty subdued and a trifle morose until the final evening when we all went out for a barbecue supper to Loch Muick and Eric got stuck into the booze and was the life and soul of the party. I drove back with the Queen that evening and she said to me: 'Why did you not let him off the leash earlier?' I suspect in her inimitable way she knew about Eric all along!

## Third Year, 1971

That winter, the Queen, apparently worried that the royal nanny, Mabel Anderson, might not be able to cope if the young princes, Andrew and Edward, were recognised, asked Jock to accompany Mispy and the children to a performance of Aladdin in the West End, where they had four seats in the stalls: their presence was no secret, but the evening passed without incident.

Jock's third year as equerry was very full. He had gained considerable experience and so was increasingly trusted. However, at Goodwood in late July there was another cock-up. Queen Elizabeth arrived at the racecourse as planned at about 2pm to be met by a clearly incensed Duke of Norfolk, who had been expecting her for lunch.[59] He left Jock in no doubt that he had failed and after the races he was summoned to the Duke's study, the four Fitzalan-Howard daughters warning him that "Daddy is on the warpath." The Duke ranted from behind his desk, but Jock defused the situation by saying that he was extremely sorry and had no idea what had happened. "Good heavens," exclaimed the Duke, "I did not think that you would say that – have a drink!" When he left the study, the girls, who were listening outside, were amazed that he had come out smiling. The royal party stayed at Arundel Castle, where croquet was a popular game, and when Jock hit a ball the length of the lawn and straight through a hoop they laughed and cried "Naval Dead Eye Dick!"

## Canada

The first two weeks of May 1971 were devoted to a visit to British Columbia. Jock had flown to Vancouver in advance to make initial plans with *Britannia* before the arrival of the royal party. One of his tasks was to carry the privy purse, a briefcase containing petty cash in brand new notes for tips. Throughout the flight he kept this close, but on arrival in *Britannia* he realised it was not with him: it was a relief when at that moment a police car with sirens blaring came flying down the jetty and a Mountie rushed up the gangway carrying the briefcase.

As usual, *Britannia* made all the difference to the life of the Queen and Prince Philip, who always seemed so much more relaxed when they were on board and able to enjoy its privacy. *Britannia* had a positive effect on even the toughest critics, such as when Pierre Trudeau, Prime Minister of Canada, who was reported by a biographer to regard the monarchy with a certain bemused contempt, asked that the president of the student council be invited on board. Steve was his name. He was a well-known anti-monarchist, determined to make his views known. All the other guests were on board for the evening reception when a colourful old car rolled down the jetty full of rowdy students shouting out "Steve for King!" Out jumped Steve, rather oddly attired, who surveyed *Britannia* before somewhat nervously making his way up the gangway, where Jock met him at the top: "Oh there you are. You're a bit late. The Queen was getting worried you weren't coming. Come on, I'll present you to the Queen." Steve was overawed and he never found the words to say whatever he had planned.

## Turnover

When Princess Anne declared that she would like a dinner and dance in *Britannia* in Portsmouth for an early celebration of her 21st birthday, it was discovered to everyone's surprise that there was a dance floor under the carpet in the dining room. There was also a lunch at the Castle of Mey for Princess Anne's proper birthday, when Jock's present was a brooch with the flags ANNE in enamel. Much of late August and September was spent at Balmoral, where Jock chatted to Prince Charles about his impending entry into Dartmouth.

Squadron Leader Peter Beer came up to Balmoral in early October to start a turnover, and the Queen observed privately that he looked disconcertingly like Peter Townsend, Princess Margaret's former admirer.[60] Jock's last royal duty came during the state visit by the Emperor and the Empress of Japan, when he noted what little enthusiasm there was as they drove through London. When he commented that he hoped the Emperor was not offended by the silence he was reminded that in Tokyo, silence was a sign of respect. He received a silver rose vase engraved with a chrysanthemum head with sixteen petals, a sign that it was a gift of the Emperor. Then on 15 October Jock received his first medal, the Queen making him a member of the Victorian Order 4th Class. By the end of the month he was established in West Cottage, West Street, Soberton, ready for a new phase in his life.

# Chapter 6: Annie's Story

When in January 1968 Jock had received an official letter to say that he was being considered for the position of equerry to the Queen, he had also been told that any appointment would be for three years, during which he would be expected to remain single. His reply was that he would be delighted to be considered but could not guarantee to be unmarried. The best thing happened in the autumn of 1971, in Jock's closing weeks as equerry: he and Annie Scott became more than friends and spent time together that Christmas when they were both in Orkney.

Annie's father was Pat Scott, managing director of Highland Park Distillery in Kirkwall. She had been educated in the local school and later in Inverness, at secretarial college in Glasgow, and at finishing school in Switzerland. Younger than Jock, Annie had been aware of him among the older boys, shooting, fishing, and playing golf with her father, but their relationship did not blossom until she came to London, where she flat-shared with other girls and took a job with Associated-Redifussion. There, at the company's administrative headquarters and transmission facilities in Television House in Kingsway, she managed the Cowboys' fan mail and worked on productions including *The Dickie Henderson Show*. She then joined the art department of *The Economist*, reporting to the broadcaster and journalist Alastair Burnet.[61]

On 15 April 1972 Annie and Jock announced their engagement and, happily, while HMS *Jupiter* languished in refit in Devonport, they made plans to wed later that summer at St Columba's, Church of Scotland in Pont Street, where the minister was Dr J Fraser McLuskey, the celebrated 'parachute padre' of the Second World War.[62] When McLuskey heard that the reception would be at The Ritz, he commented, "Oh, so it will just be an ordinary tea reception!"

Jock lunched with Prince Charles at HMS *Mercury* some weeks before the wedding, which the Prince hoped to attend but which his ship's programme would make too difficult. Princess Anne, however, was determined to attend, to the surprise of the 350 guests. The ushers were from *Jupiter* and there were so many other naval officer guests that the arch of swords stretched across the street, holding up the traffic and causing Annie's cousin Jake Stewart to remark "Oh, Cripes, there has been a shipwreck." The wedding night was spent in a bridal suite, adorned with magnificent flowers, as a gift from Claridges, and the honeymoon was spent in Madeira.

Annie had little idea of what she was buying into as a naval wife. "How could I, having been brought up on whisky?" She philosophised, however, that she was old enough not to mind being alone when Jock was at sea. And she was a brilliant hostess, whether preparing buffets for working lunches in Jock's office on the seventh floor of the MoD or for foreign VVIPs at home and abroad; she took charge of various house staffs firmly and set high standards, and was an excellent flower arranger.

For Annie "it was all great fun", and though she sometimes found formal dinners rather terrifying, she cheerfully joined Jock when turning some of their dinners into more light-hearted events. "I liked doing it, I like people, and Jock made it fun anyway. He's very generous and doesn't like being stuffy."

Annie Scott on her engagement in 1972. Slater archive.

Jock was grateful: "I could not have coped without her. Above all I certainly could not have got through the first, high-powered period at the helm of the Royal Navy without Annie's love and sterling support." There would be no doubt that Annie would play a vital role in Jock's career and, much later, when asked when there might be a First Sea Lady, he replied without hesitation: "There is already a First Sea Lady – my wife!"[63]

They had two sons, Charles and Rory.

Jock and his boys, Charles and Rory, 1995.
Source: Slater archive.

# Chapter 7: HMS *Jupiter*

HMS *Jupiter* – when Sir Eric Yarrow saw this he remarked
"Now, that was a Yarrow-built ship!" Source: MoD.

Jock was still only a lieutenant when he became equerry, and at eight years
seniority he was automatically promoted to lieutenant commander. Under the
rules then in force he would enter the zone for promotion to commander while
still serving as equerry, when reports on his suitability for future promotion

would be made six-monthly. Clearly he would be disadvantaged by not having been to sea since he was navigator of HMS *Scarborough*, and would be lacking professional naval experience. So, he was pleased when in spring 1971 he heard that after three years as equerry his next appointment would be as first lieutenant of the frigate HMS *Gurkha*, which would be the guardship in the West Indies, waters that Jock knew well. He would have to spend the first weeks of 1972 on courses, learning about discipline, first aid, organisation, and maintenance.

## The Seating Plan

However, at Holyroodhouse on 29 June 1971 there was a surprise. When Jock sent a proposed dinner seating plan to the Queen, the Queen's long-serving page, Mr Bennett, returned with an amended plan. The Queen had moved him next to her, and Jock pointed out to Bennett that there must be some mistake. Bennett insisted that this was the Queen's wish. Who was Jock to argue? Once seated at dinner, the Queen, to Jock's amazement, announced to the assembled company that he had been selected for promotion to commander and that this news would be announced on the morrow in the half-yearly promotions list. Jock was surprised, not least since this was the first possible occasion on which he was eligible, despite, he was acutely aware, having done no time in the Navy proper as a lieutenant commander. In the ensuing discussion, Prince Philip reminded the company that he, too, had been promoted to commander "first shot".

The next morning the phone in the equerry's room burned: the appointment to *Gurkha* was cancelled and, to Jock's even greater surprise, he learned that he was to command the Leander-class frigate HMS *Jupiter*. It was an exciting if somewhat daunting prospect: aged 33 he would be the youngest commander in the fleet.

There were still courses to complete, but these would be about command and operations, not ship-keeping. Among fellow students on Maritime Tactical Course Number 5, which Jock attended in January and February 1972, was the newly promoted Rear-Admiral Jock Miller, who had been Jock's popular and much-respected divisional officer at Dartmouth and who had been promoted very early to flag rank.

## West Indies

In February 1972, *Jupiter* was on exercises in the West Indies where Jock was to take over from his friend, mentor, fellow Scot, and former commanding officer in HMS *Yaxham*, Commander Ronnie Laughton. Laughton's mischievous joining instructions to Jock were to fly out via Miami to the British Virgin Islands, and from there to go to the Treasure Isle Hotel in Tortola to await the arrival of *Jupiter*'s helicopter, at an unspecified time, a day or two later. When *Jupiter*'s Wasp eventually landed on the beach on Leap Day 1972, Jock carried his own baggage across the sand to be greeted by the pilot, Lieutenant Will Hacking, "an overconfident young chap", whose first words were "Are you the new skipper? Hop in." There is an apocryphal version of this meeting in which Laughton had asked Hacking to don a Stetson hat for the occasion.[64]

Laughton greeted Jock on *Jupiter*'s flightdeck, where he introduced him to the heads of department. All bar one were older than Jock and had been senior to him as lieutenant-commanders. Laughton took Jock to his cabin for a brief turnover and a glass of gin and announced that he was leaving straight away. That afternoon, Jock sent for Hacking and told him, in no uncertain terms, that he was unlikely to go far if he addressed his new captain in such an offhand way. The message quickly reached others in the wardroom.

Laughton had planned other impishness. Peter Franklyn, *Jupiter*'s navigating officer, was not in the ship but had been sent inshore in the ship's whaler to inspect the newly constructed and, so far, unused jetty at Tortola.[65] However, the wind picked up and Franklyn decided that returning to the anchorage in the open roads off Virgin Gorda was too dangerous, and did not return until the following morning, after he too had been picked off the beach by Hacking in the Wasp.

Meanwhile Laughton sent off a signal reporting that the change of command had taken place and then promptly left the ship. The Admiral's staff assumed the signal was from Jock and, jealous of the boy-commander being promoted over their heads, warned him in reply that should he ever be lucky enough to command again he was to refer to Queen's Regulations and Admiralty Instructions, which clearly stated that no signal should be made on change of command. That evening, the commander-in-chief himself, Admiral Sir Edward Ashmore, flying his flag in the guided missile destroyer HMS *Glamorgan* invited Jock to dinner, and, next morning, *Jupiter* sailed for a short visit to Tortola.[66]

Jock would prove to be a flamboyant ship-handler but on 1 March his approach alongside at the new jetty in Tortola was notably cautious. Lacking a large-scale chart, without tugs, in an offshore wind, and with progress restricted by a coral reef it was, in the words of the report of proceedings, "an uneasy and unimpressive affair". Ashmore, who had served in the previous *Jupiter* in the Norwegian Campaign of 1940 and who had a soft spot for the present ship, had come to watch with his Captain of the Fleet. From their several vantage points on the upper deck Jock's officers, willing him to succeed, also watched anxiously to see how their new captain would handle *Jupiter.*

Post-election unrest caused a planned visit to Carriacou, Grenada to be cancelled. Instead, *Jupiter* sailed to Castries, St Lucia, but that visit ended abruptly when the ship went looking for two missing American holidaymakers and their St Lucian boat boy. The search was unsuccessful, but there was a thank you letter from the British high commissioner. This was followed by a rebuke from Princess Margaret, who was disappointed that Jock had not waited at Tortola for her official opening of the new jetty.

On 8 March *Jupiter* rendezvoused with HM Ships *London* and *Dido* and the next day they joined *Glamorgan* for a series of passage exercises with a planned speed of advance of 18 knots across the North Atlantic requiring much high-speed steaming into wind. The senior officer was *Glamorgan*'s captain Tom Baird, who, Jock recalled from his days in the Dartmouth Training Squadron from 1957–58, used to masthead cadets, sending them in the worst of weathers to sit on the navigational radar platform.[67] Jock was not surprised when Baird seemed intent on testing him, and each night he ordered *Jupiter* to keep station at two cables astern of *Glamorgan*. As Jock had yet to gauge the competence of his offers of the watch, he sat up all night in the captain's bridge chair. "However character-forming, it was a very stupid thing to do, and I often wondered how Baird became Vice-Admiral Sir Thomas. Perhaps there was more to him than met the eye." *Jupiter*'s officers, he discovered, were a nice team, but it was sad to know that having just got to know them several were due to leave as soon as she reached home. In fine spring weather on 16 March 1972 *Jupiter* anchored in Plymouth Sound and, after clearing customs and embarking families, was reluctantly moved into Devonport dockyard for a refit.

The refit formally started on 10 April 1972. Baulked by industrial action that made effective planning difficult and hindered all efforts to achieve a satisfactory outcome, *Jupiter* did not become operational again for many months.

*Jupiter's* officers kept together and dined with Prince Charles at Greenwich.
Source: Slater archive.

## Trials

Keen to force the dockyard's hand, Jock held a ceremony to mark *Jupiter*'s return to the fleet on 22 September, with a ceremonial exchange of ensigns. In glorious weather the band of Royal Marines Plymouth, supported by the pipes and drums of TS *Jupiter* from Middlesbrough Sea Cadet Corps, competed heroically with the windy hammers of Devonport dockyard. Annie Slater, at her first official duty, cut the commissioning cake.

Jock Miller, now the Flag Officer 2nd Flotilla, visited *Jupiter* in Devonport. It had been obvious to Jock Slater when they completed the tactical course at HMS *Dryad* earlier in the year that booze had become a problem for Miller and by that autumn his staff were trying to protect him. He visited the senior rates' mess for a pint or two and then the wardroom for more drink, so, by the time he arrived to have lunch with Jock and Annie he was not fully sober. Annie asked afterwards, "Are your admirals alcoholics?" It was so sad for Jock to see Miller in this state and he called privately on his staff to discuss the matter, but they chose to continue to protect their admiral.[68]

As a morale booster *Jupiter* paid a brief visit to Le Havre over the first weekend of December. Many French families were on the jetty to see what the local newspapers called *un des plus bâtiments de la Royal Navy* depart on Sunday afternoon and were impressed by the *elan* with which she left through the lock gates of the inner harbour. They did not know that Jock was allergic to shellfish and he had been fed some version of bouillabaisse for lunch: *Jupiter*'s speed was a function of his anxiety for the state of his stomach. After sea trials in mid-December much dockyard work was still outstanding and this experience of refitting a comparatively new ship in a dockyard with so many restrictive practices would be useful later, when, as Chief of Fleet Support (CFS), Jock was determined to sharpen up the dockyards.

Finally *Jupiter* reached Portland on 21 December, for a work-up that would be broken into episodes, once for Christmas leave and another in January for trials of a new underwater telephone in HMS *Valiant* submerged somewhere northwest of Ireland. Under Jock's leadership her ship's company relished getting down to their real business at last and enjoyed their two months at Portland. Jock was particularly impressed with their enthusiasm, not least because 25% of his sailors and 50% of his officers were to leave before the ship's anticipated deployment to the Far East.

*Jupiter*'s work-up ended in late February 1973 and she was assessed as 'very satisfactory'. However, Jock was furious about losing people as soon as the work-up was completed, and did not endear myself to the commander-in-chief's staff by complaining about it in a signal. Ashmore, the commander-in-chief himself, soon visited his youngest and most junior commander-in-command, arriving by jackstay and demanding to see Jock in his cabin, where he told him, "That signal you made – good point – but don't make a habit of it!"

Ashmore wanted to replace the training of seaman officers in deeply specialised long courses and the manning of frigates with officers whose specialisms included gunnery, anti-submarine warfare, and communications, with a principal warfare officer (PWO). The PWO's task would be to take command of the operations room and give tactical instructions for all fighting arms of the ship, and to share some of the burden of command with the captain. Ships of frigate size such as *Jupiter* would no longer carry deep sub-specialists (although these might still be found in squadron leaders and in larger warships).

At last, on 19 March 1973, *Jupiter* was free of the dockyard and of work-up and sailed overnight to the Hook of Holland and the passage of the Nieuwe Maas river for a visit to Rotterdam. Next was a visit to Teesside – *Jupiter* was affiliated to Middlesborough – and to the Sea Cadets of TS *Jupiter*. She then moved on to Rosyth before joining a multi-threat exercise, JMC 167, which tested the new PWO trials complement. Jock was again frustrated: while JMC was an invaluable opportunity to test out the new complement in realistic defence watch conditions, and to integrate those officers and ratings who had joined since work-up, it was frustrating to see how trickle-drafting diluted the worked-up team.

Jock celebrated his 35th birthday in Rosyth, where Nanny Gimpa visited *Jupiter*: he would always remember her standing at the top of the gangway and surveying the scene until her eyes eventually found Jock, and exclaiming, "Oh, my wee Jockie, I can't believe it!"


## Cod War

That summer *Jupiter* sailed to play her part in the Second Cod War. British fishing vessels had been taking their catch off Iceland since the 14th century and several Anglo-Danish agreements in the intervening centuries had tried to restrict British access. In the 20th century a series of disputes arose when, from 1952 onwards, Iceland, now an independent country, asserted its control over territorial waters that were unilaterally expanded from three to four nautical miles, then to twelve, and eventually to an economic exclusion zone of two hundred nautical miles from the Icelandic coast. Each of the so-called cod wars, after confrontations between the Royal Navy and the Icelandic Coast Guard, ended in agreements favourable to Iceland, not least because of Iceland's threat to withdraw from NATO and thus expose the Greenland–Iceland–UK gap, a critical anti-submarine warfare choke point during the Cold War.[69]

The Second Cod War took place from 1972–73, when Iceland unilaterally extended its fishing limits, covering the most plentiful fishing grounds off its coast. Britain, wanting to preserve the greatest possible catch quota for its fishermen and prevent a de facto recognition of other fishing jurisdictions, opposed this extension. Other European nations, both NATO and Warsaw Pact, aligned themselves with Britain, but African states, for example, keen to preserve their own fishing stocks, declared support for Iceland. They identified themselves with the Icelandic Prime Minister's argument that this was part of a broader battle against colonialism and imperialism. The left-wing Icelandic government chose to ignore provisions in existing treaties that called for the involvement of the International Court of Justice, saying that it was not bound by agreements of the previous right-wing government.

The Icelanders declared the new exclusive fishing zone on 1 September 1972 and began to enforce it by using gunboats to chase non-Icelandic fishing vessels out of the zone, and to use net-cutters on the trawls of foreign boats. By May 1973 the British Trawler Federation (BTF) still had sufficient influence to insist upon naval protection: the MoD and Ministry of Agriculture, Fisheries and Food sent maritime air patrols to give intelligence on the whereabouts of Icelandic gunboats, British support tugs and frigates went north, and Designated Fishing Areas (DFAs) or 'boxes' were designated, within which trawlers would be protected by the Navy. These boxes were promptly filled, not just by British trawlers but by other those of nationalities, including East and West German, Faroese, and Swedish. The British embassy staff in Reykjavik made a poor job of reporting the movements of the Icelandic gunboats.

The Second Cod War escalated in mid-May 1973, and in *Jupiter*, plans for summer leave before deployment to the Far East were dashed when she was ordered north to the fray. Jock took her westabout, passing St Kilda between Boreray and Stac Lee, where thousands of gannets put on a wonderful flying display. Off Iceland, Jock would never forget "my first night up there, when I was called to be told that an Icelandic trawler was practically alongside us filled with international press who requested to interview me. Needless to say, standing on the wing of the bridge in my pyjamas and silk dressing gown, there was little I was allowed to say." There were other lighter moments, and one thing *Jupiter* never lacked was fresh fish, though Jock refused the offer of fresh roe on hot toast brought to him on the bridge by his supply officer. Once, when offered fresh fish, Jock asked the fisherman if in return he would like some fresh loaves of bread, and another trawler, overhearing this exchange on VHF radio, interjected, "'ere, who does he think he is? Bloody Jesus?"

The Icelandic gunboats could try to cut the trawlers' nets by steaming across their sterns, but warships were not allowed to use force to oppose them. Instead, they tried to thwart the gunboats by close manoeuvring in the heavy seas. Visibility was poor in these crowded boxes and collisions were inevitable, when the thin-hulled frigates usually came off worse than the gunboats. Some trawlers joined the quarrel and would steer towards a gunboat, threatening to ram it. Jock found it "certainly character-forming and at times positively hairy, not least when I had to ring on full revs and place the ship on a trawler's engaged quarter [where the gunboat was] to protect it". An added difficulty was persuading the trawlers to stay together in the DFA. At the end of May a plan was made for the trawlers to move from the southeast of Iceland into a new DFA north of Iceland. Much of this was discussed on the trawler radio net and monitored by the Icelandic coastguard. To Commander Mike Rawlinson, in command of the frigate HMS *Plymouth* and Officer in Tactical Command of the forces off Iceland, it seemed that the assembly of frigates for this new phase of the war was haphazard and hurried, and he decided to stay in the southeast DFA with HMS *Cleopatra* and fifteen trawlers. He had never met Jock, but he noted that Jock's signals were to the point, unambiguous, and confident, and so he was content that, starting on the morning of 25 May, a group of trawlers should be led by *Jupiter* to a new, northern DFA.[70]

Four trawlers had already set off independently, unknown to the authorities until an RAF Nimrod reported that the gunboat *Aegir* was lying off Rifstangi, the northernmost tip of mainland Iceland.

At 12:45 on 26 May, *Jupiter* received a call for help from the Grimsby-based Consolidated Fisheries' trawler *Everton*, which was fishing alone fifteen miles off Grimsey Island, west of Rifstangi. The gunboat *Aegir* was threatening to fire on *Everton* if she did not stop and submit to arrest. Instead, *Everton* hauled her nets and headed east. *Jupiter* was about 250 miles away. A thick fog covered the surface of the sea, which had fallen flat, and *Jupiter*'s horn made a mournful sound as she rushed north, relying on her radar to know that the way ahead was clear. The Icelanders' intention was to arrest a trawler fishing within the new 50-mile limit, but the difficulty of boarding and arresting a determined vessel was soon apparent. Initially, blank shots were fired and then shots across the bow, but the skipper of *Everton* refused to stop, even when, from very close range, an inert shot hit the trawler's bow above the waterline. *Everton* and *Aegir* were in VHF communication, and fire was withheld while a trawlerman went forward to inspect the damage. The skipper was told to report when all his crew was safely aft again. Once he had, a second shot was fired into the bow. This firing and orders to stop continued with seven hits registered over the next two hours, including one that hit below the waterline and started a flood in *Everton*'s lower hold. *Aegir*, from close range, did not allow anyone to make repairs, but offered to send help if *Everton* would stop. *Everton* refused and continued doggedly eastwards, even though her pumps were defective, until in the afternoon other British trawlers arrived, some with press on board, and *Aegir* ceased firing. Throughout, it was evident that *Aegir* was under the close control of ministers in Reykjavik. The MoD in London, however, failed to react to Jock's request, which he signalled on his high-speed, eight-hour passage north, for revised rules of engagement.

At 14:45 Rear-Admiral Martin Lucey, the Flag Officer Scotland and Northern Ireland (FOSNI), on Jock's behalf asked the MoD for rules that would allow *Jupiter* to use gunfire to prevent *Aegir* harassing or attempting to arrest *Everton*. At 17:44 Jock asked permission to enter the twelve-mile limit that *Everton* had already entered. Both requests were turned down at 18:30 and it was not until later that evening that British ministers considered taking aggressive action but were advised that such an operation would be difficult without risking life and that its legality was highly dubious. Fortunately, when at 21:00 *Jupiter* reached *Everton*, the fog had lifted and – it was still daylight so far north - there was clear visibility as far as the Iceland coast, whither *Aegir* had withdrawn to avoid confrontation. Divers and a repair party, in the charge of Lieutenant Brian Raymond, were transferred by helicopter and whaler, and by next morning *Everton* was ready to proceed. Advised that his ship was only fit to steam at slow speed in calm weather, the skipper immediately returned to the fishing grounds.[71]

Having, in the passage round Rifstangi, crossed the Arctic Circle and qualified his people for 'blue nose' certificates, Jock could not resist the chance to take *Jupiter* further north and into the ice. Assuming that permission would be refused, he decided not to ask but was caught out when Lucey, commander of the fishery protection operations, flew overhead in a Nimrod.

For the next several days *Jupiter*, in company with the frigate HMS *Cleopatra* and the tug *Statesman*, guarded the northern fishing box. This cold statement of fact does not adequately convey the jostling and the gesturing at close quarters between the trawlers, the gunboats, and the frigates. On one occasion, the courtly Jock, having driven off a gunboat and prevented it from cutting warps, showed himself politely on the bridge wing to salute as *Jupiter* interposed herself between the gunboat and its intended victim, but the Icelandic skipper replied with a double handed V-sign. There were collisions and damage to other vessels, but thanks to his superb ship-handling Jock brought *Jupiter* back to Devonport unscathed.

The *Everton* incident concentrated the minds of all concerned. As a result, the BTF owners agreed to impress on their skippers the importance of close adherence to the Navy's orders and introduced penalties if their skippers failed to comply. When, on 4 June, *Jupiter* found the trawler *St Leger* fishing on her own two miles inside the twelve-mile limit, Jock admitted that this showed the splendid and determined independence of the fishermen, but it made a mockery of the Navy's protection plans, and he reported *St Leger* so that disciplinary action could be taken.

On 5 June *Jupiter* left Icelandic waters. Jock was determined to show his shiny new frigate off Scotland and took the narrow Kyle Rhea channel southbound between the mainland and the island of Skye, where tidal rates can reach eight knots. Fog intervened and visibility dropped to a cable or less, so the entire passage was 'blind', though *Jupiter*'s sound signals did produce some impressive echoes from the surrounding hillsides. Jock had hoped to continue via the sounds of Mull and Jura, but bad visibility thwarted that plan too, much to the relief of the navigating officer, Richard Sanderson.[72]

As *Jupiter* entered Devonport on 8 June the first lieutenant, John Dykes, reported that he could see Annie on the Hoe, standing by Jock's latest sportscar, a British Racing Green  Triumph Stag. Jock replied that she had only just passed her test and certainly would not have driven the car from Hampshire. How wrong he was: Annie had left home in the early hours that morning to avoid the traffic.[73]

## Beira Patrol

On 23 July 1973 *Jupiter* sailed for a nine-month deployment in the Far East. On 7 August she crossed the equator when, by tradition, 'King Neptune' came aboard, and by 15 August *Jupiter* was in Simonstown. Exercises with the South African Navy and a brief visit to Durban followed, before *Jupiter* arrived, on 29 August, in the Beira Channel to start the first of three patrols.

The Beira Channel is the stretch of water on the western side of the Mozambique channel, between Madagascar and the Portuguese colony of Mozambique on the coast of East Africa. It leads to the port of Beira, the nearest port, which is connected by railway to landlocked Zimbabwe (then Southern Rhodesia). In 1965 Southern Rhodesia had made a unilateral declaration of independence, and between 1966 and 1975 the Navy maintained one of the more unusual blockades of the 20th century, known as the Beira Patrol. It was intended to prevent oil reaching Rhodesia, in compliance with United Nations Security Council Resolution 221 of 9 April 1966, which ordered the United Kingdom to prevent, by force if necessary, any vessels suspected of carrying oil to Rhodesia from arriving at Beira.

Initially, the embargo was enforced by the full might of the British government, including an aircraft carrier and maritime patrol aircraft, but the patrol was not extended to other ports nor was the blockade abandoned, even after London became aware that Rhodesia could obtain oil through other routes. *Jupiter*, supported occasionally by the tanker RFA *Tidesurge*, was one lone frigate on patrol and was all but forgotten by planners at home, which caused logistics problems for her supply officer.

Over three months in the autumn of 1973 *Jupiter* conducted three patrols, interspersed with visits to Mauritius, the Seychelles, and Mombasa. There was little traffic in or out of Beira and the patrols were an exercise in leadership and resourcefulness for Jock and *Jupiter*'s officers. Only the brief passage of the Portuguese corvette *João Coutinho* broke the routine of sports, sailing, fishing, kite flying and a host of other competitions, reading, and studying for exams.

Alongside at Port Louis in Mauritius, the Chief Yeoman, RR 'Tommo' Thompson, brought Jock a signal with the surprising news that Lieutenant the Prince of Wales would join *Jupiter* in early January 1974 in Singapore. Next morning, Thompson brought a less welcome signal saying that Jock would be relieved early in his command and would leave the ship in Mombasa. He was incensed, as this denied him some three or four months of command that would have included the Commonwealth Games in New Zealand. "Their Lordships clearly felt that I knew Prince Charles too well to be his commanding officer. It was a huge disappointment."

On passage to Mombasa, Richard Sanderson became particularly proud of himself for having successfully taken – before the age of satnav – an accurate, high-angle sun sight using a sextant and chronometer. Jock, who was packing and preparing to leave the ship, noticed, and ten minutes later Sanderson thought he saw Jock throw his long-course navigation notebooks over the side, which Sanderson took as a complement.

On 24 October 1973 Jock was relieved by Commander John Gunning and was rowed ashore by his officers in *Jupiter*'s whaler. Annie had flown out to join him and they set off on an expedition through Kenya and Tanzania.

He was adjudged to have run a happy and efficient ship that had done well in the fleet.

# Chapter 8: Invicta, HMS *Kent*

HMS *Kent* passes through Tower Bridge for her visit in 1977 to the
Pool of London. Source: John Dukes.

To have a successful naval career every officer, however good they are at sea and in command, needs also to be successful in staff appointments and preferably in the Admiralty, or from the mid-1960s the MoD. Jock's first staff appointment was in the Directorate of Naval Operations and Trade (DNOT), whose remit covered the planning of operations, the deployment and programming of ships, and the defence of merchant vessels.[74] That such an organisation should have survived into the late 20th century was because the Admiralty had been both an administrative and operational headquarters for several centuries (whereas the other heads of service in Whitehall, the British Army and the RAF, had no operational role).[75]

## The Directorate of Naval Operations and Trade

From 1967 until it was abolished in 2003, DNOT was led by a senior captain and under the supervision of an assistant chief of naval staff at 2-star level. Gradually its authority leeched to the Commander-in-Chief Fleet at his underground headquarters at Northwood, Middlesex, but for the period under review the duty commander in DNOT, especially at weekends, was the Navy.

The Slaters returned from their African holiday in time to attend Princess Anne's wedding on 14 November 1973. They established themselves in West Cottage, Soberton and rented a flat in Dolphin Square, Pimlico. In Dolphin Square there were shops, a swimming pool, and a gym, and it was within easy cycling or walking distance of the MoD or 'Mad House'. Jock spent most of the week in London on his own. He supplemented his supper pies prepared by Annie with Loseley dairy ice creams and red wine at 47p a bottle from Justin de Blank in Elizabeth Street. He cycled to work until he suffered a minor collision when a driver failed to stop.

Jock's first director was Captain Gwin Pritchard, known as the Welsh dragon, who was "rather too bombastic with the civil servants who did not warm to him, and at his happiest sitting astride a chair backwards and relating in detail how good a ship-handler he was".[76] His next director was Captain John Cox, "a sailor's sailor but not really comfortable in the political cut and thrust of Whitehall, but who was very supportive of his desk officers, which made life relatively straightforward".[77]

DNOT was a good way to discover how the MoD functioned and Jock enjoyed being the link between the ministry and fleet headquarters. About every five days and fifth weekend he was the duty commander. There was a basic bedroom with adjoining pantry but no washing facilities and, coming fresh from command, washing up his own cups in the sink and padding down the corridor to the bathroom was a shock. As the new boy he was duty over Christmas 1973, when Annie loyally brought in all his presents in a pram.

Meanwhile, in the Pacific, *Jupiter* was in Pearl Harbor, Hawaii whence in March 1974 Jock received a call from an American officer who asked, "Say, your Queen's son is here in the HMS *Jupiter* and we want to invite him to a party. Is his surname Wales or Windsor?"

Jock also noted sadly: "Poor Annie had to spend some considerable time in the Westminster hospital before the arrival of Charles in August 1974. I would go in to visit her in the evening on my way back from work and take her laundry etc. back to the flat to deliver back the following day. We got used to the routine, but it was terribly boring for her."

On 20 July 1974 Turkey invaded Northern Cyprus, following a period of intercommunal violence between Greek and Turkish Cypriots and an attempted coup d'état prompted by the Greek military junta in Athens. British plans were laid to evacuate people from various beaches and, using his initiative, Jock spoke to the BBC and arranged for instructions to be broadcast on the evening news bulletin. "Unfortunately the central staff did not approve, having been hauled over the coals by the Foreign Secretary, Jim Callaghan. So, John Cox and I were summoned to explain ourselves – to give him his due, John was very supportive when I explained what we had attempted to do. I learnt a lot during that period about how very difficult it was to use one's initiative in the MoD – lessons that were to stand me in good stead in subsequent appointments there."

In the autumn of 1975 the Slaters bought Grenville Lodge, outside Droxford, and that October, Jock was invited, for the first time of many, to Balmoral to stalk deer. It was three hectic days:

> Travel North in the night sleeper, have a big breakfast in the Station Hotel, Aberdeen, and then straight out to Balmoral and hit the hill as soon as possible thereafter. If one arrived back in time, there was a huge tea presided over by the Queen and then we all assembled for dinner at about 8pm. Needless to say, by the end of each day, I was pretty pooped. Departure on the final day was a fast drive to catch the night sleeper South with an excellent picnic dinner which fellow guests ate together in one of our compartments, helped by some delicious claret.

## HMS *Kent*

In late 1975 Jock was appointed staff officer operations to then Rear-Admiral John Fieldhouse, who was Flag Officer, Second Flotilla (FOF2). The surface fleet then consisted of several frigate and destroyer squadrons, shared between two flag officers, and a third rear-admiral who was Flag Officer, Carriers and Amphibious Ships (FOCAS), a structure that would be maintained until 1980. Jock was due to join in March 1976 for passage home across the Atlantic, when he would get to know the job. Later that year, Rear-Admiral William Staveley would take over.[78]

Jock had formally acknowledged his appointment and was in Orkney for Christmas when the half-yearly promotion list announced his selection to captain. It was "frankly rather earlier than I thought was good for me," he wrote. Further surprise awaited when Jock called on the Naval Secretary, Rear-Admiral John Forbes, who told him that he was going in command of one of the County-class. When Jock queried this, knowing that these ships were commands for senior captains, he learned that Admiral Sir Edward Ashmore, now the First Sea Lord, had decided that senior captains should go to squadrons, which would benefit from their experience and that "you, Jock, are therefore a very lucky chap". So, the Slaters found themselves at home in Hampshire over the summer of 1976 while Jock attended commanding officers' courses again, before joining HMS *Kent* in refit in Portsmouth in August.

The guided missile destroyer *Kent*, like her sisters named after British counties, was armed with two surface-to-air missile systems – the medium range Seaslug and the short-range Sea Cat – two twin 4.5-inch guns, anti-submarine torpedoes, and a Wessex helicopter. She was a large, handsome ship, approaching the size of a pre-war light cruiser, with good seakeeping qualities and long range – ideal for the global Royal Navy of the era. The ship's company was nearly 500 and there was plenty of room for an admiral and his staff. Her crest was the White Horse of Kent and her motto 'Invicta' meant 'invincible'.

The County-class were propelled by a combination of steam and gas turbines known as COSAG. A gearbox and clutches enabled a single steam turbine fed from diesel-fired boilers, and two gas-fired turbines, working singly or together, to drive twin propellor shafts. COSAG combined the cruising efficiency and reliability of steam with the short start-up and acceleration time of gas. The gas turbines were particularly useful while steam was being raised and at high speed: at 28 knots *Kent* had a range of 3,500 nautical miles.

Jock, who had once expressed a wish that there should have been a specialisation of officers who combined engineering duties with executive functions, prepared himself thoroughly for this aspect of his new command. At the marine engineering school HMS *Sultan*, part of the briefing included a one-to-one for each new commanding officer with a senior artificer or 'tiffy' who had recently served in the class of ship to which the CO was going. On this occasion the tiffy recalled that Jock had come into the room and told him "Don't say a word but correct me if I get anything wrong." Jock then explained in detail the operation of the ship's main engines, both gas and steam, together with the complex gear box, and the parameters of the key auxiliaries, generators, fire pumps, and refrigerators. The chief was impressed.[79]

## Royal Visits to HMS *Kent*

Jock's first royal visitor to *Kent* was Prince Michael of Kent who stayed on board from 27–29 November 1976, while *Kent* undertook weapons training and a replenishment at sea of stores on her passage to the missile ranges off Aberporth. While alongside in Portsmouth during a trials period, on 2 March 1977 Princess Anne drove down from London for a short visit to the ship.

*Kent*'s sponsor at her launch fifteen years before had been Princess Marina, and after her death Katharine, Duchess of Kent took over this role. *Kent* was rededicated in Portsmouth on 21 April 1977 when, spectacularly, the Duchess landed in a helicopter of the Queen's flight on *Kent*'s flightdeck while alongside. Jock was delighted that two friends from his days in the Royal Household were in attendance, Fiona Henderson and Richard Buckley. Buckley had been at Dartmouth when Jock passed out in 1958. However, not even Jock could mastermind the end of the day that culminated with a small fire on board and, to the delight of the guests and especially of their children, the attendance of the Hampshire fire brigade with lights flashing and sirens sounding.

In December 1977 Jock was delighted to take *Kent* to the Pool of London for his final week in command. Apart from the usual formal calls and a lunch at Trinity House, the Slaters gave a lunch and dinner parties for some old royal household and other close personal friends. He recalled: "How lucky I was to have the admiral's quarters for entertaining – very grand and not designed for boy captains!" When Princess Margaret heard he was in town she rang Jock and asked whether she could bring her children to see the ship, and a happy visit ensued followed by a private lunch.

## Exercises, Visits, and Visitors

When Jock joined in August, *Kent* was not due to complete refit until the end of the 1976. Jock thought it must have been quite difficult for his executive officer, Commander George Tullis, to find himself with a captain three years younger than himself, but Tullis was imperturbable and Jock quickly realised that he was extremely fortunate that Tullis had things "most impressively under control and needing little help from me. I just got the credit!" – but he did share the frustration of getting *Kent* out of dockyard hands. *Kent* was still in Portsmouth when Rear-Admiral Staveley walked round her in mid-January 1977. He was unimpressed by her refit and it was not until 7 February that *Kent* sailed for her sea acceptance trials. Staveley, still FOF2, had only faint praise for Jock: "He has made a good start." Maybe Jock had wind of this because on 27 March he wrote to Staveley's successor, Rear-Admiral Martin 'Whiskey' Wemyss, explaining in detail the reasons for the continuing delays, all attributable to the dockyard's lackadaisical work practices. Writing from Gibraltar, where he had taken *Kent* in the hope of finding better weather to complete a tedious series of Seaslug trials, he told Wemyss, "There is a strong technical case for remaining near major dockyard support and analysis facilities, but I have insisted throughout that, from a whole ship point of view, a spell away is essential and my commanders are in full agreement."

Tullis, having achieved so much, was due to leave and his successor was to be Commander Ray Hunter, a contemporary of Jock, a submariner, and a fellow course-mate on the long navigation course. Jock's operations officer was the highly regarded Lieutenant Commander Peter Mosse. Mosse recalled:[80]

> He was charming and immediately put me at ease. I was to be the AWO(A) [Advanced Warfare Officer – Above Water Warfare] as well as operations officer, in charge of above water weapons and fighting the anti-air battle, coordinating the use of our air defence missile system Seaslug, 4.5" guns and fighter support, orchestrated by our two fighter controllers, Lieutenants Hugh Dalgleish and Malcolm 'Monty' Fuller … The relationship between the captain and his operations officer must be slick and good. Jock knew this, tested me early on, and then let me run with it, occasionally tweaking the helm to put his own mark on things, but otherwise letting me get on with it. My confidence and, dare I say it, competence grew accordingly. He would invite me to brief him on the day's activities over breakfast in his cabin each morning … when Jock would have charcoal biscuits while I enjoyed bacon and eggs … Loyalty went both ways and there were never any

misunderstandings as the result. I always knew I had his full support, and he knew he could depend on me. Shared confidence continued to build that trust throughout our time together.

Because of the refit and trials delays, *Kent* undertook a compressed and shortened basic operations sea training. Flag Officer Sea Training (FOST) reported that "the ship was well led and the ship's company worked very hard indeed to achieve satisfactory results in the time allowed. The ship sailed firmly on the upswing. There is still plenty of good potential to develop … *Kent* is an effective fighting unit and should contribute a great deal during her time in the fleet."[81]

One special visitor in 1977 to *Kent* charmed everyone. Lancelot Fleming had been an Arctic and Antarctic explorer, Bishop of Portsmouth and of Norwich, Dean of Windsor, and chaplain to the Queen. Fleming had also been chaplain in the battleship HMS *Queen Elizabeth* in the Mediterranean in the Second World War when Uncle Ned was Commander-in-Chief Mediterranean, and now Jock had invited him aboard to be the temporary ship's chaplain.

From 24–29 June, *Kent* anchored off Spithead for a fleet review to mark the Queen's Silver Jubilee. Admiral Sir Frank Twiss was Jock's special guest, but in a sign of the times a contingent of 40 Wrens were on board for the actual review and helped on the flightdeck to 'man ship' and cheer. The media did not remark on this detail, but Jock thought it might be something for the Guinness Book of Records.

At last that autumn *Kent* might be said to have joined the fleet on passage across the Atlantic and exercises in the West Indies, followed by visits to the East Coast of the USA. Jock ruefully noted that there was a surfeit of senior officers in the task group, however. The captains of HMS *Antrim*, *Hermes*, and *Sheffield* were all senior to him and he was glad when *Kent* was detached for a 'private' visit to Savannah, Georgia. His choice of port may have been influenced by his friend and mentor Ronnie Laughton, who had enjoyed a riotously successful visit to Savannah some five years before in HMS *Jupiter*. This time Jock "had a strange feeling at the outset that the arrangements were going to be shaky, when I turned into the berth from the river to find it completely deserted. It was the first time I've ever lowered a boat with line handlers onto the jetty to secure the ship! Later that morning on one of my calls I was actually taken to the wrong building and when the right one was eventually found I was clearly not expected. To conclude the morning, of the nine people invited for lunch only five materialised and four of these were of little consequence."

As an example of Jock's trust in his people he arranged with his executive officer, Hunter, that they should alternately take command for the short passages between ports. Thus, on 24 September, Hunter found himself standing on the wooden jetty of the destroyer piers at Norfolk naval base awaiting the arrival of *Kent*. She followed four US Navy destroyers into Hampton Roads and was last to berth. Hunter recalled:[82]

> The American destroyers were handled cautiously, with tugs in attendance, since berthing stern-to in tidal waters can be challenging. Eventually, all four had been secured and it was *Kent*'s turn. The faint puff of black smoke from the funnel suggested that the captain had waited long enough: the ship moved briskly ahead into a position where the allocated berth was right astern and about two cables distant. The stern board gathered pace until the stern wave was well up the counter as the ship approached the berth and it was at this point that I noticed the jetty parties, numbering some fifteen US officers and men, moving smartly back from the jetty edge as *Kent*'s quarterdeck loomed ever larger. I had the advantage over them since I was familiar with Jock's ship-handling skills and had not the slightest doubt that the ship would come to a 'half ahead together' stop feet from the jetty. It did. I was happy to acknowledge the sheepish expressions of admiration from my US colleagues, who returned to the edge of the jetty having witnessed a ship being handled with some style.

In December 1977 Jock was relieved in command of *Kent*. During his time, using his energy and leadership, he had succeeded in getting the best out of her. Wemyss told the world that Jock was "an outstanding young captain who has commanded HMS *Kent* with authority, professional skill, and style."

## Royal College of Defence Studies

Founded in 1927 and known as the Imperial Defence College until 1970, the Royal College of Defence Studies (RCDS) took the most promising senior officers of the British armed forces, diplomatic, and civil services, as well as foreign and Commonwealth students. At RCDS's home, Seaford House on the corner of Belgrave Square, these mature students were schooled at the highest level in national and international security and defence matters, in preparation for the top posts in their respective services and countries. Jock became a student in 1978.

A feature of the RCDS was – and is – its overseas tours, and Jock opted to visit the Middle East, including Israel, Jordan, Egypt, and Saudi Arabia. He prepared himself by going to see Uncle Ned's younger brother, General Sir Alan Cunningham. Alan Cunningham was famous for having defeated a numerically superior Italian army in East Africa and having entered victorious into Addis Ababa during the Second World War. He had also, briefly, commanded the 8th Army in the campaign in the Western Desert against the German general Irwin Rommel and his Afrika Korps, but had been relieved of command during Operation Crusader. In 1945–48 General Cunningham was the seventh and last British High Commissioner of Palestine, when that benighted land was ruled by Britain under a mandate from the UN. He had been beset by Zionist terrorists, the Irgun led by the Polish-born Menachem Begin, and by the Stern Gang, who murdered British soldiers and terrorised the Palestinians. In Cunningham's time, Irgun had blown up the King David Hotel, parts of which were in use as the offices of the secretariat of the British mandate government.[83]

Jock hoped to learn from Uncle Alan, and he found him, aged 90, "absolutely on the ball. He spoke at length about his time in Palestine. I only wish that I had recorded our conversation." Jock hoped to meet Begin, who by 1978 was Prime Minister of Israel, but he and Anwar Sadat were at Camp David in Maryland where US President Jimmy Carter was conjuring up the Camp David Accords, which earned Begin and Sadat the Nobel Peace Prize. The RCDS visitors were fortunate to be received and hear from many of the key players in the four countries.

That autumn, the RCDS students visited Germany and the British 1st Armoured Division, an excellent introduction for Jock to the Army and valuable when he was later to become Assistant Chief of Defence Staff (Policy & Nuclear) (ACDS(PolNuc)) in the MoD, though he began to form the opinion that the British Army of the Rhine was grossly overmanned.

A feature of the RCDS was that students were required to produce a paper on a subject of their choice. Jock was conscious that several fellow members spent much of their spare time working up their paper so before the summer holidays he assembled material to write a speech that he imagined would be given by Admiral of the Fleet of the Soviet Union, Sergei Gorshkov, when he was dined by fellow Soviet admirals to mark his 70th birthday:

> I remember well sitting at Kierfiold in Orkney over one long weekend writing my piece (such a waste of time in Orkney!) and finalising it on return to London just before the deadline set for presenting it. Much to my surprise, it clearly met the selector's eye for originality and became

part of the famous Seaford House papers for that year. Infuriatingly, before these were printed, approval had to sought from the MoD and some 'too clever by half' civil servant made some amendments to my paper without consulting me, taking out one or two of the punchy references to British politicians, etc. – pity!

Jock drew on Gorshkov's own writings and those of a wide range of western authors and analysists, reviewed Gorshkov's rise from obscurity, his wartime services, his survival of Stalin's purges, and his decades of power at the summit of the Soviet navy. Subsequently the paper was published in *The Naval Review*.

## Directorate of Naval Warfare

Jock's reward was a return to the MoD on the next rung of the ladder. He was no longer 'desk officer' but an assistant director in the directorate of naval warfare (DNW). He was not too enthusiastic about this but accepted that it was a necessary step if he were to have any chance of further sea command as a captain. His director was Captain RGA 'Dicky' Fitch, an archetypal navigator, self-assured, unflappable, and adept at making important decisions quickly. He was also a wealthy officer who knew how to play the MoD scene but, in Jock's view, did not seem to be too well versed in naval warfare.[84]

For the first time Jock realised how much time Fitch and other directors spent privately discussing the more senior appointments, flag-plotting or, as some called it, 'flagopoly', and Fitch's copy of the Navy List was very well thumbed. It was put away in his drawer not long before his departure, which indicated to all that he was about to be promoted: indeed, Fitch became Naval Secretary and later Second Sea Lord. Fitch's successor at DNW was John Webster, with whom Jock got on well.[85]

Jock also had the title of Navigational Advisor to the Admiralty Board – "a task that was hardly onerous!" – and in that capacity he received a letter from Mountbatten asking about the Mountbatten Course Ruler, an invention of his in the 1930s. "I agreed to send one to HMS *Lindisfarne* to try out and invited them to report back. Some three months later the captain of the ship reported that it was an interesting piece of equipment but had no real use in the modern Navy. However, it was useful on the bridge for putting coffee cups on! I had to be very careful how I put this over to the Noble Lord, who was particularly proud of things he had invented."

There was also a place on the Ships' Names Committee, and Jock become a Younger Brother of Trinity House, an association he would enjoy for many years to come. He did not keep a great record of his time in DNW, beyond noting that it was a busy routine, that he tended to stay in town during the week and go home at weekends, and that Annie only came up to London to attend specific events. Webster reported that "Captain Slater has made an outstanding personal contribution to the work of the naval warfare directorate. He is an officer of the highest integrity, a natural leader, and an obvious choice of flag rank in due course. A gifted and delightful person with whom it has been a pleasure to serve."

Jock's next appointment would take him from Invicta to *Illustrious*.

# Chapter 9: HMS *Illustrious* 1981–83

*Illustrious* leaves the Tyne for sea trials at dawn. Source: Alex Marsh.

Jock was delighted when in the summer of 1980 the First Sea Lord, Admiral Sir Henry Leach, told him he had been chosen to be the first captain of HMS *Illustrious*, which was being built on the Tyne. This, he later told an audience at the ship's 30th birthday dinner, was his happiest day in the Navy, particularly knowing that Uncle Ned had been the Commander-in-Chief Mediterranean Fleet in 1940 and had chosen the previous *Illustrious* for the famous raid on the Italian fleet at anchor in Taranto harbour.[86] There were lengthy courses for commanding officers: some thought that these courses were unnecessary, but Jock felt that they were an excellent opportunity, with no responsibility, for him to take stock. He also arranged to have a few days at sea in HMS *Invincible* to get a feel for one of these new carriers, taking passage from Portsmouth to Gibraltar.

## Marsh's Ship

Swan Hunter Shipbuilders had a contract to prepare their Wallsend shipyard for the construction of the second of the so-called 'command cruisers', HMS *Illustrious*, and in 1975 Alex Marsh, a young naval architect and engineer, was asked to take responsibility for the relatively lightweight structure in a yard that had been building very large crude oil carriers, completely different from warships in construction, skill sets, organisation, and management. From laying the keel in October 1976 to launch on 1 December 1978 and delivery in June 1982, the construction of *Illustrious* remained Marsh's responsibility and she would become known as Marsh's ship. He wrote: [87]

> To me she was really part of the family! Handing her over to the care
> of her first commanding officer was an especially meaningful task,
> made more so by the circumstances of the Falklands War. I recall Jock
> Slater arriving on Tyneside at the end of May 1981 amid rumours that
> the Nott Defence Review would recommend putting *Illustrious* in
> reserve or even selling the Invincible-class ships overseas. This was
> a disturbing time for the shipbuilders and the naval people standing
> by *Illustrious*. Jock Slater's contacts within the RN and the MoD, and
> his determination to get to the truth, at least gave us information and
> encouragement for us all to take a balanced view, whilst we continued
> to work at completing the ship as well as we could.

Jock arrived in Newcastle on Monday, 18 May 1981, the day before a debate in Parliament on the defence estimates, with the press full of depressing reports about the expected emasculation of the Navy in John Nott's defence review due to be announced in June. There was even a rumour on Tyneside that the construction of *Ark Royal*, the third of the command cruisers now known as anti-submarine warfare carriers, would cease. After a walk round *Illustrious,* when Jock met the first members of his ship's company, he thought she looked a shambles, and found it hard to believe that she could possibly be ready in the late summer of 1982. He realised that he was extremely fortunate to have Marsh as shipbuilding director: "He had the most marvellous can-do attitude, despite all the difficulties with a workforce that seemed all too keen to go on strike."

That week, Jock stayed at the Northern Counties Club, where, on his first evening while dining alone, the butler announced that Lord Ridley would like to speak to him on the phone. To Jock's protest that there must be a mistake, the butler insisted and so it was that he was invited to use a flat in Blagdon Hall on the Ridley estate, north of Newcastle. "Thus began a very happy friendship with Matt Ridley."

A few days later on 2 June 1981, at the launch by the Queen Mother of HMS *Ark Royal* – the second ship which she had launched to carry that name – there was some anticipation of what John Nott would say. In the event, Nott was mealy mouthed, saying that "*Ark Royal* is going forward to completion". He would not say whether all three Invincible-class ships would enter service, and he did not disclose that there were already ambitions in the MoD to sell the lead ship of the class, *Invincible*, to Australia.

Work on *Illustrious* continued apace during the summer of 1981, with the shipyard workforce and the Navy working in close harmony. Jock's heads of department became a well-integrated team under his leadership, and by November the ship was ready. Three weeks of sea trials awaited, still under Marsh's civilian control and therefore flying the Red Ensign. An Admiralty trials master drove the ship, frustrating Jock, who would have preferred to be honing his own ship-handling skills. However, his lack of responsibility gave him the opportunity to visit the nooks and crannies of the ship, to meet his 300 uniformed staff and the 350 shipbuilders and contractors, and to demonstrate his phenomenal skill at remembering names and faces. Only during short breaks in the trials programme was he allowed to take the conn – to drive *Illustrious* himself. Although largely successful, the sea trials exposed some problems and for many days *Illustrious* conducted high-speed figure-of-eight turns in Tees Bay, all at considerable cost and delay. Jock, Marsh recalled, "was extraordinarily helpful to me in ensuring that decisions then were taken in the best interests of the project rather than all parties looking to avoid blame". By January 1982 *Illustrious* was ready for final sea trials. Jock arranged for a helicopter to fly passengers and equipment between the shipyard and the ship, helping to make the trials more efficient.

## The Falklands War

The acceptance date of *Illustrious* had been set for September 1982, a target that Marsh thought was achievable but not overgenerous. On Wednesday, 31 March unequivocal intelligence indicated that the Argentinians would invade the Falkland Islands within the next few days. Leach, returning from a visit to Portsdown, thought the briefing material prepared by Nott was too wishy-washy and, in the absence overseas of the Chief of Defence Staff, went to the House of Commons in uniform and snared Prime Minister Margaret Thatcher in her office. There, Nott and others were sowing seeds of doubt in her mind, but when she turned to Leach, he persuaded her to sail a task force: "If we do not, if we pussyfoot in our actions and do not achieve complete success, in another few months we should be living in a different country whose word counts for little."[88]

Jock, Annie, and their boys were at Bembridge, Isle of Wight for an Easter break and his worst memory was watching from an Isle of Wight ferry as *Hermes* and *Invincible* sailed for the Falklands, knowing that *Illustrious* would not be ready until the autumn. That evening, however, he received a call from Vice-Admiral Sir David Hallifax,[89] the Chief of Staff to Admiral Fieldhouse, the Commander-in-Chief Fleet, asking him to report by the end of the week if *Illustrious*'s acceptance date could be brought forward. Jock replied that this was a tall order but immediately went north to Swan Hunter to consult the admirable Alex Marsh. Marsh stipulated 24-hour working and seven days a week and that he should have full authority from his company, and quickly the two men agreed upon 18 June 1982. Jock recalled: "There is nothing like the Geordie spirit when the chips are down, and we witnessed the most remarkable achievement as *Illustrious* was prepared for a premature acceptance. To this day, I am deeply saddened that this incredible success was not later recognised by an award, as there was no doubt in my mind that Alex Marsh and my commander John Tolhurst worked wonders as the ship came to life."

Marsh acknowledged that without a close relationship with Jock, and Jock's ability to lead his side of the relationship, including the MoD and Navy, he could not have achieved the goal. The workforce, who had harboured the incipient threat of a strike, became increasingly identified with the project and with the Navy, especially after 4 May when HMS *Sheffield* was struck by a missile and set on fire. Marsh wrote:

> The realisation that *Illustrious* and her crew may be sailing into harm's way focused all our minds and those of the very supportive local community. Both Jock and I were hands-on throughout the process

although, as both CO designate and chief herder of MoD officials, Jock had much more work to do away from the ship. For both of us, decisions were made quickly – and always in the best interest of the project. Trust between our teams was paramount although with different emphasis. Whilst my and the shipyard's role would come to an abrupt stop on acceptance, Jock's and his team's role would have just started.

Amid a frenzy of activity, one morning, Jock discovered two large holes cut out of the upper deck, one on the starboard quarter of the flightdeck and the other on the forecastle. *Illustrious* was being fitted with two Vulcan Phalanx guns supplied from the USA, a highly classified project: President Reagan had not formally announced that the USA were prepared to give such assistance. Later that same day the two guns were speeding up the M1 on a low loader and were promptly christened the 'Deadly Daleks'. It was proposed that both guns be fully automatic against low-flying missiles, but Jock, not liking the idea of the guns being able to spray depleted uranium shells at 100 rounds/second across a flightdeck filled with aircraft, insisted on command from the operations room. The guns were made ready for firing in record time in live test-firings in the Western Approaches and proved remarkably effective: low-flying targets were swiftly demolished, sending debris close over Jock's head as he watched from the bridge roof.[90]

Throughout, the people of the North East had taken a huge interest in *Illustrious* and on 17 June Jock invited as many as possible to come and see 'their' ship. Around 17,000 workers and their families visited, and Jock promised to return, if possible, to say a proper thank you. Acceptance of *Illustrious* by the Navy took place alongside at Swan Hunters at 10:00, 18 June 1982. Work was still going on in the background but, having signed for the ship and watched the Red Ensign being replaced by the White so that she was now a Royal Navy warship, Jock took command. Within the hour she had slipped her moorings to head out to sea and to her future. Marsh again:

> I was privileged to be able to sail with *Illustrious* down to Portsmouth. Standing on the bridge top with Jock Slater as he conned the ship down the Tyne was a once-in-a-lifetime experience. Jock's piper on the front of the ship set the tone, followed by banners from the crew thanking Swans for 'wor lass', passing *Ark Royal* under construction, cranes dipping in salute, but above all the hundreds of thousands of people who lined the banks of the Tyne to wish *Illustrious* 'God speed' – I don't think there was a dry eye on board, or on land!

Commander John Tolhurst recalled that Jock greatly enjoyed showing off his ship-handling and that speed was built up in the lower reaches of the Tyne until *Illustrious* finally exited between the Tyne piers at 20 knots.[91]

Marsh remembered: "Once through the piers the ship settled into her accelerated shakedown routine for the journey to Portsmouth, interrupted only by one of Jock's trademark first achievements – commissioning at sea. Entry to Portsmouth was met with cheering crowds, following which I disembarked for the journey back to Newcastle, sure in the knowledge that *Illustrious* was in very capable hands."

Further trials and work-up were compressed into six weeks and by July, *Illustrious* was at Portland for a three-week Basic Operational Sea Training, where John Webster was now FOST and his Commander Sea Training was Commander John Brigstocke.[92] On 20 July off Portland, Jock welcomed a weary-looking *Hermes* back from the Falklands with a high-speed steam past,[93] and on Monday, 2 August, *Illustrious* sailed from Portsmouth. Fog almost spoiled the occasion but Lieutenant Commander Tim Gedge,[94] commanding 809 Naval Air Squadron of Sea Harriers, groped his way from buoy to buoy between Spithead and Fountain Lake until he could land-on. Fortunately, the weather lifted before *Illustrious* sailed at 11:00, enabling a fly-past of nine Sea King HAS5s from 814 Naval Air Squadron to enhance the spectacle for the thousands of well-wishers on the seafront there to give her a rousing send off.

Princess Margaret, the ship's sponsor, who had launched *Illustrious*, had rung Jock to wish her "God speed". Now, Princess Alexandra came from Cowes in *Britannia*'s royal barge to wave her off at the Outer Spit Bouy. That afternoon in the Channel the rest of Gedge's squadron landed on. That evening she rendezvoused with the frigates HMS *Battleaxe* and *Amazon* and the tanker RFA *Appleleaf* for the 7,400-mile passage to the Falklands.


## Jock's Leadership

So much had been achieved in such a short space of time, thanks to Jock's leadership, his confidence in his heads of department (HoDs) led by the executive officer Commander John Tolhurst, and his willingness to delegate. "You run the ship," he told Tolhurst. "Get the HoDs right and all else will follow."

Commander (Air), head of the aviation department in *Illustrious*, was Commander Ted Hackett, who observed Jock closely and said that he was a brilliant delegator:[95]

He always let people get on with it. I admired him hugely in his ability to stand back and let his heads of departments sort the problems and drive it. And we all were right behind him. He was a brilliant leader. Tremendous style, he had natural style in terms of the way he was and how he dealt with people socially and so forth. And he was a good and wonderful man to work for. And he let me just get on with it … The thing that people don't appreciate is that the captain is the ship, and the ship is the captain. Jock was the driving force behind everything, the style, the way it's done, the way the team gets together, the speed at which we working, moving 24/7 all the time, from the maker's wall to commissioning at sea, people were working as hard as they possibly could to be prepared for when we sailed for war all the way down the Atlantic.

## The Passage South

*Illustrious* made a fast passage south while completing phase two of her work-up: on 7 August she was off Gibraltar, and she crossed the equator with due deference to King Neptune on 15 August. The following day she reached Ascension Island.

On Sunday, 16 August Jock was in his sea cabin when he heard the 'man overboard' alarm as the ship lurched to starboard. Jens Andersen, a young air mechanic, playing in goal for his team, had dived for the ball and fallen over the side, fortunately without hitting any structure. The officer of the watch saw him go and put the wheel hard over to avoid Anderson being sucked into the screws, and in the short interval before Jock reached the bridge, Anderson was already in a lifebelt, which had been released automatically, and was holding the ball above his head with the sea boat approaching. Jock recalled:

Jens Anderson, while playing football on the flightdeck of *Illustrious*, dived for the ball and fell over the side, 1992. Source: Slater archive.

It was a classic man overboard recovery. I asked the master-at-arms [MAA], Peter Hill, to bring Andersen up to the bridge so that I could congratulate him on keeping his head but to tell him not to make a habit of it. I noticed that he was shaking quite badly and, after he left, said to the MAA that he ought to be checked out in the sick bay as he might be suffering from shock. 'Shock, Sir?' he replied. 'He's not suffering from shock, Sir, he was just shit scared meeting you!' I did not know I had that effect on people!

On 27 August, just ten weeks since leaving the builder's yard on the Tyne, *Illustrious* rendezvoused with *Invincible,* commanded by an old friend Captain Jeremy Black, in the carrier operating area off the Falklands. She then assumed defence watches and maintained them for the next 60 days. Jock was somewhat surprised to be refused permission by Rear-Admiral Derek Reffell, who had taken over as task force commander,[96] to close *Invincible* for a steam past. Nevertheless, after Reffell in HMS *Bristol* had gone off some distance Jock sent a message by signal lamp telling Black to steer a steady course at 12 knots while he closed from astern at 30 knots to pass up her side at about 120 feet. Crowded onto their flightdecks, the ships' companies cheered each other, while Jock concentrated on ensuring that *Illustrious* did not hit *Invincible* "which would certainly have been the end of my career in a very big way".[97]

Jock was conscious that winter was setting in and that, whatever else happened, the weather and the seas would worsen. Over the previous months he had exchanged letters with Black. Now he flew over to talk to him. As a result of the lessons learned from the fire that had destroyed HMS *Sheffield,* everyone was required to wear oxygen bottles in satchels around their necks, but Jock put a bottle of champagne in his satchel. "It went down very well and after a brief visit to the wardroom I had lunch with Jeremy in his sea cabin."

A young protégé embarked in *Invincible* was Prince Andrew, a pilot flying helicopters in 820 Naval Air Squadron. He asked Black for permission to fly across to see Jock, who he had known since he was a boy. During the war, the 22-year-old Prince, who was then second in line to the throne, had flown his Sea King helicopter on a variety of missions including anti-submarine patrols, troop transport, search and rescue, and as a decoy against Argentine anti-ship missiles. The Prince recalled in his own words:[98]

When I think back to a day when a young man went to war, full of bravado, I returned a changed man … I was flying and saw a chaff shell fired from one of our ships that passed not that far in front of us.

For a moment it was on a steady bearing before it began to cross to our left. The terror that that was going to be that, just for a moment, has had a lasting and permanent effect on me … I put away childish things and false bravado and returned a man full in the knowledge of human frailty and suffering.

Jock could not help but feel a tinge of jealousy that Black was about to return to a hero's welcome while *Illustrious* would be left in the South Atlantic to continue the unglamorous work of wrapping up Operation Corporate, the action to retake the Falklands.

HMS *Illustrious* steams past HMS *Invincible*, off the Falklands, 27 August 1982.
Source: Slater archive.

## On Patrol

The following day Reffell embarked in *Illustrious*, which for the next few weeks kept mostly to the east of the Falklands with only occasional forays to the west to project her airpower. She made two transits of the Falklands Sound and on three occasions anchored in the outer roads of Port William.

Jock felt sorry for Reffell, who was not a comfortable boss. He was "more like a bear with a sore head". He might have expected to command an operation such as the Falklands campaign, having commanded *Hermes* and been Director of Naval Warfare and Commodore Amphibious Warfare, but the crisis had found him at his shore headquarters and another flag officer, Rear-Admiral Sandy Woodward, was already at sea and exercising ships off Gibraltar, and the Commander-in-Chief had chosen to send Woodward south. As a result, lunching with Reffell on *Illustrious*'s admiral's bridge was no great pleasure: the admiral had little sense of humour and was rather shy. Fortunately, he seemed to like *Illustrious* and did not interfere in Jock's command.

Once, Jock left Tolhurst in command and flew ashore, and while stretching his legs in the hills above San Carlos Bay he was stopped by a sentry who barked "Who Goes There?" It was typical that, when allowed to proceed, Jock engaged the sentry in small talk and on finding that he had a brother in the ship, arranged for a helicopter to pick him up the next day for a family reunion on board.

By late October the Royal Engineers, helped by *Illustrious*'s ship's company, who volunteered to spend time ashore as a break from the tedium of defence watches on board, had extended the runway in Stanley and a force of four RAF Phantoms arrived. Leaving the Falklands on Trafalgar Day, Jock ordered a farewell fly-past over Stanley by his 21-strong air group: launching and recovering them from a small flightdeck, where they could not all be ranged at once, was another organisational, engineering, and aviation triumph.

*Illustrious* returned home via North America. First she visited Roosevelt Roads in Puerto Rico, where the ship's company could vent their pent-up energies, then Fort Lauderdale and Philadelphia. Peter Payne recalled another of Jock's displays of ship-handling at Philadelphia, where, to the amazement of the Delaware river pilot, Jock simply drove *Illustrious* in and parked her alongside the jetty as if she were a big grey car. Tugs hovered nearby, their crews astonished. When she arrived in Portsmouth, *Illustrious* had been in the fleet for 125 days, 107 of them at sea, and had steamed 32,200 miles.

## Round Britain

In the spring of 1983 Jock wished to make good on his promise to return to the Tyne and chose to steam *Illustrious* anti-clockwise around Britain. He was brought down to earth a little when, on his departure from Portsmouth, the Queen's harbourmaster accused him of speeding.

He was also keen to mark *Illustrious*'s affiliation with the Cinque Ports, and after entertaining the great and good to lunch they were landed so that they could go up to Dover Castle and witness *Illustrious*, followed by the frigate HMS *Naiad*, crossing the harbour from west to east. The transit involved a difficult 90-degree turn to starboard and, as Jock later admitted, it was a foolhardy plan. The tidal stream across the entrance was stronger than anticipated, making turning without tugs inside the harbour a major challenge. *Newcastle*'s commander, Paul Haddacks, remembered "the Dover incursion quite well. As I followed two cables behind, *Illustrious* turned on a sixpence in the harbour and out we went again. My reaction was that it was a very skilled piece of ship-handling bravado carried off with great aplomb. It didn't feel reckless or unsafe, though a different view might be taken in more recent times!"[99] It was with some relief that Jock signalled his loyal greetings to the Lord Warden of the Cinque Ports, the Queen Mother, as he passed safely between the moles at the eastern end of the harbour and out into the Channel.

After intensive air defence exercises in the North Sea, *Illustrious* returned, as Jock had promised, to Tyneside, where she received some 30,000 visitors. Continuing north-about, Jock told his people that if they lived on any remote spot on the coast *Illustrious* might sail close so their families could wave. He did not recall if anyone took him up on this, but she certainly sailed close to East Haven in Angus for his mother to see *Illustrious* as the ship steamed by. In the Orkneys, she anchored briefly in Scapa Flow, when Jock was able to entertain several old friends, among them Mary Graham from Sandwick, "who I don't think had ever been out of Orkney and, dressed in her woolly hat and Sunday coat, climbed the ladder bearing a basket of eggs for me! Apparently, she said nothing on the tour, overawed by it all, but talked about the visit to her dying day."

He had hoped to make the intricate passage through the Kyle of Lochalsh, known in Gaelic as the Strait of the Foaming Loch, and down the Sound of Raasay between the islands of Raasay and Skye, but as fog grew thicker Lieutenant Commander Berry Reeves,[100] his able navigating officer, advised that it was not prudent to go on. So, *Illustrious* turned north again and instead transited the Sound of Mull, though she failed to summon Captain David Mellis to play his pipes from the battlements of Duart Castle.[101] She then continued through the whirlpools of Corryvreckan and the Sound of Jura, and past Portpatrick, where Jock's brother Tony and his family watched. Much later, Jock reflected: "Goodness knows what Their Lordships would have thought had they been aware of the details of our circumnavigation!"

A final stop before reaching Aberporth for missile firings was the Isle of Man: the Falklands War was still very much in peoples' minds and the crowds lining the shore and cliffs were most impressive. So ended a memorable eighteen-day round-Britain trip before *Illustrious* reached Devonport to embark the air squadrons for the forthcoming NATO exercise, Ocean Safari.

HRH Princess Anne visits HMS *Illustrious*, 24 May 1983.
Source: Slater archive.

## The Alraigo Incident

These last few weeks of Jock's command included a four-day visit to Lisbon, whose harbour *Illustrious* shared with the French carrier *Foch,* before both ships took part in one of NATO's regular exercises, Ocean Safari. There were not too many incidents between British and French sailors ashore, and Jock's cousin Hugh Byatt was now the British ambassador. However, while the ambassador's wife, Fiona, wanted to show off Prince Andrew, who was still in 820 Naval Air Squadron but now embarked in *Illustrious*, Jock ensured that 'H', the Prince's sobriquet, should, like any other 20-something, enjoy a run ashore with his fellow officers.

Once at sea, on 6 June 1983, a night encounter exercise was planned against *Foch*. In *Illustrious* it was intended to use radio and radar silence and send pairs of Sea Harriers to search visually, reporting what they had seen on landing back on board. The first sortie thought they had identified *Foch* and towards evening a second sortie was launched, preparatory to an attack. This ruse, known as EMCOM silence, was illegal under peacetime flying rules, but confidence was high in *Illustrious* until a grim-faced Ted Hackett asked to speak to Jock. A Sea Harrier had exceeded its sortie time and was missing.

Whether he suffered an instrument failure or misread his instruments, 25-year-old Sub-Lieutenant Ian Watson, fresh from training, had found himself in his Sea Harrier lost in growing darkness over an empty sea with only a few minutes' fuel left.[102] His radio seemed not to work, but switching on his radar he glimpsed a small contact 70 miles away and turned towards it. The contact turned out to be a small, Spanish container ship, *Alraigo*, and once alongside Watson thought to ditch in the water, but by eye he measured the containers lashed on deck to be 40ft by 16ft and, though the Sea Harrier might overlap, he thought his aircraft would fit on top. Gesturing his intentions by hand, he edged sideways onto the containers. But as he did so the swell caused everything to disappear from view except the sea and sky, and as he hit the roof of the containers the aircraft began to roll. Watson promptly collapsed the undercarriage to hold it on deck.

Meanwhile, Jock remained calm "but a little bit tense" until next morning, when he heard by a signal from the British naval attaché in Madrid where his aircraft was. For a relieved Hackett, "It didn't matter about the diplomacy or the aircraft or whatever. The most important thing to me was the pilot was all right."

Later, Jock told a journalist in *Illustrious* that it was a remarkable feat of airmanship that had saved a valuable asset and would go down in the annals of aviation history. The following day Admiral Ace Lyons, USN, flying his flag in USS *Mount Whitney*, announced his intention of coming over to *Illustrious*, where he shook Jock warmly by the hand and in his classic American drawl said: "Jock, congratulations, that was the finest f*****g bit of British salesmanship I have ever witnessed!"[103]


**The Last Alongside**

At the end of Ocean Safari, and after a weekend in Brest, Jock was keen to make an impressive departure, which nearly ended in disaster when the quarterdeck party was slower to clear the stern lines than expected and, thinking that all was well down aft, Jock went ahead too soon. Fortunately, no one was hurt: "It gave me something of a turn – there but for the grace of God!" Portsmouth on 27 June saw Jock's last ever alongside. "It was a most unhappy moment for me to give the order 'ring off main engines' knowing that this was the last time I would ever command a ship at sea – something that I truly believed I was better at than anything else, and realising that from that moment onwards I was destined for life ashore."

*Illustrious* had not been at war and Jock had not even participated in the retaking of the Falklands, as he would have wished, but his two years of command of her had been remarkable. Nearly 50 years later Jock and his heads of department, including Alex Marsh, would still hold annual reunions.

## HMS *Dryad* 1983–85

From 1983–85, Jock commanded HMS *Dryad*, a shore establishment at Southwick, north of Portsdown, which was also the home of the School of Maritime Operations. Jock was responsible for coordinating the training, while other captains, some senior to him, commanded individual faculties. Much of his duties were social and ceremonial and, needless to say, Annie played an absolutely key role in those two years. The training captain was the calm, responsible, and courteous Tony Provest, who had been second in command of *Invincible* in the Falklands War, and the main business of the school was incorporating the lessons learned during the Falklands War into tactics and operations.

To commemorate the 40th anniversary of D-Day, the map room used by General Eisenhower in June 1944 was opened to visitors and the Queen and Prince Philip came. Among other visitors was Secretary of State for Defence Michael Heseltine, causing Jock to begin to form his impressions of politicians. When Heseltine's reorganisation of defence was announced the following month, Jock reflected that "I have always watched these announcements uneasily as I had felt for some time that, slowly but surely, the senior civil servants were attempting to undermine the authority of the single-service chiefs in the hopes that they eventually could be eased out of Whitehall and thus give the Permanent Under-Secretary and his inner team greater control."

Jock wanted the MoD to buy a bridge simulator for *Dryad* and "despaired at the bureaucratic arguments that seemed to be endless knowing that, had I been given quite a reasonable sum of money, I could have had one (German made!) up and running there and then. Eventually we did get a simulator at *Dryad* and it proved first class. It was my first experience of the incompetence of the MoD procurement system run by worthy but unimaginative civil servants. The longer the delay the higher the cost."

Admiral Lord Lewin was guest of honour at *Dryad*'s Trafalgar Night Dinner in 1984 and stayed with the Slaters. "My old friend, Hugo White, who was the Principal Staff Officer to the Chief of the Defence Staff, Field Marshal

'Dwin' Bramall, rang me up that afternoon [to tell] me that … Bramall had inadvertently let the cat out of the bag that I was destined to succeed Julian Oswald in 1985 as ACDS (Policy and Nuclear). It was the first that I knew that I had even been selected for promotion and Hugo wanted me to know secretly what had happened in case Terry Lewin mentioned it [but] he kept the news firmly to himself – and so did I!"

The formal letter about his promotion and future appointment was slipped to Jock months later by Naval Secretary Rear-Admiral Richard Thomas as he walked down the aisle of Chichester cathedral at the start of a carol service. Jock should have been happy about the future but in fact he was extremely uneasy, because he did not consider himself to be "a natural MoD warrior and did honestly worry that [he] was intellectually not up to that particular appointment. Anyway, time would tell and with the tough competition up the ladder, I was lucky to get a job at all."

Jock was relieved at HMS *Dryad* by Captain Tony Norman on 7 May 1985.

Jock prepares for a live breakfast-time broadcast from the map room at
HMS *Dryad* with Bruce Parker during D-Day commemorations, June 1994.
Source: Slater archive

# Chapter 10: Nuclear Matters

As a newly promoted rear-admiral, a 2-star post, Jock's appointment to the central staff of the MoD as ACDS (Pol/Nuc) covered defence policy, nuclear affairs, and space. Outside his broad remit for nuclear weapons policy, another officer, Rear-Admiral John Grove, was Chief Polaris Executive (later Chief Strategic Systems Executive) and supervised the engineering and operational aspects of the introduction into service of a second generation of nuclear-powered submarines carrying the Trident missile. Other items in Jock's portfolio were the British National Space Centre, the Defence Policy Group (Space), the Defence Studies Steering Group, numerous inward and outward visits such as by the NATO Defence College in Italy and the Defence Review Committee from Brussels, and the impact of the newly published US Forward Maritime Strategy together with meetings of RN Athletics of which Jock became president.

**A Bad Start**

Jock and Annie moved into a bedsit in Elizabeth Street, SW1, which gave him a gentle walk through Victoria and St James's Park to the MoD. In their first week, on return to the flat after attending Julian Oswald's farewell party, they found there had been a burglary. Personal possessions and Jock's new leather case containing his personal notes were stolen. The Metropolitan Police were slow to arrive and to Jock's amazement said they were not interested in thefts under £1m in value. Fortunately, there were no classified papers in the briefcase, but Jock was concerned about the loss of his preparatory work for a conference at Ditchley on ballistic missiles, not least because it was to be his first appearance as ACDS (Pol/Nuc). He knew he was on a steep learning curve.

A week later it became clear that a policeman had sold details of the theft and Jock's name was linked on radio to the false report that the "country's nuclear chief" had lost classified papers. Later, Secretary of State Michael Heseltine had to defend him in the House of Commons. It was a terrible start to Jock's first appointment to the flag list.

## Well Served

In his new role Jock was aided by some extremely able civil servants, including Dr Edgar Buckley, who he referred to as "the doctor", and David Fewtrell, and some gifted military people, especially Brigadier Thomas Boyd-Carpenter, the Director of Defence Policy. Boyd-Carpenter wasn't "a man of much humour but [was] intellectually extremely well endowed. He invariably came up with some excellent thoughts and I could tell he was somewhat irritated when I suggested something that he had not considered!" Jock reported to the Deputy Under Secretary (Policy) David Nichols. "He was something of a challenge for me as he felt that the MoD was no place for the military and went out of his way to manoeuvre the civil servants on his staff to the disadvantage of my military team. I, therefore, spent far too much time working to mend fences and covering for him. To this day, I have no idea why he was in a job for which he was clearly unsuited. That said, I made it my business to get on with him, and think I was partially successful."

Jock set up a series of working lunches to get know his colleagues, catered for by Annie. He also began a diary, though this soon became intermittent and could not include any detail of what he was working on.

One of Jock's early visits was to the Army and RAF in Germany to better understand the role of tactical nuclear weapons on the Central Front, a key aspect of British and NATO defence posture. Once more he "was amazed to see the number of people out there and did wonder what on earth kept so many so busy". There began a continual round of defence talks and conferences at home and abroad. For staff talks, with Canada, Denmark, France, Norway, and Sweden, Jock's homework was, as ever, thorough and time-consuming. The International Institute for Strategic Studies' conference in Berlin in September 1985 was typical of these events. There, Jock was surprised to meet so many academics and diplomats who seemed to be able to talk inexhaustibly on subjects of which they had no operational experience. Privately he admitted that "I was definitely not on the same intellectual sphere as many of them."

## Strategic Defence Initiative

He took up his appointment in interesting times because there were problems of at least two decades in the making. In 1960, Britain had cancelled Blue Steel Mark II, an air-launched ballistic missile, in expectation of being able to buy the longer-range, US-built Skybolt missile. This meant that when the USA cancelled Skybolt in 1962 Britain had no alternative, until Prime Minister Harold Macmillan negotiated the Nassau Agreement with President John Kennedy. This enabled the 1963 Polaris Sales Agreement (PSA), under which the UK would operate four Resolution-class submarines, each armed with sixteen US-built Polaris missiles. Subsequently, in two rounds of Strategic Arms Limitation Talks between the USA and the USSR in 1969 and 1979, and in an Anti-Ballistic Missile Treaty in 1972, the Soviets argued for the nuclear arsenals of Britain and France to be included when counting the strategic balance in Europe.

Reagan was elected president of the USA in 1980, partly on his election manifesto promise of modernising America's strategic nuclear forces. While the British considered replacing their Polaris missiles with the Trident C-4 system, the Americans planned by 1989 to upgrade their system from Trident C-4 to D-5, a new missile with a greater range. The British were wary of how the cost of D-5 would weigh against that of keeping the C-4 and not having commonality with the USA. After some horse-trading the UK agreed to buy 65 Trident D-5 missiles as part of a shared pool of weapons to be held at Kings Bay in the USA, but the British would build their own submarines and warheads. HMS *Vanguard*, the first of a new generation of Trident missile carrying boats, was due to be ordered in early 1986, part-way through Jock's time as ACDS (Pol/Nuc).[104]

Reagan began to characterise the doctrine of mutually assured destruction ('MAD') as a "suicide pact" and instead, in March 1983, towards the end of his first term in office, called for a Strategic Defence Initiative (SDI) requiring advanced technological systems yet to be researched and developed. SDI would nullify attack on the USA by Soviet intercontinental ballistic missiles (ICBMs), an idea likened to the fictional space weapons in *Star Wars*.

The weekend after Jock's first Ditchley Park conference, where he was impressed by the US delegation led by Al Gore, Jock flew to Brussels to head the UK team for the High Level Group (HLG). The HLG was chaired by the USA and was a regular meeting of national policymakers and experts from Allied capitals and a forum for all aspects of NATO's nuclear policy, planning, and force posture. This first taste of top-level international meetings was a baptism by fire, which proved to be an excellent opportunity to get to know some of Jock's key opposite numbers. He heard the US Assistant Secretary of Defense Richard Perle, known to many as the 'Prince of Darkness' for his strong anti-Soviet views, make a strong anti-Soviet pitch on treaty violations,, and he returned to London that evening in Perle's personal aircraft and found his hawkish views almost disturbing.

Jock's first formal meeting with Michael Heseltine was to discuss Reagan's SDI. Heseltine wanted to follow the Reagan initiative but Jock saw only the Minister's burning personal ambition and little interest in defence. He suspected that Heseltine was uncomfortable in face-to-face meetings with senior military advisers, and that his Private Secretary, the equally ambitious and wily civil servant Richard Mottram, saw his task as preventing the military from having too much access to his boss.[105] At a meeting in August 1985 about the British National Space Centre, Jock sensed that Heseltine had not read the brief Jock's team had prepared so meticulously but that he had the political nose to sniff out politically important or sensitive aspects. "The rest he can dismiss with distain. I have yet to warm to him!" Opinions did not change, and in October, after a presentation to Heseltine on the UK's amphibious capability, Jock noted that "The Secretary of State is unconvinced – actually he had clearly made up his mind on financial grounds before the presentation and preferred not to listen to the pros and cons. He has four major interests, Heseltine, politics, industry, and defence [which is] a poor fourth."

At about this time the government indicated its intention to halt the 3% pa growth in defence spending, which, Jock realised, would "mean a very difficult time ahead with some unpalatable decisions to be made. I must confess that never having served in DN Plans [the Directorate of Naval Plans and senior naval directorate, whose business was the Navy's long-term budgetary plans], I do find the financial aspects of MoD life extremely difficult to get to grips with." There were other policy and financial issues, and after an interdepartmental seminar about SDI, Jock was concerned that "there has been so much nonsense talked and so many forecasts made by many who have not really studied the facts. The SDI, after all, is at present merely a research programme to establish whether BMD [ballistic missile defence] is possible. The research is also a prudent hedge against known activity in this field by the Soviets. Of course, if BMD can be achieved, we will be engaged well into the next century in ensuring stability during the dangerous transition from offensive to defensive weapons."

## Thatcher's Four Points

Britain was faced with the mass obsolescence of other weapons in its nuclear arsenal. The 1963 PSA had given Britain access to designs for smaller, lighter nuclear warheads, which became the WE177 family of bombs, the smallest version of which, with a 10-kiloton warhead, could be delivered by the small Wasp helicopter and used as a nuclear depth charge against submarines.[106] When Jock took office the MoD was looking at how the WE177 could be replaced, and he inherited from the Theatre Nuclear Weapon Policy Steering Group a rationale for the UK to continue to possess tactical nuclear weapons, which would underpin the strategic nuclear deterrent and provide a range of options, short of strategic response, to counter increasing threats from what in the Cold War were known as Third World powers and to preserve for Britain an important sub-strategic role.[107]

However, in the USA, President Reagan was developing a vision of a world free of nuclear weapons and on 16 January 1984 he delivered a speech in which he said, "Our aim was and continues to be to eliminate an entire class of nuclear arms. Indeed, I support a zero option for all nuclear arms. As I've said before, my dream is to see the day when nuclear weapons will be banished from the face of the Earth."[108] Reagan's zero option looked dangerous to Prime Minister Margaret Thatcher and at Camp David at the end of that year she told Reagan of her firm conviction that the SDI research programme should go ahead:

> Research is, of course, permitted under existing US/Soviet treaties; and we, of course, know that the Russians already have their research programme and, in the US view, have already gone beyond research. We agreed on four points: (1) the US, and western, aim was not to achieve superiority, but to maintain balance, taking account of Soviet developments; (2) SDI-related deployment would, in view of treaty obligations, have to be a matter for negotiation; (3) the overall aim is to enhance, not undercut deterrence; (4) East–West negotiation should aim to achieve security with reduced levels of offensive systems on both sides.

In November 1985, at a summit meeting in Geneva, President Reagan and Soviet General Secretary Mikhail Gorbachev met to discuss the possibility of improved diplomatic relations, human rights, the arms race, and the SDI.

## A Friend in the USA

Franklin C. Miller headed the USA's Office of the Secretary of Defense Theater Nuclear Policy Office, where he led on deterrence and nuclear targeting policy.[109] Miller was part of the team who had negotiated with the British over the D-5 missile, and he knew that, while Trident had been designed with twelve warhead carriage positions, the American Single Integrated Operation Plan intended to use only eight of these. Miller was aware that the British had contracted to buy the missile system configured for twelve positions, and after careful questioning, that eight positions had been thought insufficient for British purposes. With the increasing obsolescence of Polaris, the British had embarked on Chevaline, which needed the extra carriage positions for decoys to swamp Soviet missile defences and to ensure that enough warheads would get through an anti-ballistic missile (ABM) defence to destroy Moscow.[110]

Miller had done well to see through this veil of secrecy and grasped "the blinding reality that [the USA was] basically ignorant of how the British government thought about nuclear deterrence". He also realised that the 1958 UK–US Mutual Defence Agreement was a quarter of a century old and was in danger of expiry "just by accident". Seeking to strengthen the relationship between the Department of Defense in Washington and the MoD in London, Miller found a listening ear in Jock, but the route to Jock was not straightforward and, like many aspects of the special relationship between the UK and USA would turn on personal relations.

Captain Richard Irwin was already in Washington, seconded to the Strategic Systems Project Office in Crystal City. Irwin's British predecessor had been an RAF officer who was not very interested in naval matters, but who mentioned to Irwin before he left that "a US civil servant, Frank Miller, was very pro-Brit, very knowledgeable about strategic weapons, and should be cultivated". New in office, Irwin cold-called Miller, who told him that "There is no point in coming to talk to me again unless you are able to do so at the Top Secret Codeword level. I already know all there is to know about your system at the Secret level and have told the MoD everything I am prepared to at that level." Miller hinted that if there were talks at a higher security level he had much to offer. Irwin relayed this to Grove, the Chief Strategic Systems Executive, who consulted Jock as the appropriate ACDS.

When the British Chief of Defence Staff, Fieldhouse, a submariner with many good contacts in the USA, heard this he sent Jock to Washington. Irwin recalled that "[We] called on Frank and opened the most amazing exchange of very highly classified information about the use of nuclear weapons, which I was authorised to continue, and which I further followed up a few years later when I [became] Director of Nuclear Systems." The first of what became six-monthly nuclear staff talks was held in the autumn of 1986. The British team was led by newly promoted Air Commodore Peter J Harding, who arrived in Washington with a personal letter of introduction from Jock to Miller. These talks followed Jock's initiative but were not a one-way street. As Miller recalled, they provided a forum for an exchange of views on a wide range of subjects related to nuclear deterrence. The American and British views of the Soviet's value systems were different: the UK had a much deeper technical understanding of the effects of fire damage whereas the US tended to concentrate on blast damage, and the UK had considerable knowledge of penetration aids, which would inform US research into BMD. The talks established an enduring web of relationships among key nuclear policy officials on both sides of the Atlantic, which strengthened as the initial participants became more senior. This in turn enabled greater US–UK collaboration when changes to NATO's theatre nuclear forces were discussed at NATO HLG meetings and would eventually facilitate the sale of Tomahawk missiles to the UK, the basing of US Army Air Forces heavy bombers in the UK, and access to high and very high frequency communications.

Key to all this was the personal relationship between Jock and Miller, who rated Jock as "an extraordinary officer". The respect was mutual, and Jock would be instrumental in ensuring that Miller's role as father and architect of the US–UK dialogue on nuclear weapons policy would in due course be recognised by an honorary knighthood.[111]


**International Relations**

At the end of March 1986, in Würzburg, Bavaria, Jock attended the Nuclear Planning Group, the senior body on nuclear matters among the NATO countries. They discussed specific policy concerns associated with nuclear forces and wider issues such as nuclear arms control and nuclear proliferation. Jock, now grounded in NATO's nuclear doctrine, met and befriended many high-level delegates.

Next, he paid a first visit to San Diego and attended a conference on arms control and extended deterrence. Once more he was amazed at how "these so-called defence academics dress up fairly straightforward subjects in such a plethora of erudite words. I sometime wonder if I am missing something. But invariably conclude that words, words, words – and often other people's words! – are their bread and butter. Still, there is no doubt that those of us with massive in-trays and wide-ranging responsibilities do benefit from exposure to alternative views." In May, Jock was again in the USA for UK/US defence talks in Key West. He noted how the Americans only seemed to be able to talk on their own subject and were "seldom prepared to branch out [but] were clearly delighted to be free from the fetters of the Pentagon and we had a wide-ranging, constructive, and agreeable set of talks."

The late summer and autumn of 1986 were even busier than usual. The season began innocuously with a dinner at the Naval and Military Club to celebrate the centennial edition of Brassey's, which had originated as an annual review of the Navy, when Robert Maxwell spoke about the importance of Trident to UK defence – leaving Jock thinking that this was a surprising line for a socialist and that it would be interesting to speculate on what Maxwell would say in the red-top *Daily Mirror* in the run-up to the next election.

Jock's travel was against the background of dinners and social engagements, including invitations to the wedding of Prince Andrew and Sarah Ferguson, to the Castle of Mey, and to Balmoral. It was little wonder that one Friday night he fell asleep at a dinner party, noting that "people who entertain on a Friday night are asking for jaded guests", or that at the end of a day's stalking and a barbeque at Balmoral he was beginning to lose his voice [and] was ordered to bed by the Queen: "One can hardly disobey the Lord High Admiral!"


**Reagan and Gorbachev**

Jock's main preoccupation in late 1986 was as organiser of the steering group, the NATO Nuclear Planning Group, which was due to meet at Gleneagles in late October. The new Secretary of State, George Younger, MP for Ayr, took a close interest. Jock's efforts, however, were overshadowed by a second summit between Reagan and Gorbachev, in Iceland on 11 and 12 October 1986. The two leaders did not enjoy the same view of arms control: in simple terms, Reagan, besides his half-finished ideas about SDI, thought that he could break the Soviet economy by outspending the Soviets in an arms race, while Gorbachev needed an arms limitation treaty to provide the headroom for his reforms, *perestroika* (restructuring) and *glasnost* (openness), under which he hoped to change the Soviet economy and society.

At Reykjavik, Gorbachev proposed to reduce intermediate-range nuclear weapons in Europe and to eliminate 50% of all strategic arms, including ICBMs. He also agreed not to include British or French weapons in the count but asked in exchange for an American pledge not to implement the SDI for the next ten years. Reagan countered with his zero option to eliminate all ballistic missiles within ten years but insisted on the right to deploy SDI against remaining threats afterwards. Gorbachev then suggested eliminating all nuclear weapons within a decade. After two days of talks, they could not agree, and some held the Reykjavik summit to be a failure, but it was a turning point in the Cold War when, to the astonishment of aides and allies, the leaders of the USA and the USSR found that they shared an interest, if not in SDI technology, then at least in the principle of nuclear abolition.[112]

Britain had developed the concept of 'nuclear sufficiency', meaning the minimum of threatened destruction that would suffice to deter the Soviets. This stressed counter-value rather than counter-force targeting: destroying Moscow (the 'Moscow criterion') rather than the enemy's nuclear forces. The British government was worried about arms control, if applied to its already small force, and about the development of SDI if this prevented it meeting its Moscow criterion. Thus, Prime Minister Margaret Thatcher felt an "earthquake beneath my feet" when she heard how far the American President was prepared to go in strategic arms reduction.

Administratively, the 40th NATO NPG on 21 and 22 October 1986 was a resounding success, not least because George and Diana Younger and Jock and Annie Slater, working as a team, recognised that if they got the ladies' programme right all should be well.[113] It was the first NATO ministerial meeting after Reykjavik, and ministers chose to display solidarity with the Alliance, recognising that they should be seen to be at one with the Americans, but in practise they had been blindsided, not least by what might have been said when Reagan and Gorbachev walked in the woods with only one Russian interpreter. Jock wrote in his diary that it was incredible that Reagan had been so ill-prepared, and he worried that Gorbachev was winning the propaganda war hands down. "I fear that Reagan, despite his remarkable achievement in giving the Americans pride and confidence in themselves, is simply not up to complicated arms control negotiations off the cuff."

Not surprisingly, the communique at the end of the Gleneagles meeting was anodyne:

> We reviewed the outcome of the recent meeting between President Reagan and General Secretary Gorbachev in Reykjavik. We extended our warm appreciation to the President on his conduct of the talks and fully endorsed his bold attempt to seek far-reaching arms control agreements with the Soviet Union. We fully endorsed the President's programme presented in Iceland and stressed that this programme provides the opportunity for historic progress. We welcomed the

United States' intention to build upon the progress achieved, which provides the opportunity for progress towards very significant arms control agreements [and] We urged the Soviet Union to redouble its own efforts in this direction [and] We strongly support the United States exploration of space and defence systems [i.e. SDI], as is permitted by the ABM Treaty.

The Slaters returned from Gleneagles by helicopter and RAF VC10, which took two hours door to door; Jock called it a taste of how the jet-set live.

## Drumbeat of Business

The year ended with a familiar and exhausting drumbeat of diary engagements, including receptions, inspections, and parades, defence talks in Bergen, a weekend on the duty admiral roster, and standing in for the First Sea Lord at Westminster Abbey on the anniversary of the birth of Admiral Lord Cochrane. Work on a policy for the British National Space Centre and a visit to the space department at Farnborough took up much time. There was an annual conference run jointly by Chatham House and the MoD, when Jock reflected drily on the director, Admiral James Eberle, "'the thinking man's sailor' – I find that he is like so many of these so-called academics – too full of his own views and not enough interest in those of others. At least he has operational experience, which gives him the credibility that many armchair critics lack."

The middle of November was something of an academic test, with a defence studies symposium in London and a maritime power seminar in Dartmouth. At BRNC he stayed in the captain's house with George Tullis, was stimulated by the calibre of the officers under training whom he met, and chaired a panel that included "David Greenwood, the controversial head of the Aberdeen Centre for Defence Studies, Peter Nailor, the somewhat self-important and verbose professor of history at Greenwich, and Captain Mike Boyce".

Back in London, Jock had to fend off John Stanley, Minister for the Armed Forces, who, with a general election looming, was determined to publish an open government document extolling the virtues of Trident compared to other systems of deterrence such as cruise missiles. Jock spurned this: "The snag is that there is a very thin line between unclassified information (some 90%) and highly classified information. To make a truly convincing case for Trident it is necessary to go into the highly classified area." Stanley insisted that Jock accompany him to the House of Commons and sit in the officials' box during a debate, where it became clear that Jock was making his mark; eyebrows were raised when other politicians, including David Owen, leader of the SDP, greeted him in the corridors of Parliament. Notwithstanding Jock's opposition, the alternatives to Trident became a subject of regular review over the next two decades.

Physically, the appointment was taking a toll on Jock, who noted that "There is just too much to do and too little time to complete it. The fact that I have to work every weekend to keep pace is bad news … I am not even finding time to swim every morning or indeed walk to work. I do, however, try to find time to have a massage once a week … I am amused to see eyebrows raised when I announce that I have a weekly massage – naval people automatically cast their minds back to the massage parlour of Johor Bahru! Actually, the Dolphin Square Health Club is the height of propriety."

## Deus ex Machina

Refreshed by his Christmas holidays, Jock was surprised when the Chief of the Defence Staff, Fieldhouse, wandered into his office. Prime Minister Thatcher had declared in no uncertain terms that the United Kingdom would remain a nuclear armed power. Fieldhouse wanted Jock to go to Washington the following week to present British views and influence a study by the Joint Chiefs of Staff into the implications of Reagan's zero option. Jock was by now well-connected, and he had already, working closely with his opposite numbers in the Foreign and Commonwealth Office (FCO), helped to establish an agreed UK position on arms control. The FCO was keen to ensure that the Americans did not deviate from the 'four points' that Thatcher had agreed with Reagan, and Jock was equally certain that if he did not consult the FCO about his mission:[114]

> They would go behind our backs to the embassy in Washington … With damp rags round our heads we burned the midnight oil all weekend and I was ready to fly out [on 14 January] with one or two of my key players [Edward Buckley and Jock's military assistant David Drew]. I still remember the back upper section of the BA jumbo jet which we had reserved to continue our preparations enroute, with the most highly classified papers laid out on the table before us! There was no doubt that our subsequent presentation to the US Team was well received and Frank Miller, the US Assistant Secretary, and my old friend amongst others, was clearly impressed.

Jock soon learned that the US team were keen to hear the British views but would not be able to put their own cards on the table. He made a formal presentation to an audience of about 40, but only one or two listeners asked any searching questions, and it was only when he made one-on-one calls on senior officials that it become clear that he had made an impression "in pointing out the pitfalls of a world without ballistic missiles … time will tell that they too have appreciated the disadvantages and dangers". Frank Miller gave Jock supper, which provided an added opportunity to put across the British view.

Unusually, Jock confided some detail to his diary about the need to influence the US bilaterally:

> On what we assess will be necessary to ensure [British] strategy of flexible response and forward defence in the light of an INF agreement. There is a growing momentum, influenced in a large measure by the media, to get rid of all missiles between 500 kms and the range of the GLCM/Soviet SS20. On the face of it, an agreement would be a major step forward in the arms control process but the implications in deterrence terms are highly complex & we must not allow the US to sign on the dotted line without ensuring stability & security in Europe. Hence my talks in the Pentagon were extremely important … I had a good session with Sir Antony Acland that evening & enjoyed a drink and a swim at the Residence before dashing off to catch the night plane home.

The ink was scarcely dry on a fulsome thank you letter from Fieldhouse for Jock's report on this visit when he was off to Oberammergau to take part in a NATO planning symposium. There, like other meetings of academics, Jock found that the bureaucrats created a lot of hot air and it was debatable whether much was achieved. "Still, I found it relatively good value in making a few useful contacts and escaping from the phone and the daunting in-tray." He returned to a joint meeting of the CDS and head of the FCO seeking an agreed way ahead to ensure a coordinated programme of work between the two departments.


**Another Drumroll**

Amid the roar of meetings and travel, sublime and ridiculous, Swedish, French, and Dutch talks at staff and ministerial level, the Balance of Investments Working Group, the Defence Studies Steering Group, the British National Space Centre Board, and NATO's major biannual readiness exercise,

WINTEX, which culminated in the theoretical use of tactical nuclear weapons, all of which required detailed and careful preparation, Jock found space in his programme for the inter-services cross-country championships, which at least obliged him to take a day out of the office. After a talk to the staff course at Greenwich, Jock confided to his diary just how frustrating it was that for all his preparation and deft answers to subtle questions, there was so little reliable feedback on how he might have affected opinions: "It is so hard to get a feel for staff/audience reaction, so I never come away from these lectures with a complete feeling of success."

With another general election looming Jock listened with interest to Dennis Healey at Chatham House speaking about Labour's defence policy. "It sounds highly plausible to the uninitiated but totally inconsistent with experience and advice of the last decade. Surely the electorate won't be fooled." Two weeks later he also heard David Owen on the SDP Alliance's defence policy and that evening he was invited to a dinner party at the Grimonds' "specifically so that [he] could talk 'nuclear' to David Steel [leader of the SDP Alliance] … our conversation was … long enough for me to establish that [his] knowledge of defence matters is somewhat shaky".

## Albuquerque

Not least among Jock's personal concerns were his family and the development of his two sons, and he was frustrated when the week's leave he had planned for after Easter 1987 was cancelled, "because the infuriating David Nichols has, true to form, elected not to attend the High Level Group meeting in Albuquerque, New Mexico". Jock would go in his place, having long since realised that the only way to prepare adequately for the ceaseless round of briefings was to rise at 4am and tackle his inbox in the quiet of the early hours. Now, on 17 April 1987, he wrote "Good Friday and a marvellous day – and here I am eyes down at my desk in the drawing room desperately trying to get to grips with the complex problems of the deterrence and military implications of arms control."

Prime Minister Thatcher had had a robust, day-long meeting with Gorbachev only a few days previously, on 30 March, and the US Secretary of State, George Shultz, had just returned from discussions in Moscow on limitations to intermediate-range nuclear arms in Moscow on 13–15 April. There was much to digest and the forthcoming meeting in New Mexico was to be one of the HLG's most important. The Soviet offer to abolish all intermediate- and short-range nuclear missiles was attractive in propaganda terms, but Jock's briefing told him that the Soviets enjoyed an advantage of 10·1 in conventional forces.

Jock left home at 7.15am on a Tuesday, and on arrival in Albuquerque there was a head of delegations' dinner, so he did not get to bed for 24 hours. The next day he played a full and authoritative part in the HLG report to NATO on the zero option for intermediate- and short-range missiles, and that evening there was a formal dinner surrounded by dinosaur skeletons in the local museum. By now, Jock's standing was such that, while others went off on a classified tour of Sandia National Laboratories, Frank Gaffney, Perle's successor as Deputy Assistant Secretary of Defense for Nuclear Forces and Arms Control Policy, asked him and the German Major General Rolf Hüttel to help in drafting a paper on the implications of abolishing these missiles. The Americans were keen to see this accomplished, but, even if most of them would fall in Western Europe, the Europeans were interested in their deterrent value and demurred. Jock returned to the office in London on the Saturday, before setting out the next day for Brussels to brief NATO's Supreme Allied Commander, Europe (SACEUR, responsible for all NATO military operations) and the British delegation for a meeting of the Military Committee. The HLG met on Wednesday, when "it would have made sense for me [Jock] to lead the HLG team … but David Nichols was back from his Easter leave and whether I (or indeed we) like it or not he is the traditional leader of the UK delegation." Jock remained in London to prepare the Secretary of State and the Chiefs for the line to take on the zero option.

When, on Friday 1 May, Jock found himself at Chevening with the top MoD team as guests of the FCO for an FCO/MoD seminar to discuss arms control and the zero option for intermediate nuclear forces, he was unusually well prepared. Despite the Prime Minister having already sent her views to the US President, "Is the lady for turning? Will she accept that there are some distinct worries for the security of Europe by agreeing to 0-0 SRINF [Short-Range Intermediate Range Nuclear Forces] down to 500 kms?" Jock reflected, tentatively and modestly, "It could be that I may have taken part in an historic meeting when the UK, with all its influence, not least nuclear, within the Alliance developed its views which will not be entirely to the Americans' liking."

## Disappointment

It was a non-stop fortnight and the in-tray was full, but by 10 May the Slaters were in Scotland on holiday, where Jock was turning his mind to his next appointment as Flag Officer Scotland and Northern Ireland (FOSNI). By the end of the month he was in the USA again, with Major General Gary Johnson, lecturing on British defence policy, but when a general election was called for 11 June there was general relief that the pace of work in the MoD would slow. Jock had been ACDS (Pol/Nuc) in interesting times and his work on nuclear policy and especially the relationships he created in the USA were to have lasting effects. In September 1987, after just over two years in office, he was relieved by Air Vice Marshal Eric Macey. "Frankly, I was delighted to be leaving London as it is really not my scene, although I fear that, if I am to continue in the Navy, my future fate lies in Whitehall. That is why I am SO disappointed not to be going to sea. I suppose that I am lucky to be getting away with less than three years in the MoD although it must be said that … I expect my final year, if it had happened, would have been very productive."

He added: "To be honest, I really should have done longer as I was just getting into the swing of the arms control business and had fully established my contacts. Still, I am not sorry to be leaving – just desperately disappointed and hurt not to be going to sea."

# Chapter 11: Flagopoly

The cause of Jock's disappointment was his realisation that he might not go to sea again and command as a flag officer, and how this might affect his future appointments and prospects for reaching the top of the Navy.

In the late 20th century the promotion and appointment of admirals and, ultimately, who became First Sea Lord depended upon several variables. Formally and informally the process was administered by the Naval Secretary. Ambition, preferably covert, and raw talent were givens, and there were naturally plenty of officers with these traits. Successful command at sea was also an important qualification. Thus, engineers and logisticians (who could not command at sea) did become sea lords but none ever became First Sea Lord. Operational experience, particularly as a seagoing flag officer of a flotilla, was a highly prized qualification, and the route to the top of the Navy was perceived as being to fly one's flag at sea and to become Commander-in-Chief Fleet. The continued and continuing favour of the First Sea Lord in person was essential, but the influence of politicians was uneven and the process could be thrown out of kilter by death or resignation. Of course, luck was needed too.

**Command at Sea**

When Jock had relieved Rear-Admiral Julian Oswald as ACDS (Pol/Nuc) in the summer of 1985, Oswald took up a coveted seagoing command for a junior admiral as Flag Officer Third Flotilla (FOF3). Then, when Oswald was promoted to vice-admiral in January 1986, the rumour spread that he would be the next Commander-in-Chief Fleet. However, Jock, who was well qualified by experience to take over from Oswald as FOF3, was only eighteen months into his term as ACDS (Pol/Nuc). Instead, Rear-Admiral Hugo White relieved

Oswald in April 1987, when Jock's hopes had then focused briefly on relieving Rear-Admiral John Kerr. Kerr had relieved Jock in command of *Illustrious* but seemed to have overtaken Jock in the promotion stakes and was already at sea in one of those desirable appointments, Flag Officer First Flotilla (FOF1). Kerr was not likely to be relieved until mid-1988, implying that Jock would have to complete a full three-year term in the MoD.

Wondering about his future, Jock had written in his diary that the First Sea Lord, Staveley, the arbiter of admirals' careers "seems to be keeping his cards very close to his chest". He had added, hopefully, "Anyway, as eggs is eggs, the flag plot never works out the way the gossips forecast so we will just have to wait and see." Prophetically, he had also written, "The one other job that would appear to fall vacant in the right time frame is that of FOSNI. I hope to God that that is not our fate." Jock's anguish had not eased when at Admirals' Day in early 1987 he heard the rumour that he was indeed going to Scotland in the autumn. His state of mind was not helped by Kerr, who "seemed to be gloating somewhat on my misfortune of having no flotilla to command. His query to me whether I was 'leaving the mainstream' really incensed me."

Those two impostors, triumph and disaster, had been much in evidence at a call on the First Sea Lord, Staveley, on 27 January 1987, which caused an exclamation of joy and self-examination in the diary: "To my amazement and complete surprise, he congratulated me on my selection for promotion to vice-admiral." But this was not a welcome piece of news: "Frankly, it is far too soon, and I fear may thwart my chances of going to sea next which would be desperately disappointing. However, it is all rather exciting to be moving up before I reach 50. I look back over the last 16 years in utter astonishment with promotion first shot at every stage – I've never felt I was that good and sometimes wonder if I am really ready for the additional responsibilities thrust upon me."


## The Flag Plot

The flag plot to which Jock referred was the scheme of admirals' promotions and appointments normally kept private between the Naval Secretary and the First Sea Lord. When in March 1966 the First Sea Lord, Admiral Sir David Luce, had resigned in protest over the decision by the Labour government to cancel the Navy's new generation of aircraft carriers (CVA-01), Rear-Admiral Tony Griffin was Naval Secretary and this author recalls being told by Griffin, with a chuckle, that however he rewrote the flag plot, he came out on top as First Sea Lord.

In the early 1990s, an insider recalled that the flag plot was a physical entity, a pegboard, at least a quarter of a century old, designed to fold up suitcase-sized so that it could be carried across Whitehall from the Old Admiralty Building to the First Sea Lord's office. Lieutenant Sandy Sullivan, a junior secretary in one of the Navy Board offices, recalled that sometime in 1970 or 1971: "I can still see now the then Commander Bill Higgins, who was secretary to the Naval Secretary, carting a wooden contraption like a noticeboard with a hinged door (or maybe doors) towards 1SL's [the First Sea Lord's] office. He popped into our office for a brief chat and said that this was the flag plot. There was then a bit of banter about the possible outcome if he dropped the plot and no one could remember the exact potential appointments." This wooden board was superseded by a spreadsheet that was printed off and taken by the Naval Secretary to brief the First Sea Lord on calls: the Naval Secretary would then return to his office and make adjustments as necessary.[115]

The gossips to whom Jock had referred were those who tried to guess the flag plot in a game sometimes called 'flagopoly'. As Director of Naval Warfare, Captain 'Dicky' Fitch kept his flag plot in a heavily marked-up copy of the Navy List: he would eventually become Naval Secretary from 1980 to 1983 and then Second Sea Lord from 1986 to 1987. Captain JP Barker, five years as Secretary to the Controller of the Navy, kept his version of the flag plot in a blue ring-binder, usually locked in his desk drawer.

The playing of flagopoly presupposed that senior officers' careers, their promotions, and appointments were curated. If flying one's flag at sea was desirable, other appointments were regarded with great scepticism. In May 1987 Jock travelled out and back to the USA with Rear-Admiral Robin Hogg, who had just announced his resignation. Hogg was a rising star and in his second job as a rear-admiral but had refused to go as Chief of Staff to Allied Naval Force Southern Europe, headquartered in Naples, as a vice-admiral with the prospect of a knighthood because he saw the job as dead end. "Robin," Jock said, "has always been a most amusing raconteur … he has a good brain, and it is a pity to see the First Sea Lord, Sir William Staveley, not noted for intellect or originality, failing to hold him."[116]

## The High Road

On 18 March 1987, Staveley invited Jock to become the next FOSNI. He was, Staveley said, well aware that it would be most disappointing for Jock that he was not to go to sea. For Jock that was a major understatement. Staveley wanted to reassure Jock that this was most certainly not the end of the road, but Jock wrote:

> Frank and honest discussion is not easy with Sir William Staveley, but I told him in fairly plain language that to be selected for flag rank at the age of 46 and then not to go to sea in a flotilla was quite extraordinary; no Commander-in-Chief Fleet had ever not commanded a flotilla, so what were my chances now of fleet command? He was evasive but, in the end, conceded that it was less likely: the answer merely served to depress me in that it is quite clear that I am being channelled at present into those appointments in the MoD for which I believe I am least suited.

There was nothing to be gained from further discussion with Staveley. "I only hope that his successor, whoever he may be, is more understanding." (Staveley's successor as First Sea Lord in May 1989 would be Oswald.) Jock seized an opportunity to discuss his future with the Chief of Defence Staff, Fieldhouse, who "merely commented that it was the 'luck of the draw', and I should not assume that I was being 'put out to grass'". The Navy was shrinking and when Jock stressed to Fieldhouse how disappointed he was not to be going to sea, Fieldhouse implied that the days of a predictable, recognised path of progression from job to job had gone and that, perhaps, Jock's chances of commanding the fleet might yet materialise.

It was irritating that the news of his next appointment was embargoed until 7 April, while the rumour of it only gained in substance. A dinner party in HMS *Illustrious* for former captains and their wives, hosted by Captain Peter Woodhead, only rubbed salt into a sore. "Of course, it brought back many happy memories, but things are never quite the same again and I'm not sure if I really like going back – not least at present when I am still livid about not being able to fly my flag at sea."

# Chapter 12: Annie's Song, 1987–89

The Slaters had six weeks to move to Scotland, to close their flat at Dolphin Square (for the third time), find schools for the boys, prepare Grenville Lodge for letting, and for some pre-joining calls. Worse, Annie slipped a disc, which required three weeks of stretching in a private hospital in Havant. All was ready for the move, however, when a storm hit southern England and an old beech tree crashed onto the garage. Their car was inside, laden for Scotland. The car and its cargo were, fortunately, undamaged.

Jock also had to fit in a summons for three days' stalking at Balmoral, when, despite wild and wet weather, he shot two stags. Over tea with Prince Charles he commiserated over the difficulty of combining married life with a naval career, and slipped in the idea that maybe Prince Andrew might spend less time on 'royal duties' and more on his career.

On 20 October 1987 the Slaters relieved Vice-Admiral Sir George Vallings and his wife Tessa, who were going into retirement. Jock became FOSNI, a NATO sub-area commander, and Naval Base Commander, Rosyth, a mouthful of a title, several hats, two offices, and, he reckoned, about one-and-a-half jobs. In addition to the offices and staff to fulfil his naval tasks, the appointment came with a house, St Margaret's Hope, and a retinue comprising a secretary, a flag lieutenant who lived

Conducting the RM Band in Dunfermline: Jock later conducted the massed bands of the RM in the Royal Albert Hall. Source: Slater archive.

on the premises, a PA, several cooks and stewards, and a Royal Marines driver with car. There was also a coxswain and barge, and a Royal Marines band. Finally, Jock was supported by a childhood friend, Michael Gordon-Lennox, as his Chief of Staff,[117] and a flag captain, Alun Ryle.

## Flag Officer Scotland & Northern Ireland

The Navy was shrinking and the roles of FOSNI and naval base commander had been absorbed into one, but still occupied two offices, the former as national and NATO area commander at Pitreavie Castle and the latter in Rosyth's newly privatised dockyard, where Jock had influence but no authority. Vallings had been deeply involved in the privatisation of the yard and had kept his main office in the yard, but Jock knew that his staff were unhappy with this decision. When he met Commander Simon Fraser, his future Staff Operations Officer, and probed for his future staff's views, Fraser's evasive answer was, "That's a sensitive question" and was all that Jock needed.[118]

Despite it being rundown and shabby, he decided to refurbish the Pitreavie office and to move there, close to the 'pit', the underground headquarters at Pitreavie Castle, which was shared with the Air Officer Scotland and Northern Ireland (AOSNI), Air Vice Marshal David Brook. The General Officer Commanding Scotland and Governor of Edinburgh Castle was Sir Norman Arthur, who had been a student at RCDS with Jock. The three met regularly to discuss Scottish security issues and other problems in common. As a Scot – on his staff it was rumoured that he owned half of Scotland – Jock was warmly welcomed everywhere. His first experience of the influence the heads of the armed services had in the Scottish hierarchy came in his first week when he was guest at a dinner given by Bob Gray, the Lord Provost of Glasgow, although just before he stood to speak Gray lightly elbowed him and said, "Jock you're not a Scot – you weren't born in Glasgow!" Jock made the most of this in his speech and when next morning he called on Gray officially he was presented with a bottle of whisky, *Lord Provost's Preserve*. A year or so later, after Jock had been knighted and when the Grays dined at St Margaret's Hope, Annie offered homemade chocolates, saying "Lord Provost, have an Edinburgh sweetie." The inimitable Glaswegian replied, "Lady Slater, that is a contradiction in terms!"

Jock supported the 1988 Glasgow Garden Festival, whose strapline was 'Glasgow Smiles Better!', and, determined to contribute to its success, he lent the Royal Marines band. He also arranged for the frigate HMS *Brazen*, commanded by Captain Niels Westberg, who had been a young officer in

*Britannia* when Jock was equerry, to be alongside where he flew his flag as FOSNI. Jock was invited to a dinner at the Royal College of Physicians in Edinburgh and sat between two distinguished physicians who clearly wondered what on earth to say to an admiral and so chose to draw his attention to the portraits on the wall. After mentioning two of the subjects Jock stopped them and pointed out that the next one was his great-grandfather, Sir Byrom Bramwell, adding, "and by the way, that is my grandfather, Professor Edwin Bramwell, over there". After a pause one of his hosts exclaimed, "Good heavens! You must be JK Slater's son?" Having established his credentials, they enjoyed an excellent evening.

Meanwhile, the Slaters continued to widen and deepen their circle of friends and acquaintances. Quite apart from his official duties and titles, the appointment was neither a sideshow nor a sinecure and there were many representational tasks. These opened several doors, including that of Bute House, official residence of the Secretary of State for Scotland, Malcolm Rifkind. He was "a hugely able, fairly young politician with a wide-ranging knowledge and fast brain. Remarkably, he is also rather a nice chap, and so is his wife."

Jock asked his coxswain where his admiral's barge was. It was found in the naval base in a neglected condition and needed several months and the goodwill of the managing director of the dockyard to be restored. By Easter 1988 the barge was ready for an outing to Inchcolm, an island in the Firth of Forth. The first attempt ended with a grounding, but when Jock found himself seated next to Malcolm Rifkind at the installation of a new General Officer Commanding, Scotland, he reminded Rifkind that Inchcolm was in trust to him as Secretary of State for Scotland and suggested that they go there in his barge for a picnic, which was enjoyed by both families.

Jock's headquarters were manned during exercises by reservists and he started to visit the Royal Navy Reserve (RNR) in his area: HMS *Camperdown* in Dundee and HMS *Claverhouse* in Edinburgh where he had been a Boy Seaman, HMS *Dalriada* in Glasgow, and HMS *Caroline* in Belfast. He was saddened to find that the former close and regular liaison between the front line and the reserves was waning. The RNR now concentrated on mine counter measures (MCM) and naval control of shipping (NCS), and Jock "had an uneasy feeling that they are going to have to work much harder at their business to be effective … at the same time, we must ensure that they are properly supported to realize their potential. The calibre of commanding officer is mixed, and they have an important task to stimulate some excellent young people that they recruit both at officer and rating level and ensure that they retain them. Of course, the RNR is a good club, but it must look to its professionalism."

## Naval Base Commander

Jock's role as Naval Base Commander, Rosyth was perhaps the least onerous, but it would prove to be the most significant in qualifying him for his next appointment. Rosyth seemed likely to be chosen as the sole yard for refitting the Navy's nuclear-powered submarine fleet, and an extensive rebuilding programme had already started. There had been two 'stone frigates' or shore establishments, but artificer apprentice training at HMS *Caledonia* had been moved to Gosport and the rump of its facilities amalgamated into HMS *Cochrane*, which itself was being run down. In these circumstances Jock held considerable influence but limited authority, and no control over the budgets of the Principal Stores and Transport Officer or the Director of Marine Services. Nevertheless, the Port Board was a useful exchange of views and problems. Although it had few teeth it did give Jock a seat at the Chief of Fleet Support (CFS)'s six-monthly meetings in London.

Jock had to deal with day-to-day, often ill-informed comments about the Navy's nuclear activities. When one group was persuaded that the water running from a pipe into the Firth of Forth was radioactive, he invited them to visit the outlet, filled a glass from the outlet, and, when no one accepted his invitation to take a sip, did so himself. The eventual decision to choose Devonport for nuclear refitting work was a very close-run matter in which politics played a key role. A letter from Frank Miller reminded Jock of the close interest the Americans were taking in Britain's strategic deterrent.

## NATO Commander

Jock also held the NATO appointments of COMNORECHAN (Commander Nore Sub-Area Channel, a NATO sub-area commander reporting to the Allied Commander-in-Chief Channel and based at Northwood) and COMNORLANT (Commander Northern Sub Area North Atlantic), and was ultimately subordinate to SACLANT (Supreme Allied Commander Atlantic) in Norfolk, Virginia.[119] Only a week after the Slaters' arrival in Scotland they hosted an overnight stay by the Chairman of the US Joint Chiefs of Staff, Admiral Bill Crowe, and his wife, Shirley, who were on an official visit to the UK as guests of the Chief of Defence Staff, Fieldhouse. They bonded over a dinner of grouse:

"We gathered together a distinguished group of guests and Annie decided to give them grouse. When the platter of grouse was offered to Shirley Crowe, she looked at me and said, 'Is this BIRD?' When I told her it was grouse, she took one and for the next half hour moved it around her plate but never touched it! I knew that Bill Crowe collected hats and caps in his office in the Pentagon so, at the end of dinner, we presented him with a Glen Garry, which he proudly wore for the rest of the evening."

The following month, though Jock had not been party to the Stockholm Conference on Disarmament in Europe, which had agreed confidence- and security-building measures, he hosted witnesses from the Warsaw Pact countries to Exercise Purple Warrior, a large-scale British amphibious exercise conducted off Scotland from 4 to 19 November 1987. At the end of the exercise Jock flew out to HMS *Ark Royal* to visit his friend Hugo White, "whose job everyone (including me) thought that I would have". He wrote in his diary that "I find it so frustrating to be observing the exercise and not running it. I don't suppose I will ever really get over the disappointment of being elevated and missing the chance to fly my flag at sea. After all the years of preparation … it is a grievous blow." At the end of Purple Warrior Jock helped the Minister for the Armed Forces, Ian Stewart, host the Warsaw Pact representatives, who stayed at the imposing North West Castle Hotel, Stranraer. The dinner was "exceptionally boring, including a poor speech by the Minister". Jock had more fun at breakfast trying to persuade the Russians, Czechs, Hungarians, and Poles to eat black pudding.

After the Remembrance Sunday parade in Edinburgh, on 16 November, barely four weeks after arriving in Scotland, Jock was on his way to Norfolk, Virginia, for the three-day annual meeting of the Allied Commanders Atlantic. As COMNORLANT, this would be his first exposure to such a meeting, held at the headquarters of SACLANT, Admiral Lee Baggett US Navy. Jock recalled Admiral Fieldhouse saying that NATO meetings consisted of one long bus ride interspersed with lunches and dinners. At this meeting, Baggett mixed charm with a short temper, and stifled discussion among his juniors, but when nuclear matters were discussed, Jock, with his recent experiences of the HLG and the Nuclear Planning Group, felt compelled to speak. "You could have heard a pin drop when I held forth, [though] actually, I think that SACLANT appreciated my intervention." Afterwards, Vice-Admiral Sir Richard Thomas, SACLANT's British deputy, told Jock that he had been very brave. The other NATO delegates were secretly most impressed.

International and NATO meetings continued to call, including two days in Copenhagen in the New Year of 1988 for CINCNORTH's (the Commander-in-Chief Allied Forces Northern Europe's) study period, Exercise Viking Shield. It was a large gathering of senior NATO commanders addressed by eminent speakers such as Lord Carrington, the Secretary General, and Baggett. "As usual, these meetings are more valuable for the chance they present for discussions and dialogue in the margins. I remain pretty sceptical of those permanent members of the NATO bandwagon, not least the ambassadors and special advisers, who prance from country to country, usually with their wives, banging on about military matters wherever and whenever they have the opportunity. Still, it was fun for Annie to get away for a short break and I think she enjoyed her visit to Denmark."

There were two visits to Iceland, using the HS125 passenger jet allocated to David Brook as AOSNI for his official use, followed in September 1988 by Jock inviting the press into Pitreavie at the beginning of Exercise Teamwork 88, the biggest NATO exercise in the North Atlantic for many years, involving more than 200 ships, 500 aircraft, and 20,000 personnel over five days.

This unremitting pace of activity continued throughout Jock's tenure. Even as the Slaters were preparing to leave Scotland, Jock flew out to Newport, Rhode Island to participate in the NATO war-gaming exercise Open Road. On reaching Heathrow, British Airways announced that they were overbooked and that Jock would have to await the next flight, but on being told that this was impossible he was transferred to a Concorde flight to New York, his only experience of this aircraft. It was a "thin tube with outstanding food at the wrong time and no chance of moving about once service started".

Jock left Washington for Dulles airport to return to Edinburgh to support Iain Tennant, the new Lord High Commissioner to the General Assembly of the Church of Scotland, who was an old friend from Balmoral days. Memorably, the opening address to the assembly was given by Prime Minister Margaret Thatcher, who, when the Slaters met her beforehand, was distinctly and rightly nervous about this appearance: the Scots took exception to being lectured and christened her speech 'The Gospel according to St Margaret'.

## The Admiral's Wife

Annie's exceptional support continued, not least in Scotland, where she chaired King George's Fund for Sailors, one of whose fundraising events was the Seafarers' Ball. This she hosted very successfully in HMS *Cochrane*, where her ball committee was dominated by a formidable team of ageing Edinburgh matrons who clearly expected the Royal Navy to see to their every need. Another event was FOSNI's annual reception, a garden party in the grounds of

St Margaret's Hope, which was a test for the staff who, under Annie's guidance, acquitted themselves well.

Even though the Slaters made an effort to control the pace and content of their social and professional programme, there were many 'visiting firemen' who they always made an effort to impress. Julian Oswald, now the Commander-in-Chief Fleet in his NATO CINCEASTLANT (Commander-in-Chief Eastern Atlantic Area) hat, visited; so too did the Earl and Countess of Selkirk for the paying off of the frigate HMS *Rothesay*; the Canadian Chief of Defence Staff and his wife were on an official visit to the UK; and the Commander-in-Chief Naval Home Command, Sir Sandy Woodward, dropped in before visiting HMS *Cochrane*. Jock was sorry to miss the visit of the Duchess of Kent, but Annie handled it very well, and the Duchess's Private Secretary, Sir Richard Buckley, another old friend, told Jock how much it was enjoyed.

There were even breakfast parties for junior officers, mostly serving in small ships, who arrived five at a time, petrified, but left having enjoyed a good chat and a good breakfast: "Hearing their views on matters of the moment is important."

## The Band

The Royal Marines had not featured in Jock's early career, though he had begun to admire individual officers whom he met when he was equerry. As FOSNI, the musical Jock had his own band under his Director of Music, Captain Peter Rutterford, which he saw as a principal tool of domestic diplomacy: he deployed the band to the Glasgow Garden Festival, to play at FOSNI's summer reception, and to give Christmas concerts. Jock had hoped to make an impact by a beating retreat alongside HMS *Caroline* in Belfast. Sadly, he was obliged to cancel this and instead host a performance in the highly guarded naval headquarters at Moscow Camp. The Royal Marines band showed itself to be "a great joy, worth their weight in gold", and when the Queen's birthday was celebrated in Edinburgh, Jock proudly noted that "my Royal Marines Band acquitted themselves admirably".

The band also enabled Jock to pay tribute to Annie in a unique way. At its customary Christmas concert in Carnegie Hall, Dunfermline, Jock plotted with Rutterford for him to conduct Strauss's *Radetzky March* and for Rutterford to arrange a flute and orchestra version of John Denver's *Annie's Song* – with Jock playing the flute. It was, he admitted, a high-risk activity and his last ever public performance on the flute.

## The Troubles

Northern Ireland, at the height of the Troubles, was in Jock's area of command, though the security that surrounded his occasional visits made him not too popular with the Army if he stayed long. Nevertheless, on one visit he went out on a night patrol to observe at first-hand how intelligence of the activities of the Provisional IRA (PIRA) was gathered, and he also met for the first time the Secretary of State, Tom King, and John Stanley, Minister of State in the MoD.

Remembrance Day, 8 November 1987, was marked by a PIRA bombing during a parade at Enniskillen that killed twelve people and wounded 63 others. In March 1988, three suspected IRA bombers were shot in Gibraltar, in June an Army helicopter was shot down, and in August the first mainland bomb in four years was set off by a timing device in London. Amid these and many other killings and bombings, Jock wondered why, when in Northern Ireland he enjoyed full personal protection, there was none in Scotland. Bland assurances were given that the PIRA strongly supported Glasgow-based Celtic Football Club, that it was most unlikely to attempt an attack in Scotland, and that there was only one entrance and exit to St Margaret's Hope, which had a long drive that made it an unattractive target. Nevertheless, Jock's staff was wary, and when before Christmas a heavy parcel addressed to Jock arrived, a controlled explosion was used to reveal - and destroy - the two bottles of whisky inside: the Slaters never learned who the generous donor was.

## Royal Duties and Visits

As the Slaters' first term drew to a close they attended a dance at Claridges in London to celebrate the Queen and Prince Philip's 40th wedding anniversary. Before the event they had dinner with the present equerry, Lieutenant Commander Tim Lawrence, in Jock's old flat in St James's Palace.

Jock's knighthood was announced in the Queen's Birthday Honours on 10 June 1988 and a royal week at the Palace of Holyroodhouse quickly followed, a highlight of which was the monarch's visit to the Royal Navy. At lunch in St Margaret's Hope, Jock hatched a plan with Rutterford to enliven the event:

> When he heard what I had in mind he could not believe it and commented that he might be sacked; I reminded him that I was his boss and if my plan was carried out it would be remembered by the Queen for years to come. It was! The brass quintet played in the hall and at the pudding stage I arranged for a tray to be dropped outside the dining room and our top tuba player, Chalky Heseldine (Chalky

as that was not his colour!), fully dressed in diving kit and dripping wet as if straight out of the Firth of Forth, flopped into the dining room and played '20,000 Leagues Under the Sea' as he moved round the table. It was a huge success but nearly a disaster when Chalky, carried away by his command performance, chose to empty the spittle out of his instrument rather too close to the Captain General Royal Marines, Prince Philip.

That morning, when the Queen was visiting the dockyard, she noted the name on the brass tally on Jock's office door and asked why he was not called 'Sir Jock'? Never having used his given name 'John', Jock was delighted, unlike the unhappy Central Order of Chancery. "Who were they to countermand the Queen herself?" asked the newly minted Sir Jock.


## Two Tragedies

There were two tragedies while Jock was in Scotland. On 6 July 1988 an explosion on the Piper Alpha production platform in the North Sea, about 120 miles north-east of Aberdeen, killed 165 men on the rig and two would-be rescuers.

The second disaster was even more awful. On 21 December 1988 the Slaters were hosting a youthful supper and reels party at St Margaret's Hope to which a large number of boys and girls were invited, when Jock received a telephone call from the headquarters at Pitreavie that Pan Am flight 103 from Heathrow to the USA had been blown up over Lockerbie. Eleven residents were killed in Sherwood Crescent, where the aircraft's wings and fuel tanks crashed while on fire, and all 259 passengers and crew of many nationalities died. At first Jock had no detailed knowledge of what had occurred and he made the difficult decision that no one at the party should be told. Throughout the evening he received reports revealing the full extent of the tragedy. It was the deadliest terrorist attack and aviation disaster in Britain. "It was a strange feeling leading a conga round the house having just heard that bodies were being recovered over a wide area … an unforgettable children's party and much enjoyed by all of them but not me!"

## Prince Andrew

Among the last visitors were the Duke and Duchess of York. Jock had always taken a close interest in Prince Andrew's career and when in February 1986 the Prince became engaged, they exchanged notes, misquoting a letter from Admiral Sir John Jervis, who once wrote to a hopeful young officer: "You, having thought fit to take to yourself a wife, are to look for no further attentions from Your humble servant, J Jervis." If they had read on, Jervis had concluded that "when an officer marries, he is damned for the service".[120]

Prince Andrew was serving in the destroyer HMS *Edinburgh* and she was alongside in Rosyth when the Yorks came to lunch at St Margaret's Hope. Both young people were finding it difficult to reconcile the Prince's naval career with their married life and needed counselling of different sorts. Jock spoke to the Prince during a walk in the garden, and later to the Duchess. When she told Jock how difficult it was to be a naval wife and how little she saw of her husband, he spoke very frankly to her, causing the Duchess to exclaim, "I have never been talked to like that before!" Despite this, her six-page thank-you letter was effusive.

## *The Scotsman* Interview

Jock was also learning to manage the press and on 23 February 1989 he told *The Scotsman* that he wanted defence, and in particular nuclear matters, to be better understood in Scotland, acknowledging that "This will always be difficult in Scotland because we are here in what is essentially a socialist state and socialists are not keen on the present government's nuclear philosophy, but they don't object to the jobs that accrue from these expansions in Faslane and Rosyth." He emphasised that 15% of all naval personnel were based in Scotland, where the Navy was investing £3m a week in the Trident developments at Faslane and Coulport. Pitreavie was already an alternate headquarters to Northwood and would be developed in the next five to ten years and be able to support maritime operations in the Greenland–Iceland–UK gap, and past the North Cape towards the vast Soviet submarine bases on the Kola Peninsula in Soviet Russia.

He told his interviewer that as ACDS (Pol/Nuc) he had been involved in developing the British position on arms control in the run-up to the Intermediate-Range Nuclear Forces agreement, and while NATO and the Soviet Union "can talk and understand each other, the more we can have on-site inspection, the less chance we have of misunderstanding". However, the threat still existed and in maritime terms it was a very considerable threat; he was in the business of combating that threat. All these things worried Jock because his business was defence in depth and his aim was to keep all these threats as far away from the UK as possible. He believed that maritime forces would eventually have to be included in arms control.

Asked about the Public Accounts Committee criticism of the performance of the newly privatised dockyards including Rosyth, Jock said he had not lost faith in the changes: "I'm a great believer in privatisation … not least in the impressive personnel here in Rosyth." He concluded: "No senior officer would ever say he was happy with the budget, but it was his duty to meet the threat. It is up to the government to decide how much they are prepared to spend by way of insurance premium, and to the Ministry of Defence to decide how it should be divided up between the services. I wouldn't say I was satisfied."

## Moving On

The Slaters were enjoying their tour of duty in Scotland and both thought they had much more that they wanted to do. In addition, their boys were beginning to make good friends with their Scottish contemporaries. They were therefore disappointed when Staveley decided to curtail Jock's appointment as FOSNI after fifteen months. He was to become CFS with a place on the Board of Admiralty. Jock did not much relish the prospect of another stint in the MoD, where he never really felt at ease.

Corporal Palmer, the Royal Marines driver, and Leading Steward Noddy Holder travelled south with the Slaters to help take over Grenville Lodge again, before the Slaters set off to the Bahamas for a short but well-deserved and very welcome break.

# Chapter 13: Chief of Fleet Support, 1989–91

On 21 March 1989 Jock relieved Ben Bathurst as Chief of Fleet Support: he was destined to succeed Bathurst three more times more in the years ahead.

The office of CFS had its origins in the early 19th century and one of Jock's eminent predecessors between 1950 and 1952 had been Vice-Admiral the Earl Mountbatten, who had then revelled under the title of Fourth Sea Lord and Chief of Naval Supplies and Transport. For the first time, Jock became a member of the Navy Board and privy to its deliberations. He was lucky enough to have Captain John Roberts as his secretary to keep him on the straight and narrow.[121] "John had the most amazing capacity for hard work without making a meal of it. He seemed to relish a huge in-tray. Moreover, he had an uncanny knack of spotting the pitfalls and advising me where my priorities should lie." There was also a naval assistant, the first being Captain Chris Childs[122] and the second Captain Ned Netherclift, both engineers.[123] Seldom without a cigarette in hand, Netherclift in particular was a sharp operator who lived on his nerves. Jock valued both assistants' pragmatic advice, not least when preparing to chair interminable meetings that required detailed homework to keep ahead of the civil servants, many of whom he suspected would have liked to have caught him out.

The Assistant CFS was Rear-Admiral Toby Frere, Jock's near contemporary, a most able right-hand man. "I let him get on with it, knowing that he would invariably produce the goods. It cannot have been easy for him to have me as his boss, but you would not have known it, and I greatly valued his astute advice. He was one of the early users of a laptop computer, which, in those days, impressed everybody. How times have changed!"[124]

A civilian driver, Mr Plaster, was thoroughly reliable and made Jock's life that much easier. Plaster took *The Sun* newspaper and when he picked Jock up in the mornings from the Slaters' flat in Dolphin Square Jock would read *The Sun* until the car reached Whitehall, then switch to a more appropriate journal for a member of the Navy Board.

## More Invitations

Jock quickly came to grips with business, while the whirl of social engagements and visits continued apace. A dinner in HMS *Boxer* in the Pool of London on 3 May marked the retirement of Admiral Sir William Staveley, but passed without comment in Jock's diary. Other activities indicated Jock's breadth of interest as CFS: the Royal Institution of Naval Architects; Trinity House; the Royal Naval Supply and Transport Service; the Italian Navy's material department; the Royal Naval Supply Officers' annual dinner; the opening of the Director General Aircraft (Navy)'s Aircraft Support Executive; Anglo-French naval logistics talks in Paris; a celebration of 50 years of the Admiralty's offices in Bath; 50 years of the Royal Naval Film Corporation, and, of course, visits to the dockyards including his previous stamping ground, Rosyth.

Increasingly, Jock attended meetings and dinners of the Navy Board to which the great and good of the land were invited. At one of these dinners Denis Thatcher sat between Jock and Hugo White, and an entertaining evening passed talking about Burma Oil, rugby, gin, and much else until, during the speeches, Denis fell asleep, only to suddenly wake up and declare, "I think that the Royal Navy is f*****g marvellous" then immediately to drop off again.

There was also stalking at Balmoral, though much of the fun of the stalk was lost when Jock's knees complained, particularly going downhill:

> I was already beginning to think that I should stop but, in the event, went on for another seven years or so … on 20 September [1989]… , with Sandy Masson one of the most experienced stalkers, I was invited to take a very long shot at about 200 metres; as we lay there in the heather, me exhausted and out of breath, looking downhill, I remember debating with him about the range but in the event took the shot and to my total surprise the beast dropped down dead. 'Good Shot, sir!' made my day and I could hold my head up high when I got back to the castle for tea. Incidentally, I always suspected that the Queen and Prince Philip were briefed behind the scenes about how people had got on – but they never let on.

On more than one occasion Annie and Jock were invited to lunch at Clarence House, which was "always a jolly little party with fascinating guests and Elizabeth [the Queen Mother] invariably on sparkling form". And on 20 December 1990 the Slaters were surprised and honoured to be invited to Buckingham Palace to celebrate four royal milestones, the Queen Mother's 90th, Princess Margaret's 60th, Princess Anne's 40th, and Prince Andrew's 30th birthdays. Jock sat between the Princess Royal and Diana, Princess of Wales and Annie sat next to Prince Andrew.

Another royal event was marred for Jock by Prince Philip. An IRA bomb at the Royal Marines School of Music, Deal on 22 September 1989 had killed eleven bandsmen. There was a memorial service in Canterbury Cathedral at which the archbishop preached, and the large congregation was led by the Prince as Captain General Royal Marines and the Prime Minister, Margaret Thatcher, after which the Dean gave a lunch. The Prince chose to attack the MoD, through Jock, about the plans to close Deal and move the music school to Portsmouth: "He got so worked up that he knocked a plate of stuffed tomatoes from the hands of a passing waitress!"

## Clark's Diaries

Alan Clark, as MP for Plymouth Sutton and Minister for Defence Procurement, had kept diaries but before they were published as a book he leaked them to the *Daily Mail* at the same time as submitting them to the Cabinet Office for approval.[125] The Permanent Under-Secretary of State in the MoD was Christopher France, who warned Jock that the first volume contained a less than flattering reference to him. France said that he could object but as the book was already in the hands of the press, this would merely draw attention to the paragraph. The subject was nuclear waste disposal in Plymouth and how best it should be handled. At a meeting in London, Clark had become very excited and Jock had been obliged to say that he was confusing his constituency interests with his ministerial responsibilities. "Needless to say he did not like that and thereafter we had a very frosty relationship."

The meeting, as recorded in Clark's diary, bore little resemblance to that which Jock had attended, and Jock chose not to comment further.

## Speechifying

Increasingly, too, Jock was asked to speak at naval dinners and on other public occasions.

The invitation to speak to the General Assembly of the Church of Scotland on its chaplains' day was one of the more unusual occasions, and, typically, Jock took enormous trouble preparing his speech. Among the previous moderators of the General Assembly was Ronnie Selby Wright, who had married the Slaters at St Columba's in 1972. Wright sat with Dr J Fraser McCluskey, the minister of St Columba's and Dr R Leonard Small, who had been the minister at St Cuthbert's in Edinburgh when Jock's father was a senior elder. Jock wondered what his mother, sitting in the gallery, thought of her second son giving such an address, which was reported in the *Church Pennant*, a newsletter introduced by the Chaplain of the Fleet, Mike Henley. In it, Sam Williams, the Principal Church of Scotland and Free Churches Chaplain, emphasised Jock's call for the chaplains of all denominations to "get their act together". He quoted Jock: "I don't think that most servicemen could give a damn about what denomination a chaplain belongs to provided he is a wise chaplain and friend."

That spring the Slaters were among the guests of the Lord High Commissioner to the General Assembly of the Church of Scotland, when in the royal dining room at the Palace of Holyroodhouse Jock reminded himself that it was in that very room where the Queen had told him back in 1971 that he was to be promoted to commander. Jock was moved at Holy Communion in the Assembly Hall the following morning when the bread and wine were borne down the aisles by the Elders with stirring, unaccompanied singing.

Other speeches took a more or less standard form, though Jock varied his words to suit specific audiences. He would paint a picture of where the ships of the fleet were while he was talking, and he would give his listeners some idea of life at the top, commenting that secretaries of defence of whatever party had a real dilemma in that what the services wanted and needed to meet the threat always cost more than the country could afford. Critics questioned the nature of the threat and the degree of military imbalance between East and West. On Trafalgar Night at HMS *Sultan*, the engineering school at Gosport, he pointed out the numerical imbalance in conventional forces in Europe and said that even the major reductions offered by the Soviets would have little impact on reducing the threat. Large-scale reductions by the West would have catastrophic results for the credibility of defence and deterrence. "Now, if ever, was certainly not the time to drop our guard. Fortunately, the North Atlantic Alliance in its first 40 years had proved robust and versatile enough to face up to difficulties and challenges and adapt. Some secretaries of defence were more capable of putting this over than others."

## The Ghost of Uncle Ned

In November 1990 Prince Philip unveiled a bust to Admiral of the Fleet Lord Fraser of North Cape in the Victory Arena in Portsmouth dockyard. (The Prince had unveiled a bust of ABC in Trafalgar Square in 1967.) Jock was delighted to take as a guest Rear-Admiral Royer Dick. Dick, who, though aged 93, was remarkably alert though very frail and clearly enjoyed the outing from his London flat. Earlier, Cunningham had bequeathed to Dick the 'Coventry' decanter, given to Cunningham when he stood down as Rear-Admiral Destroyers in 1936, and a bust of Nelson, given to him by Nancy, Viscountess Astor at a lunch at Cliveden in 1949. Dick wanted Jock to have these, and as he did not seem to be dying he wanted to pass on these two gifts sooner rather than later.

A flagon-bust of Nelson presented by Nancy, Lady Astor in 1949 to 'ABC', bequeathed to Rear Admiral Royer Dick in 1963, and returned to JCKS before Dick's death in 1991. Source: Rob Powell

Dick died five months later, shortly before Martin Stephen, schoolmaster and jobbing naval historian and fiction writer, published a comparative study of British admirals in the Second World War. Stephen maintained that, however fine an admiral ABC was, he was "by no means the greatest admiral of the war and was vastly overrated because of a historical accident … [he had] walked into two victories … but interwar planning won Taranto and radar won Matapan." (Stephen, who drew on contemporary wartime papers in the Churchill Archives Centre in Cambridge, seemed to have overlooked the significance of Ultra decrypts of Italian signals.) Jock was disappointed by this judgement, a disappointment enhanced by the knowledge that Stephen had taught at his old school, Sedbergh.[126]

## Options for Change

The results of yet another defence review, *Options for Change*, were announced on 20 July 1990. Supposedly unlike previous reviews, which had been conducted primarily in response to financial considerations, *Options for Change* was claimed to be a response to the changed strategic environment of the post-Cold War era. In other words, the opportunity to reap a so-called peace dividend and to reduce defence spending was seized. The Secretary of State for Defence told Parliament that he had sought to devise a structure for the regular forces appropriate to the new security situation, while meeting Britain's essential peacetime operational needs, proposals that would bring savings and a reduction in the share of GDP taken by defence. Analysts suggested that financial and manpower pressures had made the review unavoidable, regardless of the strategic arguments involved. Pressure on the defence budget in the late 1980s had steadily increased to the extent that a review was already effectively underway, initiated by the Chiefs of Staff themselves, who felt that the procurement programme had become so far removed from defence policy that a review was necessary to force the government to make politically difficult decisions. The review proposed a major restructuring of the armed forces and was regarded as the beginning of a shift towards a capability- rather than threat-based policy. Its aim was to establish smaller, well-motivated forces that were better equipped and properly trained and housed.

*Options for Change* proposed a reduction in manpower across all three services of approximately 18% (56,000) by the mid-1990s. The most significant cuts fell on the Army, which would be reduced in strength by a quarter, from 160,000 to 120,000, the majority from forces based in Germany. Tactical air power based in Germany would also be reduced through the closure of two of the four RAF bases and the withdrawal of six RAF squadrons. The Navy would go from 48 destroyers and frigates to 40 (a similar level to that which had originally been proposed nine years earlier by Nott). The strategic nuclear deterrent would remain, but sub-strategic nuclear forces based in Germany would be marginally reduced. Thus, *Options for Change* retained the same basic force composition and balance between the three forces as in the Cold War period but on a smaller scale.

These cuts were not widely welcomed, some analysts thinking that the exact nature of the post-Cold War security environment had not yet been identified and assessed. Given the outbreak of the Gulf War in August 1990 and later civil war in the former Yugoslavia in 1992, others questioned whether the assumptions on which *Options for Change* was based were credible. Resources had been savagely cut, but commitments had only been trimmed. The Defence Select Committee was sceptical and warned that just as the Nott review had been overturned by the Falklands War, so unanticipated hostilities had followed *Options for Change* and that it was essential that ministers review their proposals.[127]

## Fleet Support

All the while, Jock was head of a large department of state. Fleet Support accounted directly for £1.5 billion and another £1 billion indirectly, and employed 20,000 civil servants and 550 uniformed staff – 5% of MoD manpower. It covered stores, spares, ammunition, the dockyards, marine services such as tugs, Fleet Air Arm aircraft maintenance and repair, afloat support and the Royal Fleet Auxiliary, building works, and the Hydrographic Service. In an attempt to pull such an eclectic and diverse department together, Jock introduced a newsletter.[128]

Within Jock's own department there were also plenty of studies, management initiatives, consultancies, and even reports, whose purposes and product are now largely lost to history. In addition to *Options for Change* there was a standing MoD efficiency exercise and an incentive scheme with savings targets of between 2.5% and 3.5% of budget. CFS had been set a target at the upper end of this range, and from 1989–90 had exceeded this target by £4.5 million. Nevertheless, Jock urged his people to manage their affairs even better, saying that "to do so we need to adopt the best possible management practices, create the best possible organisation, and acquire the best possible information on which to base our decisions".

Mindful of his own experiences as captain of *Jupiter* when she was in refit in Devonport, and *Kent* when she was in extended maintenance in Portsmouth, Jock was keen to reduce what he called "harbour hassle" and "drudgery" from ships' companies while in dockyard hands.[129] He noted ruefully that extensions and delays to the planned overall time of refits and dockyard maintenance ran into hundreds of weeks and caused severe disruption to an already tight and overcommitted fleet. Part of the problem was that the fleet was ageing. The inadequate specification of work, poor project management, and the late delivery of stores were also major factors.

Commercial management had been introduced into the dockyards in 1987. Since then 3,800 jobs had been shed at Devonport and 600 at Rosyth and further rationalisation was contemplated. In Portsmouth there was already a Fleet Maintenance and Repair Organisation. In April 1990 the Commander-in-Chief Naval Home Command assumed responsibility for the naval bases, each being formed into a single business unit for providing a service to the fleet. Management of the tugs in the Royal Maritime Auxiliary Service was also devolved to naval bases.

In other areas, the Aircraft Support Executive was considered a resounding success, with promised savings in excess of £200 million over the next ten years, and the Hydrographic Office was transformed into the MoD's first Defence Support Agency.

## MoD Accounting Officer

As CFS, Jock was one of the MoD's accounting officers – in fact, he was the only uniformed accounting officer – and, he admitted, he was unprepared for this responsibility, and a civil service course on finance and accounting only proved to show how far he was out of his depth, though it did help to prepare him for the inevitable summons before the parliamentary Public Accounts Committee.

The press was increasingly querulous about the costs of the fleet maintenance programme following a report by the spending watchdog, the Controller and Auditor General, which did not make comfortable reading. As a result, both Jock and

With typical humour, Jock hands over the 'weight of the royal dockyards' – the responsibility for them - to Admiral Sir Jeremy Black, CinC Naval Home Command. Source: MoD.

the Permanent Under-Secretary Sir Michael Quinlan had to appear before the Public Accounts Committee on 14 March 1990. It would be Jock's only appearance as an accounting officer to answer for his £2.5 billion annual budget. He spent hours preparing himself for every conceivable question, and Quinlan was most complimentary about his performance. Jock reflected that this was most encouraging, though "actually, most of the committee were frankly floundering about a subject they understood so little".[130]

## Operation Granby

Few could have imagined that Jock's next personal newsletter in December 1990 to Fleet Support would be set in the context of Operation Granby, the code name given to the British contribution to the First Gulf War, which followed the Iraqi invasion of Kuwait. The war, involving a 42-country coalition led by the United States, was conducted in two key phases: Operation Desert Shield, the military build-up from August 1990 to January 1991, and Operation Desert Storm, which began on 17 January 1991.

Jock's department was galvanised into action and in late 1990 several royal fleet auxiliaries (RFAs) were deployed: *Olna*, with two Sea King helicopters embarked, and *Orangeleaf* in support; *Fort Grange*, also with two Sea Kings; *Diligence*, to provide forward repair facilities; and *Resource*, assigned to support 7 Armoured Brigade. Four landing ship logistics (LSLs) transported the Army's heavy equipment from the UK. *Argus* was transformed into a primary casualty reception ship with four Sea King helicopters for casualty evacuation, and a shore-based logistic support team was deployed to Dubai to manage the movement of stores along an air bridge. The dockyards and the Aircraft Support Executive were working flat out to convert, upgrade, and prepare ships and aircraft to meet the emergency. Two ships of the surveying flotilla, *Herald* and *Hecla*, were nominated for Operation Granby as command and support vessels for minesweepers, and the Hydrographic Office's defence support agency at Taunton printed a huge number of extra charts and publications for urgent operational use.

All this took place against a background of work on *Options for Change.* "Savings in support must be made if we are to maintain a viable front line," Jock wrote. "We are examining the requirement for dockyard facilities, naval bases, armament, fuel and storage depots with the objective of concentrating on fewer sites … all this is taking place against intense budgetary pressures, which makes the current long-term costing probably the most difficult that we have seen for some time."[131]


## Onward

By late 1990 Jock feared that, as a gloomy Kerr had predicted, he was destined for deskbound policy work in the MoD, so a letter from First Sea Lord Oswald telling him that he was to relieve Ben Bathurst as the next Commander-in-Chief Fleet came as "a fantastic bit of news … I was absolutely delighted although very conscious that I still had much to do to sharpen up Fleet Support."

In his reply to Oswald, Jock told how relentless financial pressures were most frustrating as he was simply not able to give the fleet the support it clearly needed. He hoped that the Fleet Support Policy Group, which he had established in order to streamline and rationalise the way CFS did their business, was a step in the right direction. A very generous letter of thanks from Oswald followed, and Jock in reply commented on the frustrations of life in Whitehall: "It is depressing that so many, from ministers downwards, were hell bent on cuts at all costs and quite oblivious to the fact that they are undermining the spirit and confidence of the Armed Forces not least in the run-up to a major international conflict. The Treasury seems to be quite indifferent to the implications of what they are demanding in the light of the dangers and uncertainties of a turbulent world."

Jock's promotion to full admiral and his appointment as Commander-in-Chief Fleet was formally announced on 1 November 1990. A surprising letter of congratulations from a well-known workaholic, Admiral of the Fleet Lord Hill-Norton, soon followed, in which the old admiral encouraged Jock to take life less seriously. "Coming from him that was amazing, but needless to say I responded appropriately as I was aware that he was one of my strongest supporters."

To his surprise, Jock found himself reluctant to leave Fleet Support with so much going on and the ink hardly dry on *Options for Change* and its application to Fleet Support. Saddam Hussein's Iraq had invaded Kuwait on 2 August 1990 and Operation Granby was gearing up. That said, he was secretly relieved to be going to Northwood and knew that the command of the fleet was much more his cup of tea.

# Chapter 14: All at Sea

When Jock gave an interview to *The Scotsman* in early 1989 he was still FOSNI, and he may have exceeded his brief when batting away a question about the Women's Royal Naval Service (WRNS) and its members serving at sea. He admitted that all three services faced a demographic downturn and that most jobs at sea could be performed by women, but asserted that the female physique was not up to damage control and firefighting in a ship in action. He also maintained that putting a virile young sailor in a tin box away from home with a pretty girl was asking for trouble. *The Scotsman* blushingly reported this as "welfare problems" for the men at sea and the wives left behind.

**The Wrens**

The WRNS was formed in 1917 to 'free a man for the fleet', and numbered just under 7,000 at its peak. It was disbanded in 1919 but reformed in 1939, reaching 73,500 members during the Second World War. It lasted until 1993, when its members were integrated into the Navy. Wrens wore blue badges rather than the red and gold of the men, and their officers' sleeves bore a blue cloth diamond instead of a gold braid curl. They had their own regulations and did not come under the Naval Discipline Act until 1977: they were effectively civilians in uniform.

Wrens did not serve at sea and their anomalous position was exacerbated by the question of whether they could bear arms and fight in battle. In 1940, when Gibraltar was declared a fortress and 13,500 civilians were evacuated, women serving as auxiliaries with the armed forces stayed behind and the Flag Officer Gibraltar, Admiral Sir Dudley North, glibly commented "they are all volunteers, and we should probably all be blown up together, but they don't mind".[132] Yet in 1941, when a draft of Wrens was sent around Africa destined for Alexandria to establish a wireless interception station there, Jock's Uncle Ned, the Commander-in-Chief Mediterranean, stopped them at Durban and objected that women could not stand up to the rigours of a war zone. The unintended consequence was that ten of the party once more risked the threat of U-boats by returning across the Atlantic, and ten others were sent to Singapore, where they risked being captured when war broke out in the Far East. The response of the head of the WRNS, Commandant Vera Laughton Matthews, was to send one of her senior and most persuasive officers, Chief Officer Jessie Frith, to Alexandria to interview the Commander-in-Chief who eventually relented, writing in his memoirs about a detachment of Wrens in North Africa and that "these most useful ladies were the forerunners of many more Wrens who were presently to join us, and their services were invaluable". Meanwhile, Laughton Matthews extracted a ruling from the Admiralty that women should not be sent to places where there was considered to be a possibility of their falling into enemy hands, but that if things went wrong, women should remain at their posts in circumstances where this would be expected of men: this rule became wartime policy and was adopted by the other services.[133]

Little more seems to have been done in the next half century to examine the issue of women in combat roles in the three British armed services.[134] Despite changes in the perception of women in the wider workplace and in the law,[135] in 1977 it still took two meetings of the Navy Board to agree to place the WRNS under the Naval Discipline Act. Further change was presaged in 1984 in a comic but prescient novel by John Winton, *The Good Ship Venus*. Although taking his title from a bawdy drinking song, Winton humorously but seriously examined the issues arising in a warship with a crew drawn from both sexes.[136] When Jock, as CFS, joined the Navy Board in 1989, there was more lively discussion over whether women should serve at sea. Despite his earlier unease, Jock began to appreciate that the Navy needed women at sea and, as he reflected later "the tide was rising fast and … the best thing to do was 'get on with it'".

When the question of women at sea arose formally, Rear-Admiral Michael Livesay, Assistant Chief of Naval Staff from 1986–89,[137] advised the Board that the retention of experienced men was a critical problem and that using Wrens ashore to make up numbers would not suffice: he wanted Wrens to have a wider role, and to make them more employable. The Navy interpreted previous governmental statements regarding women in combat as extending to women at sea, and Livesay proposed a study that would review this policy.

## West

A six-month study was commissioned in June 1988, though the Navy Board dampened expectations by "noting that there [was] little enthusiasm in the Navy (shared by the WRNS) to employ WRNS at sea". Captain Alan West, who had spent most of his career at sea and had little experience of working with Wrens, was appointed to lead.[138] He recalled that his instinctive reaction was against women serving at sea, and he thought this was typical of most people in the Navy. He soon found that senior officers, even at Navy Board level, thought that it would be a disaster. Looking back, he thought that he had been picked because he was expected to say that women at sea was "totally impossible and we can forget it".[139]

West and his study team spent four days and nights at sea with the Royal Netherlands Navy, where women had already been serving in ships for about ten years and whose mixed-crew ships performed well in operational training, which was run by the Royal Navy at Portland. Curiously, another group of civilians in uniform, the Royal Naval Auxiliary Service (RNXS) was overlooked: the RNXS was a volunteer service dressed, administered, and trained by the Royal Navy, which had appointed its first female skipper, Denise St Aubyn Hubbard, in 1978.[140]

After examining many options, in March 1989, to the surprise of many, West recommended that Wrens should go to sea from April 1990 and that the WRNS should merge with the Royal Navy on 1 April 1991. Women should be given full career opportunities, which would solve both quality and quantity issues in recruitment and, by reducing the strains caused by shortages of male personnel, would, it was hoped, improve male retention. To take account of suggestions that women were not strong enough to carry out some of the communal duties, such as storing ship and damage control, and the need to divide messdecks between men and women, West proposed a maximum of 10–15% of billets in any one ship should be filled by women. When it came to which ships, the terms of reference given to West for his study recognised "successive governments' policy that women should not be employed in combat areas". He interpreted this narrowly and thus rather pulled his punches by identifying five supposedly non-combatant ships suitable for women to serve in.[141]

The issue was sensitive, and even these limited proposals were regarded by many as going too far too fast. There were some supporters, but West's recommendations were deeply unpopular among contemporaries, who used strong language to assert their views. Misogyny among men was matched by angst among their wives and sweethearts. It would be the responsibility of

Admiral Sir Brian Brown, as Second Sea Lord and Chief of Naval Personnel, to make an unpopular policy work, and he had other, principled reservations about women at sea. He doubted the morality of employing women in combat roles while men were in safe jobs ashore, and, remembering media coverage of the Falklands War, he recoiled from the thought of female burns victims appearing on television. Nor was he persuaded that Wrens' career prospects were inadequate: rather that there was a queue of high-class volunteers for the WRNS. Brown kicked West's report into the long grass, took three months to circulate it to departments and headquarters for consideration, and allowed a further three months for comment.[142]

## Hamilton

However, at about this time, Archie Hamilton, newly appointed Minister of Defence for the Armed Forces,[143] received a note from Prime Minister Margaret Thatcher that said something like: "Dear Archie, I feel that there should be wider opportunities for women in the armed forces. What do you think? Margaret." Hamilton began a round of individual discussions with the Chiefs of the three services, during which he learned from Admiral Oswald, who had become First Sea Lord in May 1989, about the West report. Hamilton was unimpressed by its limited proposals, and at the suggestion of his military assistant, Commander Roy Clare,[144] he too visited the Dutch Navy. To Hamilton, the gap between the Dutch experience and West's recommendations for women at sea was glaring.[145]

Then, when Hamilton read a paper that described the official position regarding women in combat as a precept rather than a policy, he asked for further advice. Told that "historically … departmental [i.e. MoD] and Parliamentary discussion on the employment of women in the Services [had] been based on the premise that the British public would not accept that women should be placed in a position where they could be required to kill or be killed", Hamilton concluded that the employment of women in combat was a matter of social, military, and, above all, political judgement.

## Oswald

First Sea Lord Oswald was cautious about sending women to sea, though publicly he kept an open mind saying that he wanted to listen to the arguments. While the debate raged within the Navy, the Army and the RAF watched nervously. Hamilton's ministerial interest was in Oswald's view the least good reason to make any significant change. What largely persuaded Oswald was the realisation during his visits to ships and establishments that many younger members of the service, men and women, thought that women at sea would happen, and that it should happen.[146] His Naval Assistant, Captain John Lippiett, and his Secretary, Captain Nick Wilkinson, ensured that during visits he met female reservists who already went to sea for training, and that he could sound out naval officers. Wilkinson also canvassed the opinion of the naval staff, reporting back that "people thought that if we were going to do it, do it properly and get on with it".

Still Oswald hesitated, and sent for West to ask whether he thought that women at sea was the right decision and whether it would damage the Navy. West replied that it was the right and only decision and that, although there would be uncomfortable moments, it would not cause critical damage to the Navy. The final clincher seems to have been a visit to HMS *Collingwood* when, over lunch, Oswald chatted to a very bright Third Officer WRNS, a weapons engineer who clearly hoped to go to sea and who astonished him by telling him that she played in the front row for Llanelli Women's XV. In the car going back to London he turned to Wilkinson with a sigh and said, "OK, Wrens to sea, we'll do it."[147]

Eventually it was Oswald who insisted in January 1990 that the first contingent of Wrens should be at sea by 1 October 1990, and that the first tranche of 300–400 Wrens should be at sea by the end of that year.

## Brown

Brian Brown was Director General, Naval Manpower and Training (formerly Director General Naval Personnel Services) from 1986–88 and Second Sea Lord and Chief of Naval Personnel in 1988 , placing him at the centre of the argument about women at sea.[148] He remained unconvinced, and the paper that the Navy Board was due to take in the New Year of 1990 reflected this, and his views were likely to sway the Board. Brown was visiting the Falklands when Captain Peter Dunt, his secretary, who was minding the shop in London, remembered very clearly talking to Roy Clare, who told him that no matter what the Navy Board recommended, Hamilton had decided that women were going to sea. Clare's report later appeared in officialese as: "Informal discussions with Minister (AF) have indicated that there should be strong support for this from the Secretary of State." Dunt relayed this message from London to Brown in the South Atlantic over a poor line and by the time he had returned from the Falklands, Brown had rewritten the paper to ensure that it recommended sending women to sea. In the re-draft, Brown also proposed that West's restricted group of ships should be extended to include aircraft carriers and landing ships. The Navy Board discussed the WRNS study informally on 11 January 1990, and a final, revised paper, NAVB/P(90)1, was circulated on 24 January 1990, when members were given 48 hours to approve it out of committee.[149]

The Navy Board's decision was thus relatively easy: the harder part for the implementation team, under Brown's supervision, was to meticulously draw together all the strands and complexities for getting the first tranche of women to sea and the full integration of the WRNS into the naval service.[150]

**Women at Sea**

Given a new, political perception of women in combat roles, instead of the five ships proposed by West, or the larger group of ships proposed by Brown, the first ships with mixed crews were the carriers HMS *Invincible* and HMS *Ark Royal*, and several destroyers and frigates of which the frigate HMS *Brilliant* was the first. What had begun in comedy in 1984 nearly ended in farce six years later, however, when *Brilliant* was about to deploy to the Persian Gulf to take part in Operation Granby at the start of the First Gulf War. Oswald rang Commander-in-Chief Fleet Bathurst to ask on behalf of ministers "who were rather worried [and wondered] whether another ship might be sent, rather than putting women in harm's way", only to be told firmly by Bathurst that if he did that the whole concept would be "dead in the water … ministers have said that they want this to happen and it's a very good opportunity for them to find out the consequences of their decision".[151] *Brilliant* and the female members of her crew acquitted themselves well in the Gulf and, subsequently, when redeployed in the Adriatic to enforce a United Nations arms embargo, they starred in a BBC documentary series produced by Chris Terrill and broadcast 1995.

Also in 1990, after several years of senior WRNS officers gradually breaking new ground in posts previously held by male officers, Chief Officer Pippa Duncan hit the jackpot and became the first WRNS officer to command a shore establishment, HMS *Warrior*, responsible for supporting the materiel infrastructure of NATO and Royal Air Force and naval staffs at fleet headquarters.[152] The women adopted naval ranks in December 1990 and the officers hoisted gold braid stripes instead of the traditional blue cloth of the WRNS in April 1992. By 1 November 1993, when Jock had become Vice Chief of Defence Staff (VCDS), there were 25 ships with facilities for women, and nearly 1,000 women at sea.[153]

Looking back, Jock asked himself "What was all the fuss about?" Attitudes had changed markedly and most of his concerns had been proved unfounded.

# Chapter 15: The Globe and Laurel

Jock was still CFS when in 1990 Lieutenant General Henry Beverley, Commandant General Royal Marines (CGRM) from 1990–94, called to brief him informally on his proposals for the Corps.

## A Savings Measure

Since the end of Konfrontasi, the three-year conflict on the island of Borneo and the Malay Peninsula in the mid-1960s, the Corps had been stable at about 7,500 men. This was largely agreed to be the minimum strength at which the Corps was viable and could offer a worthwhile career. Below this, overheads would rise, the training system would become too top heavy, and uncertainty would affect morale, recruiting, and efficiency. It was feared that the dissolution of the Corps would be self-fulfilling. However, the 1981 Nott review proposed – at its simplest – to reduce Britain's defences to a nuclear deterrent and to a defence against the Soviet Union on the Central Front in Germany, and to significantly reduce the capacity for expeditionary warfare. The main cuts were to fall on the Navy, which, although it took on the Trident submarine force, was to lose around one-fifth of its 60 destroyers and frigates. One of the three *Invincible*-class carriers and the two amphibious ships, *Fearless* and *Intrepid*, were to be cut. If implemented, the Nott review would have been the death knell for the Royal Marines and could have meant disbandment or, worse, absorption into the Army. If this had been proposed the then CGRM, Lieutenant General Steuart Pringle, made it clear to the Navy Board that he would recommend disbandment. Some naval officers thought of the Corps as a savings measure that could be offered to save some ships.

The palpable success of the 1982 Falklands War brought the Royal Navy and Royal Marines to their collective senses and returned sanity to the wider defence debate. By 1985 the concept of amphibious warfare was written into the defence policy of the government of the day, and from it flowed all the costed capability requirements for specialist shipping.

## Beverley's Brainwave

Now Beverley was the architect of a revolutionary plan for the Royal Marines. With the growing power and influence of the central defence staff, the status of CGRM as advisor on amphibious warfare to the Secretary of State could no longer be justified and it was clear to Beverley that the time had come for the Royal Marines to reintegrate fully into their parent service. He proposed to the First Sea Lord, Oswald, that CGRM and his staff be relocated to the Portsmouth area and become a type commander reporting to the Commander-in-Chief Fleet. This would resolve a budgetary anomaly: CGRM was top-level budget holder and thus a member of the Navy Management Board, which was synonymous with the Navy Board itself. As a type commander he would become a high-level budget holder on a par with Flag Officer Naval Aviation and Flag Officer Submarines.

It was also clear to Beverley that the Corps could no longer sustain its own promotion structures. Though the Royal Marines supported a lieutenant-general and two major-generals with their staffs, this was a glass ceiling and very few senior Royal Marines officers made their mark outside the Corps. Beverley proposed that the two major-generals and their staffs be amalgamated into one headquarters, and, more importantly, that the management of Royal Marines officers' careers should become the responsibility of the Naval Secretary. Oswald was surprised when he first heard these ideas, and he asked Beverley to return after he had had more time to consult his peers and confirm their support.

## Evolution

As Commander-in-Chief Fleet, Jock gave his wholehearted support to his staff and to Beverley's while they worked out the details of the changes, and it would be the spring of 1994 before Lieutenant General Robin Ross took over as CGRM and Headquarters, Royal Marines was inaugurated.[154] As Beverley would write: "I [am] delighted at the way that it has all worked out.

The abundant talent within the Royal Marines [has been] unleashed … [and] Jock's terrific interest and support was absolutely crucial to the success of this (dare I say) rather historic evolution." Beverley recognised that, while serving Royal Marines officers would see the logic in all these changes, some retired officers would be more difficult to win over, used as they were to centuries of deep suspicion of the Royal Navy. There was a hiccup, however. In July 1991 Jock visited ships in Plymouth and was guest of honour at the Armada Night dinner in HMS *Drake*. He had, as usual, taken considerable trouble preparing his speech and blamed himself for what went wrong. Another guest was Robin Ross, who had just returned from leading an Anglo-Dutch force in Operation Safe Haven, a humanitarian initiative to protect the Kurds in northern Iraq. Ross was an old friend of Jock and after dinner complained of the omission of any mention of the Royal Marines' recent success in Iraq. In retrospect, Jock realised that he was in error, even if he did not like the force with which Ross had made his point.

On 31 October 1991 Jock was able to make amends and at dinner in the Royal Marines Officers' Mess at Stonehouse he made a keynote speech welcoming the decision to draw the Corps under the fleet umbrella, which was planned for April 1993. He promised:

Flexibility and mobility are the cries and what could be more flexible, more mobile than a maritime capability with an amphibious component … I welcome with open arms the work we are currently doing to align more closely the Corps with the Fleet … I'm absolutely certain we are moving down the right lines [and] am determined to see the widest possible delegation under the new command arrangements, which will ensure that the Commandant General remains very much the boss: arrangements that will ensure that the Corps and its business will be well represented in the corridors of power; arrangements that will guarantee that the individual identity, the professionalism, the traditions, and the esprit de corps of the Royal Marines will not be undermined … I'm in no doubt that Joint Operations will be the cornerstone of any future conflict. I'm also in no doubt that those daunting challenges will take place at the boundaries between different elements or areas of extreme climate and geography – and that is exactly why we must continue to have Royal Marines – to fight on the boundary between sea and land and in extreme places and tough conditions. That is why we must continue to argue strongly for the ships, aircraft, and equipment that are central for the task.

Jock concluded by telling the assembled company: "In me you have one of your strongest supporters." Privately, he noted: "I was very glad that Henry Beverley presided at the dinner as it was he who had the guts to persuade the Doubting Thomases in the Royal Marines, both serving and retired, that this was the right thing for them to do … Julian Oswald, the First Sea Lord and I were convinced that if we did not make this move, the Corps would be seen as an elitist vine and that the vine would wither and die. I was in no doubt that there were those in the Army and Civil Service in particular who saw the Royal Marines as 'rich pickings'. Our challenge was to get the Royal Marines back at sea and doing what they do best."

## The Band Was His!

Jock had further amends to make to Ross. The musician in him was a great fan of the Mountbatten Festival of Music, hosted each year by the Corps in the Royal Albert Hall, and when Ross retired as CGRM Jock could think of no better way of thanking him for his service than by secretly arranging to conduct the massed bands. In retrospect it was a high-risk plan but he asked his former director of music in Scotland, Peter Rutterford, to coach him and on the morning went to a rehearsal. Annie knew something was up but not precisely what, when, after the interval, Jock was announced on the stage to pay tribute to the Royal Marines Band Service, especially after the bombing at Deal, and to the Commandant General. At the end of a short speech he disclosed that he intended to put his command of the Marines to the practical test of conducting their regimental slow march, the Preobrazhensky. "Judging by the applause of the audience, they approved, but to this day I cannot think why I did it!"

Jock's early contact with the Corps came in December 1958 when he received the Queen's telescope from General Sir Hardy Campbell, Commandant General Royal Marines. Slater archive.

Having paid tribute to Ross in the Royal Albert Hall, the following week Jock hosted a Navy Board lunch to say farewell. It was lunch with a typical Jock joke: after drinks in the drawing room of Admiralty House the guests moved into the dining room where to everybody's surprise the table was bare. As they sat down "Chief Steward Keith Farrow and Leading Steward Brian Humphrey dressed in khaki fatigues, doubled in and placed individual boxes of compo rations in front of us. Actually, each box contained a delicious picnic."

## Royal Navy and Royal Marines

Jock's regard for the Royal Marines was not theatre and his words were no lip service. In September 1991, when he took the salute at the passing out parade of the newest Royal Marine young officers, he commented, "What an impressive team they were, clearly very proud to have achieved their green berets." Jock presented the sword of honour to Second Lieutenant Russell Corn, just as the then CGRM, General Sir Campbell Hardy, had presented a sword to him 34 years before. He was delighted at lunchtime when he met among the families of the young Royal Marines officers, a father, Lieutenant Commander James Ashby, who had joined the Navy with him.[155]

On 16 November 1992 the Navy gave a dinner in HMS *Ark Royal* in Portsmouth to celebrate the 40th anniversary of the Queen's accession, hosted by the First Sea Lord, though it was Jock's team at Northwood who made all the arrangements. Major General David Pennefather recalled that "we were each given the dinner plate from which we ate, given, washed up and boxed, as we left the ship – such style!" Every available commanding officer in the Royal Navy and Royal Marines attended, and Jock took the opportunity to invite them all to HMS *Dryad* that morning for a meeting. General Beverley's thank you letter showed how genuinely thrilled he was by the way in which the Royal Marines had been welcomed into the fleet. Jock noted: "Much credit for the integration goes to Henry himself, who, I suspect, had quite a hard battle behind the scenes with his predecessors."

For his part thereafter, Jock rarely referred to the naval service without calling it the Royal Navy *and* Royal Marines.

# Chapter 16: Commander-in-Chief Fleet, 1991–93

Jock took over as Commander-in-Chief Fleet from Bathurst in January 1991. He was based at Northwood in Middlesex and had as his Chief of Staff Rear-Admiral Roy Newman[156] and Paul Haddacks as his Captain of the Fleet. As usual, Jock delegated to men he could trust, and Haddacks recalled that he was given a very wide brief to visit all elements of the fleet, surface, submarine, Fleet Air Arm and Royal Marines, and that he would debrief Jock in person, not by written reports but verbally usually about every fortnight over a working breakfast. "He was as always, sharp and incisive, and quickly drilled down to the nub of any issue. I always felt he was an absolute master of his business." Haddacks also sat in on Jock's regular meetings of fleet flag officers, which gave him valuable insights, demonstrated confidence in his Captain of the Fleet, and eased his relationship with those flag officers who did not always appreciate someone from headquarters "dipping his toes into their command business". [157]

**Northwood, Middlesex**

Jock kept a seat at the Navy Board and wore two NATO hats. Firstly he would be a major NATO commander, Commander-in-Chief Allied Command Channel (CINCHAN), a post that existed from 1952 to 1994, responsible for defending the sea areas and allied shipping around the English Channel. . Secondly, he would be CINCEASTLANT, a major subordinate commander, a post that existed from 1952 to 2004, reporting to the Supreme Allied Commander Atlantic, whose headquarters were in Norfolk, Virginia. There was a large NATO staff at Northwood, though Jock was "frankly not sure what they all did but they seemed incredibly busy when the annual exercises took place. They were headed up by a Dutch Rear-Admiral, Paul Leertouwer, a nice man with firm views on maritime affairs and I appreciated his advice and guidance."

As flag lieutenant, Tom Karsten proved absolutely first class and fitted into the family admirably: "Educated at Charterhouse, he was not a conventional naval officer, and I much enjoyed his originality and relaxed but efficient style. He often would set off to London to play football with his friends in Hyde Park – or at least that is what he said he was doing. I got used to the pretty girls, who I thought had come up to speak to me but made a beeline for Tom." In return, Karsten found Jock to be an extremely generous and supportive boss.[158] Sub-Lieutenant Mandy McBain was the PA who ran Jock's office affairs well.[159]

One of Jock's first briefings was in his capacity as Commander of Task Force 345, Britain's nuclear deterrent. It took place in 'the Hole', the underground part of the headquarters, and was given by the Flag Officer Submarines. There would be regular exercises of nuclear command and control arrangements. Jock noted that there was a small French team whose only role was to deconflict the movements, or 'water space,' of the nations' respective strategic missile-firing submarines. The French were not then part of the Integrated Military Structure of NATO, and he soon became aware that the US Navy were chary about the French presence.


## Operation Desert Storm

Operation Desert Storm, the First Gulf War, began on 17 January 1991 and ended with the liberation of Kuwait on 28 February 1991, when the Navy played a significant role in the early stages of the war. Lynx helicopters destroyed what there was of an Iraqi navy in the Battle of the Bubiyan Channel, British minehunters cleared near the Kuwaiti coast, allowing the US battleships *Wisconsin* and *Missouri* to launch devastating bombardments against Iraqi ground forces, and a Seadart missile from HMS *Gloucester* destroyed a Silkworm missile aimed at coalition warships.

Many of Jock's ships and aircraft were under the operational command of Air Chief Marshal Paddy Hine at RAF High Wycombe,[160] where, until 29 January, Jock's Chief of Staff, Newman, was doubling as naval deputy. Newman's nickname was 'the Rottweiler' and some people saw him as a bit of a rough diamond; those who knew him better affectionately called him 'Uncle Roy'. His style was sometimes aggressive, and some found this disconcerting, but Jock appreciated Newman's professional, pragmatic, sometimes tough, and always well-considered, advice. Newman's loyalty and integrity were impressive and the two got on well together.

The in-theatre commander, Commander British Forces Middle East Lieutenant General Sir Peter de la Billiere, was based in Riyadh. Also in Riyadh was the Chief of Staff, Air Vice Marshal Ian MacFadyen, whom Jock remembered flying a Phantom jet into Stanley Airfield before *Illustrious* sailed home at the end of Operation Corporate in October 1982.[161] Commodore Chris Craig was the Senior British Naval Officer Middle East and, having done particularly well in command of HMS *Alacrity* in the Falklands nine years previously, again acquitted himself well. Jock was slightly envious: "Some people have the good fortune at finding themselves at the front at critical times." Craig's signal on 22 April 1991, indicating the end of Operation Granby, marked an important historic moment, and as the ships returned to the fleet's operational control, Jock flew out to congratulate his people. He was accompanied by his director of operations, the "most able" Captain Paul Canter, and by Karsten.[162 163]

Jock would never forget flying into Kuwait and seeing the sabotaged oil wells still alight and thick, dirty smoke everywhere. That evening he flew out to visit the MCM squadron, which was based on RFA *Sir Galahad*, and dined in the middle of a minefield with the commanding officers in HMS *Hecla*. The next day he visited several ships off Bahrain, finishing for the night in HMS *Exeter*. There he met for the first time Captain Nigel Essenhigh, and learned of Essenhigh's strong views about the organisation of the fleet; he was left in no doubt that here was an officer who should be watched for future promotion. Jock thought it was good for his people to see their commander-in-chief, but was very conscious of not overstaying his welcome. Nor could he escape his private disappointment that the people he was meeting had taken part in operations while he had not. It was the same feeling he had experienced after the Falklands – "envy and a slight inferiority complex".


**Slicing the Defence Budget**

The MoD has suffered a continuous succession of defence reviews since the Second World War. After the Nott review in 1981 the major reviews in Jock's time as an admiral were *Options for Change* in 1990, *The Defence Costs Study* aka *Front Line First* in 1994, and – to come – the *Strategic Defence Review* and the *SDR New Chapter* in 1998 and 2002 respectively. In between there were numerous minor or stealth reviews and white papers.

*Options for Change* in 1990, which affected force levels, stranded the MoD looking very oversized compared to the reduced front line, but there was no pause in the pace of defence reviews to give an opportunity for *Options for Change* to be bedded down. The next review was *Prospect*, a stealth review in 1991 of MoD headquarters, which sought to reduce MoD overheads and streamline working practices to match reductions in front line strengths. *Prospect* looked at the future size and structure of the MoD and its relationship with the commands, including headquarters manpower, and sought savings at all levels of at least 20%, and a significant relocation of posts out of London. Specifically, *Prospect* would produce a leaner, tauter, and more responsive MoD after a net reduction of 20% in 2-star service and civilian posts, overall reductions of 10% in staff numbers in London by 1993, rising to 20% in two years, and slightly more following the move of the Procurement Executive to Bristol.

As far as the Royal Navy was concerned it meant the move of the Second Sea Lord to Portsmouth in 1994, the merger with the Commander in Chief Naval Home Command (CINCNAVHOME), the establishment of the Naval Support Command at Bath under the CFS, and turning the Royal Marines into a type command with headquarters in Portsmouth.

## Type Command

The surface fleet would be given similar management status as the Fleet Air Arm and the Submarine Service. Jock created a Flag Officer Surface Flotillas under Vice-Admiral Nick Hill-Norton, based in Portsmouth, who would also be Commander Anti-Submarine Warfare Striking Force Atlantic. Rear-Admiral John Brigstocke became the Commander of the UK Task Group and the fleet's amphibious authority. He was based in Plymouth, where 3 Commando Brigade and the Commodore Amphibious Warfare headquarters were already collocated. Jock was content to know that he had two very able officers to complete all changes by vesting day, 6 April 1992, when the new type command, the Flag Officer Surface Flotillas, was stood up. Rear-Admiral A Bruce Richardson deserved much credit for the work of his implementation team in reaching this milestone in the reorganisation of the fleet and in ensuring the best possible start, but Nick Hill-Norton, the first holder of this new appointment, was in his element. In his speech, Jock paid tribute to Rear-Admiral David Bawtree, the Flag Officer Portsmouth, for his cooperation, although he was surprised not to see him at the ceremony. In fact, Bawtree, though a most competent officer, was uneasy about all the changes afoot, which directly affected his role as commander of the naval base.

## Health Warning

On New Year's Eve 1991 an old friend and naval doctor, retired Surgeon Captain David Dalgliesh, with whom Jock had served in *Britannia*, used his experienced eye to diagnose a man under great pressure. Dalgliesh told Jock how shocked he had been 40 years before when he had seen the then First Sea Lord, Admiral of the Fleet Sir Rhoderick 'Wee' McGrigor, exhibiting similar signs of being under pressure and wondering how long he could last. Jock was already concerned about his blood pressure and high cholesterol. Dalgliesh regarded cholesterol as an American fad but was worried about Jock's hypertension and encouraged him to take as much time off as he could, free of social nonsense. He regarded quiet periods of inactivity as a form of vital medicine. Jock took the warning well, replying:

> Your ancient medical and most experienced eye was not deceiving you. I have been working under pressure for some years now and the last year has been particularly demanding and at a pace that younger people would find daunting. You are absolutely right, I ought to ease up but it's easier said than done sitting at the forefront of major changes in the Alliance and an internal and complex evolution in naval affairs – not to mention commanding the Fleet. The only real way is to step down and let others have a go but I'm not ready for that yet. Nevertheless, I take your wise advice – and indeed that of others recently – very seriously and am doing my best to ease the pace a little.

But Jock took little real notice. In January and February 1992 he went shooting with his sons in Hampshire and with his friends, the Hunters, in Herefordshire; he corresponded with members of the royal family; flew to the USA for a SACLANT wargame, Open Road, with some 50 flag and general officers participating; visited Copenhagen for Exercise Viking Shield and took an active part in a SACEUR meeting about the NATO command structure; and paid a visit in rough weather to HMS *York* and HMS *Beaver* in the Atlantic off Gibraltar. In Gibraltar he stayed with Derek Reffell, who was now the governor, and noted that Reffell still lacked a sense of humour and was clearly not best friends with the Flag Officer Gibraltar, Jock's old friend Geoffrey Biggs. Biggs was obviously well established on the Rock and respected by all three services. He was his long-haired, scruffy old self but had adopted a purple woolly-pully to indicate his tri-service command, of which Peter Harding, the new CDS, did not approve. When Harding told Jock that this must stop, Jock replied, "We are lucky to have a man of Geoffrey's calibre and intellect out there, leave him alone!"

Next, Jock and Annie flew to Scotland to celebrate Rory's 15th birthday at Gleneagles. By early February Jock was on his way to the Caribbean to visit the Standing Naval Force Atlantic, where he was battered in a bad winching from a USN helicopter into the deck of the Dutch frigate *Jacob van Heemskerck*. His day off on Great Abaco in the Bahamas was spoiled by unusual cold, wet, and wind – and the expense. He visited HM Ships *Ariadne*, *Broadsword*, and *Brazen* and entered Miami in *Brazen* for talks with US authorities about counter-drug smuggling operations in the Caribbean, before flying off via calls in Kingston, Jamaica to Curaçao and Venezuela for official visits.

Jock was home on 20 February to fly his flag in the minesweeper *Soberton*, which he had commanded briefly in 1964, as she made her way up the Thames to paying off after some 35 years of service in the Fishery Protection Squadron, and that evening he attended a dinner hosted by her captain, Lieutenant Commander Justin Wood, in the RNR headquarters, HMS *President*. (The ship was determined that their own chef should cook dinner for all 60 guests, including 18 of the former ship's commanding officers, bringing everything up from the jetty: "Needless to say, it took rather a long time, but a good effort.") Next day, the Slaters were guests of General Sir Henry Beverley in the royal box at the Royal Albert Hall for the Mountbatten Festival of Music. Those six weeks in early 1992 were typical of Jock's punishing schedule.

## NATO Reorganisation

It was not all travelling and handshaking, and a persistent issue was the NATO command structure, about which Jock disagreed with the MoD. Annie had accompanied Jock to Copenhagen for a NATO meeting, but when Exercise Viking Shield was finished she flew home with the Vincents and the Oswalds while Jock stayed on for a meeting of SACEUR.

Few, not even Jock, had foreseen the tumultuous transformation of the political landscape of Europe at the end of the Cold War. The Treaty on Conventional Armed Forces in Europe (CFE) had been conceived in 1989, signed in 1990, and would enter into force at the end of 1992. CFE imagined broad parity of conventional forces from the Atlantic to the Urals between NATO and the Warsaw Treaty Organization of Friendship, Cooperation and Mutual Assistance (The Warsaw Pact), mirroring agreements on strategic and sub-strategic systems. Meanwhile, Poland had elected its first non-Communist prime minister, and Poland, Czechoslovakia, and Hungary had participated on the side of the US-led coalition in the Gulf War. On 1 July 1991 the Warsaw Pact itself was dissolved after 36 years of military alliance with the USSR, and the USSR disestablished itself in December 1991. The risks of general war in Europe were greatly reduced and NATO faced very different defence and security challenges.

NATO required a new strategic concept, new force, and new command structures, and NATO strategy was reorientated towards reacting rapidly to regional crises. CINCHAN was to be disestablished and there would be only two major NATO commanders, SACEUR and SACLANT. Jock presented his proposals for collocating the new Commander-in-Chief Allied Forces North West with CINCEASTLANT at Northwood. This was not the MoD's policy, and Jock's advocacy earned him a reprimand from the outgoing CDS, Vincent, which was relayed to him by the First Sea Lord, Oswald. However, Jock was convinced that Vincent had no idea what he was talking about as regards maritime affairs and was disappointed that Oswald had failed to support him. Nevertheless, "I would have been failing in my duties if I were not to put forward what I believed to be right and in the best interests of the Alliance."

## A Fleet for the 90s

In the closing weeks of his tenure as Commander-in-Chief, on 26 November 1992, after nearly two years at Northwood, Jock was invited to address the Royal United Services Institute. His subject was a fleet for the 1990s. His first point was that those who, in the modern, technologically agile world, believed that military matters could easily be categorised into land, sea, and air were making a facile and anachronistic judgement. The audience had already heard from the Commander-in-Chief UK Land Forces and from the RAF's Commander-in-Chief Strike Command, who had highlighted their own key aspirations for the future of their commands. In some ways, said Jock, it would have been more appropriate and more fruitful to explore common requirements and to be given some insight into how British assets could most effectively be coordinated. For his part, he was absolutely in no doubt that joint operations would be the cornerstone of any future conflict, especially given the wide range of possible scenarios that might arise, and that joint meant multi-service and more than likely multinational. There had, he pointed out, been some 80 significant conflicts since the Second World War, most of which had involved early and sustained commitment of naval forces.

For half a century the Royal Navy and Royal Marines had adapted primarily in response to one immediate and massive threat in the European theatre and its adjacent waters. This had been the principal concern of NATO, and the free world had relied on and contributed to the United States' *Forward Maritime Strategy*. Now faced with a wider spectrum of challenges, NATO had agreed a new strategy in a new command structure tailored for the remote possibility of general war within a credible warning time, while at the same time making adequate provision for a wide variety of less intense tasks and for the promotion and protection of British interests, international peace, and stability. Jock was ahead of the game when he talked about a 'hybrid' structure capable of providing fully regenerated forces for general war while operating a cost-effective fleet.

He referred to the recent Defence White Paper called *Defence in the 90s*, which he described as a reasoned judgement about where resources could best be targeted to provide value for money and a credible level of readiness in the new strategic environment.

NATO remained, geostrategically, a maritime alliance with critical linkages across the Atlantic and key maritime access routes to the North Sea, the Channel, the Baltic, the Norwegian Sea, and the Mediterranean. The alliance's two halves were separated by 3,000 miles of ocean and one of the cornerstones of British strategy must be the ability to protect those routes. Crises of varying intensity would continue to occur regularly despite international efforts to prevent or forestall them, and there was a real problem in the proliferation of weapons of mass destruction and other advanced military technology.

The specific features of future threats that were the Commander-in-Chief Fleet's business were maritime forces, primarily equipped for high-intensity and complex operations, which were also eminently suitable for low-intensity operations. Given long lead times, new dangers and tasks would have to be met with ships-in-being. Strategic lift was critical for any serious military operation, and Jock gave the example of the Gulf War where, despite the massive airlift, some 85% of the cargo went by sea and, after the initial build-up, some 5,000 tons of ship capacity had been needed every day.

As for freedom of the seas, Jock reflected that the leading maritime nations had most to gain from protecting trade and maintaining international security at sea. At heart he was a Mahan-ist, but he hinted at Corbett when he recognised that when it came to sea power it was difficult for anyone other than the United States Navy to concentrate sufficient naval power in overwhelming force, except in local areas for limited periods. The fact remained that the sea gave access to almost every region of the globe, its peoples, and its resources, and it sustained the vast bulk of international economic effort: 90% of world trade moved by sea. Mahan's words rang true: the sea is a great highway, a wide common over which men may pass in all directions. Nevertheless, it was naive to suggest that sea power could subsist on the fleet alone. Sea power was not special or superior: it could be applied in some situations but not in others. Rather, Jock could not stress enough that joint warfare was crucially important at all levels of military command.

He set out his own plans for the formation of a naval contingency force capable of fulfilling the most important national and alliance tasks. This force was likely to contain a carrier, an amphibious group with a helicopter capable ship and LSL, nuclear submarines, and a dozen destroyers and frigates, with mine warfare support and logistic platforms. He referenced the navy's radical restructuring of naval bases, dockyards, training establishments, armament, fuel, stores, and victualling depots to ensure the right level of support for the front line, but no more. It was essential, he said, that the fleet for the nineties struck the right balance between its front line, its support and its people.

It was a rousing and well received speech, which Jock finished with "we need the ships, we need the men, we need the money too!".

# Chapter 17: Buggins's Turn, 1992

As Commander-in-Chief Fleet 1991–93, Jock was expected by many to succeed Oswald as First Sea Lord if Oswald became CDS. However, during a weekend in the spring of 1992 when Jock was at home in Hampshire, Oswald, who lived locally, invited himself for coffee. Jock hoped that Oswald was bringing some good news and he was totally surprised to learn that the Chief of the Defence Staff, Harding, had asked for Jock to be the next VCDS.[164]

**The Chiefs**

In the beginning of the 20th century, the political heads of the Royal Navy and the British Army were the First Lord of the Admiralty and the Secretary of State for War. Both were ministers heading powerful and independent departments of state, and each had a seat in his own right in the Cabinet. At the end of the First World War they were joined by the Secretary of State for Air, as political head of the Royal Air Force, which had been created on April Fool's Day 1918 out of the Royal Flying Corps and the Royal Naval Air Service. For much of the rest of the century the professional, uniformed heads of the services were the First Sea Lord and (from 1917) Chief of the Naval Staff (First Sea Lord/ CNS), the Chief of the Imperial General Staff (1909–64) then Chief of the General Staff (CGS), and the Chief of the Air Staff (CAS).[165]

In the 1920s and 1930s concern was expressed over the need for greater coordination between the three armed services. The Lloyd-George government (1916–22) rejected the idea of a Ministry of Defence, but a Chiefs of Staff Committee was formed in 1923. In 1936 the Baldwin government created a Minister for Coordination of Defence, and Admiral of the Fleet Lord Chatfield, a former First Sea Lord, held this appointment until the fall of the Chamberlain government in 1940. Chatfield's effectiveness was limited by his lack of control over the service departments and his limited political influence, and, on forming his government in 1940, Prime Minister Winston Churchill, intending to take ministerial control of the Chiefs of Staff Committee, appointed himself as Minister of Defence. In 1946, Atlee's postwar government introduced the Ministry of Defence Act, and a new Minster of Defence, AV Alexander, who had been the wartime First Lord of the Admiralty, was given a seat in the Cabinet. The three service ministers lost their seats but remained as the political heads of the separate departments of the Admiralty, the War Office, and the Air Ministry.

This centralisation of defence activities into a single ministry mimicked the precedent set by the American National Security Act of 1947 and was intended to curb inter-service rivalries. Until the late 1950s the heads of each of the three services took it in turn to chair the Chiefs of Staff Committee, but in 1956, Marshal of the RAF Sir William Dickson, formerly an officer in the Royal Naval Air Service, became the first permanent chairman.[166] As CAS in 1953–55, Dickson's work focused on building up the V-bomber force while the armed forces were being reorganised against a background of cuts in the defence budget. Dickson welcomed Prime Minister Sir Anthony Eden's plan to create a separate chairmanship, but no sooner had he been appointed than he was confronted by the Suez Crisis. In practice, Dickson was the only appointee, because Eden's successor, Harold Macmillan, as part of post-Suez restructuring of the armed forces, converted the appointment into a more fully-fledged Chief of the Defence Staff, and in July 1959 Admiral of the Fleet Lord Mountbatten became the first CDS, a position he held for six years. The separate departments of defence merged in 1964, and the defence functions of the Ministry of Aviation Supply merged into the MoD in 1971.

Over time the CDS accreted power and influence, and was recognised as the professional head of all the British armed forces, and the most senior uniformed military adviser to the Secretary of State for Defence and to the Prime Minister. The CDS focused on operations and strategy, while a civil servant, the Permanent Under-Secretary of State concerned himself with administrative and financial policy. After Mountbatten, it became normal for the CDS to complete an approximately three-year term and until the late 1970s the CDS post was filled by Buggins's turn – the appointment being rotated between the three services. Implicit in this system was that every six years or so each service would produce a candidate who was suitably senior and experienced. This usually meant having been Chief of Staff of his own service.

The first break in this pattern was precipitated by the death in early 1977, after only three months in office, of Marshal of the RAF Sir Andrew Humphrey, who caught pneumonia while visiting the Royal Marines on their winter exercises in Norway. Admiral Sir Edward Ashmore was then the senior and longest-serving single-service chief and was near the end of his three-year term as First Sea Lord, and his retirement was postponed while he temporarily filled the vacancy. By the end of the year the RAF had freed Air Marshal Sir Neil Cameron, who had served less than a year as CAS, and he completed the RAF's Buggins's turn as CDS from 1977–79. The normal pattern was then resumed and the next two CDSs were a sailor, Admiral of the Fleet Sir Terry Lewin, from 1979–82, and a soldier, Field Marshal Sir 'Dwin' Bramall, from 1982–85.

## The Lewin Reforms

Lewin was an opponent of the Buggins's turn concept, arguing that each third round left the choice of CDS in the gift of a single service. He also observed that the Navy did rather better in the scramble for resources when the CDS was not a naval man. Early in 1982 Lewin proposed to the Secretary of State for Defence a reform of the top echelons of defence based on five principles. The first was that the CDS should become the principal military adviser to the government in his own right rather than merely as the chairman of a committee with collective responsibility. Secondly, the Chiefs of Staff Committee should become the forum in which the CDS sought the advice of his colleagues; no longer would it be a fulcrum of collective responsibility. The third principle was that the Chiefs of Staff should remain the professional heads of their single services and be responsible for the fighting effectiveness, efficiency, administration, and morale of their services, and remain responsible for advice to the government on strategy, resource allocation, and their own single-service matters; they should retain their right of direct access to the Prime Minister should they not like the advice from the CDS. Fourthly, the central staff should be responsible to the CDS in his own right and not merely in his position as the chairman of the Chiefs of Staff Committee. Finally, the CDS should become chairman of a senior appointments committee comprising the Chiefs of Staff and have responsibility for overseeing the promotion and appointment of all 3- and 4-star officers of all the services, and the appointments of some 2-star officers to important appointments. This latter qualification was intended to preserve the careers and the promotion prospects of those officers who might serve with objectivity in central appointments, to the disappointment of their own services.[167]

These reforms were not in place when the Falklands War broke out in the spring of 1982. Lewin was in New Zealand and the First Sea Lord, Admiral Sir Henry Leach, was able to use Lewin's absence to advocate a naval answer to the problem: sail the fleet! In doing so, Leach bypassed Air Chief Marshal Sir Michael Beetham, who was coming to the end of an unusually long five-year term as CAS and who, as the senior Chief, was the acting CDS. Leach also bypassed the VCDS, who was another airman.

After the Falklands War Lewin clarified the chain of command in operations, which even in single-service operations would run through the CDS. Finally, the CDS was supported by a deputy, normally of a different uniform, and this post had been initially occupied by a 3-star officer and titled Deputy Chief of the Defence Staff, though since 1978 it had been held by a 4-star officer, the first being Bramall. Lewin persuaded Heseltine, Secretary of State for Defence from 1983–86, to confirm the deputy as Vice Chief of Defence Staff and as a 4-star appointment, and in July 1984 Heseltine told the House of Commons that "The defence staff will be headed by a Vice Chief of the Defence Staff who will report jointly to the Chief of the Defence Staff and the Permanent Secretary. These changes will further consolidate the position of the Chief of the Defence Staff as the principal military adviser to the Government." An accompanying White Paper, Central Organisation of Defence, made it clear that the VCDS would be a member of the Chiefs of Staff Committee and the Defence Council, thus becoming one of the Chiefs in his own right.

## Harding Becomes CDS

The next test of Buggins's turn came in the autumn of 1985 when Bramall, who had succeeded Lewin, retired and it was the RAF's turn to provide the CDS. Buggins's turn was discarded because Prime Minister Margaret Thatcher had formed a close working relationship with Admiral Sir John Fieldhouse during the 1982 Falklands War, and she chose him as CDS. Much as Jock disliked Buggins's turn, he realised that, once it was abandoned, individual services would no longer be in the driving seat for CDS selection. The power of appointment would now lie with the Secretary of State, the Permanent Under-Secretary, and the incumbent CDS; one could not argue against an additional, sixth principle to Lewin's - the best man for the job.

Jock was pleased that Fieldhouse had been appointed but wondered, "If the Falklands campaign had not happened in 1982, would he have reached the very top? On the meetings that I attended with him, I remember he had a habit of apparently dropping off during the briefing and then declaring his chosen way ahead, which he had clearly decided before we went in! That said, he was a wise and pragmatic CDS."

After Fieldhouse had his three-year term as CDS the Buggins's pattern seemed to be re-established: Fieldhouse was followed by an airman, Marshal of the RAF Sir David Craig, from 1988–91, and a soldier, Field Marshal Sir Richard Vincent, from 1991–92. Vincent's appointment was remarkable because he had been neither a commander-in-chief nor CGS, but instead was promoted from VCDS, marking the growing importance of that appointment.

In 1992 Buggins's turn would have been the Navy's but the pattern was again interrupted. Marshal of the RAF Sir Peter Harding succeeded Vincent on 31 December, winning the appointment against the claims of his quiet, scholarly, naval rival, Admiral Sir Julian Oswald. Oswald enjoyed good relations with the senior civil servants in the MoD and possessed great integrity. Though few knew what he thought, however, though it was suspected that he felt that he had let the Navy down by not becoming CDS. The only other contender was General Sir Peter Inge, the CGS, who had only been in office a year.

Harding, who had joined the RAF aged 19 in 1952, had a brilliant mind and incisive brain and was widely admired for his presence and charisma; he was tall, debonair, and affable, and was so devoted to the RAF that colleagues joked that he was "the sort of man who even sleeps in light-blue pyjamas". He achieved his ambition to fly more than 100 types of aircraft, including a MiG-29 during a visit to Russia. He was a bon viveur and known for his gregarious, clubbable nature out of hours, listing his interests in *Who's Who* as "tennis, pianoforte, bridge, birdwatching and shooting (normally separately)". He was a consummate Whitehall warrior, having been Vice Chief of the Air Staff from 1983–85 and VCDS in 1985, Air Officer Commanding Strike Command 1985–88, and CAS from 1988–1992.

## A Surprise Offer

Over coffee at Grenville Lodge, Jock demurred over becoming VCDS, but Oswald pressed, saying that Jock, with his national, tri-service, and NATO experience, was the right man for the job and that in replacing one central admiral, Bathurst, with another, the Navy would get the key appointment of VCDS twice running. Oswald, who was nursing his own disappointment at not having become CDS, suggested that Bathurst, who had been VCDS since 1991, could be the next First Sea Lord, while Jock, with age on his side, could be a prime contender for CDS at the next turn. Somewhat reluctantly, Jock accepted the challenge. Only later did he learn that the Army had put up General Sir

John Waters, then Commander-in-Chief, Land Forces, for VCDS, but Harding had rejected the nomination because he did not like Waters' abrasive style.[168]

These senior appointments were promulgated on 5 July 1992 and Jock reccived messages congratulating him, including one from Lord Lewin, who, as CDS, had promoted the status of the VCDS, and who told Jock that he regarded it as being much more influential than any single-service chief, particularly as VCDS was now chief in his own right.

Jock was VCDS for the next three years.

# Chapter 18: VCDS 1993–94

VCDS's team in 1989: from left to right (top) Leading Steward Phil Varly, Cook Eve Williams, Assistant Military Assistant LtCdr Karen Pearce, Sergeant Paul Kimberley, Petty Officer Steward Noddy Holder, (bottom) Secretary David Murtagh, Annie, JCKS, Military Assistant LtCol Keith Pople. Source: Slater archive.

In January 1993 Jock took over from Bathurst as VCDS and began a busy round of calls orchestrated by his new office staff. They were led by Colonel Keith Pople of the Army Air Corps, a most able staff officer with a sharp brain and incisive mind who coped admirably with a daunting workload and was not frightened to state his views. He was a shrewd and observant critic of the Whitehall scene, though when things were not going his way he could display a rather irritating dismissive manner, which could annoy people. His assistant was Lieutenant Commander Karen Pearce, a former Wren and a Russian interpreter. She was a tower of strength and had irrepressible humour, and was the life and soul of the office. She looked after Jock's daily programme and his external visits at home and abroad, and understood how to get the best out of the MoD machine. She was sensitive to individual personalities and impressed everyone she met, although Jock observed that sometimes she obtained her own way by flirting. The third member of his team was a civilian secretary, David Murtagh, a steady pair of hands with a dry sense of humour, who served Jock very well.

The Slaters were supported by a personal staff: Petty Officer Steward Noddy Holder, Leading Steward Phil Varley, Leading Wren Cook Eve Williams, and driver Sergeant Paul Kimbley. Noddy Holder had been in the retinue for seven years, and his cheerful, loyal, and most helpful nature were huge assets. Phil Varley was smart, cheerful, reliable, relaxed, and confident. Eve Williams, who followed the Slaters from Northwood, was clearly happy running her own kitchen and proved an excellent and most professional member of the team. Sergeant Paul Kimbley was strong-minded and rather brash, but drove exceptionally well, if a bit too fast; he was reliable.

**Tensions at the Top**

In preparation for becoming VCDS Jock undertook some familiarisation visits, including to Germany where, as ACDS (Pol/Nuc) in the mid-80s, he had gained insight into operations and strategy on the Central Front. His visit to British Forces in Germany was something of an eye-opener, however. "All the generals and air marshals were very helpful and ensured that their business was fully understood by me [but] there seemed to be an inordinate number of staff officers seeing to their every need and my movements were programmed to the n'th degree." Jock stayed one night with General Charles Guthrie in Rheindahlen, where the general was Commander-in-Chief, British Army of the Rhine. This was their first meeting and Jock found it hard to gauge just how good Guthrie was professionally. "Although he clearly had style and … was obviously ambitious, I had the impression that behind his somewhat oily front lay an iron fist and a strong determination to predominate." Jock also detected that there was little love lost between Guthrie and Air Chief Marshal Sandy

Wilson, the Commander-in-Chief RAF, Germany, who "was a fairly typical senior airman with traditional views about the indivisibility of air power".

When Jock became VCDS in 1993 Malcolm Rifkind was Secretary of State for Defence, Harding was CDS, Bathurst was CNS, Inge was CGS, and Graydon was CAS. The PUS was Christopher France. As CDS, the charismatic Harding proved popular in the MoD, where he was seen as a robust and experienced leader who fought for the cause of all three armed services. Harding did not like the fact that in his absences the chairmanship of the Chiefs of Staff Committee still rotated between the single-service chiefs, and he introduced a further reform – that VCDS, Jock at the time, would deputise for the CDS and chair meetings in his absence. This did not please Inge, who, despite the role of air and sea power in the simmering war in Bosnia, had played himself into a lead position in advising the Cabinet, much to the irritation of Harding. Inge was thought to be withholding from the CDS information about the land campaign and Jock, if he was to be effective as CDS deputy, also needed to be kept in the picture. He thought Harding should have been firmer with Inge, to ensure that the CDS was seen to be in the driving seat.

Tall, imposing Harding was well established as CDS and he and Jock got on well. He recognised VCDS as a 4-star post in his own right and delegated well. Of the other Chiefs, Inge was much the more influential. It was supposed that the CAS, Mike Graydon, had been selected by Harding as a safe pair of hands. The CNS, Ben Bathurst, held the Navy's corner very satisfactorily during his tenure, his previous experience as VCDS giving him a most useful hand with the Centre. The RAF was best at MoD staff work, was run from the top, and presented a unified view. The Army was less impressive and operated inefficiently, not least because it was run as a set of fiefdoms – that of the Quartermaster General, the Adjutant General, and the Master General of the Ordnance – and the CGS seemed to have little overview. Navy staff were less well trained but the Navy was more democratic and amenable to change.

The key civil servant under VCDS was the Deputy Under Secretary (Policy), David Omand, one of the leading civil servants of his generation, and Jock admired and valued his intellectual calibre, his undoubted integrity and wise counsel. He was, however, very private and not easy to get to know, and had a rather shy, academic style and disconcerting deadpan expression that tended to raise suspicions about what he was thinking. Other civil servants in senior positions in the MoD were professionally able but no longer enjoyed the respect once they had once enjoyed. They swapped jobs and departments too much for Jock's liking, seemed to take pleasure in suggesting changes that would unsettle the services, and there was an agenda to increase their influence over the military that could never be underestimated. The uniformed people in key positions in the MoD tended to be just as sharp and competent as their civilian counterparts, and they had operational experience outside the MoD. While the services were good at handling change, it became clear to Jock, particularly as the forthcoming *Defence Costs Study* would reveal, that the Chiefs needed to identify the key issues on which they were not prepared to compromise. Jock encouraged everyone, military and civilian, to work constructively together.

## The Aesculapian Club Speech

In his first week as VCDS Jock attended the Chiefs of Staff Committee at a meeting about the Allied Rapid Reaction Corps, which he felt well able to discuss, having only recently visited its headquarters in Germany. In his first month he attended a conference at Ditchley on international disaster relief, and then had a non-stop round of meetings, state visits, and invitations to stalking at Balmoral, which took him around Britain, to Europe, and to North and South America.

He used an invitation to speak to the Aesculapian Club, one of the oldest medical dining clubs in the world, at the Royal College of Physicians in Edinburgh, as an opportunity to collect his thoughts on what he should say in public about defence. The audience heard about the challenging times they lived in, times of great turbulence, uncertainty, and incredible change. The Warsaw Pact was no longer the main threat to security and the chances of an East–West conflict had disappeared for the time being, even as he prophesied that the Russian Bear would one day start growling again, and that the risk of a resurgent Russia with an awesome arsenal of nuclear and conventional weapons was real. He spoke of the increasing risk of ethnic and territorial conflicts, compounded by economic and political instability in central and eastern Europe and in the former Soviet Union. Outside Europe, the proliferation of ballistic missiles and nuclear, chemical, and biological weapons of mass destruction, and the destabilising transfers of conventional arms, posed a threat to Britain's interests and those of her Allies.

Having unsettled his audience sufficiently, Jock moved on to a more positive theme, pointing out that NATO, with its increased emphasis on flexibility and mobility of Alliance forces, remained key to providing stability and security in Europe. His listeners were reminded that the ongoing fundamental reassessment of Britain's defence needs were set against a bleak financial outlook. Britain was engaged in a major reduction and streamlining of her armed forces, including a one-quarter reduction in BAOR from 155,000 down to 119,000, a 50% reduction in RAF Germany, and major cuts in maritime and air defence forces with support being cut proportionately. This was proving a painful process for everyone, from the front line through to those in support and in industry, at a time when there was little if any reduction in commitments or increased world stability. Politicians had to decide if new force structures were sufficiently robust to cope with the uncertainty of the future. What level of risk were they prepared to take? Ironically, since the collapse of Communism, British forces had never been so busy. Deployments included Kuwait, Iraq, the Balkans, Cambodia, and a host of other UN tasks around the world, not to mention Northern Ireland, the South Atlantic, Belize, and Hong Kong.

He told the Aesculapians that the elastic was stretched, and this was Rifkind's judgement when he decided in 1993 to add 3,000 men to the Army, including two infantry battalions, the Royal Scots and the King's Own Scottish Borderers, paid for from the existing Defence budget. The total cost of these additions was £700m: what should be cut to pay for them? Should it be air defence of the UK, the fleet, the amphibious capability, or the Territorial Army? These questions had major defence and political implications, and were the issues that Jock as VCDS was tackling.

"One thing was for sure," Jock concluded. "He is a brave man who can forecast what lies ahead. Our history is littered with failures to predict trouble spots with two obvious examples of late, the Falklands in 1982 and Kuwait in 1990, and there is absolutely no doubt that there will be others in the years ahead. Of course, preparing to deal with the unexpected leads to difficult political decisions and politicians are always reluctant to look beyond the life of their current Parliament."

The speech became the template for others, though each was tailored to Jock's audience. When he was Commander-in-Chief Fleet and then First Sea Lord, he would also recite from memory where the individual ships of the fleet were while he was speaking to his audience.

**Ceremonial and Social**

VCDS's duties were wide and varied and included the ceremonial. On 1 April 1993 he attended the Royal Air Force's 75th anniversary at RAF Marham; the micro-detailed planning was hugely impressive and Jock felt sorry for Graydon when the wild, wet weather forced the cancellation of the 148-aircraft fly-past. He was left wondering what the costs of such a jamboree were, bearing in mind how defence as a whole was struggling for funds.

Admiral Sir Jock Slater in the uniform of one of the Elder Brethren of Trinity House.
Source: Slater archive.

He also attended a briefing and dinner at 'the Fort', the secret service's training centre, and was amused to note that, while its official name was Browndown Battery, the Gosport taxi drivers knew it as 'the spy school'. Later that month Jock hosted the official visit to the UK by the Deputy Head of the Saudi Arabian National Guard: the Foreign Office was keen that this should be a success but Jock was unsure of whether the talks were of much value. Representing the CDS he attended a Portuguese state visit during which Annie slipped and fell on the parquet flooring between two rooms in Buckingham Palace, breaking her wrist: next morning she received a letter and a bunch of flowers from a concerned Queen.

In that first six months Jock visited the Cinque Ports Training Area, including the Hythe counter-insurgency ranges where the Northern Ireland Training Advisory Team was preparing soldiers and Marines for their demanding tasks in the province. He found it very humbling to meet young Royal Marines, many looking as if they had just left school, who soon would be faced with some very difficult tasks in dangerous situations. For this and subsequent visits there was a helicopter, sometimes a Gazelle from 32 Squadron RAF, and if it was fitted with dual controls Jock asked to fly it himself. At a small lunch party at Lancaster House, hosted by Malcolm Rifkind in honour of General Colin Powell, the retiring Chairman of the US Joint Chiefs of Staff, Jock sat next to Powell and enjoyed an excellent discussion about US–UK relations. He noted that some believed that Powell might run for the United States presidency and was in no doubt that he would have been excellent in the role, but his wife, Alma, whom the Slaters knew well, feared that as a coloured man he would be assassinated. The Slaters, representing the Defence Secretary, flew to Bavaria as the guests of SACEUR, General John Shalikashvili, for the opening of the George C Marshall European Center for Security Studies at Garmisch. The Chiefs also invited the Queen and Prince Philip to dinner in Admiralty House.

In the same period, on the principle that 'give a busy man a job and he will do it well', Jock also agreed to chair the newly formed Younger Brothers' Committee of Trinity House, and became Vice Chairman of the Royal United Services Institution – where, as always, he was irritated by "pseudo-intellectuals who held forth on Defence matters and liked the sound of their own voices, sometimes talking off the tops of their heads".

## Anglo-US Relations

In June 1993, the Slaters visited the United States as guests of Admiral David Jeremiah, the Vice Chairman of the Joint Chiefs of Staff: Pople, Pearce, and Varley accompanied them. The visit started in Colorado Springs, where the party looked at the American Air Defense System in Cheyenne Mountain, followed by a morning at the US Air Force Academy and talks and dinner with the Commander-in-Chief Space Command, General Chuck Horner. He had commanded the air forces in the Gulf War and was surprised that Jock could engage him in a wide range of professional issues. Afterwards, Pople told Jock that he had heard that Horner's staff were not used to visitors who were prepared to challenge their boss.

Next stop was MacDill Air Force Base in Florida, where the host was Major General Waldo Freeman, the Deputy Commander-in-Chief Central Command. The Commander-in-Chief, General Wayne Downing, had not planned to be there but word spread from Colorado Springs that Jock was worth engaging with and Downing changed his itinerary to meet Jock over lunch, leaving Jock to wonder "what the buzz net up to Washington was saying".

Then at Fort Bragg, headquarters of the US Army's XVIII Airborne Corps, Jock was briefed by 82nd Airborne Division, which was evidently comprised of extremely dedicated and single-minded people. The programme ran late and when Jock arrived at Camp LeJeune to see the US Marine Corps under training, he saw young US Marines already at their positions in 80°F, ready for the afternoon demonstrations. He had little success in persuading his hosts to cut lunch short, so when the demonstrations were complete, he asked his host, the Commanding General USMC, William M Keys, if he might address the marines. Keys frowned, Jock smiled, and, while standing on the steps of an armoured vehicle, held forth. After a few moments, he heard the marines *grunting*, something he had not known about. He subsequently discovered that this was their way of showing their approval of what they were hearing. Jock was glad that he had thanked them for their efforts.

The final stop was Washington for a day of calls and discussions in the Pentagon, including with the Chief of Naval Operations, Admiral Frank Kelso. It had been "a most successful week's visit which contributed markedly to enhancing US/UK relations, which should never be taken for granted."

## Colombia

While Annie returned home, Jock flew on to Colombia to inspect British forces operating alongside the counter-narcotics police at the height of that country's struggle with the Medellin Cartel. He was met by a heavily armed security contingent who, every time his car stopped at traffic lights, jumped out waving their weapons threateningly: it seemed that the chances of being shot by his own protectors was high. Next day in the jungle he met Major Jamie Lowther-

Annie launches RFA *Fort George* at Swan Hunter's yard on 1 March 1991 (Alex Marsh stands behind Jock). Source: Slater archive.

Pinkerton, who oversaw a 20-man group of SAS soldiers. Lowther-Pinkerton was an old friend who had been equerry to the Queen Mother in the mid-1980s and who would go on to be the first Private Secretary to Princes William and Harry. Jock was impressed by the young team, but over a picnic lunch it soon became very clear that General Peter de la Billiere's recent book, *Storm Command: A Personal Account of the Gulf War*, revealing details of SAS operations in the Middle East, was a no-no subject. This was the first time Jock had come face to face with the depth of feeling about de la Billiere's book and why de la Billiere had become *persona non grata* at the SAS headquarters in Hereford: "For such a brave and highly decorated officer, this was very sad – not least as I gather his book had been approved by the MoD." After lunch he flew over the poppy fields in a small two-seater aircraft, his pilot telling him that his colleague had been shot at the previous week, the bullet going through his wing and hitting him in the chin. When he told Jock that they were flying at about 100ft, Jock suggested that he'd seen enough poppies for one day. At the ambassador's high-powered dinner party that night Jock was left in no doubt that the Colombians were extremely grateful for British help, appreciation that was well received by Ambassador Keith Morris.

Once home it was something of a relief for the Slaters and both sons to attend the commissioning of RFA *Fort George* in Newcastle. Jock asked John Webster to paint a picture of the ship, which Annie, *Fort George*'s sponsor, presented, and for a change Jock was in attendance and Annie was the guest of honour.

## Downing Street

In late September 1993, Prime Minister John Major visited the MoD to be briefed by the Chiefs. Major had been Prime Minister for three years and Jock was impressed by his grasp of strategic issues. Furthermore, he was also a good listener, and the Chiefs took the opportunity to warn him of the dangers of hollowing-out the armed forces so that the front line looked satisfactory but overall support was left lacking. Next month the Chancellor of the Exchequer, Ken Clarke, also crossed the road for a briefing at the MoD accompanied by Chief Secretary to the Treasury Michael Portillo and other leading Treasury officials. As the Chiefs eloquently made their pitch Jock thought that Clarke was not listening, and Portillo remained silent, perhaps knowing that he would be the next Defence Secretary. Clarke was in an arrogant mood and the Treasury team who accompanied him were clearly ignorant of Defence issues, were disinclined to engage in discussion, and did not wish to be deflected from their agenda, however powerful the arguments. Jock would find the same four years later when engaged in the Strategic Defence Review (SDR), "though by that stage I had got used to Treasury intransigence".

Jock prepared a handwritten brief for Harding's call on the Prime Minister and the case he presented would become depressingly familiar. He included disappointment at the level of senior debate about defence – decisions were being taken in a cavalier fashion; the fact that the armed forces were reaching a turning point in terms of the part they could play in crises; the risks being taken by reducing equipment and training for the armed forces; the huge role the professionalism of the armed forces in the Falklands War played in the Conservative Party's 1983 General Election success; the government was taking regeneration for granted but any reduction in the services' capabilities could result in irreversible change. Jock asked what had changed since the last defence review and what plans there were for unforeseen and unpredictable events. And while the calibre and achievements of UK armed forces were second to none, this could not be assumed. The key to British security was US involvement in NATO. How would the Allies view further drawdown of forces in the run-up to a summit? The arguments were powerful but, regrettably, would need to be repeated in the years to come. Looking back, Jock could not remember what Harding said when he returned from 10 Downing Street, "But I am sure he would have told me that all the points were well made!"

## Lobbying Against Defence Cuts

Secretary of State Rifkind was being primed by the Chiefs in the MoD to resist pressure from Clarke in the Treasury for cuts. In October there was a two-day debate in the House of Commons on defence and the message from backbenchers was that cuts would be firmly resisted. Michael Evans in *The Times* appeared to have inside knowledge and was particularly eloquent about the effects on the Navy. Rifkind's "battle with Clarke" was rebuffed by some officials who insisted that some changes in expenditure were not related to the public expenditure round. For example, the sale of the dockyards, in which Jock as CFS had been deeply involved, would bring in revenue, though the aim was greater efficiency; and the decision to give Trident submarines a secondary, tactical role would incur minimum funding – in fact, about £100m for the so-called Trident sub-strategic option. The debate deterred the government from a full-scale defence review, Jock noting that ministers simply did not have the stomach for it.

In mid-November Annie accompanied Jock on official visits to Egypt, Cyprus, and Italy, and by the end of the month he was back in town to chair a two-day conference for senior British officers in NATO. For light relief Jock became president of the Royal Naval Piping Society, which had been formed in 1951 under Uncle Ned.

Jock had never courted the press but in December 1993 he gave a non-attributable press briefing over a sandwich lunch to a dozen leading members of the London press corps. He told them how he hesitated to look further into the future than tomorrow morning's breakfast news, but that the growing pattern of instability in the world was set to continue. While delighted to see the end of the Cold War and the Communist system, which had oppressed so many for so long, the fact was that it had been a very stable world. Communism had suppressed centuries-old ethnic, religious, and nationalist rivalries, while the two superpowers, America and Russia, had restrained post-Cold War conflicts. With that system of restraint gone there would be eruptions of conflict on a scale more widespread than before. The scale of global instability and unrest was worrying. The former Republic of Yugoslavia encapsulated many of the new challenges that Britain faced. Already there were 3,000 British troops on the ground and many more in support. Civil war on the borders of Europe threatened British interests, which was of concern to NATO and the UN.

He then spoke in general terms about British defence, pointing out that defence spending had already dropped by 15% in real terms over the past five years. The changes had been dramatic: 33% fewer destroyers and frigates,

57% fewer submarines, 43% fewer armoured regiments, 30% fewer artillery regiments, 40% fewer air defence squadrons, and a cut of 27% in strike attack. What was more, he told the journalists, the armed forces were engaged in a major savings programme to realise £4 billion by 1995–96. Service manpower was being cut by 25% and some 37,000 civilians were being shed. The Navy was closing or rationalising 70 sites including half of its training establishments and 14 Royal Naval stores and transport service depots. The Army was also restructuring, disbanding, or amalgamating more than 300 units, and the Royal Air Force was closing 21 air stations.

Jock repeated what Rifkind had told the recent Conservative Party conference in Blackpool, that Britain was in danger of creating "a paper tiger": to maintain the front line it had been forced to reduce war stocks, spares, and maintenance – it had been hollowed out. He thought that he may have been a little too frank and the questions that followed were lively. He drew it to a close when someone commented on the number of admirals versus the number of ships in the Navy. Jock answered that in a service then of 60,000 people it was perfectly reasonable to have 40 senior executives. The trouble was that they were called admirals; many big organisations had a much higher number of senior executives for a workforce of similar size.

His final message was that the country was renowned for the quality of its armed forces and the calibre of its people, but they must never be taken for granted: the government must never throw away its trump card.

**Tomorrow's News**

In February and March 1994 Jock had an eighteen-day visit to the Far East, starting at the Asian aerospace exhibition in Singapore. Four days in Indonesia followed, including a visit to a marine infantry brigade, but he was not allowed to visit any of the Indonesians' elderly ships. The Philippines and Thailand were next, though the Thais were reluctant to engage in any substantive discussions. The Slaters returned via Hong Kong, where Jock discussed the withdrawal plans with the Commander British Forces, and they boarded their plane on Sunday, seven hours ahead of London. While Jock was airborne and asleep, the Sunday papers in Britain were being printed and distributed.

Admiral Jay Johnson USN, aware of Queen Victoria's strictures against her officers accepting foreign awards, without warning, makes Jock a Commander of the US Legion of Merit. Source: Slater archive.

# Chapter 19: The Fandango, 1994

On Monday, 14 March as Jock stepped into his official car at Heathrow after landing from Hong Kong, his driver, Sergeant Paul Kimbley, gave him a copy of the day before's *News of the World*. On the front page was the claim that Harding was involved in a sex scandal. The story was also carried in the *Sunday Times*.

**Sunday**

That Sunday, Secretary of State Malcolm Rifkind had barely finished reading his newspaper when Harding rang him at home to announce his resignation. Rifkind rang the Permanent Under-Secretary of State, Christopher France, for advice and then spoke to Prime Minister John Major.[169]

In Germany, Lieutenant Colonel Richard Shirreff heard the rumour of Harding's resignation. Shirreff was military assistant to General Sir Charles Guthrie, who was spending the weekend at a health farm in Bavaria. Shirreff had not heard any prior rumours about Harding and knew no more than what was in the newspapers, but he called Guthrie to advise him to pack his bags for London at once. Shirreff knew that Guthrie had followed Inge in several previous appointments. Both were steeped in Cold War operations in Germany and in counter-terrorist operations and, though neither was well versed in joint operations, Shirreff advised his boss that there was a good chance that, "after shuffling the pack", Inge would become CDS and Guthrie would succeed him as CGS.[170]

## The Spanish Firecracker

On Harding's death, his obituary in the *Daily Telegraph* was coy about the circumstances, while *The Times* wrote of the Falstaffian aspects of his character.[171] Harding had been married for 39 years, was a father of four, and had just authorised a military code in a ten-page booklet on personal morality in the armed forces, which placed emphasis on a stable domestic life and told officers to set an example to their men. It warned that married or single officers might jeopardise their status by having affairs. Harding himself, however, had a reputation as a ladies' man and, said one colleague, "was always very appreciative of attractive women".[172]

Hubris took the shape of the Spanish-born Bienvenida Pérez Blanco, the wife of former MoD minister Sir Anthony Buck.[173] Pérez Blanco's story, detailed in her book *The Making of a Modern Mistress*, was the rags-to-riches "rise of a contemporary courtesan, who emerged triumphant from the poverty of the backstreets of Valencia to enjoy the five-star lifestyle of the upper echelons of British and American society … [she] practised the secret art of pleasing powerful men and supporting them in their ambitions". Her lovers in the wealthy drawing rooms and bedrooms of London, Dallas, Morocco, and Bahrain included a wide and influential group of men as well as Harding: Sir Anthony Buck, whom she had married; Ahmed Kano, one of the richest men in the Middle East; and Thomas Enders, former US ambassador to Spain and Cambodia and a former high-ranking CIA operative. Her book told how, as Lady Buck, she had entertained the internationally rich and powerful, and made an exotic and chaotic impact on the British political scene.[174]

Harding's affair with Pérez Blanco had begun while he was CAS, after meeting her at a dinner at the Indian High Commission. He had invited the Bucks to dinner at his official residence in Kingsley Court, Knightsbridge, where he exchanged numbers with her. They met again a few days later at the Belvedere restaurant in Holland Park, when Harding was in a sombre mood: it was the day the first British servicemen's bodies had come back from the Gulf. "This is the first time I have received my men back in coffins," he is supposed to have told her. Their favourite place to meet became the Halcyon Hotel, also in Holland Park, where he would arrive in his official car. They would take her spaniels for a walk. Allegedly, on the day that Harding became CDS, he met Pérez Blanco at Le Meridien Hotel, Piccadilly for lunch and they celebrated his appointment over scallops and caviar. Harding's affair was blatant, and after he had a private telephone line installed in the CDS office the Home Secretary allegedly signed warrants authorising taps on Harding's and Pérez Blanco's phones.[175]

Sometime in early 1994, having divorced Buck, ended her affair with Harding, and married again to become Countess Sokolow, Pérez Blanco consulted Max Clifford, a publicist who dealt in kiss-and-tell stories. He sold her story to the *News of World* for £175,000.[176] She then arranged to meet Harding at the Dorchester hotel while a journalist sat nearby in the restaurant and a photographer waited outside. They were pictured kissing as they parted and it was these Judas kisses that were published in the *News of the World*.[177] Later, in a series of tell-all interviews with headlines such as 'Defence chief was a tornado in bed', Pérez Blanco described how Harding had showered her with love letters. "You have the body of a young girl. I long to envelop you in kisses," he allegedly wrote in one.

Years later, Jock was astonished at these revelations. "How Peter Harding could have been so seduced by such a high-class whore we will never know but it certainly torpedoed my chances of succeeding him!" Jock was not the only person to be surprised and astonished. Despite Harding's reputation as a ladies' man, the private telephone line in his office, his use of the official car and driver to take him to assignations, his lunchtime walks in the park, the time he found for cinq à sept, and the alleged warning he'd been given about Pérez Blanco, there were few politicians or senior officers in the Ministry of Defence who later admitted knowledge of the affair.

**Monday**

Monday's papers carried the news that Harding had gone. On reaching Whitehall Jock consulted Christopher France, who told him that, as the longest-serving Chief, Inge, who had been CGS since February 1992, would temporarily take over until Malcolm Rifkind had had time to consider the way forward.

The newspapers summed up the arguments for the two candidates and were full of speculation about whether Inge or Slater would take over permanently. There was universal appreciation of the urgency to fill the vacancy left by Harding, both to restore morale in the forces and to pursue the war in Bosnia while resisting the Treasury's calls for cuts in defence expenditure. Commentators noted that, even though Buggins's turn was a discredited principle, the Navy had not filled the appointment for some years. However, Bathurst, the First Sea Lord, did not think himself a front runner. The CAS,

Air Chief Marshal Sir Michael Graydon, was ruled out because he had been obliged to apologise to Clarke and Portillo after accusing them of denigrating the RAF in order to win the Treasury's case for cuts in the RAF's bloated administrative structure.[178]

*The Scotsman* described Jock as "a smooth operator, displaying charm and military acumen … a safe pair of hands who is unlikely to embarrass the government" and who therefore had a strong claim, but it was the only newspaper to be unequivocal in its headline: 'Scot in the running for top forces job', meaning Jock. Another newspaper, noting that Jock was three years younger than Inge, suggested that he was the man of the future rather than one whose time had come.

Even though CGS General Sir Peter Inge, 58, had less MoD and senior NATO experience than anyone else in the running, his career having been in the mainstream Army and his commands in Germany, he emerged as the front runner. He was variously described as dynamic, articulate, and forward-thinking, and as a wily and skilled political operator who had been successful as CGS in persuading the Conservative government to reverse some cuts in the Army.


## Tuesday

Without Harding's disgrace and given the customary three-year term in office Inge would have retired as CGS in early 1995 and Harding as CDS in late 1995, leaving the door open for Jock to succeed Harding. Jock learned later that Harding had indeed recommended that he should be the next CDS, and, it was rumoured, had said the same in a letter stored in the CDS's personal safe. This, apparently, had the support of Christopher France. But Rifkind was keen to make an immediate appointment and decided that, with the Balkans in full swing, Inge should have the job. Inge seized the opportunity, which he could not otherwise have expected, and made it known that he would not be an interim CDS as Ashmore had been in 1977, but would serve a full term. This implied that the next vacancy for CDS would be sometime in 1997, when it might still, under Buggins's turn, be a Navy appointment. Rifkind sent for Jock to explain that Inge would retain the appointment but reassured Jock that age was on his side and that his time would come.

*The Times* was still speculating on who would be the government's choice when on 16 March Guthrie rang Kenneth Rose to tell him that he, Guthrie, was to become CGS and Inge was to be CDS. Rose was a former officer in the Welsh Guards, Guthrie's parent regiment, and a longstanding diarist at the *Sunday Telegraph*, and he and Guthrie discussed what Rose could "usefully write in [his next] column".[179]

Disappointed, Jock settled back into his role as VCDS, determined to do his best to help the newly promoted Field Marshal Inge take on a task for which some felt him ill-prepared.

Jock and Annie as Prime Warden of the Shipwrights
Shipwright and his lady. Source: Worshipful Co of Shipwrights.

# Chapter 20: VCDS II, 1994–95

The remaining months as Vice Chief of the Defence Staff were to be some of the busiest in Jock's career. The leading themes were the war in Bosnia, the announcement of the findings of the *Defence Costs Study* (aka *Front Line First*) in July 1994, and overseas diplomacy, which included a speech in New Zealand in November when he gave a definitive exposition of British defence policy and strategy in the post-Cold War era.

There was the usual whirl of visits and invitations, "which frankly I could well have done without although they were important in terms of keeping in touch with a wide variety of people. Breakfast with the Director of Naval Plans, Commodore Stephen Meyer, was a typical example, though it [was] interesting to note the subsequent success of many present including two future Second Sea Lords, James Burnell-Nugent and Adrian Johns, and another guest, the Director of Air Plans, Air Commodore Jock Stirrup, who eventually became Chief of Defence Staff." Jock was so busy that on 27 March 1994, his 56th birthday, he reflected on how life was flying by at a hectic pace, and he wondered how he could survive a further few years under such unrelenting pressure. He also knew that he had to work extremely hard, later writing: "Few people, if any, appreciated that I did not feel that I was really suited to life in Whitehall. That said, the Royal Navy had prepared me well for life at the top and I was determined not to let them down!"

**War in Bosnia**

Clashes between Bosnians, Croats, and Serbs had started in early 1992 and full-scale civil war had broken out by April that year. Over two million people were displaced and thousands of women were raped, making it one of the most bloody and violent conflicts in Europe since the Second World War. Intervention in Bosnia and Croatia was authorised by UNSCR 776 in September 1992 and the war ended after the General Framework Agreement for Peace in Bosnia and Herzegovina was signed in Paris at the end of 1995. When the United Nations Protection Force (UNPROFOR) handed over to NATO's Implementation Force (IFOR) in winter 1995, an uneasy peace fell over those unhappy lands.

The British contribution to UNPROFOR and then IFOR, Operation Grapple, had started with the deployment of 2,500 troops, rising to 7,500 men and women. The Navy's contribution consisted of helicopters from 845 and 846 Naval Air Squadron, warships in the Adriatic Sea, and RFA ships based in the Croatian port of Split. The RAF provided trooping flights into Croatia. The main land-based contribution was an Army headquarters, an infantry battle group with armoured reconnaissance, and engineer and logistics support including a workshop. A second British battalion group was sent in March 1994 to guard the lines of communication from the port of Split into the interior of the former Yugoslavia. It was the deployment of the Army on this scale that had given Inge the edge over Slater when it came to choosing who the CDS would be.

### *Defence Costs Study* aka *Front Line First*

While Inge, first as CGS and then as CDS, fought the war in Bosnia, Jock was left as VCDS to fight a battle at home. One defence review, *Options for Change*, had begun in 1990 was not due to be fully implemented until end of 1995, and some were already arguing for yet another instalment of the so-called peace dividend. Ministers shied away from a full-scale defence review and some civil servants were critical of Secretary of State Rifkind, suggesting that he was not interested in defence, though in the opinion of Jock, who knew and liked Rifkind ("first class and brilliant on his feet in front of an audience"), this was a rumour spread by civil servants who knew that Rifkind did not like them. Even Jock, normally mild-mannered, had at times to remind civil servants that the MoD was not a business and that it would undoubtedly fail operationally if it became too bureaucratic. The fact that operations in Bosnia were underway reinforced his point.

The Chiefs firmly believed that the services needed a period of stability while there was war in Bosnia, but in November 1993 Chancellor of the Exchequer Clarke gave notice of a major spending review. Clarke wanted £3.2 billion cut from the defence budget over the next three years including £750 million in the first year. After discussing this with his junior ministers and the Chiefs, Rifkind made the Treasury the offer it least expected. He proposed cuts of £1 billion in year one on the condition that if these could be identified the MoD would be permitted to retain the extra £250 million for whatever front line, operational capability improvements were needed. Formally known as the *Defence Costs Study*, Rifkind gave this new review the name *Front Line First*. David Hart was brought in as a special adviser and his ideas ranged from selling off the married quarters estate to buying cruise missiles from the USA.[180]

Arguably, *Front Line First* was rushed: 33 separate studies, 20 of which were major and 13 minor, were started in January 1994. Interim conclusions were reached by April and the report to Parliament was made on 14 July 1994. The basic question was by how much could the support be reduced while maintaining the front line? Looking back on *Options for Change*, Jock thought that while those most closely involved might have been satisfied with the depth of its strategic analysis, he, when CFS, was blindsided. He was therefore agreeably surprised that ministers, not least Jonathan Aitken and Robert Cranborne, became involved. While Rifkind stood back from the detailed cut and thrust of the work, Hart strode the corridors of power with a cigar in his mouth holding forth about his views on defence, some of which were valuable and others just troublemaking.

Hart put his knife into the RAF's infrastructure. Graydon, the CAS, said that this was unfair, but he was not supported by Air Marshal Sir John Walker, Chief of Defence Intelligence 1991–94,[181] who sided publicly with Hart. The Navy and the Army were content to let Hart's criticism gather momentum – they regarded it as justified – although they too had to answer tough questions. It was a "brutal period" for the RAF.[182]


## Doctors

Defence Costs Study number 15 into the Defence Medical Services went awry. Rifkind recalled that "the savings we had identified were successfully achieved but we made at least one significant mistake. We had announced the reduction of service hospitals from three to one and the establishment of military hospital units in NHS hospitals. This change was severely criticised, and, in due course, the mistake was acknowledged", but it was not reversed. The Select Committee on Defence later described the reductions in the DMS as being "dramatic, [and] warned that these reductions may have gone too far and too fast … the Defence Medical Services are not sufficient to provide proper support to the front line … and show little prospect of being able to do so in the future … Defence

Costs Study 15 has not enhanced the front line but has seriously impaired it."

Jock also admitted that *Front Line First* did not get everything right. There was no doubt that medical services were essential operationally, but the doctors were their own worst enemies, unused to and out of their depth in the cut and thrust of the MoD. Notably Surgeon Commodore Ian Jenkins, who would later become the Surgeon General, was enlightened about the need for change but the same could not be said for many other service doctors. Fundamentally, the doctors could not agree on assumptions about casualty rates, which were key to measuring the medical support required, and many were reluctant to embrace change, not least those moonlighting in private practices. Nevertheless, the service had to be modernised and costs cut, but the net result was that the confidence of the doctors was undermined.

It was a very unhappy time for the DMS and Jock thought himself one of the people primarily responsible. He would be happy to know that the DMS has settled into the 21st century and recruitment and retention are satisfactory.

## Dentists

On 20 January 1995, at a dinner to mark the 75th anniversary of the Royal Naval Dental Service, the head dentist, a surgeon commodore, harangued Jock in a 35-minute speech on the failure during *Front Line First* to provide a satisfactory future for defence dental services.[183] During this diatribe, Jock rethought parts of his prepared speech: "I did wonder if I should have brought a gumshield for the after dinner drinks!"

After warming up his audience with a joke he launched into a critique of what he had just heard. The aim of the Defence Costs Studies No 15 into the medical services was to transfer spending from the support services to the front line: medical and dental services could not be exempt. Typically, Jock had the numbers at his fingertips. The dentist:patient ratio was supposed to be 1:1095, and the ratio in the Second World War, when there had been 700 naval dentists on the books and some 800,000 men under arms, had been 1:1143. Today that ratio was about 1:690. "But of course," he told his listeners, "You can do anything with statistics and I assure you that I will do everything I can to ensure that not only your numbers are satisfactory but also that your conditions of service are acceptable and your administration is sound."

In Jock's view, things were not looking bleak and signs were encouraging, and he was pleased to find after dinner that he had won over at least part of his audience.

## Permanent Joint Headquarters

One high-profile issue already prevalent before *Front Line First* started was the matter of forming a Permanent Joint Head Quarters (PJHQ). Jock was convinced from his time as Commander-in-Chief Fleet that there should be permanent headquarters for the command and control of operations. At first he could not persuade Harding (the CDS) nor the Chiefs, Bathurst (CNS) Inge (CGS), or Graydon (CAS) to support this idea, which encroached on single-service sensitivities, not least the status of their own headquarters at Northwood, Wilton and High Wycombe. However, Rifkind's opinion was that the MoD and other headquarters at all levels were too large, too top heavy, and too bureaucratic. Jock was on to a winner.

Jock admired Secretary of State Michael Portillo whom he hosted here at the opening of the new Permanent Joint Headquarters, Northwood.
Source: Slater archive.

As VCDS, Jock wanted a general to set up the PJHQ, and his private consultations suggested that there were only two who could carry through this historic change. One was Rupert Smith, who was already destined for Northern Ireland, and the other was Christopher Wallace, who the new CGS, Guthrie, instantly made available for the task. As the PJHQ progressed during 1994 the Chiefs were persuaded, and Inge, from being uneasy about the whole project, became very supportive. Wilton became the frontrunner while some felt that a greenfield site was the answer; analysis favoured Northwood. There is no doubt that Malcolm Rifkind's personal interest and staunch support was the key to the success of the whole project. Wallace duly conducted a most successful implementation phase and thereafter became the first Chief of Joint Operations.

## Results of the Defence Costs Study

On 14 July 1994 Rifkind began his report to the House of Commons by announcing three main conclusions from *Front Line First*. Certain management and command structures could be streamlined, many defence support functions could be outsourced to the private sector, and many command, training, and support structures could be provided by the armed forces jointly, rather than by the three services separately.

There would be a reduction of 5% (11,600) in uniformed people, the majority from the RAF, and 7% (7,100) of civilians, including more than 20 senior military and civilian positions at rear-admiral (2-star) level and above. MoD staff in London would be reduced from 5,000 to 3,750, the Procurement Executive would have 500 fewer staff, and there would be similar cuts elsewhere. Seventeen stores depots, two military hospitals, three RAF bases (one in Germany), the Fleet Air Arm base at Portland, and the Royal Marines School of Music at Deal in Kent would close, and the separate Army, Navy, and RAF headquarters would merge into a single joint headquarters at Northwood. For operational as well as cost-effective reasons, he would create a Joint Service Staff College and other joint facilities for the three services, which were long overdue.

These announcements caused qualms about redundancies, but these were offset by new equipment orders after Rifkind told Parliament of improvements to the front line. An order for 259 Challenger II tanks was confirmed, together with an upgrade of 142 Tornado GR1s to GR4 standard, 7 *Sandown*-class minehunters, £300 million for laser-guided bombs and laser designators, 400,000 rounds of 51mm from British Aerospace's Royal Ordnance, there would be a new Batch 2 *Trafalgar*-class nuclear submarine (the future *Astute*-class), two new amphibious assault ships (the *Albion*-class landing platform dock), and a promise of Tomahawk cruise missiles. Twelve Harrier aircraft from the reserve fleet would be moved to the front line. Rifkind also recommended that the United Kingdom dispose of all its freefall nuclear bombs so that Britain's only nuclear arsenal would be in its Trident submarines. These changes, said Rifkind, "would ensure that every penny which is spent is absolutely essential for the support and operational effectiveness of front line forces, and enable the armed forces to discharge their military tasks and commitments properly, to the full and with formidable capability".

Jock was suspicious and, knowing that politicians were adept at sugaring the pill, wondered whether these promised orders would come to fruition. In the event they nearly all did. Critics rightly contended that the cuts were driven by the Treasury, while Rifkind argued that the reductions did not affect the front line of the armed forces, but rather targeted support staff and assets. Jock regarded the PJHQ as the most significant contribution that he was able to make as VCDS.

After the dust had settled Rifkind gave a personal overview of the work at the Royal United Services Institute (RUSI). As RUSI vice chairman, Jock was in the chair but forbore to comment or sum up. Defence as a proportion of GDP had fallen from 3.4% to 2.9%.


**Taking Stock**

An address to the Joint Service Defence College in his final few months as VCDS gave Jock an opportunity to take stock of what had been achieved after an unprecedented period of restructuring and streamlining. Even before *Front Line First* the MoD had been engaged in a major savings programme that had realised £4bn by 1995/96. It was infuriating to Jock that there was no credit for having already made major cuts in the size of the armed forces. There was a drawdown of 43% in armoured regiments, 30% in artillery regiments, 33% in destroyers and frigates, 57% in submarines, 40% in air defence squadrons and 27% in strike attack squadrons. In parallel, 87,000 uniformed personnel and 37,000 civilians and support personnel were being shed. On top of this 'efficiency' there would be savings of £3bn each year by 1997 and a *New Management Strategy* aimed at savings at all levels.

In the light of the uncertain and turbulent international scene Jock found it increasingly difficult to justify such cuts. However much Prime Minister John Major appreciated this, Britain had reached a watershed in terms of the part its armed forces played in the life of the nation and as an arm of foreign policy. Reviewing operational commitments, Britain was underplaying its contribution on the international scene. The armed forces were as busy as ever, but all too often overstretched, under supported, and sometimes unnecessarily endangered. He detailed those commitments, in Bosnia, in Iraq and in Rwanda, where there were some 500 engineers, logisticians, and medics. Then there were the garrisons, large and small, in the Falklands, Hong Kong, Cyprus, Brunei, Gibraltar and Belize. And in Northern Ireland where, despite the ceasefire, there were 19,000 troops.

On the policy side he had been deeply immersed in a plethora of subjects such as counter-proliferation, readiness and regeneration, preparations for strategic and sub-strategic Trident, and a host of national and international issues, not least a real chance of revitalising NATO and an even better chance to re-emphasise the continuing need for trans-Atlantic cooperation and for drawing the French in closer.

Despite the war in Bosnia, the *Defence Costs Study* was a preoccupation in the MoD. Of course, implementation would be the test, and the savings were still very immature and needed budget holders to turn the studies into reality. All this activity was running alongside the normal Long Term Costings Cycle, LTC 95, well underway.

As VCDS, Jock was very conscious of the dangers of change after change leading to turbulence and uncertainty, and consequent demotivation. In his mind, *Front Line First* fuelled unease, which would be exacerbated by the Bett Review of career structures, conditions of service. Proposals to place married quarters into a housing trust were also unsettling.

If this made 1994 a demanding year, 1995 would be no easier. The task of managing change superimposed on international turbulence was enormous. Jock called it a revolution. He was deeply impressed – indeed humbled – by the understanding and constructive way people were facing up to the pressures and uncertainties, not least because many were seeing reduced career prospects and others knew their jobs were on the line. However, he remained "distinctly unhappy" that the overall drawdown of the armed forces was high risk in the light of the dangers and uncertainties in a divided world.

He was conscious that with a change of government would come another defence review that would expose these risks, but not at all confident that there would be any major reversal of this downward trend: "there are no votes in defence".

Looking forward, he knew that the Royal Navy would need strong leadership, and his experience as the VCDS would stand him in good stead in the bureaucratic battles that lay ahead: "Yes, the standing and influence of the UK's armed forces remained high and the calibre of our people and their achievements were legion; but we must not fall into the trap of taking their loyalty and commitment for granted and must do nothing to destroy the unique characteristics that made them second to none."

## France

Jock continued to accept invitations to speak to a wide audience, and he especially liked to visit universities, where he knew that young people would be critical and ask penetrating questions. However, he was disappointed at the newly established Centre for Defence and International Security Studies at Lancaster University, where his listeners were not well informed about defence matters. Moreover, it was a long way to go for an evening engagement and then be driven straight back to London, to be ready to leave for France the following morning and lead the British delegation to the Anglo-French bilateral talks. The main subject on the agenda was the establishment of an Anglo-French Air Group, but Jock could not forget the charming General Jean-Philippe Douin, who took him aside to ask about his friend Peter Harding: "Jock, what is wrong with you British? Peter was merely proving his virility."

That autumn of 1994 President Francois Mitterand hosted the Annual Anglo-French Summit in Chartres, where Prime Minister John Major's team included several senior ministers, and Malcolm Rifkind headed up the MoD team in which Jock represented the CDS. There was a series of bilateral discussions in which British and French defence links were a leading theme. But, though defence ministers issued a joint statement, the resumé had been written in advance. Jock noted: "All the talking was done by the President and the Prime Minister with the occasional intervention by a Secretary of State, no doubt endeavouring to make his mark. I think that eyebrows would have been raised had I spoken!" When it was clear that Jock and the French Chief of Defence Staff, Admiral Jacques Lanxade,[184] would not get a word in edgeways, it was arranged that they should sit next to each other for lunch, and afterwards they took coffee à deux.

Jock had other foreign visits including a private trip to Saudi Arabia, Australia and New Zealand, and a visit to South America and the West Indies accompanied by his personal staff. It was at an evening reception in Guatemala that Jock noticed for the first time that Keith Pople and Karen Pearce were paying more attention to each other than to the guests.

## Trafalgar Night

In October 1994 Jock was guest of honour at three Trafalgar Night dinners. Typically, he spent time preparing these speeches, topping and tailing them with the usual Trafalgar and Nelson content, and after a few jokes to gain the guests' attention he delivered his message. He told an audience of NATO officers at Mons that they were on the threshold of a new era, marked by increasing instability and uncertainty in a world where pressure on resources was exacerbated by ethnic, religious, and territorial disputes, and in which a new world order was yet to be established. If Nelson had gazed into a crystal ball, he would have been amazed to see NATO but would surely have applauded the remarkable way the Alliance was adapting to new circumstances. Nelson would also surely have warned against dropping guard in the face of international tension and turbulence.

The following day was spent at Dartmouth (Jock commuted by HS125), on the invitation of Captain Simon Moore.[185] Jock looked back on his seven terms there with the happiest of memories, and, as always, enjoyed meeting young officers and hearing their views. He had the opportunity to address the next generation of officers including a dozen youngsters attending an international nautical competition and the foreign and Commonwealth students at the college, and he told them about Nelson's professionalism, bravery, and patriotism, and about an officer dedicated to making his country great through the Royal Navy. He warned that this could not be taken for granted and he emphasised the importance of working together for the common good. Next day he did what he liked best, a Q&A session with the young officers. Answering a question as to whether Britain was doing enough on the world stage, he said he thought that Britain was selling itself short and underplaying its key contribution on the international scene: 76,964 servicemen were deployed that very day (typically Jock had such a number at his fingertips). And to a final question about the future, Jock was upbeat:

> I envy you – I wish that I were starting all over again. Yes, the Royal Navy was very different to the one I joined 38 years before, but it continues to play a vital role in responding flexibly to calls worldwide and you should be in no doubt about the inherent versatility of maritime power to respond to these calls. Furthermore, we, the Navy, have the temperament, the experience, and the expertise that qualifies us uniquely for this role … There will, of course, be changes, difficulties, and challenges, but one thing is for sure – the key importance of the

Royal Navy will not diminish, and the future lies in the hands of the new generation, your generation.

Jock was especially keen to speak at the British American Forces Dining Club, which 50 years earlier Uncle Ned as First Sea Lord and Ned's close friend, Admiral 'Betty' Stark USN, had attended.[186] Their friendship, Jock noted, had epitomised what lay at the heart of victory in the Second World War and the special relationship, a relationship that was especially strong between the two navies.

Jock quoted Bismarck, who had said that "the supreme fact of the 19th century was that Britain and the US spoke the same language". Without doubt, Jock told them, this was also the key to the 20th century, and they had to ensure that it continued to be so into the 21st century. In phrases that might be questioned today (2025), Jock said that the 50th anniversary of D-Day had served to remind different generations in Britain, the USA, and elsewhere of that great enterprise and what an irresistible force Britain and the USA could be when united and pulling together towards a common goal. It was, he said, in the USA's national interest to remain fully engaged in Europe: the USA needed Europe just as much as Europe needed the USA, but he was concerned that more recent events in the USA were challenging that view.

## Health

During this period Jock enjoyed his last days of stalking at Balmoral, including two disappointing blank days, during which he found his knees ached agonisingly. The weekend after Mons and Dartmouth was spent in Scotland, where Jock caught "the most ghastly fluey cold in that weekend, which was infuriating as I was billed the following Monday to speak at the British American Forces Dining Club, attend a Chiefs' lunch for the Queen Mother on the Tuesday, attend, with Annie, a big dinner given by the CAS, Mike Graydon, on the Wednesday and host the Senior British Officers in a NATO Conference on the Thursday and Friday before leaving for New Zealand on the Saturday. "Mad! Yes, absolutely mad! – but I went ahead with the whole week coughing and spluttering except sensibly backing out of the Queen Mother's lunch. The trouble was I always hated letting people down, a feeling that went back to early days at Dartmouth when I regarded those who reported sick as weak! Still do!" He was feeling "extremely grotty" at the British American Forces Dining Club and in New Zealand, to preserve his voice for the Q&A, his major speech had to be read for him. Others might have taken this as a gypsy's warning.

## The Baltic States and Belarus

In early March 1995 one of Jock's last tours as VCDS was to the Baltic states, Estonia, Latvia and Lithuania, and to Belarus. One of the first units he met was the Baltic Battalion, BALTBAT, where a Royal Marines unit was led by an impressive young officer, David Stewart, who was substantive captain, acting major, and local acting lieutenant colonel.[187] Jock was impressed that the Royal Marines detachment, with their drive, determination, and professionalism in the face of local difficulties, was making a huge impact. The Soviet legacy was appalling: military equipment was in poor repair or inadequately supported by spares and fuel, and infrastructure was in a poor state. As they withdrew, the Russians had embarked on a wanton and savage scorched-earth policy, destroying buildings and facilities and scuttling small craft in the harbours. Jock called on ministers and senior civil servants, visited academies and military formations, and received requests for English language training and for defence staff talks. British largesse included the offer of a place on the war studies course at King's College London for Enn Tupp, a former officer of the Soviet army and Estonian minister for defence from 1994–95.

Jock appreciated that, despite the long history of their peoples, the Baltic states were three new nations, fiercely proud of their independence but facing an enormous struggle to rebuild the structures of state after 45 years in the Soviet yoke. National budgets were small, and defence forces faced severe competition from social programmes. It was difficult to think of Belarus as being separate from Russia: economic and cultural ties were close, the architecture was drab, and aspects of western democracy were quite foreign, particularly the apolitical nature of the armed forces and the control of defence forces by civilian politicians.

In Latvia there was another historical resonance when Jock laid a wreath at the memorial to British dead in the combined actions of the British and French fleets at the liberation of Riga in 1919. His visit to the Baltics was nicely bookended when on 15 March 1995 he heard the Russian ambassador speak at RUSI: "Not an impressive performance and included a justification transmission on the rights of the Russian attack on Chechnya."


## Good News

In April 1995, Ben Bathurst kindly stood down earlier than usual to allow Jock to relieve him as the First Sea Lord and to position Jock as the likely next Chief of Defence Staff when Inge eventually retired.

# Chapter 21: First Sea Lord I, 1995

The turnover from Admiral Sir Ben Bathurst was its usual brisk affair and Jock became First Sea Lord on Monday, 10 July 1995, nearly 40 years after marching up the hill to the naval college in Dartmouth at the start of his career. The Slaters moved into the Mall House flat in Admiralty Arch, where Uncle Ned had been the first incumbent in 1944, and Annie immediately set about turning it into their London home. On the Thursday, the Queen received Jock, and then Annie and he went to lunch with the Queen Mother at Clarence House. Afterwards they attended a garden party at Buckingham Palace and that evening in the survey ship HMS *Hecla,* hosted by the hydrographer of the Navy, Rear-Admiral Nigel Essenhigh, Jock celebrated the bicentenary of the Hydrographic Office.

Sadly, in his first month, Jock closed two naval establishments – the naval air station at Portland and the Royal Naval Engineering College at Manadon – as part of savings measures. Soon he was back in the USA, with James Arbuthnot, the Minister for Defence Procurement, to witness the first Trident D5 missile firing from the submarine HMS *Victorious*: he hosted a dinner at which the US Secretary of the Navy, John Dalton, was guest of honour and visited the Trident training and refit facilities at Kings Bay, Georgia. He returned to London in time to take the salute at the Royal Tournament at Earl's Court.

Jock had resumed work at his usual furious pace.


**New Teams**

After the results of *Front Line First* were made known, there were ministerial changes at the MoD and a few days before Jock became First Sea Lord, Rifkind, with whom Jock had enjoyed an excellent relationship, moved to the Foreign

Office. Jock liked his successor, Michael Portillo, who turned out to be a most able political animal, though Jock sometimes found it hard to judge what he was really thinking. He was extremely good on his feet – despite a habit of telling the same joke more than once. Jock recalled later that year that when he invited Portillo to address the retired admirals and generals, the Minister had asked what particular points Jock wanted him to make. Jock gave him five key topics and "in a fifteen-minute address without notes he had covered all five in the same order. [It] was most impressive, and his Q&A session was excellent."

Other new ministers were: Minister for Defence Procurement James Arbuthnot, who was well regarded and dependable and whose legal expertise was highly beneficial; Parliamentary Under Secretary of State Freddie Howe, who demonstrated similar good nature and was pleasant to work with; and Jock's old friend Nicholas Soames, Winston Churchill's grandson, whom he had met when equerry to Prince Charles in the late1960s, who became Minister for the Armed Forces. Soames was a popular and energetic minister, if more comfortable dealing with the Army than the other services. Despite their friendship, Jock made a point of telling him the bad news as well as the good, and not buttering him up, especially when, after visits, the new minister returned to Whitehall having promised something that he was quite unable to deliver.

Jock's official diary was already full. "There were key meetings and lunches and dinners, many of them working, at every possible moment. How fortunate I was to have a very hard-working staff both in the office and in the flat: I could not have coped without them. Above all I certainly could not have got through the first, high-powered period at the helm of the Royal Navy without Annie's love and sterling support."

He inherited a strong supporting team. The Assistant Chief of the Naval Staff was Rear-Admiral Jeremy Blackham, who was making a great success of a most demanding appointment. He was an experienced, politically tuned, natural MoD warrior and understood the art of the possible in Whitehall. Jock had complete confidence in him as regards his knowledge, judgement, and integrity, and he was agreeably relaxed, modest, and even-tempered. "He very definitely merited the 3-stars that would shortly become his."[188]

Jock's Secretary was Captain Peter Tribe, who was very much at home in Whitehall and professionally most competent. He had good working relationships with the other outer offices and kept his ear to the ground. Jock liked his calm manner and easy style of leadership; he was clearly well respected and a person to whom people came for pragmatic advice.[189] The Naval Assistant, Captain Jamie Miller, proved enormously loyal and threw himself into every aspect of his demanding job, even if he found the going tough. He had a genuine and fatherly respect for people, but his best qualities were his old-fashioned values, his sharp seaman's eye, his dislike of inefficiency, and his remarkable gift for engaging the affection of one and all. He was particularly effective during visits in noticing matters that might not have been brought to Jock's attention.[190]

## On the Defensive

Very soon Jock found himself defending the decisions taken under *Front Line First,* telling the *Daily Telegraph* that "We have to make absolutely certain that if the crunch were to come then we can regenerate, but overall, our people are pretty stretched now. We are in the process, in the light of new circumstances, of a regeneration study to look to see exactly what it is we need to do and how we should do it." He was reflecting the views of senior officers of all three services when he said that he was concerned that the 25% cut in manpower in the armed forces since 1989 had been hasty and ill-conceived: "We must keep up our capability at the top level: anti-submarine warfare [and] anti-surface warfare are not just things you pick up overnight and send your ships to sea. They require a huge amount of training, training, and training again, both ashore and at sea." *Front Line First* as an exercise and analysis of how to streamline the support of the three services was outstandingly successful, but "implementation of that analysis is extremely uncomfortable and turbulent for our people … The reality is that if you reduce the number of frigates, destroyers, submarines, and the number of small ships [but] you maintain the number of tasks, then inevitably the stresses and strains on the fleet are greater. The opportunities for maintenance are less, the opportunities for leave and recreation are less, and the opportunities for training at the higher level are not so great." He was worried about the effect on morale, the increased workload for sailors, and eroded job security: "I am concerned about the effect it has on our people now redundancy is an inevitability because it is the only way you can regulate your numbers in a hurry."

Nevertheless, Jock told the *Daily Telegraph*, he was confident that the Royal Navy was about the right size, although "it would be quite wrong to give a sort of 'everything's fine, everything is rosy in the garden' impression – of course it is not, we have a series of extremely difficult problems to tackle but I believe on the whole we're tackling them pretty positively".

David Zwirek of the *Western Morning News* was critical of the effect that *Front Line First* would have on the Devonport naval base and the West Country at large, where 21,000 jobs had been lost in the defence industry since 1985. Jock's line was that he would prefer the naval service to be under pressure than underemployed, but he was all too conscious of the need to monitor 'stretch', telling Zwirek that *Front Line First*, with its increased workloads and erosion of job security, was a major challenge and that good leadership at all levels was critical. Specifically, he reassured the newspaper that a contract for nuclear submarine refits would go to Devonport. However, when Zwirek quoted the Flag Officer Plymouth's belief that Devonport should become the centre of excellence for amphibious shipping, Jock was not so sanguine: "It is not a straightforward decision, Plymouth or Portsmouth, because it is tied to manpower and sea:shore ratios." Jock denied that Devonport had ever played second fiddle to Portsmouth or that the southwest "remains in the shadow of its South Coast rival".

## A Poor Sermon

That autumn the Slaters flew up to Edinburgh to represent the Chiefs at a service in St Giles' Cathedral to mark the 50th anniversary of VJ Day, which was marred by an "appallingly insensitive" sermon given by the Roman Catholic Archbishop of St Andrews and Edinburgh, Keith O'Brien.[191] He outraged the veterans, some of whom had been Japanese prisoners of war at the time of Hiroshima and Nagasaki, by delivering a sermon critical of nuclear weapons. "Some of his comments were absolute nonsense and I could hear Sir Eric Yarrow, a member of the Burma Star Association, murmuring 'Nonsense!'" Jock, with his Church of Scotland background, was never shy to engage with the clergy and what happened next is best described in his own words:

> I followed Princess Anne and Tim Laurence out and she very swiftly bade farewell to the clergy as she clearly knew I was going to take the archbishop to task. I did! I told him, in no uncertain terms, that his sermon had been irresponsible, inappropriate, and most insensitive on such an occasion; furthermore, his comments about the potential for an accidental nuclear explosion if a nuclear convoy was on the Edinburgh ring road were absolute nonsense. He retorted that that was what his briefers said. My response was 'Well you had better get better briefers!'

O'Brien chose not to attend the subsequent reception given by the Secretary of State for Scotland in the Chamber Street Museum.

## Washington and Norfolk

Jock had already called on his French and Spanish opposite numbers and other senior European naval chiefs at a meeting of the Channel Committee in Paris,[192] when in October 1995 he flew to the USA to renew his acquaintanceship with his old friend Admiral Mike Boorda, Chief of Naval Operations. The visit included two Trafalgar Night dinners, the first at the British ambassador's residence, with a Royal Marines band and the Secretary of the Navy, John Dalton, as the guest of honour. The toast to the Immortal Memory was proposed by the Vice Chairman of the US Joint Chiefs of Staff, Admiral Bill Owens. The second dinner followed during a visit to Norfolk, Virginia, organised by Vice-Admiral Ian Garnett, the British Deputy Supreme Allied Commander Atlantic, and chaired by Captain John Hance, who had been Jock's commander in HMS *Dryad* ten years before.

Between dinners, much business was done, and Jock was left in no doubt that another old friend, Rear-Admiral Tom Blackburn, head of the British Defence Staff in Washington, was doing a sterling job of keeping alive the special relationship, which in the post-Cold War years was particularly strong. A few months later he received through the post a certificate making him an associate member of the United States Naval Institute. He noted that any additional maritime links with the United Sates were to be welcomed.

## Broadsheet

*Broadsheet* was originally an annual, green-ink newsletter from the First Sea Lord to retired senior officers. By the 1970s it had become a magazine in which the First Sea Lord's letter served as a foreword to news articles from other departments of the Navy. In Jock's time as First Sea Lord, the key to *Broadsheet*'s success was its editor, Commander Laon Hulme, who "sought future, relevant topics, and adhered to firm self-imposed timelines while fine-tuning the current edition. *Broadsheet* offered a platform to project senior views and strivings, and all knew that *Broadsheet* would provide an appreciative audience, so few declined the opportunity to promote their achievements."[193]

Its circulation was in the region of 44,000 and Jock used it to promote the message he wanted everyone to hear: that the strategic scene was changing fast and that sporadic regional conflicts had replaced the monolithic threat. He underscored the need for the versatility and reach of balanced maritime forces, usually within joint and combined operations, and highlighted updates and enhancements to the Navy's three core capabilities of power projection: carrier-borne air, amphibious forces, and nuclear submarines, and he emphasised the modernisation of escort forces including a new generation of air defence destroyers, mine countermeasure forces, and RFAs. He told his readership that he knew, "perfectly well that to deliver all this would call for huge powers of persuasion in the coming years to impress the politicians (who seldom liked to consider long-term issues) and indeed my own Chiefs of Staff colleagues who had to fight their own corners and knew that my shopping list would inevitably be expensive."

He was able to do this before the dead hand of central control of media fell over Whitehall departments, knowing that some copies of *Broadsheet* would find their way to the press and the public.


## Unwelcome Presents

Two items marred Christmas. On 31 December Andrew Gilligan in the *Sunday Telegraph* speculated on the outcome of a MoD study of homosexuality in the services. Jock was conscious that attitudes were changing, and he was already consulting privately and widely as to what the Navy might think if current MoD policy were to be changed.

The second matter concerned the Mall House flat in Admiralty Arch, which had been the London residence of the First Sea Lord since Uncle Ned had moved there in 1944. Though ministers in the MoD supported its continuing use by the First Sea Lord, others in the government wanted to include Admiralty Arch in a sale of government property. After news of this broke in the *Daily Telegraph*, Admiral Lord Hill-Norton, "not the most diplomatic of senior officers", criticised Michael Portillo for allowing such a sale to be considered and called him a "little creep". Jock hurried to disassociate himself from these remarks, but damage may have been done.

# Chapter 22: The Trojan Horse

When Jock became First Sea Lord in July 1995 he remembered trying to digest the *Naval War Manual* and thought that the subject of maritime doctrine needed to be brought up to date and made more readable. He was also determined that maritime doctrine should recognise and be recognised for its contribution to joint operations. He was therefore delighted to find that a new publication, *British Maritime Doctrine* (*BMD*), was already at an advanced stage of drafting. He took no credit for its preparation, but *BMD* would be an enormous help in the months to come.

**The Naval War Manual**

The *Naval War Manual* was first published in the 1920s, republished in 1959, and last revised in 1961.[194] The author recalls seeing shelves of unissued copies of the *Naval War Manual* in the bookstore at Dartmouth when he was there on the staff in the late 1970s. However, no doctrine, no theory of war whether by land, air, or sea, was taught at Dartmouth, not to the third-year Murray scheme officers of the 1960s, who were supposedly the navy's first undergraduates to be taught at the naval college, and not to the ready-made graduate officers recruited in the 1970s. Nor was the *Naval War Manual* taught at the lieutenants' course at the Royal Naval College, Greenwich, nor on the staff course there and, most tellingly, it was never part of the ship-command examinations that were so important to officers wishing to command at sea.

## Fighting Instructions

Instead, the Navy relied on *Fighting Instructions*, which had existed since the 16th century and down the years had been reissued and revised repeatedly. Julian Corbett was one of the first to catalogue and analyse the changes in these instructions, which had as much to do with fighting in fleets as with the manoeuvre of ships in formation under sail and later steam. Corbett's first analysis, *Fighting Instructions 1530–1813*, was published by the Navy Record Society in 1905.[195] This aroused new interest in the instructions, and three years later Corbett issued another volume, *Signals and Instructions 1776–1794*, where he included as addenda to his previous work.[196] The two volumes dealt with battle at the tactical and operational level of combat.

Corbett realised that there was little interest in warfare at strategic and political levels and in 1911 he published his seminal work, *Some Principles of Maritime Strategy*.[197] Since the early 20th century discussion of naval strategy had turned on the writings of Alfred T Mahan, whose book *The Influence of Sea Power upon History* was a study of decisive battles and campaigns between large, organised fleets and was addressed to the nascent US Navy. By contrast, Corbett's principles of maritime strategy were written for the largest and most powerful navy of the day. Corbett assumed that British naval officers knew how to win wars and campaigns, but he also appreciated that, however glorious and important it was to beat the enemy in battle, officers needed to know what could be achieved before and afterwards.[198]

Corbett recognised that command of the sea could be relative rather than absolute, and favoured the strategic defensive, intense local offensive, the projection of land forces, blockades, raids on enemy trade routes, and, only once the enemy has been sufficiently weakened on sea and on land, a shift to the strategic offensive. Corbett also recognised the primacy of politics in war and society and the need for an appropriate strategy to protect national interests. More than other strategists, he was also interested in alliances and coalitions, the economic and financial dimensions of war, and the material and technological aspects of war.

He was commissioned to write the official history of naval operations during the First World War but died before he could agree the final corrections to the third volume, which covered the Battle of Jutland. When the Admiralty perceived that Corbett had smuggled his ideas into the official history, a note was cruelly inserted saying that "The Lords Commissioners of the Admiralty find that some of the principles advocated in this book, especially the tendency to minimize the importance of seeking battle and forcing it to a conclusion, are directly in conflict with their views."[199] Subsequently, little of Corbett's principles of maritime strategy was reflected in the *Naval War Manual* of 1925, nor in the revised *Fighting Instructions* of 1928, which incorporated the Navy's lessons learned in the First World War.[200] Fighting instructions continued to be written and reviewed throughout the 20th century, and for much of the Cold War they spilled into two volumes, Fleet Exercise and Training Instructions (FXTIs) and Fleet Operational and Tactical Instructions (FOTIs).

There had never been a lack of innovative military thinking in the British armed forces, as CE Callwell, Julian Corbett, JFC Fuller, and Basil Liddell Hart attest, but by and large British officers – of all three services – did not care about doctrine and were reluctant to engage in intellectual debate. Yes, there were tactical instruction manuals whose use was largely confined to the classroom and to exercises, but operational experience was handed down informally, often by word of mouth, through generations of officers. For example, the preface to the 1939 edition of *Fighting Instructions* made clear that these were: [201]

> Guiding principles … not to be regarded as orders. Extensive reference to these instructions should not be necessary on the bridge at sea in time of war. In the event of war, the Fighting Instructions may be further defined by supplementary orders, which would depend on the circumstances of the war and the composition of opposing fleets. It is the duty of Captains to acquaint officers of the rank of Lieutenant and above, and other appropriate officers, with the contents of the Fighting Instructions, in particular as far as they apply to the tactics and duties of their own ships or aircraft in war.

As Mäder observed: "In the absence of formal statements on the overall role of the British armed forces, a common starting point for the study of conflict did not exist. In such an organisational culture, innovation was left to coincidence, largely steered by what was already known or physically available."[202]

## Army and RAF Doctrine

This was about to change after the fiery General Nigel Bagnall became CGS and established the Higher Command and Staff Course (HCSC) to educate senior Army commanders at the operational level of command. Bagnall wanted to change the Army's pragmatism and mindset of improvisation, an attitude particularly strong in the Army's 'small wars' culture. He argued that the operational level of command, the coordination of a military campaign at the corps level and above, was a highly complex matter that needed to be studied. In 1989 Bagnall oversaw the publication of *Design for Military Operations – The British Military Doctrine*, whose principal author was Granville-Chapman.[203]

After *Options for Change* in 1990, the RAF followed the Army with its own *Air Power Doctrine*, though this addressed different problems because its conceptual thinking was preoccupied with technology.[204] Procurement programmes dominated conceptual considerations, and the role of the RAF was defined by what technology was affordable and available: "There was a somewhat natural tendency of aviators to reject contemplation in favour of action and to focus on technical and tactical issues rather than complicated operational or even military strategic concepts, which, so was the perception, at best would be ignored and at worst made the RAF vulnerable to inter-service rivalries."[205]

## British Maritime Doctrine

The Navy remained institutionally ignorant of these developments in doctrine, until in 1993 two rising stars, Captains Alan West and John McAnally,[206] were invited to attend the fourth HCSC, which was still run at Camberley. (It was later moved to the newly established Defence Academy at Shrivenham.) As a student at the RCDS, West had written a Seaford House Paper on why Britain needed a grand strategy. Now, as part of the seventeen-week HCSC, he and McAnally were exposed to British Army doctrine and were required to write papers about the operational art of warfare. West's paper addressed the Navy's need to be able to state what British maritime doctrine might be and he took this with him when he became Director of the Naval Staff Division (DNSD) from 1993–94, when he was responsible for providing administrative support and advice to Oswald, First Sea Lord and Chief of Naval Staff.

Some of the early ideas about post-Cold War maritime doctrine and strategy were discussed in DNSD in West's time as director, while Jock, as Commander-in-Chief Fleet, had already set out in a speech to RUSI in late 1992 his vision of the fleet in *A Fleet for the 90s*. Jock had emphasised the relevance of the Navy's existing force structure and the operational experience gathered at the end of the Cold War. There were three overlapping defence roles, identified in the 1992 Defence White Paper, including national security and support of NATO and the UK's wider security interests outside Europe. The latter spawned a very wide range of tasks for which Britain needed to retain an intervention capability. In turn, the fleet, Jock told his audience, had its own three overlapping fleet roles: directed tasks, fleet priorities, and the unexpected.[207]

Jock was still VCDS but knew he would be the next First Sea Lord when he was consulted about West's relief as DNSD. He chose McAnally, who when he duly called on Jock to discuss his pending appointment, recalled being asked if he "was signed up to the three core capabilities", which McAnally understood to mean carriers, amphibious ships, and nuclear submarines, and replied that he was. Privately, he thought that "there should be more to our rationale than that",[208] and so, in November 1994, a doctrine seminar was convened at the Royal Naval College, Greenwich. There, in an exchange of ideas between naval officers and academics, it was noted that at successive defence reviews during the Cold War the Navy had been unable to articulate its case strongly enough and that it had entered the post-Cold War years with fighting instructions orientated towards a long, anti-submarine war in the Atlantic. In a changed strategic environment, the seminar noted that despite the perceived success of the Army's *British Military Doctrine* and the RAF's *Air Power Doctrine*, the Navy's senior officers were still sceptical about the value of writing down any doctrine.[209] However, at desk-level in DNSD, a different opinion was emerging: the increasingly joint character of operations raised the question of whether Britain's armed forces might in the not too distant future conceive a joint doctrine, when the contributions of the three services would be based on their respective single-service doctrines. If so, it was argued, the lack of any naval doctrine would be a serious disadvantage, making it more difficult to advance any separate 'naval case'. A decision was made to write what would become *BMD*, and the work fell to Commander Mike Codner, whose self-effacing manner hid his great intellect. Codner had been an alumnus of and lecturer at the US Naval War College, Newport Rhode Island, and was familiar with US maritime thinking. He was helped by a civilian, Eric Grove, a maverick but genius academic. Grove had recently completed, for the *Classics of Sea Power* series from the US Naval Institute Press, an annotated edition of Corbett's great work, *Some Principles of Maritime Strategy*, in which Grove had included Corbett's previously unpublished notes for lecturing to the naval war course, Corbett's so-called *Green Pamphlet* of 1909.

Codner and Grove wrote the first draft of *BMD* in six weeks, but whereas Corbett's prose was limpid and legally precise, the draft *BMD* was almost unreadable. McAnally "remember[ed] editing it rather severely on two occasions because I thought it could be made more readable and the ideas set out in a more logical order … In an effort to increase its interest I also commissioned side paragraphs containing historical narratives to illustrate particular themes." Codner remembered the process slightly differently:[210]

Lacking both an institutionalised doctrinal process and top-down guidance, the Royal Navy's first doctrine project was organised on an ad hoc basis. The project officially started in April 1993. Some midcareer officers were tasked with collecting relevant material which was then discussed in the Committee of Taste … While the Royal Navy's senior leadership did not oppose the project, which was largely pushed bottom-up, they did not express great interest either. As some of the involved doctrinalists remember, the feeling at the time was that some senior commanders "thought it a bit of a nuisance". However, once the final draft was presented, the Navy Board accepted it as formal doctrine and considered it to be an authoritative starting point for future debate.

When Jock saw a late draft he was particularly keen that the principles of war should be explained and that the doctrine behind the Falklands War should be included as a case study. Then, with the inclusion of a glossary (which took up some 50 of the 250 pages), *BMD* was ready. In his foreword Jock wrote:[211]

We in the Royal Navy must be careful to avoid a dogmatic approach in thinking about the principles that govern our maritime actions. We must maintain our reputation for innovation and for responding to political changes and technical opportunities. Yet there has always been a doctrine, an evolving set of principles, practices and procedures that has provided the basis for our actions. This doctrine has been laid out somewhat piecemeal in various publications and there has never been a single official unclassified book describing why and how we do our business. This publication aims to fill that gap by drawing together the fundamentals of maritime doctrine.

Doctrine draws on the lessons of history. So this book fuses historical experience with current thinking and terminology and I hope you will find this thought provoking … To claim that the result is perfect would be nonsense. Indeed it would be contrary to the best traditions of the Service for any such codification of thinking to be regarded as unchallengeable. What follows has been accepted as doctrine by the Navy Board and thus represents an authoritative starting point for future debate … It is thus a necessary foundation for the formulation of joint doctrine with the other Services. I expect this publication to be taught, applied, discussed, and tested within the Naval Service and I commend it to all who have an interest in the profession of arms at sea.

At the launch of *BMD* at RUSI in November 1995 Jock was accompanied by McAnally as DNSD and Captain Bob Williams, director of the Maritime Warfare Centre at HMS *Dryad*, where a maritime doctrine cell had been established to keep doctrine under review – though in fact editorship of *BMD* remained in DNSD and the next edition would be published in 1999 under the imprimatur of the Head of Defence Studies.[212]

## Joint Doctrine

Some argued that the Army's doctrine in focusing on the operational art of war was little more than the equivalent of the Navy's FXTIs and FOTIs, but that *British Maritime Doctrine* was different. BMD took the discussion to the next level, and thus was Britain's first real military strategic doctrine.

In the minds of its lead authors, Codner and Grove, the purpose of *BMD* was twofold: to present a coherent rationale for post-Cold War maritime strategy and to provide a Trojan Horse by which maritime thinking would be injected into the joint debate. First, the extensive glossary captured the language in which the debate over joint doctrine would develop. Second – a novelty – it was maritime doctrine as opposed to naval doctrine, concerned with the application of maritime power drawn from all three services, sea- and land-based, supported by national and commercial resources, and exercising influence over sea, land, and air environments. Third, *BMD* contained the underlying thesis that maritime power is inherently joint and demonstrated the Navy's clear understanding that future military operations would be joint operations. And fourth, *BMD* was unclassified, and thus accessible to and indeed aimed as much at politicians and their advisers, journalists, scholars, and other influencers, as at serving officers.[213]

In sum, *British Maritime Doctrine* recycled Corbett's ideas and presented them anew for the post-Cold War environment. This chimed well with Jock, who was keen to press his joint credentials, and he sent copies under covering letters to ministers and others. A general election and a change of government was in the offing and having no inkling who Labour's new Secretary of State for Defence would be, Jock sent copies to several members of both Houses of Parliament. This was well received, not least by the current Defence Secretary,

Portillo, who was particularly pleased that it emphasised its place within the framework of joint doctrine, and by Jim Callaghan, the former Prime Minister, who hoped that it would open some peoples' eyes to "the truths that had been in great danger of being forgotten".

In the foreword to first edition of *BMD*, Jock emphasised that doctrine was not dogma. Rather it was an anvil upon which ideas were forged or, as Jock called it, a "starting point for future debate". In the light of what Jock would achieve during the forthcoming SDR and his speech at RUSI, the *Maritime Contribution to Joint Operations*, a second, revised edition of *British Maritime Doctrine* was published in 1999.

Jock and Annie at HMS *Dryad* in the rain for the 50th anniversary of D-Day, 4 June 1994. Source: Slater archive.

# Chapter 23: People Matter

When in July 1995 Jock became First Sea Lord, he inherited a system of career management of officers of the Royal Navy and Royal Marines, a pattern of specialisation and subspecialisation, and personnel management that was well established but that belonged to a much larger body of officers. Changes were underway.

## Management of Personnel

The office of Second Naval Lord had been created in 1830 and was restyled Second Sea Lord in 1904. In 1917 the title was changed to the Second Sea Lord and Chief of Naval Personnel (2SL/CNP) and by the late 1970s and early 1980s, in a Navy of 65,000 people, he was supported by half a dozen directors-general and directors. Through these directors, who mainly inhabited the attics and warrens of the Old Admiralty Building on the north side of Whitehall, 2SL/CNP was responsible for the policy of recruitment, training, pay, and conditions of service, while the Commander-in-Chief, Naval Home Command (CNH), which had been created in 1969 with headquarters in Portsmouth, was responsible for the execution of that policy. These roles were merged into 2SL/CNP-CNH when the old Admiralty personnel departments were rusticated to Portsmouth. However, while the Naval Secretary belonged in the organisational pyramid of the Second Sea Lord, he continued to report directly to the First Sea Lord for certain aspects of his work. There was more than one Second Sea Lord who was irked by this.

The Naval Secretary, an office established in 1800 when it was styled 'Private Secretary to the First Lord of the Admiralty', used to have direct access to the political head of the Navy, and in 1912 a new and reforming First Lord of the Admiralty, Winston Churchill, chose Rear-Admiral David Beatty to fill the appointment.[214] Later, the Naval Secretary reported to the First Sea Lord, the professional head of the service, and advised on flag officers' appointments.

The WRNS had already been absorbed into the Navy proper; in 1993 the Officers Study Group (OSG) recommended an end to the schoolmaster or Instructor Branch and medical officers' careers were seriously affected by *Front Line First*. Rear-Admiral Alan West, Jock's Naval Secretary for his first few months as First Sea Lord, had supervised the move of the personnel departments to Portsmouth. Now a Naval Manpower Agency (NMA) under the Second Sea Lord would be set up. NMA's purpose was to ensure that sufficient manpower was available and effectively deployed in peace, crisis, major crisis, and war.

West had already been appointed by Bathurst as Commander of the UK Task Group, thus setting him off on the trajectory which, after being a successful Chief of Defence Intelligence and Commander-in-Chief Fleet, would see West become First Sea Lord from 2002–06. "Actually, he was lucky because, at that stage, I did not rate him as highly as others … He has merely proved that luck plays a very large part in senior careers!" Jock chose Rear-Admiral Fabian Malbon – "much more my cup of tea" – as the next Naval Secretary and the chief executive of the NMA. He had great confidence in Malbon's understanding of the needs of senior officers and their appointments.[215]

## The Captains' Plot

The Naval Assistant to the Naval Secretary was always a long-serving captain and advised on captains' appointments. Below him there used to be other senior captains as directors of naval appointments for each specialisation: seamen, engineers, supply and secretariat (logisticians), instructors, and the former WRNS, who curated the careers of more junior officers. (The Royal Marines had their own military secretary.) Admirals' appointments – the flag plot – were the prerogative of the First Sea Lord but promotion to flag rank from the captains' plot was slightly more by consensus. Although the First Sea Lord was absolute (Jock claimed that as First Sea Lord "I could do anything"), this lack of direct influence over the selection board was an irritant to successive First Sea Lords.

In 1982 Rear-Admiral 'Dicky' Fitch, who was Naval Secretary from 1980–83, provided a rare glimpse of the system in action. In a personal letter to each serving captain announcing redundancies and reductions under the Nott defence review, he told them that eighteen captains would be leaving early in a first round of redundancies and that five flag posts would be disestablished. He reminded his readers that:[216]

> Officers are selected for promotion into vacancies by the Promotion Committee chaired by the First Sea Lord and comprising the four other Naval Members of the Admiralty Board, the two Commanders-in-Chief [Fleet and Home], and, when appropriate, the Head[s] of Specialisation. As far as practicable selections are spread amongst the four GL [General List] specialisations in proportion to their size … It has never been the custom to promulgate the resultant career factor for promotions to the Flag List and First Sea Lord does not intend to change this. I can, however, tell you that overall, during the next few years (up to 1986), about one Captain in five is likely to be promoted. Thereafter prospects should be somewhat better (since there will be fewer Captains) unless there are further cuts in the Establishment.

Jock was in the South Atlantic in HMS *Illustrious* when he received his copy of the letter. His comment was, "such a nice letter to receive after almost 100 days at sea!".

Fitch did not mention another important decision, that the opportunity and performance of officers in the Falklands War would not alter the captains' and flag plots: pre-war decisions would not be changed. Thus, although he had done well as Commodore Amphibious Warfare and had commanded the amphibious assault group Task Group 317.0 with some success, Captain Mike Clapp retired as a captain in 1984, while the commanding officer of HMS *Intrepid*, who had been junior to Clapp and who was perceived by some not to have had such a good war, was promoted in 1985 to rear-admiral. Other captains who had done well during the war were also passed over for further promotion.

The precise system varied over time and by the 1990s the board for promotion from OF5/6 to OF7 (a scale of rank used by NATO) from captain/commodore to rear-admiral, was known as the flag promotion board and consisted of the uniformed Navy Board and the professional heads of service, sitting without the First Sea Lord. Several First Sea Lords were disconcerted by not having a greater input into this board, which voted on lists prepared by the Naval Secretary. Six to twelve months before promotion, captains were short-listed and presented to the promotion board in an order of priority. After voting, the board would forward perhaps three names for two slots on the flag plot.

## Pollock's Problem

Jock was aware that 20 years before, when Admiral Sir Michael Pollock was First Sea Lord from 1971–74,[217] he became concerned that the naval appointments and promotion system did not give his potential admirals time to gain the breadth of experience they needed for the highest appointments in defence. Consequently, he exercised his prerogative to 'dip down' the list to choose two captains to be promoted to rear-admiral three years before the earliest date that could have been expected. The officers he chose were captains AJ Miller and JHF Eberle.

The gifted Miller had been Jock's divisional officer at Dartmouth, where the young men worshipped him, and he had enjoyed several commands at sea. He had just six years' seniority as a captain before he was promoted aged 45. He became Flag Officer Second Flotilla in 1972, and attended the same tactical course as Jock, who was about to command HMS *Jupiter*. However, Miller took to the bottle and was retired 'sick' two years later.[218]

Eberle, known in his youth as 'Brainbox', became Assistant CFS in 1972, then FOST from 1974–75, Flag Officer Aircraft Carriers and Amphibious Ships from 1975–77, CFS and a member of the Admiralty Board between 1977 and 1979, and Commander-in-Chief Fleet from 1979–81, before his favour with the incumbent First Sea Lord ran out. He was sent sideways to be Commander-in-Chief Naval Home Command from 1981–82. Having been groomed for stardom for ten years, it was still thought that he might become First Sea Lord or chair the NATO Military Committee, or even be CDS. However, after a vetting by Prime Minister Margaret Thatcher's closest aides, she, quite rightly in Eberle's view, appointed Sir John Fieldhouse, who had just won the Falklands War for her, as First Sea Lord. Instead, Eberle, whose outspokenness included his views that Britain had an over-sufficiency of nuclear weapons and that the nuclear deterrent should be paid for by the central defence budget and not by the Navy alone, was offered the appointment of VCDS. Perhaps he misunderstood the rising power of VCDS, but he declined, saying, "being vice anyone would not be my choice". He resigned, aged only 56 to spend the next ten years at Chatham House as an influential and successful director of the Royal Institute for International Affairs.[219]

Pollock's experiment was not repeated, though the problem he had tried to address persisted, as appointments common between the services became more numerous and more significant, and the length (and pattern) of naval officers' promotions and appointments was too brief to produce strong candidates for some of the most important joint or tri-service appointments.

## Officers Study Group

Jock was VCDS and therefore not on the Navy Board when in April 1993 the OSG, under the chairmanship of the Second Sea Lord, Vice-Admiral Sir Michael Layard, made its report.[220] The OSG recognised that the structure of the officer corps had remained essentially unchanged for 37 years and the many proposals for change in its 100-page report would have far-reaching effects.[221]

It recommended that the distinction between General List officers who joined for a full career, Supplementary List officers, who joined for short careers, and Special Duties officers who were promoted from the lower deck, should all be removed. While recognising the need for higher education, it rejected the idea of in-service degrees in favour of degree courses at state universities, a decision that would lead to the closure of the Royal Naval Engineering College Manadon. The OSG also described the use of rank by Royal Marines officers depending on whether they were serving ashore or afloat as "anomalous and unfair".

While recognising the requirement for 'platform-based' skills (that is, surface ship, submarine, aircraft, or Royal Marines commando), which must be the basis on which the officer corps was structured, the OSG also saw the need for more senior officers to develop business skills and it was proposed to address 'Pollock's Problem', the need for high-calibre officers to be fast-tracked to flag rank and promotion to lieutenant commander, by selection, thereby allowing early promotion for more able officers.

## One Star

Captains (OF5) served nine years in the rank or until aged 55 before they were retired or were promoted. The rank of commodore (OF6 or 1-star) was not used in the Navy except as a non-substantive appointment to denote the most senior captain in a naval base or barracks or of a flotilla. Commodore rank was only held while in a specific appointment, after which the holder reverted to the rank of captain. There was a pay anomaly too in the Navy, whereby captains, on gaining six years seniority, were paid as OF6 or 1-star and qualified for a commodore's pension. This gave some flexibility in appointing captains, since an appointment could be filled by a junior captain or by a senior or 'over six years' captain. Similar rules applied in the Royal Marines, where the rank of brigadier was also non-substantive.

This caused some jealousy in the other services, where promotion from OF5 to OF6 was by selection, and scorn from the Treasury, which sought to reduce the number of naval officers who qualified for 1-star pay and pensions. Arguing that the Navy should align closely with the other services, the OSG recommended that rank of commodore (OF6) in the Navy should be made selective and substantive.[222] After a 1-star review led by the Naval Assistant to the Naval Secretary, Captain Bryan Burns, an officer structure that included substantive commodores and brigadiers was approved by the Navy Board chaired by Jock in 1996.[223]


## Schoolies

Concern over the OSG and criticism of *Front Line First* merged into general unhappiness about change, and Jock, as one of its architects, had to face disapproving comment as defence in general and the Navy in particular moved into the implementation phases of these studies.

The OSG had recommended that the future officer structure of the Navy should be based on four platform skills: warfare, engineering, supply, and the Royal Marines. The platform skills of the 'schoolies', or schoolmasters in the Instructor Branch, meteorology, and oceanography, should be subsumed into the warfare branch. Other skills such as training, which the schoolies brought to the Navy, would be reallocated, so while a significant proportion of instructor officers might transfer to other branches, the branch would cease to exist after some three centuries.[224]

In July 1996 Jock bravely accepted an invitation to attend the historic final dinner of the schoolmasters held at HMS *Sultan*. Many of those present objected to the changes, and it was not an easy evening. In his speech, Jock looked back with pride at what the branch had achieved in its long history but, he said, the time had come for change as part of the revolution being experienced at the end of the Cold War, the consequent downsizing of the armed forces, and the recent streamlining of support structures designed to maintain and enhance the front line. Inevitably, such a revolution could not be conducted without an element of pain and grief for those who saw their hard-earned prospects eroded. Jock appreciated only too well why some schoolies had mixed feelings about the OSG and the 'platform-derived structure' at the core of its recommendations. However, he was unsentimental that the skills of the instructor branch would in future be nurtured under the auspices of the warfare and engineering branches.

## Royal Marines

Royal Marines officers' ranks were out of kilter with the Navy and the Army. A major Royal Marines was equivalent to a commander in the Navy when serving afloat and to a lieutenant colonel in the Army when serving ashore. This was just about manageable in a single-service environment, but with the increasing number of joint appointments it was becoming confusing. Also, the issue rankled with the Army because their commanding officers of battalions were lieutenant-colonels, while the equivalent Royal Marines commandos were commanded by Marines colonels, who were therefore better paid (and more experienced).

The OSG proposed that the Royal Marines officers' rank structure be aligned with its Royal Navy counterparts, and that command of Royal Marines commandos be at the rank of colonel and, even more controversially, that Royal Marines officers adopt naval badges of rank. This proposal was about to be put to the Navy Board when the CGRM, Lieutenant General Sir Robin Ross, consulted by phone two of his senior subordinates, the commander of 3 Commando Brigade, Brigadier David Pennefather, and Brigadier Jonathan Thomson. They were thoroughly, intensely against the idea, and in consequence Ross baulked at the rank changes to the surprise of the Board and not least the First Sea Lord Bathurst. Bathurst is alleged to have said of this incident: "Never let this issue be tabled again at a Navy Board meeting."

Nevertheless, later, when the matter did return to the Navy Board, the choices were starker: either naval badges of rank and titles, or alignment of ranks and seniority with the Army. Major General Pennefather was now CGRM and Jock was First Sea Lord. This had to be sold to the Royal Marines and Jock noted that, whereas those serving in the Corps could see the logic of the changes, some retired officers were more sceptical. The outcome was that all Royal Marines officers up to the rank of lieutenant colonel were advanced by one rank, as shown in this table:

| NATO code | Stars | Royal Navy – new | Royal Navy – old | Royal Marines – new | Royal Marines – old | Army |
|---|---|---|---|---|---|---|
| OF10 | ***** | Admiral of the Fleet | Admiral of the Fleet | | | Field Marshal |
| OF9 | **** | Admiral | Admiral | General | General | General |
| OF8 | *** | Vice-Admiral | Vice-Admiral | Lieutenant General | Lieutenant General | Lieutenant General |
| OF7 | ** | Rear-Admiral | Rear-Admiral | Major General | Major General | Major General |
| OF6 | * | Commodore | Captain | Brigadier | Colonel | Brigadier |
| OF5 | - | Captain | | Colonel | Lieutenant Colonel | Colonel |
| OF4 | - | Commander | Commander | Lieutenant Colonel | Major | Lieutenant Colonel |
| OF3 | - | Lieutenant Commander | Lieutenant Commander | Major | Captain | Major |

It was also clear to Jock that the Royal Marines were losing much talent because of a glass ceiling, and at about this time the service produced a report proposing the integration of its officers into the naval appointing system. In the words of the author:[225]

> It was one of the most straightforward and least controversial pieces of work that I have ever undertaken. Everyone to whom I spoke thought that it was a good idea and that the continuation of the Dedicated Appointments System was out of date and unhelpful to RMs [Royal Marines] and appointers alike … RMs should cease to be appointed to dedicated RM appointments and should become members of the Common Appointments System – the Naval Assistant [Burns] was in favour, CGRM [Pennefather] was in favour, and Jock [First Sea Lord] said 'yes'.

Jock was fully supportive of bringing the talented and cerebral Royal Marines into the fold after he met Colonel Rob Fry, who commanded 45 Commando in Arbroath from 1996–97. He wanted to bring him into the Whitehall front line and Fry became the first Royal Marines officer in modern times to head a naval staff division. Beverley, who had led much of the reform within the Corps, was delighted that the abundant talent within had been unleashed: "Jock's terrific interest and support had been crucial to the success of this rather historic evolution".[226]

## Common Appointments

Twenty years after Pollock's experiment Jock saw that with an even smaller officer corps it would be ever more important to oversee the captains' list and to determine who might be promoted to rear-admiral; he wanted more control over who would be promoted to the rank.

When in London, Burns, the Naval Assistant, had discussed captains' appointments with the First Sea Lord in his office, but after being rusticated in 1994 to Portsmouth and with Jock becoming First Sea Lord in 1995, he grew accustomed to calling on Jock at Grenville Lodge – usually on Monday mornings or Friday afternoons. The OSG had foreseen a greater role for what it called the Common Appointments Committee, which effectively became a two-man committee consisting of Jock and Burns. At first, they did not discuss how the captains' plot dovetailed into the flag plot, but eventually Jock made Burns privy to this. Burns had by now added new-style Royal Marines colonels to the captains' plot, and while Malbon was preoccupied with the NMA, Jock acquired near complete control over the promotion and appointing plot for all senior officers.

## Senior Appointments

Earlier, White, while home on leave from Gibraltar, had exchanged handwritten letters with Jock in which they discussed the flag plot including the future of Admiral Peter Abbott, who was currently Commander-in-Chief Fleet.[227] White agreed that Abbott should relieve Jock as First Sea Lord, since Abbott had more experience of the MoD than White and would be better at winning Whitehall battles over the Navy's need for a new generation of aircraft and aircraft carriers. White generously concluded that: "You should without hesitation count me out [as a future First Sea Lord] … you should not allow friendships or kindness to influence your decision, which must be in the sole interests of the Navy and defence."

Jock's problem was that having been asked to nominate an admiral as VCDS in 1997 the flag plot needed to be adjusted. Admiral Sir John Brigstocke, who had enjoyed a dramatic rise through the Navy, had been earmarked to go as Deputy Supreme Allied Commander Atlantic by Bathurst, but for family health reasons he was unable to accept. Instead, Jock told him in late 1996 that he would be promoted to full admiral (4-star) and become Second Sea Lord, and that it was "one of the most demanding and influential appointments and one to which you could bring strong leadership and the enviable experience you have been fortunate to accumulate as a captain and on the flag list. I was incidentally particularly attracted to having a Second Sea Lord with the credit of [having been] a senior fleet flag officer and ACNS."

Jock, feeling the need for a collegiate view, consulted his predecessors Bathurst and Oswald, and over a lunch outlined his determination "that the Royal Navy should not be seen off again". Jock thought that Abbott was the right man to become VCDS and a strong candidate to become CDS in succession to General Charles Guthrie, and that he should be relieved at Northwood by Vice-Admiral Mike Boyce, who would in due course relieve Jock as First Sea Lord.[228] Vice-Admiral Jeremy Blackham was the right person to return to the MoD as the 3-star Deputy Chief of the Defence Staff (Equipment Capability), and Jock had already earmarked Vice-Admiral Ian Garnett as the next Chief of Joint Operations (CJO). "This was quite a change round at the top for my final year, but I was determined to have two possible contenders for the next CDS and Abbott and Boyce fitted the bill."

Rear-Admiral Nigel Essenhigh, who was ACDS (Programmes) during the SDR, had impressed everyone in the MoD and particularly Secretary of State Robertson, who was keen to see him as the next CJO. Essenhigh was preparing himself for this.[229] However, when Robertson rang Jock to propose this, Jock saw the request as interference in his professional responsibilities and emphasised that Garnett, who was already nominated, was particularly well suited for the job – and so it proved. Besides, Jock had an altogether different plot for Essenhigh, as the relief for Boyce as the next Commander-in-Chief Fleet in 1998, an appointment that would require a double jump directly from rear-admiral (2-star) to admiral (4-star). The plot was kept in great secrecy between Jock and Malbon, and when Essenhigh was eventually told by Jock, Essenhigh wondered "if he was talking to the right person".

Jock was hoping to enjoy a close relationship with Brigstocke as Second Sea Lord and, during a routine call in November 1997, revealed his intention regarding the senior flag plot, not least Jock's own plan to stand down in October 1998. Further, he had recommended to Robertson that Boyce should be the next First Sea Lord and that Essenhigh should be Boyce's successor as Commander-in-Chief Fleet. No such rumour had reached Brigstocke, who was convinced that he would only spend a short time as Second Sea Lord before becoming Commander-in-Chief Fleet. Brigstocke pointed out that it was extraordinary that an officer, currently a rear-admiral, should be earmarked as Commander-in-Chief Fleet. Brigstocke regarded Essenhigh's elevation as blocking future possibilities for him, and he surprised Jock by his vehemence.

Strangely, Essenhigh's double promotion mirrored another one that had taken place half a century earlier, when Jock's Uncle Ned heard from the wartime First Sea Lord, Admiral Sir Dudley Pound, that his relief as Commander-in-Chief Mediterranean was to be Rear-Admiral Henry Harwood, who would receive a double-jump promotion to full admiral. Not only did Cunningham doubt whether Harwood was the right man for the job, he was also concerned that several vice-admirals would be passed over. When he met Pound, he noted: "I had a two-hour interview with DP [Pound] and told him just what I thought about Harwood's appointment. I shook him very badly, I could see that, but it was too late."[230]

Fifty years later Jock was similarly shaken, and saddened, too, that Brigstocke, one of the most able officers of his generation who had risen to the top after a most distinguished career, should be so dissatisfied with his lot. To Jock's great disappointment and discomfort this wrecked their relationship. Over subsequent months, Jock would need to rely on the Naval Secretary Malbon to keep him informed of the mood in the Portsmouth headquarters, whither, like Achilles, Brigstocke withdrew.[231]

Essenhigh's promotion was welcomed in *The Times* and more importantly by the fleet. He was two years at Northwood as Commander-in-Chief and when Boyce did indeed become Chief of the Defence Staff, Essenhigh took over as First Sea Lord in January 2001. However, fifteen months later he stood down for personal reasons that were never disclosed to Jock, who felt badly let down, ruefully confiding in his diary: "I could just hear poor John Brigstocke saying, 'I told you so'."

# Chapter 24: Unfinished Business

The MoD's policy regarding homosexuality in the armed forces rumbled on throughout Jock's time as First Sea Lord. It was something he could well have done without as there were so many other more important topics in the in-tray. His firm views were consistent with MoD policy, but he was disappointed to discover that the other Chiefs "were keeping their heads down and allowing me to make the running … I was very well aware that I had widespread support in the naval service, although I was also aware that attitudes in the country were changing."

## Don't Ask, Don't Tell

While serving in HMS *Newcastle* in 1994, Lieutenant Commander Duncan Lustig-Prean was approached by a blackmailer who had discovered that he was gay. Lustig-Prean reported the incident but was subsequently interrogated himself and discharged from the Navy with the loss of his commission and his pension rights. He became leader of the campaign to lift the ban on gays serving in the armed forces, was chairman of Rank Outsiders, a group campaigning for gay men and lesbians in the armed forces, and was its spokesman and campaigns adviser when he addressed a meeting of the RUSI in 1999.[232] Lustig-Prean's case was cogent and he took no pleasure in dragging his country through the courts: "Indeed, I think that it is quite wrong that our armed forces should be run by the judiciary, and it is a crying shame that we have reached this stage five years on from the start of legal proceedings." He agreed that there was no place in the military workspace for sexual conduct of any kind. There were other nations, with whom British armed forces operated, that did not have a ban on homosexuals and had codes of conduct and regulations controlling the behaviour of their people. A policy of 'don't ask don't tell', however, would be "an expression of institutionalised hypocrisy". What was needed was a policy like that of the Australian armed forces with regard to women – a policy of 'no touch'. The MoD was unique in having an absolute ban based upon orientation rather than sexual activity: this, he said, was like the bans of earlier eras regarding Jews, black people, and women at sea.

Lustig-Prean, invited to speak at RUSI, said that if Jock had used similar language about black people as he had been quoted as using in the national press about homosexuals, he would have been charged with incitement to racial hatred. Lustig-Prean saw little difference to incitement to homophobia. The MoD's present policy was based on a perceived prejudice in some people's minds, resulting in the dismissal of people of excellent character and unblemished record whose usefulness to the service had never been in dispute. These people were discharged only because of a private aspect of their private life. They were not discharged because of any misconduct or any inappropriate misbehaviour. Rather, the reason for their dismissal was intrusive and unpleasant surveillance or interrogation by the authorities. Lustig-Prean thought that it was Kafkaesque to argue that homosexuals were susceptible to blackmail if the very ban itself placed them at that risk.

Whatever personal views Jock held he strongly denied ever having used prejudicial language against homosexuals, and through the Director of Public Relations protested that he was only implementing government policy, which he advocated should remain unchanged. He firmly believed that he was expressing the views of the Navy at large, something that Lustig-Pean eventually acknowledged was so.[233]


## Less than *Brilliant*

Public opinion regarding homosexuality was changing. After the decision recommending that Wrens should be able to go to sea, concerns about 'loss of femininity' were sometimes a code for the discussion of sexuality. The West Report did not pass without a civil servant minuting that "we must do nothing which might make more difficult the defence of the continued treatment of homosexuality as an offence in law for service personnel."[234] Among those opposed to women in ships there was a genuine concern about heterosexual liaison, and in his research, West was often asked whether, if the rules regarding women at sea were changed, would there be new rules for homosexuals? He had found that a significant number of officers felt it wrong if they were not.[235]

August 1995 saw the release of a fly-on-the-wall BBC TV documentary about life in HMS *Brilliant*. A film crew spent ten weeks in *Brilliant* during a deployment to the Mediterranean and the producer had, not unexpectedly, concentrated on some of the seamier sides of service life. The overall impression of the six-part programme (published as a book, *HMS Brilliant – In a Ship's Company*, by Chris Terrill) was that young men, when not preoccupied with their duties on board, tended to think about women, alcohol, and how safe their jobs might be. "Well!" commented the *Portsmouth Evening News*, "Isn't that what you would expect of any young men?" There was an unpleasant misogynistic undertone to the series, however, and comments made by some of the ship's company about women at sea were included in the broadcast. One surprising effect of the programme was to turn one particular misogynist and homophobe sailor into a hero for some of the programme's ten million viewers.[236]

Jock made his views clear, telling Radio Scotland, "I am extremely disappointed in the production. What I'm getting is a distorted image of the Royal Navy. It fails to show the deep professionalism, and the high calibre of its people. The audience gets a view of the Navy which makes me extremely uncomfortable: it is not the Navy I know, and those I have spoken to within the Navy are deeply disturbed by what has been shown. I think there is far too much concentration on peripheral activity. There's an inference that all sailors do is get drunk ashore and the reality is not that."

Nevertheless, the Director of Naval Recruiting placed advertisements in national newspapers which stated that 'Every episode is worth watching. If you like what you see, fill in the coupon or contact your local careers office'. Recruitment jumped.


**The Leaked Letter**

During autumn of 1995 the campaign for an end to the ban on homosexuals in the military appeared to be approaching resolution. The case had already passed through the Court of Appeal and campaigners were preparing to go to the European Court of Human Rights. Some 250 sacked military homosexuals wished to claim their jobs back and the MoD feared a wave of compensation claims. Lord Justice Brown had noted that "the tide of history is against the Defence Ministry" adding that "old prejudices" were breaking down and that "Lawrence of Arabia would not be welcomed in today's armed forces".

Minister for the Armed Forces Nicholas Soames was reported to be searching for a compromise and appeared to be surprised that such stern resistance had come from the military and, most tellingly in his mind, from the Navy, which he thought, having allowed women to serve in warships, would not object to lifting the 'gay ban'. Meanwhile, Admiral Sir Hugo White, Jock's successor as Commander-in-Chief Fleet, had conducted a survey in the fleet and wrote to Jock as First Sea Lord, summarising his findings. White's letter contained fifteen points, all against the lifting of the ban on gays, and ended strongly:[237]

> The top brass are all too vulnerable to social politics and possible fluctuations of Ministerial view. If military top management is really alert to and shares the deeply felt concerns of the front line over preserving current rules on homosexuality, why is it not more overtly and vigorously fighting the corner? It seems to many that the PR battle is being left to retired officers who, despite their best intentions, seem to be out of touch with the real issues as seen from wardrooms and messdecks … This issue is widely seen as yet another potentially fundamental change and erosion in conditions of service to add to women at sea, options for change, defence cost studies, and the current fleet tasking overload, to name but a few … the fleet … should not be used as an arena for what they perceive to be social experimentation as a result of a vociferous lobbying by a minority group … The services are trained fighting forces, used to privation, and in the case of the fleet, its people are cooped up in very crowded conditions with little escape from one another for weeks and often months on end. In the last resort they accept that they are expected to fight and if necessary to die in order to protect a country and society whose freedoms they cannot always themselves enjoy, and in the case of homosexual tolerance strongly do not wish to. It is not at all clear to the sailor why the Armed Forces have to mirror society when their conditions of service are so very different … Hugo.

The letter was widely circulated and leaked to the *Daily Mail*, which commented that White's views carried much weight since they were the opinions of a fighter and not a deskbound administrator. There was no leak enquiry and the identity of whoever leaked the letter is not known. At the time it was thought that Rank Outsiders had leaked documents to *The Guardian*, whereas leaks to the *Daily Mail* were by government sources. However, the *Daily Mail* missed an essential feature of White's letter: that he was not alone in his views about homosexuals at sea and that his letter was a consensus of the views of the fleet.

December 1995 brought a fresh blow when on New Year's Eve the *Sunday Telegraph* picked up the *Daily Mail*'s story and included a quote from Jock stating that he and his colleagues were in no doubt that the existing policy should stand. Jock said that the reporting was "absolute nonsense!".[238]

## Changing Attitudes

Reinforced by White's letter, Jock still felt that it was his duty to oppose any change in government policy regarding the ban on gays in the Royal Navy and Royal Marines. There was no doubt in his mind that his stand had the full support of the vast majority in the Navy, who judged such activities to be incompatible with service life. However, he was becoming increasingly uneasy about how the matter was being managed, was privately horrified at how some sailors had been hounded out, and felt that there should be much more sensitivity in addressing the issue. He was not supported in his personal or professional views by the other Chiefs, and compared to the Navy, the Army and the RAF were much more tolerant of homosexuality.[239]

It was always supposed that the kai-tais (transvestites) in Bugis Street, Singapore were airmen from RAF Changi, and, as revealed in Peter Parker's *Some Men in London: Queer Life, 1960–1967*, 'a bit of scarlet' had long been a euphemism for homosexual activity by guardsmen who used to hang out in a named set of public houses.[240] One very senior soldier told this author that "it was 'not on' in a civilised society to be so beastly to gays and the whole thing [would not fall] apart because there are a few gays in the Navy."[241]

The other Chiefs saw an end to the gay ban as inevitable, while Nicholas Soames chortled that in the Second World War "the Guards, and the Welsh Guards in particular, were full of homosexuals; some of the best officers were homosexuals". As far as the government was concerned, ministers would defend the status quo until the issue went to the European court and at that stage "we would decide [to] give way rather than defend a hopeless case". Soames was sorry if Jock had become a target for the gay community.[242]

At the time of the debate Simon Moore was captain of BRNC. Moore's brother was a homosexual, "a good man but who had recently died after contracting AIDS". From talking to his young officers under training, male and female, Moore gained the strong impression that they would object greatly if the Navy "flew in the face of the changes in society generally by refusing to accept gays". This resonated with Moore's own views and at a routine call he told Jock so: "I remember him being considerably surprised, but he listened carefully and clearly took in the message"[243]

Jock's mind was not closed; he registered that young officers simply did not understand why he was taking such a strong line, writing afterwards that "The modern generation fresh from school were perfectly used to such activities and took them for granted! I did wonder if I was terribly out of touch, and I knew this issue would become increasingly high profile in the year or two ahead. [Moore] certainly made me sit up and think."

## The End of the Ban

New Labour was elected to power in 1997 and when Jock retired in 1998 the matter of ending the 'gay ban' was unresolved. Subsequently, however, Lustig-Prean won his argument in the High Court and Court of Appeal, but the judges said that while the ban was not justified they could not overturn it. The case was taken to Strasbourg and the European Court of Human Rights, and, while public opinion was running strongly in favour of ending the ban, the new Commander-in-Chief Fleet, Essenhigh, wrote to the new First Sea Lord, Boyce, setting out his strong moral and practical objections to any change in the rules and encouraging Boyce to resist change.[244]

In the event, the European Court of Human Rights vindicated the rights of lesbians and gay men, and the Chiefs were blindsided when Secretary of State George Robertson, aided by his top civil servants, and bypassing any objections that the military might have, announced a policy change. The government conceded, and the ban on gays was formally lifted on 12 January 2000.

# Chapter 25: Portillo's Poll, 1996

Six years earlier, when it had become clear that Inge, having become CDS in the fallout from Harding's affair with Bienvenida Buck, intended to hang on for a three-year term, Bathurst understood that the only way that a sailor could be lined up as Inge's successor was for him, Bathurst, to stand down early to give Jock a two-year stint as First Sea Lord. Jock would then be only 59 when the next CDS was due to be appointed. When Bathurst told Rifkind of his plan to nominate Jock as his relief, Rifkind asked: "What about Hugo White?" White was the incumbent Commander-in-Chief Fleet. Bathurst replied that, sadly, he had no further employment for him and he would be placed on the retired list.[245] Rifkind was not content, and he arranged for White to go to Gibraltar as governor while remaining on the active list and available to relieve Jock as First Sea Lord, if, as expected, sometime in 1997, Jock were chosen as CDS.[246]

Michael Portillo replaced Rifkind as Defence Secretary in July 1995 and in the same month Bathurst retired as First Sea Lord and was promoted Admiral of the Fleet, the last First Sea Lord to be promoted to 5-star rank. Bathurst's promotion was not straightforward. For many incarnations the First Sea Lord had been an admiral of the fleet, a 5-star officer, and, when this practice ceased and 5-star rank was preserved for the CDS himself, it had been the custom for many years to promote the First Sea Lord on the day he retired to Admiral of the Fleet, so that notionally he remained on the active list and received an extra £10,000 per year (at 1990s pay scales) for having been head of his service. The Bett report had proposed the end of this practice, and Secretary of State Rifkind had pocketed this saving. It took a 40-minute argument with Rifkind and his Private Secretary Margaret Aldred, and a further delay of six weeks after Bathurst's promotion had been approved by the Queen, to convince the

Secretary of State that Bathurst should indeed be Admiral of the Fleet. "I only just got in under the door," Bathurst said.[247]

## Newspaper Rumours

The year had opened well for Jock, with a profile in the *Sunday Times* under the strapline, 'The Navy's lucky to have Jock at the helm but they won't have him for long – he's a contender for Chief of the Defence Staff'. The newspaper described how "the smart money is already on him succeeding Inge."[248] Discussions about who would take over from Inge opened in Whitehall in early 1996, when Jock learned that it was hoped to make an announcement before the summer break. There was a hot debate raging behind the scenes about whether it should be him or the CGS, Guthrie, as the next CDS. Jock had many friends and supporters in the MoD and especially in the central defence staff of all three services and among the senior civil servants, including his successor as VCDS, Air Chief Marshal Sir John Willis, but Jock was disappointed to learn that Inge was working hard behind the scenes to undermine his candidacy as CDS and to promote his own protégé, Guthrie. Jock also heard a rumour that the Minister for the Armed Forces, Nicholas Soames, was rooting for Guthrie. The new Permanent Under-Secretary, Richard Mottram, was thought to favour Guthrie, who he thought would be easier to manipulate, and was against Jock and his very public advocacy of new ships. Other ministers were thought to support Jock's candidacy. Jock himself chose to remain silent, knowing that his advocacy of joint operations, his tri-service, national and NATO experience qualified him for the top job.[249]

On 5 September 1996 the Air Force Board gave a dinner at Bentley Priory to which they invited all the Chiefs of Staff. Before dinner, Inge took Jock aside to inform him that tomorrow's *Daily Express* would carry an article saying that he, Inge, would be relieved by Guthrie. The article did not appear, but Jock was left wondering how Inge knew: he suspected that no final decision had been made but detected some underhand work. During an official visit to Turkey and Oman in early October Jock was shown an irritating article in the *Daily Telegraph* that profiled Guthrie as the next CDS. This, together with a piece in the *Sunday Telegraph*'s gossipy 'Albany at Large' column that chronicled the doings and sayings of the great and good, was written by Kenneth Rose.[250]

## Portillo's Poll

Jock correctly assumed that, while no decision had been announced about Inge's successor, the ground was being prepared. In retrospect, he wondered if he had been too reticent in the process and whether he should have brought his predecessors into play sooner, particularly Lord Lewin, a highly respected former CDS. While Inge pressed for Guthrie should be his successor, Portillo, who did not consider himself bound by anything Rifkind had said, agonised over who should relieve Inge. Memories differ about the decision-making process, but it seems likely that Portillo asked his ministers not to consult their officials but to write down the order in which they would recommend the next CDS. The consensus was that, while the courtly Jock was better qualified, the gruff Guthrie was wilier and would be better able to stand up to New Labour, among whose leaders he had already made friends. Jock was campaigning hard for a future that included new carriers, and to some this exhibited a loss of credibility. There was a war in Bosnia, which, despite the role of RFAs and carrier-based aircraft, and of the Royal Marines, Inge and Guthrie represented as an Army matter and that therefore the CDS should be a soldier.

Once Portillo had decided on Guthrie and consulted Prime Minister John Major, he wanted to speak to Inge about how the news should be given to Jock. Inge was in Brunei when Portillo called, and his personal staff officer, Commodore Mark Stanhope (himself, a future First Sea Lord), listened in. "The Secretary of State had rung to talk about the handling of the announcement of Guthrie as the next CDS, and if Inge had known the subject I am sure he would have asked me not to listen in on the call. Nothing astonishing came out of the call to give me a hint of why Guthrie rather than Jock [was chosen], but [on] recognising the colour of my uniform, Inge was embarrassed enough on completion of the call to justify the decision to me saying 'best man for the job'."[251]

## Breaking the News

On the morning of 15 October 1996, once Inge and Jock were back in London, Portillo asked to see Jock. Portillo understood that no sailor had been CDS since the mid-1980s and that Jock was well prepared for the appointment and better qualified than anyone else. He also knew within the MoD that Jock was the clear favourite of the defence staff. However, the decision had been swayed by Inge's belief that the CDS should more often than not be a soldier and that current operations in Bosnia required a soldier. Sitting opposite Portillo at his table, Jock could see that Portillo was extremely uneasy imparting this bad news, even if there was no surprise after a series of "dishonourable leaks". Jock restricted himself to commenting that the handling of this whole matter had been a disgrace and that as the Navy's candidate with national, tri-service, and NATO experience second to none, the decision would simply not be understood by the Navy, nor by many others. This was the first time that a soldier had relieved a soldier as CDS and the decision paid little regard to reasonable rotation. Otherwise, Jock said little more than he was obliged to say – that Guthrie would make an able CDS and would have Jock's support.

Courteously, Portillo showed Jock out of the main door, which led directly onto the corridor, instead of through the outer office, thus avoiding the eyes and sympathy of his staff. As Jock looked along the corridor, he saw Inge standing by the main door of his office nervously waiting for him. Inge was clearly embarrassed as he invited Jock in. There, Jock accused him of outrageous conduct in the handling of the succession and questioned his rationale in recommending Guthrie. Inge became extremely nervous, and his reply was "pathetic and irrational". Jock met this with silence and left by the same door as he entered. Walking back down the corridor to his own office he saw that his star, which had risen for so long, had just fallen out of the sky. Cancelling his engagements, Jock and Annie lunched alone in the Mall House flat reflecting on the future. He sent Guthrie a note of congratulations and Annie sent Guthrie's wife, Kate, a bunch of flowers. The news travelled fast and that evening, as principal guest at the Anchorites' dinner in the Café Royal, Jock was greeted with a standing ovation.[252]

By coincidence, Jock had already invited the admirals of the fleet to come to the MoD for a briefing on 16 October. Those present were Prince Philip, Ashmore, Bathurst, Hill-Norton, Leach, Lewin, Oswald, Pollock, and Staveley. They then retired to the Mall House flat for lunch, where they were joined by several wives. No discussion about the succession of CDS took place until Prince Philip had left and the wives had moved with Annie into the drawing room. The Admirals then gathered round the lunch table and a fierce debate commenced. After Jock gave an account of what had happened, Hill-Norton, "not one for anything other than the full-frontal attack", argued that collectively they should complain immediately to the Prime Minister. Lewin, although supporting some form of formal objection, counselled against such a move because the decision had already been made and it was important that Jock's standing, which remained high, should not be undermined. Ashmore and Leach, although furious that Inge had promoted Guthrie at the Navy's expense, agreed with this.

The Navy Board's Trafalgar Night Dinner was held in Admiralty House on 17 October and the Princess Royal was guest of honour. Among other guests were Portillo and Inge. Portillo's fulsome thank you letter on the morning after carried no hint of the personal drama that had unfolded over the previous few days. Jock was due to fly to Italy on 20 October to visit British personnel serving there, but once Guthrie's appointment was announced he flew via Gibraltar to discuss the situation with White. Their meeting is best described in Jock's words:

> Thank heavens Hugo was an old friend as our meeting could otherwise have been extremely awkward … [As] Hugo and I walked in the garden of the Convent … I asked him, under the circumstances, if he would like to return to London to do the second half of my time as First Sea Lord. Without hesitation, in his selfless way, he absolutely refused to consider this as he thought that it would be bad for the Navy and that I was the right person to lead us through the inevitable defence review that lay ahead. He only had one request and that was to leave Gibraltar as soon as possible in view of his wife Jo's ill health. I, of course, said that I would set this in hand with the Foreign Office as soon as I could, bearing in mind that Malcolm Rifkind was now the Foreign Secretary.

Jock later lobbied for White to be made KCMG. Rifkind agreed that White had done an excellent job as governor of Gibraltar but failed to persuade the wider Foreign Office, and replied that he was "immensely saddened that the original plan did not work out, not least because you would have made an excellent CDS and it would have been good for the Navy".

## The Chiefs' Revolt

It was not just the Admirals who were angry. In December 1996, six of the eight living former CDSs wrote to Prime Minister Major arguing that a principle of reasonable rotation had not been respected. They were Admiral of the Fleet Sir Edward Ashmore, Field Marshal Lord Bramall, Marshal of the Royal Air Force Lord Craig, Admiral of the Fleet Lord Hill-Norton, Admiral of the Fleet Lord Lewin, and Field Marshal Lord Vincent. Field Marshal Lord Carver was sympathetic but refused to join the revolt, and Harding, though willing to join, was black-balled from participation by his own people.

Prince Philip knew and had asked to be kept in touch, but Major's Private Secretary John Holme did not show this letter to the Prime Minister until the end of February 1997, by which time, on 15 January, Bramall, Craig, and Lewin had met Portillo. The meeting allegedly turned fractious when, according to Holme, they were "very rude to Portillo in substance and quite out of order in their approach. I understand that he was furious afterwards – hence the delay in providing advice." This seems to have been an exaggeration, as Portillo recalls no such meeting. However, the PM's Private Secretary further denigrated the former Chiefs by a reference to "Hill-Norton's behaviour, which has become increasingly eccentric"; he has "behaved insultingly to Michael Portillo on several issues of recently".[253]

Meanwhile, Hill-Norton had written to the Cabinet Secretary to complain about the discourtesy of not even acknowledging the former CDSs' letter. The upshot was that on 27 February Major replied politely to each of the former Chiefs: he understood their concerns and was grateful for letting him know, but, he wrote, since 1982 the most important principle of appointing the CDS had been that each appointment should be made on merit. That derived from a view that rotation by service might not always be in the national interest. However, within the defence staff there should be a broad balance of appointments between the services. Major went on to say that the selection of Guthrie to succeed Inge as CDS was made after most careful consideration. "I was fully consulted and agreed with the choice on its merits although there were other excellent candidates whose abilities I much admire. We were fortunate to have such a choice."

There was also some, perhaps deliberate, misunderstanding of the former Chiefs' position: they were not objecting to Guthrie *per se* but to the process by which he had been chosen, and at the end of March 1997 the former Chiefs wrote again to correct "misconceptions and misunderstandings that still seemed to exist". The Prime Minister was wrong in suggesting that a new principle had been introduced in 1982, which, they wrote:

> Refers to a memorandum sent by the then Secretary of State, Sir John Nott, to the then CDS, Lord Lewin, in connection with the change of responsibilities of the CDS and did not reflect the appointing of the CDS … We cannot accept the implication that the Chiefs of Staff can stand aside when it comes to the appointment of the Chief of Defence Staff because their personal interests might sway their professional advice. The service Chiefs of Staff are responsible to the Crown through Parliament for the loyalty and fighting efficiency of their individual services. They are senior professional advisors to the government on matters of defence policy. They are accordingly

intimately concerned in the choice of Chief of Defence Staff and uniquely well placed to give valuable advice.

The letter ended, "we have no wish to prolong this correspondence at this present time, but we would ask that our letters are placed on record for future reference".[254] In March, when the retiring Inge called on the Prime Minster to say his farewell, Holme's brief to Major dismissed the Chiefs' revolt as "a fuss".

Guthrie became Chief of Defence Staff on 2 April 1997; a month later Tony Blair's New Labour won the General Election and on 22 May 1997 Rose was able to record in his diary, after the Welsh Guards annual dinner, "I talk[ed] to Charles Guthrie, who has formed a favourable view of the Labour Cabinet during the past three weeks. He had already, of course, made some contact with the Blair circle before the election and received a friendly reception. He particularly likes the Secretary of State for Defence, George Robertson, who had expected to be made Secretary of State for Scotland. Charles took him to Bosnia, where he declared his admiration and support for our forces."[255]

Jock returned to London after his visit to Gibraltar and Italy, determined not to look back and to do the best he could for the Navy during the remainder of his time as First Sea Lord. However, he harboured a deep sense of injustice and felt deeply the lingering sense that he had failed the Royal Navy.

# Chapter 26: Project Celery

Project Celery was one of the names of the search for a ship that would be suited to a promotional role and be available as a royal yacht. The principal ministries involved, the MoD, FCO, and Department of Trade and Industry were not keen to bear any great proportion of the costs, and British industry was not willing to pay for costs outside the times they were using the yacht.

## Hospital Ship

HMY *Britannia*'s primary role of hospital ship was practised once in 1972 but when the opportunity arose to do so again during the 1982 Falklands War, she was found wanting.[256] She lacked the necessary stability to be used as a hospital in the South Atlantic, and would have been the only ship, besides the carrier HMS *Hermes*, using furnace fuel oil (FFO), which, given her limited range, would have presented a logistical problem. Worse, she was unsuitable for modern medical needs and there were no heads or bathrooms on the deck that was designated as the main hospital ward. There was also some suggestion that the enemy might make her a prestige target. Later, another reason was given: *Britannia* lacked a modern helicopter capability.[257]

Reportedly, *Britannia*'s failure to go to war was a "major blow to the yacht's ship's company who wanted to play their part in the conflict … The decision [not to use her] was also disappointing from a PR perspective as it handed easy ammunition to the critics of the Yacht."[258] In hindsight, if, despite her limited functionality as a hospital ship, the distinctive glossy blue paintwork of her hull had been sacrificed for a coat of white and a few red crosses, she might as a Falklands veteran have won a place in the heart of John Bull. Instead, in the spring and summer of 1982, *Britannia* undertook royal duties and during the winter of 1983–84 was fitted with a sewage treatment plant, the lack of which had stopped her making further visits to North America. She was also converted from FFO consumption to diesel (NATO F76), something that had previously been judged too difficult.[259]

In 1986 *Britannia* was used for evacuating around a thousand people from Aden, the only time in her career that she remotely fulfilled her primary role. However, six years later the Commons was told that in view of her age, *Britannia* was no longer suitable as a hospital ship and, given the availability of other more appropriate vessels, she would be released from her defence role.[260]


## Business Centre

The idea that the royal yacht might have another role was first raised during the administration of Prime Minister Harold Wilson, when the Queen's Private Secretary Michael Adeane wrote to Wilson to say that "Her Majesty and the Duke of Edinburgh have been thinking about ways in which they might be able to help the country during its present economic difficulties. They have in mind the value of an example as much as that of some tangible saving. As a result, I am to say that The Queen hopes that you and the Secretary of State for Defence may feel free to consider the future of the Royal Yacht in connection with any discussions which you may be undertaking about the Armed Services." Wilson "profoundly appreciated Her Majesty's gracious offer and the spirit which prompted it", but after consulting the Chancellor of the Exchequer, the Secretary of State for Defence and (at the Queen's bidding) the First Sea Lord, Admiral Sir Varyl Begg, took "the view that the Royal Yacht should continue to be employed broadly in her present role and that additional use should be made of her as opportunity occurs".[261]

It would be eight years, during the Queen's state visit to Brazil and Chile with Jock in attendance, that this "additional use" would manifest as two 'sea days' off Rio de Janeiro, when *Britannia* took guests to sea to help promote British industry.[262] In the same year off New York, and then in the 1980s, events in which the yacht was used for conferences and commercial events involving industrialists, bankers, financiers, and politicians became regular features of the yacht's programme. The guests would be hosted by their opposite numbers from the UK and there would be presentations, possibly a ceremonial contract signing, and then a reception and a formal lunch or dinner. Sometimes, as an additional draw, the yacht would take visitors to sea. While the Navy met the overheads of staff, services, and fuel, any additional costs were borne by the British companies involved. These trade days, as they became known, were regarded as successful in attracting many millions of pounds of business, far outweighing the lifetime running costs of the yacht.

*Britannia* was again mooted as a savings measure in the 1970s but she survived even the Nott review of 1981.[263] Instead, a major refit in 1987 was intended to prolong her service life for ten years, though no sooner was this complete than the rules changed after the sinking of MS *Herald of Free Enterprise*.[264] This tragedy led to urgent amendments to the International Convention for the Safety of Life at Sea (SOLAS), which were strongly advocated by the British government and covered stability, subdivision of watertight compartments, remote surveillance, and lifeboats (*Britannia* only carried life rafts).

## Project 96

*Britannia* was beginning to look her age and when in 1991 the American General Norman Schwarzkopf was shown round the yacht he is alleged to have remarked in her engine room: "Okay. I've seen the museum piece. Now, where's the real engine room?"[265]

A small team was set up in the MoD at Bath to produce a minimum viable design for a new royal yacht, and a naval staff requirement, number 7089, was raised and became known as 'Project 96', which indicated when the authors thought the new ship might be ready.[266] If she were to carry passengers for trade days she also had to meet the new SOLAS regulations. The royal barge would be kept and the royal apartments would be comparable in size to those in *Britannia*. There would be a dedicated conference room with state-of-the-art facilities, and, because Civil Aviation Authority standards for a light helicopter called for a landing deck, that deck would be significantly larger than the Navy's standards and would give space below for a proper business centre where presentations and other related events could be held, rather than using the royal dining room, which had been the practice in *Britannia*. These design criteria led to a much smaller vessel. However, the team was criticised for not including any naval officers, let alone anyone with experience of *Britannia*, nor any representative from the Palace.

But support for *Britannia* was slowly collapsing and in September 1991 a note between officials said: "It is clear from talking to Sir Robert [Fellowes] that the Royal Family entertain very few hopes of acquiring a new yacht and that they wish to follow a strategy of spinning-out the life of the present vessel as long as possible though successive refits." This note was copied to the FCO, the Treasury, and the Cabinet Office, and to desks in the MoD.[267]

By the early 1990s the Navy had shrunk to 71,000 people and 35 destroyers and frigates. While the Navy was immensely proud of the standards of excellence in *Britannia*, this was at the expense of the manpower needed for the fighting fleet. The option of somehow taking the yacht's costs outside the defence budget was rejected by the Treasury, and the idea of turning *Britannia* into a Defence Support Agency was examined and rejected when FORY argued that the "MoD is not my primary customer … I am so closely involved with the workings of the Palace that it would, in my opinion, be totally inappropriate for me to be subject to Treasury or PAC scrutiny."[268]

The Navy Board, of which Jock was a member as CFS from 1989–91 and as Commander-in-Chief Fleet from 1991–92, felt it would welcome a replacement, but if asked whether a frigate should be paid off to man *Britannia* or whether the build costs should be set against the current naval budget, felt that the fighting fleet should take priority. Jock, as VCDS from 1993–95, was outside the chain of decision-making when two years later the First Sea Lord, Admiral Sir Ben Bathurst, prioritised keeping the naval college at Dartmouth open over running *Britannia*, telling an interviewer in an echo of Prince Philip's words of 25 years before: "There was no way I could tell the fleet that I was prepared to spend money on manning the yacht and not on manning a frigate … I thought the yacht was rather super, but when it came to the choice between the yacht and a frigate, I had to choose the frigate."[269]

When in 1994 Rifkind announced that *Britannia* would be decommissioned in two years' time, Michael Evans, defence correspondent of *The Times* and author of several well-informed stories about *Britannia* and her possible replacement, disclosed that the Queen felt that she no longer needed a yacht to transport her around the Commonwealth. Although the government would examine the possibility of replacing *Britannia*, Evans wrote that there were few who believed that the yacht would be replaced. One of the strongest arguments for decommissioning the yacht, he added, was that she had not been used in her role as a hospital ship either in the Falklands in 1982 or in the Gulf War in 1992.[270]

After Jock became First Sea Lord in July 1995 he was dismayed by a front page article by Evans describing a vessel that would double as a sail-training craft and "would continue the role of promoting British trade and industry on world trips". This was the 'Cadland' ship, which was being promoted by Maldwin Drummond, Libby Purves, and others, which would cost up to £60m to build.[271] Jock was incensed at the suggestion that he was prepared to consider MoD funding. "Nonsense! I had made it quite clear from the start that if there was to be a successor it should not be funded by the MoD apart from the ship's company."[272]

Evans was later awarded the Desmond Wettern Award for Best Journalism after a vote strongly supported by naval staff.[273]

## Project 2002?

Decisions about *Britannia* and her replacement were being taken elsewhere. A small group of ministers comprising the Defence Secretary, the Deputy Prime Minister, the Foreign Secretary, the President of the Board of Trade, the Chancellor of the Exchequer, the Lord Privy Seal, and the Chief Whip, chaired by Prime Minister John Major, were working up a paper on the options for replacing the royal yacht.[274] Jock was not consulted. On 18 December 1995 the group examined a proposal based on the 1991 minimum viable design, which assumed that a reduced royal party would fly between ports, outside caterers would be employed, and the Royal Marines band would be accommodated ashore. The cost would be £55m, though quite soon it was recognised that that figure could reach £80m. This new vessel was known as Project Celery (cost efficient elegant royal yacht).[275]

The group agreed that there were strong arguments for replacing *Britannia*, which enhanced the prestige of the monarchy and the nation and was valued by British industry:[276]

> A few major trade or investment deals would easily recoup the cost … on the other hand … the public's limited appetite for expenditure on the monarchy had been revealed by the reaction to the suggestion that the damage from the Windsor fire would be repaired entirely by public funding … The Queen herself has given no clear indication that she wanted the Yacht replaced since her statement in 1994 that a new Yacht was not necessary for the purposes of royal travel alone … If a decision were taken to replace the Yacht, great care would be needed to avoid creating embarrassment for the Royal Family.

The group rejected novel designs but agreed that a new yacht would be publicly funded from the Treasury's reserve, and Major undertook to seek the views of the Queen. Subtly, the rhetoric was changing. Officials had begun to describe the new yacht as a "proud symbol of Britain's long and noble maritime tradition … a working showcase for the excellence of British design and engineering".[277] Lord Ashbourne told the Lords, "We see the Royal Yacht as a national yacht, which is both a status symbol for Britain and, indeed, a symbol of British excellence."[278] The prose waxing stronger, officials wrote that she "will represent the nation overseas … [be] a showcase for the excellence of British design and engineering … [and be] a proud symbol of Britain's long and noble maritime tradition … enhancing the country's status and position in the eyes of the world".[279] However, the replacement royal yacht would need some of the fittings and furniture from *Britannia* that *Britannia* would need herself if she was to be preserved as a museum ship.[280]

Major dithered. "In the light of the current debate about the Royal Family and the Monarchy, [he] did not feel it was the right time to take a decision on a new Royal Yacht. The matter should, however, be kept under regular review," wrote his Principal Private Secretary to the Cabinet Secretary. "Once the divorce between the Prince and Princess of Wales had been completed, for example, public sentiment could turn quickly."[281] There the issue rested for much of 1996, though Number 10 was lobbied for a decision by the Parliamentary Maritime Group, the All-Parliamentary Group on the Royal Yacht, and several government ministers.[282] There was also an editorial in the *Daily Telegraph* on 19 August that echoed officials' words that "a royal yacht should serve as a reminder to the world of the proficiency of British engineering and seafaring skills" but veered off into party politics: "if minsters want to put a time bomb under Labour, let them order a replacement immediately, and dare the Opposition to denounce the move".

Early in 1997, ministers led by Malcolm Rifkind, now the Foreign Secretary, pressed Major for a decision, and almost a year after Major's first meeting about the royal yacht a timescale for the decision was drawn up,[283] but on 20 January Major sought advice on ways of delaying this.[284] At last he agreed that a new yacht should be ready for the millennium and, if not, for the Queen's Golden Jubilee.[285] Confusingly, Major wrote in his autobiography: "Keep *Britannia*? Well, that was very much my position, although it wasn't the view of the whole Cabinet, since Ken Clarke was opposed, believing such expenditure would backfire and damage public support for the royal family. For that reason, the fate of the vessel remained unsettled."[286]

## Politicking

Events now moved rapidly. Options for private sector funding were ruled out because they were seen as undermining the prestige of the project and of the monarchy, and would give rise to awkward presentational questions if adequate funds were not forthcoming or if the source of any funds was questionable. Instead, at a Cabinet meeting to discuss the forthcoming General Election,

Major tasked Portillo with making the announcement. Overnight a draft was sent to the Palace.[287] Next morning, 22 January, Jock heard that Portillo was about to make a statement in the Commons and grimaced wryly thinking that that was probably the end of a royal yacht. He was surprised, therefore, when Portillo told the Commons:[288]

> The Government have decided to commission a new purpose-built royal yacht ... we believe that a royal yacht is an important national asset, which projects a prestigious image of Britain, adding powerfully to official occasions and assisting greatly in promoting British economic interests ... The vessel will be a symbol of the Crown, of the kingdom and of its maritime traditions. It will be designed to exhibit an enduring level of style, elegance and dignity ... and should act as a showcase for Britain's design and engineering skills ... She will be crewed by the Royal Navy and fly the White Ensign. The Queen will contribute to the furnishings and fittings of the state rooms and the royal apartments, drawing some items from *Britannia* ... The running costs should not be much more than half those of *Britannia* ... I trust that she will enter service in time for Her Majesty's golden jubilee in 2002.

Britain's unwritten constitution required that the Opposition be consulted, and from the back benches of the Commons Conservative Douglas Hurd had already volunteered to sound out Tony Blair informally. A pencilled note suggested that the leader of the Labour party should be given advance notice "on Privy Council terms" of any decision, but despite Portillo declaring himself anxious that the replacement should not become an election issue, the matter was not referred to the Opposition.[289] Instead, Portillo told the Commons, "I do not regard today's statement as a constitutional one. I regard the yacht as an important aid to Her Majesty and to this country's economic interests, but not as a constitutional matter ... I should like to contrast that with the announcement of the previous royal yacht, when a Labour Government, during the 1951 General Election campaign, issued a press notice from the Admiralty announcing that there would be a new royal yacht."

Portillo's statement was well received. In Hansard, only Dennis Skinner MP, nicknamed the 'Beast of Bolsover' and known for his left-wing views and acerbic wit, was recorded as being churlish: "£60 million should not be spent on a yacht for the royal family when it could be spent ... on people who are waiting in [hospital] corridors on trolleys; on schoolchildren who do not have pencils or even classrooms, in some cases; on pensioners, who are being robbed blind; or on the 4 million people who do not have a job … we should not spend any more money on this aristocracy, which has been pushing its own self-destruct button for the past decade."[290] Labour, however, was hurting from not having been consulted, and many sympathised with Skinner's views.

## The Prince's Alternative

In February 1997 a new project team was formed, headed by Commander John Prichard, who had been *Britannia*'s senior engineer from 1982–84 and who had recently retired from the Navy.

The team turned their attention to having a new yacht ready for the Queen's Golden Jubilee Review in 2002. Rear-Admiral Sir Paul Greening, a former FORY and now Master of the Royal Household, and Commodore Anthony Morrow, the current Commodore Royal Yachts, attended meetings; the design work was undertaken by members of the Royal Corps of Naval Constructors at MoD Bath. The 'minimum viable design' of 1991 was quickly rejected and a ship's company of 122 Royal Navy personnel was established, compared with 240 for *Britannia*, most savings coming from the use of modern machinery and surveillance systems. The royal party of dressers, chefs, footmen, hairdressers, protection officers, ladies in waiting, equerries, and secretaries was reduced from 50 to 34. The ship was to be built to commercial standards and was to be capable of operating, but not carrying, a helicopter. To make the new yacht less dependent on tanker support, her range was to be 6,000 nautical miles at 15 knots, against *Britannia*'s 2,000 at 14 knots, and she was to have a top speed of 18 knots, against *Britannia*'s 21 knots. Her endurance was to be 45 days compared to *Britannia*'s 30 days.

There was another option favoured by Prince Philip. He knew that the steam turbines in the Cunard liner *Queen Elizabeth 2* had been removed during her 1986–87 refit and replaced with diesel engines, and he thought that this option for *Britannia* had not been properly considered. These ideas were sponsored by Devonport Management Limited (DML) and underwritten by Sir Donald Gosling. There was no doubt that Devonport could do the job: they had just rebuilt Getty's 1907 yacht, *Talitha G*, in which Prince Philip had spent Cowes Week, and he was much taken with her. DML was keen to move into the luxury yacht market and would have carried out the conversion at a very reasonable price. The idea was heavily canvassed in 1997 but it was going to cost at least as much as a new build and was felt to be a classic case of pouring new wine into old bottles, which would not have projected the image of a 21st-century yacht at the leading edge of technology.

Jock recalled: "Prince Philip was angered that the possibility of running HMY on diesel engines had not been properly addressed and he never really forgave me for not pursuing this. Actually, the Navy Board had concluded that to spend £20m on taking the yacht to bits to establish what needed to be done in the light of new Safety at Sea Regulations and then spending £60m to refit her to run on for perhaps another fifteen years was not sensible and that it would be much better to build a new yacht."

The debate rumbled on until after the coming General Election.


## Prince Andrew

One other matter affected Jock's relations with the royal family, and the anniversary of Jock's first year as First Sea Lord was ruined, when on Friday, 2 August 1996 the *Daily Express* ran a front page with the headline 'Why Andrew Quit The Navy' and a story by its defence correspondent Nicholas Assinder. According to Assinder's sources in the MoD and the Palace, the Prince "loved the sea and was a good officer, but he lacked that little bit extra" and "was out of his depth". Assinder found someone who described a decision by Jock regarding Andrew's naval career as "honourable and even courageous", while on the inside page he wrote that the Prince himself "had taken a look at the prospects for his naval career and decided to bow out gracefully – before the Navy did the bowing for him". Jock condemned the report as scurrilous nonsense and untrue.

In fact, earlier that summer Jock had requested a meeting with Prince Philip to discuss Prince Andrew's future. Jock knew that his call would be tricky, and was not surprised when Prince Philip challenged him: "The trouble with the Navy is that they do not know how to handle a royal prince."

Jock's reply, "Of all people, Sir, I probably do!" was received with a resigned smile.

"So, you are telling me he has bogged it?"

"No, but his heart is not in it."

It was a particularly sad occasion for Jock, who was mindful of what the Queen had said to him some time before: "Do try and persuade Andrew to stay in the Navy." Jock felt that he had failed his monarch and knew that his close rapport with the Queen and Prince Philip was undermined. Later, Jock discussed the future with Prince Andrew and together they planned an alternative London-based, deskbound career for his final years in the Navy. The Prince was promoted to commander on 27 April 1999 and moved from the Directorate of Naval Operations and Trade to the Directorate of Naval Staff Duties.

Jock was confident that he had made the difficult but right decision.

# Chapter 27: First Sea Lord II, 1996–98

The end of the Cold War heralded new strategic circumstances. *Front Line First*, which Jock had steered while VCDS, meant that the front line would be leaner, and a radical restructuring of the armed forces was underway. The process brought turbulence and upheaval but, as Jock noted to himself, it was both long overdue and absolutely essential for the armed forces to enter the new century fit and healthy, albeit on a limited budget. The Navy enjoyed an enviable reputation on the world stage, a reputation enhanced by the scale and quality of its operations, which ranged from the Adriatic to the South Atlantic, from the Caribbean to the Middle East, and from the North Atlantic to the Far East, and Jock would impress on ministers that this was what the taxpayer was paying for: "There was no doubt in my mind that we had never in peacetime asked more of the fleet and of all those involved in training and support."

### *First's Report*

In the New Year Jock recorded *First's Report*, a personal video message to the Navy. He described his programme of visits to ships and submarines, to Northwood, Yeovilton, Plymouth, Rosyth, Scotland, and Gibraltar, ceremony and social, briefings for retired admirals and generals, the First Sea Lord's conference, and two days in Northern Ireland to see the Royal Marines at work, which would have been exhausting to a lesser person. Jock regretted the fact that he had not spent as much time in the front line as he would have liked. He was determined to keep his finger on the pulse, to listen to people's views and concerns, and to keep them as well informed as possible. Like *Broadsheet*, *First's Report* was widely distributed and was frank about the strategic situation remaining cloudy and unsettled. Against the backdrop of reduced budgets, lean manning, and gapping, the fleet was busier than ever.

In the Gulf, the Armilla patrol had begun its fifteenth year and was likely to continue for the foreseeable future, *Vanguard* had completed the first Trident patrol, and *Victorious* was about to take the first sub-strategic missiles to sea. The West Indies guardship was busy, particularly in the aftermath of hurricane Luis and the eruption of the Soufriere volcano on Montserrat at the end of the previous year. Jock repeated his mantra that he would rather have the fleet under pressure than underemployed. The FA2 Harrier had a new look-down, shoot-down radar capability, there was a new command system for Type 23 frigates, Tomahawk land attack missiles were being bought for nuclear submarines, the new helicopter carrier, HMS *Ocean*, would soon begin fitting out, and the plum in Jock's pudding, the Permanent Joint Headquarters, would be formed at Northwood and backed by a Joint Rapid Deployment Force. "We are the biggest, most balanced maritime force in Europe, and ship for ship, marine for marine, sailor for sailor we are the best in the world. I aim to keep it that way."

Jock's visits took the form of forums, one in the wardroom, one with the senior rates, and one with the junior rates: ten minutes or so from Jock and then a Q&A period. Filming for *First's Report* included a day at sea in HMS *Richmond* from Portsmouth: "It was a rough old day at sea in the Channel and I did wonder if my sea legs would survive when visiting all departments, but fortunately all was well and we got full value from the day before flying back to Northolt in a Lynx."

## Proceedings 1996

Jock reinforced his message in an article written for the United States Naval Institute Proceedings in March 1996:[291]

> Britain's armed forces' posture was shifting towards power projection. For the Royal Navy, this meant expeditionary warfare, focusing on littoral operations and warfare from the sea. There were three core capabilities to provide this task: carrier air groups, amphibious task groups, and nuclear submarines. Future effectiveness would depend on the successful development of a range of emerging defence, communications, and information technologies. These would provide power projection technology for the fleet, essential for the conduct of operations that would be increasingly joint service in nature and most likely would involve allies. Power projection technology would

provide the capability to strike enemy targets at long range with a high degree of accuracy, minimum attrition, and low collateral damage. Cruise missiles enhanced naval fire support, and other sophisticated weapons would be central elements of the projection force. Over land and sea, fast and stealthy fighter attack aircraft and advanced helicopters, deploying their own suite of smart new munitions, would be key participants. Advanced joint reconnaissance, intelligence, surveillance, and damage assessment systems would be needed to provide precision targeting and command and control information. Many linked sensors would contribute to the overall picture.

Parts of Jock's new navy were visionary: unmanned air and underwater vehicles were set to play an increasingly important role. To sustain operations within the littoral, the projection force must be protected and the technology to achieve mine detection and clearance in shallow water and to counter the proliferating and ever-quieter submarines would be of key importance.

In sum, Jock told his audience at home and abroad that the Royal Navy was seeking a new power projection technology that would blend above and below water warfare, command and control, computers and intelligence, and strike technologies. These would give Britain and its allies highly capable forces able to conduct intensive, incisive expeditionary warfare and be able to undertake responsive humanitarian work and sensitive peacekeeping operations.[292]

## Jane's

In May 1996 a new addition of *Jane's Fighting Ships* was out, edited by the doughty Captain Richard Sharpe, who told Press Association News that one of the greatest areas of concern was the delay in orders for new amphibious assault ships to replace *Fearless* and *Intrepid*. "How much longer can one go on playing this game?" he asked. "These delays are causing annual running costs of £40 million on the ships. It is the Treasury seeking by any means possible to delay the contracts; [this] is the economics of lunacy."

Jock was in Scotland to welcome HMS *Repulse* back from her last deterrent patrol when at a press conference he was quizzed about this and had the opportunity to tell PA News that orders for new vessels to replace the 30-year old ships were needed now as those ships could not enter service until 2000–2001. "I will only be happy when I have seen HMS *Ocean* flying the White Ensign and orders for replacements for *Fearless* and *Intrepid* are firmly on the stocks." He emphasised the flexibility of the modern Royal Navy and its ability to undertake different operations. "We have a much smaller but much sharper fleet than we have had for a long time. With a fleet of twelve nuclear attack submarines, the Type 23 frigate, the new Merlin anti-submarine helicopter, and the arrival of Tomahawk cruise missiles, the make-up of the Navy is 'about right'." However, Jock was concerned about orders for the next generation of attack submarines, which were not expected to be placed until 1997 at the earliest: orders for five were vital to maintain the overall fleet size. In addition, the tri-national Horizon project, involving Britain, France, and Italy, to develop a replacement for the navy's Type 42 destroyers (this would become the Type 45 destroyer) was not likely to produce its first ship until 2005, although the Type 42 destroyer *Birmingham* was being paid off in 1998.[293]

"What we have is stability at sea, but the ships and aircraft are wearing out and that stability is no longer sustainable," commented Richard Sharpe.

The PA report irritated Secretary of State Portillo, or rather his senior civil servants, who suspecting that Jock and Sharpe had colluded and accused Jock of having taken an unprecedented step in expressing his concern about delays for new ships. "That was certainly true but not in such words. I was referring to the *Fearless* and *Intrepid* replacements, which, frankly, were well overdue. Fortunately, I was able to get hold of the Press Association News report of what I actually said and sent this straight round to Michael Portillo and heard no more."

Jock continued to hold the working lunches that he had begun when a newly appointed rear-admiral, and some weeks later the Permanent Under-Secretary Richard Mottram was a guest. When Jock asked again what had happened to the orders for the new ships, Mottram replied offhandedly that they would be announced the following week, saying, "I don't find the requirement compelling, but you have won the argument."[294]

## Christmas 1996

December 1996 meant carols at the Guards Chapel, the RNLI ball at the London Hilton, the annual banquet of the Guild of Freeman of the City of London, a Chiefs' briefing for the Prime Minister, and the passing out parade at Dartmouth. Christmas Day was spent in the company of Anthea Turner on an ITV special from HMS *Belfast*, which included a proposal of marriage for a sailor in HMS *Victorious*, a Trident submarine somewhere underwater on patrol.

The season brought the usual crop of cards from the Queen and Prince Philip, the Queen Mother, Princess Anne, and Princess Alexandra and the

Kents. Jock had wondered whether his Christmas card from John Major at Chequers would be the last from him, and he speculated what the effect would be of a review of the armed forces, which had been promised by Tony Blair, leader of the Labour Party.

By 8 January, Jock was in the USA to meet the Joint Chiefs of Staff and the Chief of Naval Operations. He was made a commander of the US Legion of Merit, and Portillo wrote at once to congratulate Jock on a well-deserved honour.

There was good news in March: Jock was able to announce that a contract was to be placed for two new fleet tankers, *Wave Knight* and *Wave Ruler*. His personal view was that this was "very good news to get them ordered before the election is announced". On 17 March it was "even better to get these ordered before the election" – this time these were the Trafalgar-class nuclear submarines *Astute*, *Ambush*, and *Artful*. On 20 March the *Daily Telegraph* carried a positive article under the headline 'Royal Navy proves it is still a world force' with a news story that RAF Harrier pilots were spending five weeks in HMS *Illustrious* improving their carrier-borne flying skills in the ground-attack GR7, a slightly larger version of the Navy's fighter, the Sea Harrier FA2.

## Proceedings 1997

In March, the US Naval Institute's house magazine *Proceedings* published another round of its forum in which it asked naval chiefs outside the USA to answer one simple question. This year the question was: "How does your Navy intend to exploit the capabilities of your Air Force and Army to conduct littoral warfare more effectively?" [295] For Jock, this was an opportunity to burnish his 'purple' or joint credentials, and his response is worth publishing in full:

> I do not like the way this question is framed. The key to success in littoral operations is undoubtedly the ability of all three services together with our allies to interoperate and thereby allow the joint force commander to exploit the particular capabilities of each discipline. Navies traditionally have taken part in international operations involving other services and often exercise what must be the ultimate joint capability in the littoral – an amphibious operation. Maritime operations are joint by definition, as they involve forces operating afloat, ashore, and in the air. Furthermore, naval forces can provide afloat headquarters for joint forces offering advantages

in flexibility and access. Naval forces are also autonomous and can operate successfully without host nation support or overflying rights. There are many recent examples of countries becoming increasingly wary of allowing foreign forces to operate within, through, or from their territory. Thus, the ability to operate in the littoral and to project power ashore will rely more than ever before on naval units capable of organic air operations, amphibious operations, and of stand-off attack by sea-launched missiles. The Royal Navy for the 21st century is configured to do just that and practices these capabilities on a regular basis.


## Nelson Mandela

At Easter 1997 the Slaters visited South Africa for the South African Navy's (SAN's) 75th anniversary, when, as the 'mother' of the SAN, the Royal Navy enjoyed pole position. Jock was privileged with a memorable 20-minute audience with the President and knowing that the SAN was in dire condition, Jock used every opportunity to press for an upgrade to its ships. He reiterated that with almost 2,000 miles of coastline and a corresponding economic exclusion zone through which well over 100 supertankers passed each year, South Africa needed a strong navy.

During a fleet review Jock was invited onto a dais to join Nelson Mandela while he waved his baseball cap at HMS *Chatham* as she steamed passed. She was commanded by Chris Clayton, who had been the second helicopter pilot in *Jupiter* 24 years before. Jock looked to the horizon where he could see Robben Island, which had been Mandela's prison for so many years.

Jock also met Captain Bill Leith of SAN, who had completed the navigation course with him in 1964, and other old friends there for a defence industries exhibition – Rear-Admiral Sam Salt, and Alex Marsh, who had built HMS *Illustrious* and who was now the marketing director of the Babcock International Group.

In the garden of Admiralty House the Slaters found a magnolia that had been planted by the British King and Queen when they visited South Africa in HMS *Vanguard* in 1947 – a visit Jock remembered because of an Edinburgh Academy school task for which he had kept a scrapbook of the royal tour; and he wrote to Queen Elizabeth the Queen Mother to tell her that the tree was in good shape.

Annie then returned home and Jock flew to Hong Kong for ceremonies to mark the closure of the naval base HMS *Tamar*, in advance of the Chinese takeover later that summer.


## Portillo's Goodbye

When Labour won the General Election on 1 May 1997 Portillo expressed his profound gratitude for the loyal service given to him and his ministers: he had been much impressed and influenced by the Services' enthusiasm, devotion to duty, loyalty, and commitment to solve problems. "I cannot believe that any minister was better served in these respects. It is all the more impressive given the changes through which you have all been required to pass. I look back with pride on the things we worked on together where Britain, the MoD, and the armed forces played an important role for good. But I think also of the small things done well and of people in junior posts who made the difference with their devotion and good cheer."

Jock and Portillo exchanged handwritten letters, Portillo writing, "I have enormous respect for your talents and leadership, and it was a privilege for me to work with you. You know how much I admire the Royal Navy and it has a First Sea Lord worthy of it. You were extraordinarily helpful to me, not just with advice but also in the way that you worked to resolve problems. Despite all the external pressures upon us, from finances, parliament and press, we worked within the building to find solutions."

He concluded with a warm thanks to Jock, to Annie, and to the Royal Navy.

# Chapter 28: Strategic Defence Review

On 2 May 1997 *The Times* headline was 'Landside Victory for Labour'. After eighteen years of Tory government New Labour was elected on the promise that it would maintain the level of government spending for two years but that there would be a defence review. Jock kept hold of a copy of New Labour's manifesto with its promise to retain Trident and to maintain a strong defence through NATO, writing in the margin, "We must hold them to it!"

There was irony in the fact that Guthrie had been preferred as CDS for his perceived ability to accommodate the new government. George Robertson was the new Secretary of State and John Reid was the new Minister of State for the Armed Forces, two excellent Scots whom Jock much looked forward to working with.

Robertson wanted to build a consensus across the political spectrum and consult widely, and encouraged outside views and ideas, an approach that Jock fully supported. However, Jock would not forget his first call on Robertson, who pointed at his own broken nose and irregular features and asked, "Jock, do you know why I look like this?" For once Jock was wordless. Robertson explained that he had once been involved in a very nasty car accident in which he was hit by a Royal Navy Land Rover. "But don't worry," he continued, "I won't hold it against you when you come to argue the case for new aircraft carriers!"

John Reid was a plain-speaking Glaswegian who was determined to get to grips with his defence portfolio. Reid's office was next to Jock's and once, after hearing cheering, Jock discovered the minister's outer office deserted. Further inside, Reid and his staff, holding cans of beer, were watching Celtic v Rangers on television. As a Catholic Reid was a Celtic supporter, but he raised his can and said, "Come away in, Jock, I suppose you are a Rangers fan? No matter – have a beer!" Such was the different style of the new government.

## First's Business

The Queen's speech at the State Opening of Parliament on 14 May contained notice of the review of defence, the fifth since the last review by a Labour government – the Mason review in 1975. Then, the defence budget had comprised 4.5% of gross domestic product but by 1997 it was 2.56%. "Oh dear – here we go again!" wrote Jock. "But not unexpected."

Before the end of May the SDR, with its strapline *Modern Forces for the Modern World*, was launched. Robertson outlined its aim – to build on the developing consensus on defence and to establish the widest possible shared vision about Britain's future security needs and the tasks of its armed forces. He stressed that the review would not be an in-house defence study, but foreign policy led, and that the MoD would jointly work with the FCO to establish a policy baseline that would build on MoD strengths and on the best features of existing policies and capabilities. The review was expected to be completed around the end of the year and to give the armed forces a coherent and stable planning basis into the 21st century.

The SDR would be conducted against a background of social and ceremonial affairs: the presentation of the Duke of Westminster's gold medal to Dr Andrew Gordon "for his book on Jutland";[296] a SSAFA (the armed services charity) service in Westminster Abbey; the induction at Lambeth Palace of a new archdeacon for the Royal Navy; the state opening of Parliament; a gala seafarers' dinner in the presence of the Princess Royal; the Chiefs of European Navies meeting in Copenhagen; the visit of the chief of the Spanish naval staff; celebration of the Glorious First of June in HMS *Excellent*; and a service of thanksgiving for the life of Captain Nicholas Barker, who died of cancer a few days after his book *Beyond Endurance* was published;[297] dinner at Trinity House; lunch at Lancaster House in honour of the retiring SACEUR; official visits to the Netherlands, Wimbledon, and the Royal Tournament; and not forgetting a garden party at Buckingham Palace.

Daringly, the Royal Naval Association (RNA), under its president Vice-Admiral Sir Roy Newman, held its annual conference in Belfast, when Jock told the gathering that naval forces were being stretched to the limit to play a greater worldwide role in preserving peace, and that while superpower rivalry was over, paradoxically there was less peace around the globe. To adapt and to provide a strong maritime capability in the 21st century the Navy had to change gear – not down, but up. Trident was now operational, three submarines of the new *Astute*-class had been ordered, updated Harriers had entered service, and Merlin helicopters were soon to do so. At present, there were 80 ships of the fleet at sea, over half of them outside UK waters, and 20 ships led by the carrier *Illustrious* were taking part in the global deployment Ocean Wave 97, exercising with international forces and showing the flag in 34 countries. Among establishments to be closed was the Royal Naval College, Greenwich. Jock read a lesson from Ecclesiastes: "To everything there is a season, and a time to every purpose under the heaven: a time to be born, and a time to die; a time to plant, and a time to pluck up that which is planted." With a defence review underway, some of his listeners feared that he might have been referring not just to the college in Greenwich but to the Navy at large.[298]

Jock invited Lieutenant Commander Prince Andrew to a working lunch and to take stock of his progress as a desk officer in DNOT. In his thank you letter, the Prince said how much he was enjoying his exposure to the workings of the MoD and the wider aspects of responsibilities of a department of state, assuring Jock that he would continue to give him and the Navy his fullest loyalty and commitment. "I am deeply grateful for the understanding you give me and I'm determined not to disappoint either you or the Navy."

That summer the Slaters enjoyed ten days in the Mediterranean in Sir Don Gosling's yacht *Leander,* but returned to the sad news of the death on 1 August of Princess Diana.

## Japan and South Korea

The new Joint Services Command and Staff College, a project close to Jock's heart, opened on 8 September. Soon after, Jock left for official visits to Japan and South Korea, which were well reported by Jock's Naval Assistant, Captain Tony Rix, in his usual, inimitable style. While the Japanese would always be hospitable and courteous, he wrote, it was evident that the warm reception that Jock received wherever he went was sincere and genuine. It was clear that the Japanese Maritime Self-Defence Force, its navy, was very keen to deepen its relations with the Royal Navy, and much could be achieved through regular high-level visits, ship visits, staff talks, and personnel exchanges. Jock and his party went on to visit South Korea. Rix again: "A fascinating visit to a country where the security situation is unique, unpredictable, and volatile, and while Britain had no legally binding agreement to assist South Korea, it was clearly in her best interests to maintain close links in the cause of Britain's wider interests in the Asia Pacific region."

**Autumn 1997**

In the continuing row over the flat in Admiralty Arch, the *Evening Standard* claimed that, although it was still the Slaters' home, the new government was going to turn the magnificent building into a 60-bed shelter for homeless young people. The news was greeted as gesture politics: if the government was serious about sheltering London's homeless it would have found somewhere suitable earlier. The row continued in the newspaper for several days.

Jock's foreword for the Association of Royal Navy Officers' yearbook of 1997 reprised what he had told the RNA in Belfast earlier. A task force of twenty ships had set sail for the Asia Pacific rim and that carefully judged and balanced restructuring of the Royal Navy and Royal Marines was underway, focused on streamlining support and enhancing the front line, and producing:

A force package which in terms of capability, influence, projection and effectiveness is well matched to our defence planning assumptions. It is no coincidence that some of the major navies of the world, having seen what we have done to reshape our forces for the future, are keen to learn from that experience, and I welcome this. Lest there be any doubt about the size and capability of today's fleet, the Royal Navy currently comprises 130 ships, submarines, and RFA, 234 aircraft and three Royal Marines commandos with some 46,000 uniformed and 22,000 civilian personnel, all maintained by an operating budget of £3.8 billion … There is no doubt that we make a significant impression on the world stage and I'm proud of that … but it is important to be aware of the pressure which we face as we go about our duties. Much is demanded of our ships, sailors, and marines as we maintain a particularly high level of activity at sea and ashore. More and more is being asked of them and yet they continue to deliver with their professionalism, which is second to none and a can-do spirit that puts others in the shade. We cannot take this work for granted and I place the greatest importance on the well-being and the care of our people and their dependants.

This was also the message Jock carried to the International Seapower Symposium hosted by US Admiral Jay Johnson in Newport, Rhode Island in November 1997.

**Academe**

Jock made time to review for *The Times* Tom Pocock's life of Sidney Smith, *A Thirst for Glory*, and Nicholas Rodger's new book, *The Safeguard of the Sea,* with the assistance of his Head of Defence Studies.[299]

When Guy Hudson, who in 1940 had been commissioned into the Royal Naval Volunteer Reserve, died leaving a bequest for the education of naval officers at Oxford, Jock's Head of Defence Studies liaised closely with Professor Bob O'Neill, chairman of the military education committee and Chichele Professor of the History of War, over how the bequest should be used.[300] The Guy Hudson Memorial Fund as it became known was established to provide bursaries for young men and women in the Oxford University Royal Naval Unit. It paid for a mid-rank officer to be the Hudson fellow and to study at Oxford for a term or so, and for an annual address by a senior officer. Jock strongly supported these proposals and gave the first talk. The proof of the pudding came when, several months after he had spoken, O'Neill repeated Jock's speech almost word for word at an academic conference.

That autumn there were royal events in Windsor Castle and Westminster Abbey to mark the 50th anniversary of the marriage of the Queen and Prince Philip, which ran in awkward parallel to preparations for paying off *Britannia.*

# Chapter 29: Farewell to *Britannia*

On 20 January 1997 *Britannia* sailed from Portsmouth for the Far East. During the election campaign, old-style Labour politicians such as John Prescott made a virtue of the scrapping of what he presented as a millionaire's toy, and at every stop of his battle bus he began his set speech with a rant about the yacht: "The Tories want to build yachts. We're going to scrap it." The fact that *Britannia* had originally been commissioned by Labour Prime Minister Clement Attlee was overlooked.[301]

Whatever Prime Minister Tony Blair's views were, he knew little about *Britannia* and first went on board during the ceremonies at Hong Kong to hand over the territory to China. Blair and Prince Charles talked together while Blair's party toured the yacht, where even such an inexpert as Margaret Cook, wife of Robin Cook, the Foreign Secretary, recalled that the engine room looked like a museum piece "with highly polished brass pistons and rods, and everything spotless", and picked up on the gossip that "one of the reasons that *Britannia* was to be decommissioned was that the engine room was so old and out of date that the upkeep was impossibly costly in terms of staff and materials".[302]

Blair, urged by the Prince ("Oh you must, Prime Minister, it's fascinating"), was then given an impromptu tour of the yacht by Commodore Tony Morrow. This persuaded the PM, who, once ashore and in his car, turned to his press secretary Alastair Campbell and exclaimed, "We must keep *Britannia*, what an asset!"[303 304]

Robin Cook was also won over, and judging by an editorial and several well-informed articles in *The Times* it seems that *Britannia* might be reprieved through a public–private partnership.[305 306] Later that month it was rumoured that the Labour Cabinet was due to sign off the replacement yacht, which then was expected to cost £60m. The Cabinet, however, was divided. Blair was strongly supported by Peter Mandelson, Minister without Portfolio, who was sure that the Cabinet would approve a replacement,[307] but at the end of September Chancellor Gordon Brown was clear that the £12m annual cost of a royal yacht could not be justified.[308] Evidently, he had inherited the same brief as his predecessor Ken Clarke, who had "adamantly refused to contemplate spending £60m of public money on anything as nineteenth century as a royal yacht at a time when we were cutting back on public spending … I was also unpersuaded that the yacht would make any practical difference to our export performance."[309]

While the eventual outcome of the SDR would be seen as a triumph for Jock and the Navy, it was prejudicial to the royal yacht, felt Jock:

> I simply could not go round the MoD waving a White Ensign and shouting that, in future, we must have a Royal Yacht when I was struggling to persuade Whitehall about nuclear submarines, aircraft carriers, and amphibious ships. Sadly for me, I did not endear myself to Prince Philip, who simply could not understand why *Britannia* could not be refitted with diesel engines and run on for longer. The Navy Board had repeatedly pointed out that in the light of the new Safety of Life at Sea regulations it would be much better (and indeed more economical) to spend the money on a new yacht.

By early October a brochure for Project Celery was ready, but Brown's arguments won the day and on 10 October 1997 the government duly announced that *Britannia* would pay off in December and would not be refitted or replaced.[310] The press release quoting the Secretary of State for Defence said: "*Britannia* has served the nation well for over 40 years and earned a special place in many people's affections. We made clear that we would not spend public money on a royal yacht, and I am keeping that promise. We in the MoD have to justify every penny of the taxpayers' money that we spend and, in this case, I could not do so, particularly given a yacht is not needed for royal travel. We considered private finance options, but this would only have been viable with a substantial annual subsidy from public funds."

Jock, who had not been party to this decision-making, noted:

> [It] was a very sad day for the royal family, royal yachtsmen past and present, and all their supporters when the government formally announced that *Britannia* would pay off that December and would not be refitted or replaced … In my personal signal to Commodore

Tony Morrow, the last Commodore Royal Yachts, I paid tribute to all who had served in *Britannia* … their professionalism, loyalty, and dedication had been the hallmarks of the Yacht's success under the White Ensign and she had become a legend in the second half of the 20th Century … I knew that the right decision had been made but I also knew that it would not endear me to the Queen and Prince Philip, not least the latter who clearly felt that the Royal Navy had let them down and I, in particular, had failed to push for a refit with diesels to run her on for a further 15 years.

## Cry-Bye

There were only a few more ceremonies to be performed. *Britannia* paid her last visit to the Pool of London, when the Queen invited the Chiefs and their predecessors to lunch on board. Jock was less than comfortable to find himself sitting next to Prince Philip, but "happily we had a very good chat about other things and the [decommissioning] was not mentioned". The yacht played host to the Royal Navy Presentation Team, the normal venue being the Palace of Westminster, and afterwards Jock took questions from a packed and lively meeting. Lord Jellicoe, the only son of Jellicoe of Jutland, was fulsome in his speech of thanks.

Later, Jock was setting off for the Guards Chapel for the SSAFA carol concert, "where Annie had done some magnificent flowers", when he heard that the Secretary of State wanted urgently to speak to him. The Slaters and Robertsons had been invited to lunch with the Queen in *Britannia* and "Robertson was uneasy about how to play it. I pointed out that my position was equally difficult, as many thought (not least Prince Philip and the Royal Yachtsmen), unfairly, that I had not given the future of the Yacht great support." Jock advised Robertson that there was only one way to play the following day, "with a very straight bat!"

On decommissioning day, 11 December 1997, the Slaters drove to Portsmouth: "We all tried to make the best of it but there was an atmosphere of great sadness, not least for me, with so many happy memories of days long since passed … It was all very emotional, and tears were in many eyes." Fourteen members of the royal family attended with former royal yachtsmen and their families, who watched 337 years of tradition draw to a close. When the Queen spoke, she said, "Looking back over 44 years we can all reflect with pride and gratitude upon this great ship, which has served the country, the Royal Navy, and my family with such distinction. *Britannia* has provided magnificent support to us throughout this time, playing such an important role in the history of the second half of this century … It is now with sadness that we must say goodbye."

*The Sun* newspaper unkindly carried the headline 'Cry-bye Britannia'.

Jock reflected: "To this day I simply don't know what HM really thought about the demise of the Yacht. Prince Philip's views were well known but I had a strange feeling that she knew that there was no way the First Sea Lord could major on a new or refitted Yacht with so many defence pressures on his shoulders and with little political enthusiasm." Nearly 30 years later he would still fret that he might not have done enough to ensure that there was a replacement for *Britannia*.

# Chapter 30: Joint Force 2000

There was much work still to be done in 1998. Jock, however, had another problem.

**Prostate Cancer**

There had been self-confessed health warnings in Jock's diaries before, but it was reading Stuttaford's medical column in *The Times* at the start of Christmas leave, 19 December, which made him realise that the urinary trouble he was experiencing and which had only been confided to Annie, might be more serious than he suspected.[311] At a routine medical check Jock was told that he was impressively fit for a 59-year-old but he insisted on a PSA blood test. A few days later, Surgeon Commander David Tulloch, head urologist at the Royal Naval Hospital at Haslar, rang to invite Jock for further tests, and rang again on the following Monday to invite him to return later that week. "No," said Jock, "I will come down this afternoon." An MRI scan confirmed the worst: "I will never forget the body blow sitting in my study the following day when Tulloch telephoned to say that I definitely had prostate cancer and the sooner it was operated on the better."

Roger Kirby, urology specialist at St George's Hospital, Tooting in London, was the recommended surgeon. Jock checked with his brother, Tony, on Kirby's qualifications and was reassured that he was one of the best in the country. In his Harley Street clinic at the beginning of January Kirby reassured Jock that he was doing the right – and the only – thing. But Jock cursed: "I regretted insisting at my annual medical on a PSA test … Could I possibly have survived another nine months and then had surgery?" Thursday, 15 January 1998 was selected for a prostatectomy.

Jock spent what remained of the Christmas holidays planning the way ahead as the SDR work reached fever pitch. "What an absolute bugger this all was in my final ten months as First Sea Lord and at such a critical time for the future of the Royal Navy."

Jock wrote to inform Robertson, who replied that he did not want him to rush his convalescence and that he would not expect him in office again until after Easter. Jock had other ideas but kept these to himself. The last week in London before retiring *hors de combat* was filled with calls and briefings and preparing Admiral Mike Boyce, the Commander-in-Chief Fleet (whose appointment to relieve Jock the Queen had coincidentally just approved), to stand in at top-level meetings about the SDR. Jock's last task was to give a lunch for the family of Sir William Staveley, who had died the previous autumn, before a thanksgiving service in St Martin-in-the-Fields, where Jock read a lesson: few knew that three days later he would undergo major surgery.

At Haslar, Jock was well looked after, particularly by the smart and starched naval nurses, but he was unimpressed by the general coordination of the hospital where "quite clearly an old-fashioned ward sister or matron was missing". However, he was released after eight days, when Annie drove him home and put him straight to bed. He aimed to return to London in early March, and it was not long before boxes started to arrive and Jock, determined to keep in touch with the fast-moving events in London, began to take calls. Although he had expressly said that he did not want get-well messages, it was heart-warming to receive good wishes from the Queen, Prince Charles, the Defence Secretary, and the Chaplain of the Fleet.

## Christmas Card for Saddam

Two of Jock's problems in the SDR were the replacement in the Navy's order of battle of the three *Invincible*-class carriers (a project known then as CVF), and of the Sea Harrier.

Meanwhile, in the Middle East the prospect of a second Gulf War loomed when Saddam Hussein expelled six American weapons inspectors from Iraq and the United Nations decided to pull out its own weapons inspectors, setting the conditions for conflict. After an emergency meeting between Prime Minister Tony Blair, Foreign Secretary Robin Cook, and Defence Secretary George Robertson, Jock was asked to send the carrier HMS *Invincible* from the West Indies to the Mediterranean. Robertson described it as a purely precautionary measure, while Cook talked about the seriousness of the crisis: "We cannot let up the pressure on [Saddam] until he's abandoned his biological weapons programme and until we have adequately verified that. Stopping people developing weapons of mass destruction entirely fits with our policy. Poisoning whole cities is not ethical."

The mounting crisis in the Gulf required a military option should all diplomatic negotiations fail, and the fastest way for the UK to contribute would have been to deploy RAF aircraft. But many of the Gulf states were unwilling to provide bases for the aircraft. For Jock, there could be nothing better than a call for an aircraft carrier in the Middle East and he was quick to emphasise that the Navy could deploy early and poise almost indefinitely – waiting in a state of high readiness and out of sight over the horizon. Also, besides carrying aircraft, *Invincible* could be a command platform for multi-service or multinational operations, and the deployment of ships sent political messages to allies and enemies alike without commitment and without risk. It would be a classic demonstration of maritime power, and, coming as this did in the midst of the SDR, be "a very good message to [the government] on the utility of aircraft carriers … There was nothing new in all this to those who understand maritime affairs. What was becoming increasingly significant was the Navy's ability to project power ashore, whether it be carrier-borne air power or the potency of the Royal Marine commandos or the deadly accuracy of the submarine-launched Tomahawk Land Attack missiles. Actually, Saddam Hussein deserved a Christmas card from me for helping me to make the strongest maritime case in the SDR debate."


## Operation Bolton

*Invincible* was in the western Atlantic when on 13 November 1997 she was ordered to proceed to Gibraltar to embark additional aircraft. She crossed the ocean at 25 knots – 600 nautical miles per day – and six days later seven Harrier GR7s embarked. Her enhanced air group now consisted of seven GR7 ground-attack Harriers, eight FA2 fighter Sea Harriers, four airborne early warning Sea King helicopters, and six anti-submarine Sea Kings, four of these in RFA *Fort Victoria*. *Invincible*, commanded by Captain James Burnell-Nugent, then took part in Operation Deliberate Guard in the Adriatic, flying 53 sorties over the former Republic of Yugoslavia, which was an effective work-up for what was to come. She spent Christmas off Cyprus before returning to Operation Deliberate Guard in January, when Guthrie visited her, and then passed through the Suez Canal. On 25 January 1998 *Invincible* traversed the straits of Hormuz to participate in Operation Bolton in the Gulf. Her principal tasks were day and night missions over Iraq using GR7s as interdictors and FA2s for force protection. These operations required close coordination with three much larger US Navy carriers, *George Washington, Nimitz,* and *Independence.*[312]

Burnell-Nugent wrote in his report of proceedings:[313]

> This was the definitive post-Cold War aircraft carrier operation … In the full public gaze, Operation Bolton provided a clear demonstration of the diplomatic signalling power of maritime forces, a capability endorsed at the highest levels in London, Washington and New York. The Royal Navy provided a defence platform for a joint offensive maritime air capability, not seen deployed from the UK for many years … flying nearly 800 hours in theatre, many over a belligerent country 6,000 miles from home. Operational integration of FA2s and GR7s, particularly at night, was repeatedly demonstrated over Iraqi missile engagement zones. This was a very substantial achievement of which all on board felt justifiably proud … The rapid evolution of this new defence capability from a CVS [the Royal Navy's light aircraft carriers] must be harnessed and further developed.

Robin Cook told the House of Commons that *Invincible* and "the people who sail in her or fly from her have played a very important role … If we get a diplomatic solution, it would only be because we have assets like *Invincible.*"

## FA2 and GR7

The Harrier was not one aircraft type, but a family of aircraft that shared a name and a similar profile. All were single-engine, short take-off and vertical landing subsonic jets powered by variants of the Rolls-Royce Pegasus engine.

The Navy's Sea Harrier FA2 was a fighter aircraft optimised for air defence of the fleet, a role in which an earlier version, the Sea Harrier FRS1, had proved so effective during the Falklands War. Made of metal and measuring 46ft 6in (14.17m) in length and 25ft 3in (7.7m) in wingspan, the FA2 had reached the limits of its development. The RAF's Harrier GR7 was a second generation or 'big wing' Harrier with a larger wingspan of 30ft 4in (9.25 m), optimised for ground attack and lacking a fire-control radar for air-to-air combat.[314] Both the Sea Harrier FA2 and the Harrier GR7 suffered from reduced engine performance in hot weather, which limited vertical landings when returning to the carrier while still carrying full payloads. However, the performance of the GR7 was better because it was constructed of carbon fibre and thus was 2,000lbs lighter. For continued hot weather operations both versions of the Harrier would need a more powerful engine. This would require larger air intakes and exhausts, and a larger body, but the manufacturer, British Aerospace, had pulled the plug on further development, preferring instead to invest in later generations of aircraft.

During the SDR, before he was hospitalised, Jock had put in hand a far-reaching piece of inter-service staff work addressing the future of the Harrier force and the CVF: the work had historical precedents stretching back to his Uncle Ned.


## Second World War Precedent

By 1918 the Royal Navy operated one of the largest air forces in the world, but when, in April that year, the Royal Naval Air Service was merged with the Royal Flying Corps in order to form the RAF, the Navy lost its aircraft, its air and ground crews, its air stations, and many of its air-minded officers. It took two decades of argument before the Navy won back control of the Fleet Air Arm, on 24 May 1939, just before the outbreak of the Second World War. In the meantime, the RAF, obsessed with the alleged accuracy and efficacy of high-level bombing, had neglected torpedo and dive bombing and the fleet's need for aerial air defence. In consequence, the Navy opened the war with a ragtag of inadequate shipborne aircraft. The Admiralty also wanted control over some land-based aircraft, but this was denied, and all it got was operational control over aircraft allocated by Coastal Command.

In parallel, fleet exercises in the Mediterranean in the 1930s had shown that naval operations would be severely prejudiced if the fleet did not possess command of the air. Consequently, when Jock's Uncle Ned was Commander-in-Chief Mediterranean from 1941–43 and based in Alexandria, he wanted his own air force, trained for operations over the sea and for long-range reconnaissance. Cunningham argued well and a reluctant RAF was obliged to set up 201 Group, but it took a meeting at Chequers and some head-banging to give this group its proper title, which was 201 (Naval Cooperation) Group. Even so, Cunningham had cause to complain that Air Marshal Arthur Tedder, Air Officer Commanding-in-Chief Middle East Command, had refused to allocate new aircraft to the group, aircraft that had been brought to Egypt in ships escorted by the Navy.[315]

As a young man during his visits to Palace House Jock had heard Uncle Ned's criticism of the RAF, of the difficulties he had worked under to obtain air support in the Eastern Mediterranean, and of the personal problems in dealing with Tedder.

## Royal Navy/RAF Cooperation

Air Chief Marshal Sir Richard 'Dick' Johns became CAS on 10 April 1997 and at informal meetings Jock and Johns agreed to avoid public arguments and hoped not to be divided and ruled by the Treasury.[316]

The evident success of Operation Bolton inspired them to discuss an idea that was so revolutionary – the creation of a joint force of Harriers – that Jock decided that only a tight circle of his staff should be involved in talks. Flag Officer Naval Aviation Rear-Admiral Terry Loughran was excluded because it was feared that he and his people, especially the 'Sea Harrier community', on seeing a threat to fixed-wing naval aviation, would be instinctively opposed.[317] Subsequently, at a Defence Council meeting on 18 December 1997, Jock and Johns were ready to put forward an initiative, which was being developed by teams led by the Assistant Chief of Naval Staff, Rear-Admiral Jonathon Band, and by the Assistant Chief of Air Staff, Air Vice Marshal Tim Jenner.

Jenner had noted other opposition from civil servants, who thought that a joint force of Harriers would not in the short term save much money. "It looked good on paper, but it was," he noted, "very much a side show, an administrative move rather than operational … a Chief-level trade-off regarding how much support the RAF would give to a new carrier programme."[318] Band's and Jenner's paper outlined three basic tenets: the continuing need for long-range precision air attack, emphasis on expeditionary operations, and the need for carrier-borne air power. They proposed a two-phased process. First, a joint Harrier force would be formed of the GR7 and FA2 fleets, a force that would transition to a fully joint organisation. Second, there would be a common airframe solution to the Future Carrier Borne Aircraft and the RAF Harrier replacement. They told the Defence Council that these proposals were pragmatic and affordable, and overall would improve operational effectiveness. Jock and Johns undertook to develop their thinking in a paper called 'Joint Force 2000'. Jock was adamant: "We knew perfectly well that, if such a paper were to be given the usual circulation it would be staffed to bits and all the critics would want to have their say. So we decided that the paper would be finalised over Christmas and then sent, signed by Dick [Johns] and me personally, straight to the Chief of the Defence Staff and the Permanent Under-Secretary."

The paper was ready on 19 January and arrived at Jock's bedside in a red box: it was his first signature on recovering from his prostatectomy and he felt confident that it was an historic document.

JF2000 reiterated the three basic tenets and fleshed out the two-phased approach. These were supported by the emerging findings of the SDR, placed emphasis on joint force operations, and proposed that the CVF should be considered a "joint defence asset". Also, operational analysis showed that flexibility could be maximised by a common aircraft solution to the FCBA and Future Offensive Air System, and this common aircraft was likely to be the Joint Strike Fighter (JSF) then in development in the USA. A common aircraft solution should form part of a joint force in which all aircraft could contribute to land- or sea-based operations. This offensive air capability would be in addition to planned investment in Eurofighter and Tomahawk land attack missiles (TLAM).

Summarising the equipment programme, the authors noted that the CVF was fully funded with an in-service date of 2012, though the type of aircraft had not yet been decided; the FCBA was funded for the same in-service date and the UK had invested US$200m in the concept demonstration phase of the JSF; the Harrier GR7 replacement had yet to be funded; and FOAS was assumed to be a fleet of manned aircraft in the 21st century, for which feasibility studies and a technology demonstration programme had been funded.

A common airframe solution would allow for common basing, support, personnel management, training, and operations. Some of these advantages would accrue "by maximising the joint approach to current Harrier capabilities". Cost and performance studies predicted that JSF would be the replacement aircraft for the FA2 and GR7, and planned collaboration with the USA offered UK industry the best opportunity for significant aircraft work. A joint requirements office should be established "to capture the joint requirement for common aircraft solutions to FCBA/GR7 replacement programmes [and] CVF compatibility would be ensured by inclusion of the carrier project in the joint office".

## Joint Force Harrier

Jock was particularly pleased when George Robertson, in announcing the outcome of the SDR, described JF2000 as an "historic proposal" and spoke of his intention to replace the *Invincible*-class with two larger, more versatile carriers.

JF2000 became the Joint Force Harrier when the Royal Navy's Sea Harriers were merged with the RAF's Harrier GR7s, a force ready to operate as required from the *Invincible*-class aircraft carriers or from air bases. No 3 Group RAF would be formed on another April Fool's Day, 2000, commanded by a rear-admiral, with two deputies, one air commodore as commander of Joint Force

Harrier, and another for the Nimrod maritime patrol aircraft (transferred from the former No 11/18 Group).

The pinnacle of Joint Force Harrier's achievements would come in 2000 when a mixed force of Harriers operated from *Illustrious* during Operation Palliser off crisis-torn Sierra Leone.

# Chapter 31: The New Carrier

By December 1997 Jock's arguments for a future generation of CVF were proving successful. His resolve, as if he needed it, was reinforced by two visitors. The first was US Navy Chief of Naval Operations Admiral Jay Johnson, who said, "As a carrier aviator, my interest in the CVF was more than casual so we spent considerable time talking about it … [I found] Jock's belief in the need for newer, more capable/flexible carriers was resolute, though not universally appreciated at the time."[319] Jay's visit was quickly followed by that of an old friend, Frank Miller, Assistant Secretary of Defense at the Pentagon, and over a working breakfast Jock updated him on the progress of the SDR: "Behind the scenes [Miller] was being most helpful in Washington in a discrete way by telling the Americans to support the UK proposal to build a new class of aircraft carrier."

**New Approaches**

While Jock was contemplating surgery he had approved a paper, *New Approaches to the Use of Maritime Forces*, in which he eloquently set out what he called "the emerging maritime issues in the SDR". The paper described how maritime-based forces could be developed in future, consistent with the emerging themes and requirements of the SDR, which were reinforced by recent and encouraging experiences of operating with the USA who "have the undisputed lead in expeditionary operations". Jock hoped that the paper would be considered an important contribution to the development of joint doctrine and concepts of joint operations, and key aspects of defence policy.[320]

However, he missed a series of key meetings about decisions in the SDR, at which he was represented by Boyce, who remained Commander-in-Chief Fleet. Boyce was well-supported by Band as ACNS, Commodore Rory McLean as Director of Naval Plans, and Brigadier Rob Fry as Director of Naval Staff Duties, who were successful in pushing Jock's agenda of shifting British defence policy away from the Central Front in Germany and towards an expeditionary strategy. Nevertheless, Boyce found this period "comprehensively knackering".

Jock returned to his office in London on 8 March. Perhaps he should have waited another month for the long-term effects of the anaesthetics to wear off. He used the lifts to get to his office on the 6th floor of the MoD. "The great thing was I was back in harness … negotiations on the SDR had reached fever pitch and I wanted to ensure that all the right naval balls were in play. I sought a meeting with George Robertson as soon as possible to assure myself this was so. By that stage, I was pretty confident that the two aircraft carriers were in the programme." At a meeting with Roberston to review the naval front line on 24 March, the CDS, Charles Guthrie ("whose grasp of maritime affairs was limited"), and the Permanent Under-Secretary Richard Mottram ("not an enthusiast for naval matters"), were present. Jock was delighted that against the odds Robertson had decided to give his support to the CVF and that he also supported a future amphibious capability. Jock had won an historic victory, though at a price. He had argued throughout for twelve nuclear-powered attack submarines and had to accept ten, and there was another contretemps:

> We then got on to the question of frigates and destroyers, I will never forget my exchange with the Defence Secretary. Throughout we had argued for 35, 12 Destroyers and 23 Frigates. George then said to me 'Jock, I'm going to give you three more.' I said: 'That's great – 38 – three more than we suggested!' 'No he replied – three less.' I then for the first time realized that, unbeknownst to me and the naval staff, the civil servants led by Mottram had privately put forward a figure of 29; so George intended to give us 32 i.e. 3 more! I was hugely irritated by this but concluded that the overall result was as good as we could really expect.

## Outcome of the Strategic Defence Review

Jock tackled the closing months of his term as First Sea Lord with fervour. Events included the inward visit of Admiral Guido Venturoni, the Italian Chief of Defence Staff, who had just been appointed Chairman of the Military Committee of NATO; dinner with the House of Commons Speaker Betty

Boothroyd to pay tribute to the Armed Forces Parliamentary Scheme; an RAF reception at High Wycombe to mark the 30th anniversary of Strike Command; lunch at Trinity House to brief some great and good; a major event in Portsmouth to celebrate the 25th anniversary of the UK/Netherlands Amphibious Force; the summer meeting in Greece of the Chiefs of European Navies; a second address to the General Assembly of the Church of Scotland in Edinburgh; the launch of a new HMS *Kent*; a farewell visit to the Royal Marines at Lympstone; a First Sea Lord's conference in HMS *Dryad* entitled 'Into the 21st Century', which John Reid addressed; an official visit to Chile, which brought back many memories of the Queen's state visit there 30 years before; a final Navy Board dinner; and a last Admiralty Board meeting.

Even Jock was obliged to record that looking at his programme, "I simply do not know how I kept pace and indeed how my hard-pressed staff kept up."

Understandably, there was a triumphal tone to Jock's message to the fleet after the announcement of the SDR on 8 July. The Navy had emerged with a clear operational concept, a plan for a powerful and balanced front line, increased funding for some projects, and a strategy to address the overstretch issues of the past few years. Some changes in emphasis would occur, including reductions in the front line, which would be challenging, but overall the plans for the Royal Navy and Royal Marines were designed well to carry them into the 21st century.

The SDR recognised a shift from confrontation on the Central Front of Western Europe towards a strategy of expeditionary warfare. Crises and threats to British interests could arise anywhere, necessitating joint, versatile, and rapidly deployable forces, and the importance of maritime forces had been recognised in the review. Operations would be undertaken in cooperation with other services and with allies. The Navy's participation in the Joint Rapid Reaction Force and initiatives such as JF2000 and the Joint Helicopter Command for battlefield helicopters would enhance future operational capabilities.

The decision had been made to replace the current *Invincible*-class carriers with two larger aircraft carriers capable of operating fixed-wing aircraft from the Royal Navy and RAF, and helicopters from all three services. In addition, a brigade-sized amphibious force would include HMS *Ocean*, two replacement LPDs (*Albion* and *Bulwark*), two replacement LSLs, and four additional ro-ro ships, enhancing sealift capacity alongside improved heavy airlift for the Joint Rapid Reaction Forces.

Continuous at-sea nuclear deterrence would be maintained through four SSBNs (nuclear-powered, ballistic missile-firing submarines), as it had been for 30 years. All *Trafalgar*-class submarines would be capable of firing TLAMs, extending the Navy's ability to influence events up to 1,000 miles inland. However, while orders for three *Astute*-class submarines and plans for two more were confirmed, there would be a reduction from twelve to ten attack submarines. The number of destroyers and frigates would decrease from 35 to 32, and the mine warfare force would increase from 19 to 22 vessels. The total number of anti-submarine Merlin helicopters would remain at 44, and more Lynx helicopters would be upgraded to a higher standard.

The review supported the Royal Navy's aim of a balanced fleet, with improved equipment procurement, spares, and support. A Chief of Defence Logistics, a new tri-service post insisted upon by ministers, would consolidate the three single-service support commands in order to deliver best practices, avoid duplication, and improve support to joint operations. Logistics shortfalls in all three services, especially for overseas deployments, would be addressed, including the Navy's ammunition stock levels.

Defence Medical Services were affected, but there would be increased medical recruiting, new equipment, and improved medical support for operations overseas including a new 200-bed primary casualty receiving ship.

A key aim of the SDR had been to prioritise people and to eliminate overstretch and gapped complement billets. Flexible approaches to programming ships and submarines would align commitments with resources while maintaining a strong presence in critical areas. The reduction in hulls for destroyers, frigates, and attack submarines would allow redeployment of personnel until improved recruiting and retention measures took effect. No redundancy scheme was anticipated from the review, though there might be some voluntary targeting of specific specialist categories. There would be a substantial increase in training days for both Navy and Royal Marines reserves and an increase of 350 personnel in the RNRs.

Jock concluded his message to the fleet: "The Strategic Defence Review has been a rigorous and comprehensive analysis of the role of the country's Armed Forces and how that role should be carried out. In our case, the task for the Royal Navy and Royal Marines is clearly set out. The plans stand us in good stead and ensure that we remain one of the most powerful and effective navies in the world."

## Paying for the Carrier

The centrepiece of the SDR's new strategy of force projection was two large, 40,000-ton aircraft carriers with a complement of up to 50 aircraft and helicopters; the first would have an in-service date of 2012. The fixed-wing component would probably be provided by the JSF under development in the USA, but the MoD was also studying a marinised Eurofighter, an upgraded Sea Harrier, and other existing US and French naval jets for its Future Carrier Borne Aircraft requirement. The two new carriers would replace the three existing *Invincible*-class light carriers: these were of 20,000 tons, could only deploy a maximum of 24 aircraft and helicopters, and had been designed for anti-submarine warfare rather than force projection. The new size, it seemed, was arbitrary but was based on the US Navy's amphibious assault ships, which operated a mix of helicopters and Harrier jets. This turned on the assumption that the Harrier and its successor would be aircraft of comparable sizes. Though not part of Jock's story, that ambition would prove impossible.

Johns, the CAS, had signed the RAF up to JF2000 and the notional 40,000-ton ship, but there were huge misgivings both in the RAF and the Navy, especially in the Fleet Air Arm, which did not like the secrecy with which the agreement had been reached. Further, after Rear-Admiral Iain Henderson (1998–2001) and Rear-Admiral Scott Lidbetter (2001–03) there was no succession plan for a 2-star naval officer to fill the unhappy attempt to combine the roles of Air Officer Commanding No 3 Group and Flag Officer Maritime Aviation.[321] Meanwhile, Max Hastings, an influential journalist, campaigned strongly against the JSF, or F35B as it became, claiming it was an unaffordable aircraft and that it had disappointing ground-attack capability, a short-range, and insufficient payload. The future Navy needed many more, smaller, affordable bottoms, the journalist wrote, and flight platforms should be cheap and cheerful, with an eye to operating unmanned aerial vehicles in the future: "Our admirals should abandon big willy pretensions [and] join the 21st century."[322]

The SDR decision regarding the carriers turned out to be the easiest part of the process for the Royal Navy, wrote Nick Childs, BBC defence correspondent, but would turn into a nightmare and be one of the most troubled and controversial defence programmes displaying the worst traits of procurement mismanagement. After BAe Systems became the prime contractor and the preferred design rose to almost 70,000 tons, the carrier programme, which at £2.7 billion had been described in the cost of the SDR as fully funded, rose to £3.8 billion, the aircraft capacity fell to from 50 to 40, and the in-service date slipped.[323] Within a few years, in order to keep the new carriers in the programme while paying for the ongoing wars in Afghanistan and Iraq, and while also making further instalments of the so-called 'peace dividend', the MoD was obliged to cut submarines, destroyers, frigates, minehunters and people from the Royal Navy's order of battle.  Further in 2010, under the Strategic Defence and Security Review, the Invincible-class carriers and the Harrier force were prematurely retired.[324]

Jock was dismayed at the concessions of 1997/98, which were made to win the new carriers, and 30 years later, looking back in retirement at the number of submarines, destroyers, and frigates in the fleet of the 2020s, he knew that he would have been hard pressed to argue the case for the carriers against a surface and sub-surface fleet so reduced.

# Chapter 32: First Sea Lord III, 1998

Jock was justifiably pleased with the outcome of the SDR and received several letters of congratulations for what had been achieved, including a note from Admiral Lord Hill-Norton observing that the Navy had come out of the SDR much better than he had feared. He added that very personal and enormous credit was due to Jock for what must be regarded as an unqualified success, and that nobody knew better than him what a battle it must have been. "Gosh! From him, praise indeed!"

Jock had indeed ensured that the Royal Navy remained one of the most powerful and effective navies in the world, but in his final three months as First Sea Lord he now had to sell his ideas and answer many questions. There was no let-up in the pace of events:

> I had little time to reflect … I went straight off to address the Naval Members of the Advanced Command and Staff Course at Bracknell that very evening. Actually the whole of that week was extraordinarily high tempo – inter alia: address to the Royal College of Defence Studies on the Monday with Equerries Dinner for the Queen and Prince Philip that night; a Chiefs of Staff and Senior Appointments Committee before the Admiralty Board above; lunch on the Wednesday with the Chamber of Shipping before the formal press conference announcing the SDR, and later that evening the Chiefs of Staff dinner with Prince Charles at York House; Financial Planning and Management Group Meeting in MoD on the Friday, before flying by helicopter to Southampton to address the Missions to Seamen AGM in the liner *Oriana*. I suspect that I was pretty pooped by the end of that week so I am surprised to see that Annie and I attended a dinner and dancing with the de Laszlos at Pelham Place on the Saturday night. Phew!

## Pople and Pearce

When VCDS and on a visit to South America and the West Indies in 1995, Jock had noted that his Military Assistant Keith Pople and his Assistant Military Assistant Karen Pearce spent more time chatting to each other than engaging with the guests. Once back in London, he spoke to each, making it clear that what they chose to do in private was their business but when it became Jock's business, they should stand from under. Nor should they again accompany him abroad together. Pearce was reappointed to HMS *Illustrious* and that appeared to be the end of the matter, but when Pople tried to rekindle their affair, Pearce accused him of sexual harassment and a court martial followed in April 1998. The charge against Pople was conduct to the prejudice of good order and military discipline by committing adultery with Pearce while he was her immediate superior officer. Although the relationship was admitted by both sides, the court accepted Jock's evidence that Pople was not Pearce's superior officer in the chain of command, even though in the outer office he held higher rank and had an input into her personnel assessment reports; they had separate duties under distinct lines of reporting. At the end of a nine-day court martial, during which the judge advocate was alleged to have taken a prurient interest by allowing "cross-examination in an arguably more in-depth fashion than that seen in civil courts", Pople was cleared of the allegations.[325]

It was, said a BBC reporter, a tale of love and lust, of infidelity and promiscuity, of betrayal, revenge, and, finally, regret, which exposed the military's outdated attitude to adultery, and it highlighted the extent to which senior officers in the armed services are out of touch with the rest of society. Jock would enter the history books as the most senior officer ever to have been called as a witness at a court martial.[326]

## Blood Red Dinner

The doctors' and dentists' discontent at the outcome of *Front Line First* rumbled on throughout Jock's time as First Sea Lord, and in 1998 in the final weeks before retirement he accepted an invitation from the Medical Director General (Navy), Surgeon Rear-Admiral Mike Paine, to the 'Blood Red Dinner' of the Royal Naval Medical Club in the Painted Hall at Greenwich:

> I simply cannot think, with everything else going on in my final weeks, why I agreed to be the guest of honour, but Mike Paine had been my Principal Medical Officer in *Illustrious* so I felt I should do it for him. Every living naval doctor and dentist was present, all deeply unhappy

that the Defence Medical Services were still in a state of disarray post the Defence Cost Studies. I was very conscious of their deep unease and decided that I must face them but knew I could not, at that stage, allay some of their fears. Nevertheless having one's health proposed by so many health experts was a new experience.

After some light-hearted remarks and expressions of gratitude for the work of the medical professionals, Jock addressed the state of the DMS. He admitted responsibility when VCDS, when he led the defence staff through *Front Line First*, for not always identifying the best solutions. The situation was not ideal, but changes had been necessary. There were ongoing efforts to implement improvements and renewed focus during the recent SDR. He highlighted the urgency of resolving uncertainties, pointed out that the secondary care organisation required core facilities, and that alignment with the NHS was essential. The Royal Naval Hospital at Haslar was identified as playing a critical short- to medium-term role and required adequate staffing and resources, but there were gasps when he mentioned its potential closure within five to seven years.

He also discussed the newly established MoD hospital units (departments of large, regional, NHS hospitals), which were beginning to demonstrate improved performance. Nonetheless, concerns about achieving a critical mass and meeting military training requirements persisted. He concluded by stressing that the success of any chosen structure depended on securing the right medical personnel. He observed that the declining strength across the DMS was causing strain and jeopardising retention. While acknowledging that there were no simple solutions, Jock said that the government had prioritised these issues, and mentioned innovative interim measures, such as increased use of reserves and better terms and conditions of service. As he proposed a toast to "The Royal Naval Medical Club", his audience appeared to respect his honesty, though their concerns about the future lingered. At the end of the evening, Jock felt relieved to return to his car.


**Russia**

In the closing weeks of 1996 Jock had spoken to the economic and current affairs forum of the Reform Club. The chairman, Anthony J Capo Bianco, appreciated Jock's attendance and his handling after dinner of questions in a testing Q&A session, when Jock had described in chilling detail the Russian nuclear submarine fleet's state of readiness even at a time when, despite the

Russia's acute financial problems, the Russian leadership was querying the expansion of NATO into eastern Europe. There, the embrace of democracy, Jock told his audience, had to be carefully balanced against the inherent suspicions of Mother Russia. Bianco took issue with Jock's assertion that Europe had insufficient wealth to finance the forces necessary to turn Europe into a world power and that it was NATO – the USA – that should provide the basis for European defence: Bianco called this "an interesting concept".

However, Jock's views were informed by personal contacts with the Russians and by an unusual set of Anglo-US-Russian meetings.

In July 1996, as part of the tercentenary celebrations of the Russian Federation Navy (RFN), which had been founded by Peter the Great, he had met and heard Admiral Igor Kasatonov speak at RUSI about the Russian navy, and he had toasted the Russians in iced vodka: "Who would have thought that one day we would all be friends – or sort of!" Later that summer he flew with Annie to St Petersburg for some historic and memorable few days as the personal guest of Admiral Felix Gromov, Commander-in-Chief of the RFN. Jock was supported by HMS *Cornwall* and a full Royal Marines band.

At lunch on the second day of the trip Gromov's wife beautifully recited Pushkin without a note. "Annie nearly had a cardiac arrest when I whispered to her that it was her turn next with Shakespeare!" That afternoon there was a re-enactment on the lake at the summer palace of the Russian tsars of the 1770 Battle of Chesme in the Russo–Turkish War, and when the hosts discovered that Annie was descended from the Scottish-born Russian naval officer Admiral Samuel Greig, who had distinguished himself at Chesme, she was treated with great respect.[327] Jock recalled: "Almost every Russian admiral that I had ever heard of was present and they had been well briefed about me and [were] clearly thrilled to come face to face with representatives of their adversaries during the Cold War. The presence of my brilliant interpreter, Robert Avery, was an absolute godsend: he had the incredible talent of instant interpretation, so I was able to strike up a great rapport with the hosts."[328] Jock also noted that "The Russians did things in a big way but were incredibly bureaucratic, chaotic, and rather inefficient with all decision-making at the highest level." He had good conversations with Prime Minister Viktor Chernomyrdin, substituting for President Boris Yeltsin, and the Defence Minister General Igor Rodionov.[329]

Unexpectedly, the following morning Jock was invited to a working breakfast with Admiral Gromov: "Little could I have imagined during my long career that one day I would sit face to face with the head of the Russian navy and enjoy a healthy rapport … We had a full 90-minute, very open and friendly discussion, helped along with a glass or two of Stolichnaya. Inevitably, the expansion of NATO to the East and European security were key subjects where Gromov made a prepared statement before he invited me to comment. We also discussed naval cooperation and the importance of trust and understanding."

Jock also had a one-to-one meeting with the Russian hydrographer Admiral Anatoly Komaritsyn, who, impressed by the history and work of the Hydrographer of the Royal Navy, wished for enhanced cooperation. An unforgettable weekend was helped not a little by Jock's Russian, which he had learned at Dartmouth and in which he was coached by Avery.

Arriving at the Russian naval headquarters to sign an historic memorandum of understanding, September 1998, Jock met by Admiral Vladimir Ivanovich Kuroyedov, Commander-in-Chief Russian Federation Navy (r is Rear Admiral Pyotr Mikhailovich Avdeichik, Deputy Chief Main Naval Staff). Source: Robert Avery

Jock opens his speech in Russian. "No wonder they all look so uneasy," he joked. Robert Avery interpreting on Jock's left. Source: Robert Avery.

## RUKUS

Jock had another, unique source of information about the Russian navy in which his three successive Royal Navy's Heads of Defence Studies, Wilson, Page, and Hore, played no small part. Informal confidence-building measures at the end of the Cold War had grown into secretive – and deniable – staff talks between the navies of Russian, the UK and the USA, known as RUKUS. The Royal Navy and the RFN soon discovered that, while there was a shared maritime history since the time of Peter the Great, approaches to operating at sea, the role of warships, and the contribution of naval power to their respective military doctrines were quite different. The RFN, for example, was unfamiliar with the concept of rules of engagement (ROE), which were well developed within the Royal Navy, and the RFN had little concept of the broader utility warships such as in embargo or humanitarian operations. Further, the Royal Navy's emphasis on breadth of training contrasted with the Russian emphasis on the depth of capability. Above all the RFN was autocratic with little delegation, whereas the Royal Navy was governed by mission command.

The end of the Cold War saw talks about the avoidance of incidents at sea develop into ship visits, table-top exercises, real-life exercises, and detail discussions of ROE and joint procedures. A key feature of RUKUS was the engagement of senior officers, the repeat attendance of a small band of civilians such as Avery and Professor Eric Grove, and informal exchanges between the lower-level participants often involving some late-night hard-drinking.

The zenith of these Anglo-Russian relations was arguably 25 September 1998 in Moscow when Jock signed a memorandum of understanding (MOU) with the RFN covering naval cooperation in a wide spectrum of maritime activities, one of the most successful pieces of defence diplomacy of the post-Cold War years. "[How] could I have imagined that, in the month of my standing down, I would be sitting in the Russian main naval staff headquarters and signing such an agreement with the Commander-in-Chief of the Russian Federation Navy, Admiral Vladimir Kuroyedov?"

The Russians clearly attached tremendous importance to their relationship with the Royal Navy. Annie once more accompanied Jock:

> It was an extraordinary feeling waking up in our room and looking out at the Kremlin about which I had thought so much for many years. It was then on to the main Russian naval headquarters. When I wrote my Seaford House Paper at the RCDS on Fleet Admiral Gorshkov and his grand design little did I imagine that twenty years later I would be having talks with a successor in his very office. The signing of the agreement, the first ever concluded by the Russian Federation Navy with a Western counterpart, marked the culmination of a most successful set of negotiations and was seen as a most significant event in terms of defence diplomacy. The Russians had clearly appreciated the exchanges and contacts between professional experts and the high degree of mutual respect that had been built up between our two navies. Considering that Russia's bilateral military programmes with some of our key Allies such as the USA and Germany had virtually dried up, their commitment to our naval cooperation programme was seen in Whitehall as a great achievement.

Jock presented Kuroyedov with an engraved decanter and a bottle of Highland Park, and on the way to a press conference they stopped to admire the portraits of previous Russian commanders-in-chief, not least Annie's ancestor, Admiral Samuel Greig. These meetings were indeed voyages of discovery of each other's people and ships, but despite the personal camaraderie there was little sign of any change of the RFN into a more westernised model of empowerment and delegation of authority, but rather a continuing culture of paranoia and distrust. In this sense, Jock's speech at the Reform Club, with its reference to the suspicions of Mother Russia, was well informed and prescient.

There was no opportunity to build on this historic visit and to develop the friendly and seemingly productive relationships that had been so successfully fostered with erstwhile adversaries. Sadly, when in 2000 the Russian submarine *Kursk* sank in the Barents Sea after suffering a high test peroxide explosion, the Russians reverted to their old Soviet style and it was five days before President Putin authorised a UK/Norway rescue operation. The MOU did not cover underwater operations but Kuroyedov was still in office and Jock wondered whether, had he been able to speak to him personally, he could have urged the Russians to accept immediate assistance.

## Farewell to Arms

On 29 September 1998 Jock addressed a full house of RUSI and was more than usually determined to deliver an upbeat message. The naval staff, led by the brilliant, cerebral, Brigadier Rob Fry, Royal Marines, had worked up a paper called 'The Maritime Contribution to Joint Operations'. It had been heralded earlier in the year in a paper to the Financial Planning and Management Group, had been rehearsed during Jock's visit to Chile, and this was his opportunity to present it publicly and take questions. Jock told his audience:

> Next week I hang up my seaboots after nearly six years in the Ministry as Vice Chief and latterly as First Sea Lord. Six years that have seen a revolution in our affairs through the Defence Cost Studies and the recent Defence Review. I leave at a most exciting point – one might almost say a watershed point – at which we have reaffirmed the Royal Navy's joint tradition; a point where we have seen a swing from a continental to an expeditionary strategy; a point at which we now envisage an operational scenario much more complex and much less singular than in the past, with a joint, integrated, and indivisible battlespace and a point at which maritime forces have a clear and pivotal role. I wish I was starting all over again.

Sir Michael Alexander, the chairman, called it an exemplary lecture, just what RUSI needed to hear and importantly what the Royal Navy needed to comprehend. The full text of this important paper is annexed.

## Vale

On his last morning over a glass of champagne Jock gave each member of the Navy Board a personal copy of John Winton's biography of Uncle Ned[330] and then processed to the south concourse of the MoD where he addressed the assembled naval staff. He was stepping down after 1,185 days as First Sea

Lord, 798 days as VCDS, 687 days as Commander-in-Chief Fleet, 4,845 days as an admiral, and 15,356 days in the Royal Navy, and, given the chance, "I would do it all over again."

He was optimistic about the future. The SDR had given a renewed focus to operational readiness, joint capabilities, sustainability, and versatility, all pivotal themes in shaping the Navy's future. The Navy maintained its excellence while transitioning from the Cold War to a new strategic landscape. Notably, the SDR emphasised the Navy's role in expeditionary warfare, recognising its ability to project force globally. The importance of maintaining an integrated approach to operations was central to his message; he stressed that joint operations were key to advancing the Royal Navy's capability.

While expressing confidence in ongoing projects such as new aircraft carriers, submarines, and other advancements, he also acknowledged the challenges ahead. The defence review had set ambitious goals for equipment renewal and there were seventeen platforms currently under construction, including HMS *Ocean* and the *Astute*-class nuclear submarines. These projects underscored the Navy's commitment to staying technologically advanced. However, he urged vigilance, highlighting the need for ministers to ensure that these ambitious plans would come to fruition without compromise.

Operationally, the Navy maintained a high level of activity worldwide, yet he noted the strain on readiness for contingent requirements. The pressures on personnel and platform availability remained significant concerns. He recognised the Fleet Commander's increased flexibility as a positive development, yet acknowledged the continued need for targeted solutions to ease the burden on sailors.

Welfare and the morale of personnel were also central to his reflections. Efforts by the Second Sea Lord to improve conditions and reduce billet gaps were vital steps forward, but challenges in recruitment and retention remained. He stressed that the calibre and spirit of naval personnel were exceptional, and their dedication was both humbling and crucial to the Navy's success. Ministers' promises to prioritise people's welfare was an encouraging development, but he urged continued attention to improving terms of service.

Finally, he emphasised the importance of fostering support beyond the Navy. Advocacy of the *Maritime Contribution to Joint Operations* was a responsibility shared by all who cared about the naval service. Reaching out to broader society, to policymakers, and to industrialists, was also necessary to ensure a better-informed and supportive public. This, he believed, was key to sustaining the Navy's pre-eminence. In concluding his address he expressed gratitude for the dedication and professionalism of the naval service at sea and ashore.

Jock shook hands with the Navy Board and departed through the south door of the MoD to the applause of his people and then waved his cap out of the passenger window of his car. He departed secure in the knowledge that the Navy's future was bright and its leadership prepared for the challenges ahead, but he entered retirement with mixed emotions – a combination of relief, emptiness, and frustration. Sitting back in the car, he felt and thought three things:

> First, an overwhelming feeling of relief that the enormous weight of responsibility I had held for so long was suddenly lifted. Second, a feeling of emptiness that all I had worked towards for years was finally over. Third, a feeling of utter frustration that, with my national, NATO, and tri-service experience, I still had so much to offer the defence scene and thus a feeling of abject failure that the Royal Navy had prepared me so well for the ultimate top job and I had failed to secure it. The latter reaction would remain with me for the rest of my life.

Jock in contemplation: "Well, Granny was right when she said this would bring me luck!"
Source: Rob Powell.

# Chapter 33: Great and Good

To use a 21st-century recruiting slogan, Jock was made in the Royal Navy, a making in which his Uncle Ned, Admiral of the Fleet Viscount Cunningham of Hyndhope, had had great influence. Jock's own attributes were manifested by the quiet authority he always radiated and by a ruthless mastery of the subject, however new or unfamiliar to him, as Commander Barry Goldman recalled when he accompanied his admiral on a visit to the USN-run, direction-finding station at RAF Edzell, Aberdeenshire:[331]

> The journey was about 1½ hours and one which clearly demonstrated Sir Jock's work ethic. I was bundled into the back whilst he sat in the front seat doing his files. In this mode, he was not one for small talk or pleasantries and I quickly realised that I was not expected to engage him in conversation. Having left in good time and being ahead of schedule, the driver was directed to pull over and wait so that we could arrive exactly on time. He spent the additional time carefully studying his brief to ensure that he had all facts and figures to hand and the names and identities of all those that he was likely to meet firmly fixed in his mind. He was a master of detail and had a photographic memory for names and personalities, but this demonstrated to me that he worked hard at it as well as having such amazing recall.

Jock also had a strong empathy for his people, as Lieutenant Peter Payne, his assistant navigator in HMS *Illustrious*, recalled. When appointed to *Illustrious,* Jock, despite the frenetic activity to prepare her for sea, wrote by hand to welcome Payne to the ship. Later, Payne was stunned when, during a pleasant exchange on the bridge, Jock asked him about his wife by name and inquired whether they liked living in Totnes:[332]

And it wasn't just me; he could do this sort of thing with all of us. We loved him for this and discovered in his leadership style a technique that seemed to know instinctively the safe limits of any given navigational or operational situation, so that he permitted his subordinates the freedom to make their own decisions, keeping him advised. I never saw him lose his temper and the nearest he came to an expression of displeasure was a switch to crisp, pithy comments that were more than enough to warn people that their decisions, or lack thereof, were leading matters too close to the boundaries of what he considered safe and professional. *Illustrious* was a happy ship, brand new, and a crew united in common endeavour. But it was our captain's remarkably capable, caring and yet understated personality that was the bedrock of our high morale.

Jock's ability, known to psychologists as super-recognition, enabled him in *Illustrious* to address by name just about anybody in the ship's company and air group of over 1,000 men, right down to the lowliest junior mechanic, and to recall their backgrounds.[333]

Jock stood down as First Sea Lord on 8 October 1998 and like his predecessors he remained on the active list, but unlike them he was not promoted to Admiral of the Fleet (5-star). Briefly it was mooted that there might be a seat in the House of Lords, where there were few active naval peers, but there was no precedent for this. A plaque in the Mall House flat recording Uncle Ned's residence there as First Sea Lord and his postwar successors, but a proposal to bring this up to date and add Jock's name, so that the list of occupants began and ended with a Cunningham was rejected. Instead, Jock opened a new portfolio of private and public service in which he applied the qualities the had made him so successful in the Navy.

In an interview for an oral history project at Dartmouth, Jock reflected on his career, telling the interviewer that "The key to a successful career, and I learned this at Dartmouth, is to surround yourself with people of great quality, delegate to them mercilessly, and never stay long enough to be fully tested."[334] But this is too modest, for his achievements whether as non-executive director of Vosper Thorneycroft and of Lockheed Martin, Elder Brother of Trinity House, where the Princess Royal succeeded Prince Philip as Master, Prime Warden of the Worshipful Company of Shipwrights, where he skilfully oversaw arrangements for Prince Charles to succeed his father as Permanent Master, chairman of the Imperial War Museum, or Deputy Lieutenant of Hampshire, chairman of the RNLI, among other offices, were met with unanimous praise.

Music had always given Jock great pleasure and he was pleased to become President of the Royal Navy Pipers' Society, formed in 1951 when Uncle Ned was its president and Prince Philip its patron. After his performances on the flute at Carnegie Hall, Dundee and conducting the massed bands at the Royal Albert Hall, he was even more thrilled to be asked to be the first president of the Royal Marines Association Concert Band.

Outdoor sports continue to appeal and he played golf at that haunt of retired admirals, the Liphook Golf Club, and long after he could no longer stalk the Scottish hills as a guest of his monarch he enjoyed many days shooting with, among others, Donald Gosling at Broadlands and the Princess Royal at Gatcombe.

He has always been a good, quick-thinking orator, who chooses his words wisely and delivers them effectively, and he possesses great people skills. Two anecdotes from his days as chairman of the RNLI suffice. On visits to lifeboat stations he would speak to everyone, often making a beeline for the lady behind the tea urn in the boathouse or others around the periphery of the gathering. Then, in a new lifeboat, he asked if he could take the helm in rough weather when an impromptu man overboard exercise was simulated: Jock was not fazed in the slightest and he recovered the man perfectly, gaining the full respect of the boat's coxswain. This became a regular event with other admirals, but none did it better.[335]

From the turn of the 21st century until today, Admiral Sir Jock Slater, still on the active list, has given more than a quarter of century of remarkable public service in those industries, societies, and charities in which he has become involved. An account of these services would fill another book, but this volume has looked exclusively at his life and times and his influence on defence and naval policy at the end of the Cold War when, as Max Hastings told this author, "Jock was an outstanding First Sea Lord, by far the best holder of the post in the past 25 years, and should have been Chief of Defence Staff."[336]

Installation of Prince Charles as Prime Warden of the Shipwrights in the Painted Hall at Greenwich in the presence of HRH Prince Philip, Permanent Master. Source: Worshipful Co of Shipwrights.

# The Maritime Contribution
## to Joint Operations

**First Sea Lord's Valedictory Address to the Royal United Services Institution**

I am delighted to be invited to address the Institute in my final few days in office. It was tempting for me this afternoon to take stock of the Royal Navy and Royal Marines over the period of my service (some 42 years) and then talk in detail about where we are today – in terms of operations, support, equipment and people. I have decided to concentrate on 'The Maritime Contribution to Joint Operations'.

The subject arises naturally out of the Strategic Defence Review (SDR) which has had at its heart a view of future operations which is, above all else, expeditionary and joint. Although those of us within the Navy have been thinking in those terms for some time, this is one of the first opportunities I have had to make a public statement on the subject (and there could be no more discerning and informed audience than at the RUSI!). I also take considerable pleasure and some pride in the fact that my valedictory address at the RUSI comes at a time when we see emerging a fresh and intellectually stimulating approach to maritime power (I can at once claim authorship and avoid subsequent responsibility!). Less flippantly, I am delighted to have been involved in a Defence Review which has accurately caught the grand strategic mood of the time, established a broad military strategic doctrine in response and called on practitioners like me to deliver at the operational and tactical levels. Furthermore, I have been hugely impressed by the way Ministers, Officials and the Military have come together so constructively to plan a defence strategy that I am fully confident will stand the country in good stead in the years ahead.

I want to speak in some detail about the practicalities of the maritime contribution but, before I do, I would like to set the scene by reviewing historically the Navy's joint credentials and reflecting a little further on the strategic dynamics we face today.

## The Navy and Joint Operations in History

As First Sea Lord I am the inheritor of two separate traditions which, although they have been as enduring as the application of Naval Power, have been placed into particularly sharp focus by the history of the Royal Navy since 1805 – an arbitrary date, but one with an obvious significance which will not be lost on this audience.

The first tradition is the old-fashioned view, a view which contends that the twin principles of the decisive fleet engagement and command of the sea represent the proper application of maritime power, particularly British maritime power during a period which started with Naval pre-eminence and is still today characterised by Naval prominence.

This is a tradition which its advocates would argue saw its consummation on 21 October 1805 and, while such singular victories have more or less eluded the Royal Navy in the twentieth century, it is a tradition which has been carried on by the American victories in the Pacific campaign in the Second World War. These same advocates, not least Mahan, would go on to say that when fleets have met without decisive result – and the obvious example is Jutland – this was the result of local, tactical factors and indicates no change in the main principle; had, in Beatty's pithy phrase, the 'bloody ships' behaved properly, normal historical service would have been restored, the German High Seas Fleet destroyed and the British Grand Fleet permitted to go about its normal business of the unchallenged exercise of command of the sea.

It is a tradition which draws on a history of battles which were not only decisive but also annihilating, citing a history which includes not only Trafalgar but also Navarino, Tsushima and the US Pacific campaign.

It is a tradition which sees the Royal Navy as the ultimate instrument of victory in the wars of national survival of the nineteenth and twentieth centuries.

It is, of course, a view not unique to this country and one which perhaps reached its peak in America in the 1940s, when it was wryly described by Secretary for War Stimpson as 'the particular psychology of the Navy Department, which frequently seems to retire from the realm of logic into a dim religious world in which Neptune is god, Mahan the prophet and the United States Navy the only true church'.

It is a tradition which is both attractive and compelling and one which has driven military strategic policy in this country for long periods. I only have to look as far as the development of the Dreadnought and a Grand Fleet designed solely for decisive battle to find an example.

## The Second Tradition

To look on the other side of the coin, I am also the inheritor of a second tradition which has run in parallel with the first (whose main spokesmen are Corbett and Richmond), which sees the application of maritime power as inextricably linked with operations on the land. This is a view which is joint rather than navalist and one which sees the coveted fleet engagement as relevant only in so far as its effects can be measured in the prosecution of a land campaign.

As an illustration let me remind you of Corbett's revisionary view of Trafalgar: the battle coincided with Napoleon's masterpiece at Austerlitz. The first, Corbett claimed, did little more than confirm an existing strategic situation; the second destroyed the only viable continental coalition and established French hegemony in Europe. In Schurman's words 'from under the muzzles of the guns of Trafalgar he thundered again to all who would hear the message: without a supporting army, imaginatively led, the Navy is not a decisively effective offensive weapon'.

Yet the same period showed a definitive example of the use of maritime force to complement land operations. The Peninsular campaign was preceded by the amphibious withdrawal of Sir John Moore's army at Corunna and its re-insertion under Wellington through the port of Lisbon. It was a campaign sustained by maritime power and one which used frequent and imaginative tactical manoeuvre from the sea.

To the advocates of this second tradition, an overview of the Peninsular War shows all the features which Liddell Hart would later characterise as 'the British way in warfare': that is limited expeditionary operations in a minor theatre sustained from the sea and accompanied by the subsidy of local allies. Indeed, our conduct of grand and military strategy in the Napoleonic era is well worth looking at again today; incidentally I am pleased to see that the Institute will shortly be staging a panel discussion on the legacy of Liddell Hart – thinly disguised under the title of 'Manoeuvre'! – would not be at all surprised if we see Liddell Hart's work rehabilitated after a period of neglect as we rediscover the realities of expeditionary operations.

The two traditions I have described cohabited for most of the nineteenth century but became perilously close to divorce in the early twentieth century.

Having already chronicled the Russo-Japanese war, Corbett was invited by the Committee for Imperial Defence to be the official Naval Historian of the war with Germany. His death in 1922 after the publication of three volumes spared him the mortification of seeing in the following year the issue of an Admiralty disclaimer for what they saw as 'a tendency to minimise the importance of seeking battle and forcing it to a conclusion'.

So far, all that I have said looks back, but by way of introduction I wanted to emphasise the combination that exists in our naval heritage: on the one hand a simple and direct inheritance of the Nelsonic tradition of seeking battle on the sea and, on the other hand, the application of maritime force as part of an integrated, joint approach to war. The first remains a glorious tradition of which I am extremely proud, but it is the second which establishes the precedents which I suggest will influence the future.


**Changed Operational Scene**

So, what of that future? Volumes have been written on the changed strategic circumstances in which we now live, and I have little to add to what seems now to be the general view that we are moving away from a military strategy of predisposition on the North German Plain and the North Atlantic and towards a doctrine of expeditionary operations. I will, though, selectively quote others to make a few points.

I will start on safe ground by turning to Lawrence Freedman, who has offered the following definitions: 'Operational space defines the combat zone, political space that which must be protected and logistic space links the two'. From this I would contend that where operational and political space overlap – as was the case in Northern Germany and to a lesser extent in the Norwegian Sea – forces need to be pre-deployed as far forward within the operational space as is possible. In turn this has temporal implications and when logistic time – in Freedman's words 'that which is required to prepare for war and sustain operations' – is limited, we have to depend on high readiness and war stocks which are based well forward and available for instant use.

It was this vicious circle of condensed operational space, the coincidence of operational and political space and limitations in logistic time which characterised the Cold War. Now, of course, these relationships are inverted, and we see the separation of operational and political space and the creation of greater logistic time and space or, stated more simply, what we now recognise as expeditionary operations.

I wanted to make these rather technical points to draw out the importance of the two fundamental components of manoeuvre and indeed all warfighting – time and space. Why have we become so interested in manoeuvre in recent years, to the extent that we all claim to be manoeuvrists now? The answer is simple: by the re-ordering of the relationship between operational, political and logistic time and space, manoeuvre has been restored to the battlefield.

If you were occupying a general defensive position along the inner German border, manoeuvre was a tactical indulgence which was simply not available to you. Now, however, when operational and political space may be separated by large distances, or where political space, in the traditional and absolute sense, may not even exist at all, there is a capacity for manoeuvre because time and space have again become available for its conduct.

Herein lies the key and it is a vitally important point because the logistic space which will characterise expeditionary operations will, typically, be occupied by the sea, and it is the capacity for deployment and sustainment of seaborne forces which will define logistic time. In the same way, deeper operational space will permit manoeuvre by Land, Air and Naval forces, but it is in the air and on the sea that the capacity for manoeuvre will frequently be greatest because of the permissive nature of those elements. Quite simply, it is easier for a self-sustained Naval Task Group to move 400 miles in 24 hours than it is for an Armoured Division. For these reasons, what I will now title 'Maritime Manoeuvre' has a relevance for the future which it has not had for the immediate past – and it was on that basis that the maritime aspects of the Strategic Defence Review were argued.

Those of you who read the June edition of the RUSI Journal will have seen Brigadier Robert Fry's article entitled 'End of the Continental Century'. Without rehearsing its arguments again, I agree with what he said about the historical point we now occupy between periods of continental and maritime pre-eminence. We now have a military strategy, clearly laid out by the SDR, which is essentially maritime. Let me be absolutely clear what I mean by that. I do not mean that we have a Naval strategy, a return to the first tradition of which I spoke earlier. Rather I suggest we have a military strategy which links directly into the second tradition I described; one that will depend on maritime deployment and sustainment and will permit the prosecution of operations from the sea to the land; but one which is demonstrably joint and for which divisions between the land, sea and air environments are unnecessary and artificial.

The SDR White Paper states that 'success in modern warfare depends on joint teamwork'. Battles and wars are won by maritime, ground and air forces operating effectively together in support of shared military objectives. What I want to do now is to explain the maritime contribution to that joint enterprise.

## New Operational Challenges

Let me start by comparing the operational challenge we will face in the future to the one we faced in the past – and if you detect a note of wistful nostalgia, it is not because I carry any vestige of Cold War baggage, but because, no matter the scale of the Soviet threat, it was part of an operational environment which was beguilingly simple.

Operations would have been conducted within well-defined geographical limits against an enemy which could be assessed in precise capability terms and with a style of warfighting based on linear escalation at the heart of which was the aim of inflicting maximum physical destruction. All very straightforward.

This grim prospect was set within an alliance architecture of command which was well established, frequently exercised and tailored to the specific requirements of the naval and land/air campaigns; and the fact that these environments could have been so neatly compartmentalised is a telling comment on the relative simplicity of the operational circumstances.

Today's and tomorrow's operations will be conducted at global range against an ill-defined enemy by forces likely to be brought together by diplomatically expedient circumstances; indeed, the participants may have to learn the business of combined operations on the job. That is a big enough task in itself, but to superimpose on that a situation where campaign aims may be imprecise at the outset, may change over time and may be directed against an enemy whose centre of gravity is psychological rather than physical and you have a pretty complex cocktail. Indeed, the traditional concept of an enemy – a well-defined set of capabilities unified by hostile intent – may not be appropriate to the threats of what we have come to define as Asymmetric Warfare.

Taking all this together illustrates the need for forces which are adaptive and capable of reconfiguration within a campaign, which transcend old environmental boundaries, and which share a warfare doctrine based on universal principles, but which avoids prescriptive operational solutions. This represents a real challenge, but much progress has been made already, and the Strategic Defence Review will build on this further. The Permanent Joint Headquarters and the Joint Service Command and Staff College are already in existence and will be complemented in due course by a Joint Defence Centre. Together they will variously devise, teach and practice a doctrine which I confidently expect to establish us as world leaders in the business of joint operations. I am in no doubt that these institutional reforms will one day take their place alongside those bearing the names of Haldane and Fisher and will be recognised as being of equal importance.

## Maritime Contribution

Let me now describe what maritime forces will bring to this environment and, just as importantly, what they will not. You need no reminding of the reach, self sufficiency – in both tactical and logistic terms – and independence from host nation support which are the traditional hallmarks of maritime forces. But let me also emphasise the wide spectrum of the operational choices which they offer.

Maritime forces can deploy, withdraw and redeploy simply by exercising freedom of navigation. From a sea base, they can provide transport, mounting bases, airfields, stores depots, barracks, fire support, hospitals and refugee havens, all without infringing sovereignty and frequently with complete invulnerability. They can provide collectively, or as a single unit, a capacity for everything from constabulary operations to high-intensity warfare. And, in certain circumstances, they can even act independently of the traditional levels of war. A single ship ostensibly operates at the tactical level, but when, as with HMS Cornwall in Sierra Leone recently, it can bring all the qualities I have listed together in a single theatre, it can have a palpable impact at the operational level in pursuit of strategic objectives.

Finally, maritime forces provide the quickest means of deploying a logistically self-sustaining and tactically coherent force over long distances, providing an invaluable capacity for timely presence and thus the ability to nip trouble in the bud. If this fails, they have recourse to demonstration, coercion and war fighting; they can shape the joint operational environment in advance of heavier forces and play a role in support of them once they are established in theatre.

Above all else, I suggest to you that it is this range and subtlety of choice within a single campaign which is the key contribution that maritime forces will make to the complex and demanding operational environment we now face. What maritime forces cannot do is match the rapid initial deployment, range and fire power of land-based aircraft, nor the weight and territorial presence of land forces. But by adaptive force composition and joint integration we can minimise these shortcomings, and it is to these themes that I will now turn.

## Naval Task Force Role

A Naval Task Force is precisely that – a force brought together to discharge a specified task, or range of tasks. It has no prescriptive composition but is likely to be designed for self-sustainment, for the contribution it can make within the single, joint battlespace, and for its own protection.

It is likely to be preceded by one or more nuclear submarines. The very dispatch of a nuclear boat represents a powerful signal if, indeed, we choose to advertise it. Its unrivalled capacity for timely deployment (600 miles per day) will get it into theatre fast and its multi-faceted ability to launch TLAM from up to 1000 miles, carry out the clandestine insertion of Special Forces and gather information and intelligence means it will simultaneously provide presence, a capacity for coercion and the preparatory moves for warfighting; equally, it will simultaneously figure in the prospective enemy's calculations at both the operational and tactical levels.

The Task Force following on will be preparing for operations in the most complex joint environment – the littoral; and it is complex as it draws together the three disciplines – land, air and sea, in three dimensions.

At the heart of the Task Force will be a capacity for advanced command and control to facilitate power projection. Projecting from the sea has many elements. I have already mentioned the submarine-fired Land Attack Cruise Missile. I now come to the new Amphibious Flotilla and the new larger carriers, but I must take care here not to describe future capabilities in the rather inadequate language of the past. Our amphibious capability has been historically light, slow and designed for single insertions in largely positional warfare. The fact that it won back the Falkland Islands owed more to extraordinary ingenuity than innate capability. The future force will have only passing resemblance to that which exists today. It will be served by new LPDs and, crucially, an LPH capable of operating Troop Transport and Utility and Attack Helicopters to deploy and support its embarked force. Attack Helicopters will provide a completely new dimension, not only making good a long-standing weakness in anti-armour capability, but more importantly by allowing the simultaneous prosecution of the close and deep land battle. Neither would I see the Embarked Force solely defined by the capabilities currently embedded in the 3 Commando Brigade. The force we project ashore would need to be designed for task in the same way as the maritime force. It may require the armour and the logistic depth to sustain it. The increased powers given to the Chief of Joint Operations to coordinate our exercise programme, so that these disparate force elements can routinely train together, is yet another important legacy of SDR. In exactly the same way, whilst I am obviously pleased that we are operating both the Sea Harrier and the RAF Harrier GR7 from our Carriers, that is only the first step in an integration which I hope will eventually see the replacement of the Royal Navy and Royal Air Force Harrier force by a single, high-performance aircraft flown, supported and maintained jointly. Joint Force 2000, the historic agreement between the Chief of Air Staff and myself, which emerged as part of the SDR, forms the basis for this integration.

The Air Group operating from the Future Carrier will, again, transform the combat power we will apply to the joint battle. It will give us an organic capability for both battlefield support, as well as air defence; indeed, we might have to reinvent the procedures for the close support of ground manoeuvre which the new operational environment will demand.

The Air Group will dramatically change the proportion of indirect fire support available to the force ashore; it will conduct – in coordination with attack helicopters – the simultaneous close and deep operations of which I spoke previously. When used in conjunction with a ground combat element enjoying the tactical advantage of protected mobility, the support of 155mm artillery, armour, extended range Naval Gunfire Support and tactically targeted TLAM, you will recognise immediately the distance which separates this vision from the 'boots and bergen' amphibious operations of popular imagination. It will be a potent force, bristling with sophisticated capabilities able to accept battle at formation level against a range of threats.

## Maritime Manoeuvre Qualities

It is at the point of transfer from sea to land that the particular qualities of maritime manoeuvre will come into their own. The ability of a task force to move over distance, concentrate and project force interestingly in a manner closely described by Corbett in a different context – means that we can achieve the dislocation of the enemy which is the central aim of manoeuvre warfare.

By exploiting time we will gain space and by exploiting space we will be able to use our future formidable combat power to establish high tempo operations and thus exploit the dislocation we will have already created.

As the doctrinaires amongst you will know, and as I learnt as the Vice Chief of Defence Staff, it is the ability to transition which is the key to tempo and, in projecting force from the sea to the land supported from the air at a time and place of our choosing. We will achieve a transition which even the most tactically agile enemy will be pressed to match.

The operational sequence I have just described is, of course, not a one-shot effort. By using the advantages of sea-basing, the force would have a limited logistic footprint on land, could re-embark with the same facility with which it moved ashore, and be capable of geographically displaced operations after a short period of recuperation and transit.

In saying this I make no claims for maritime-based forces to exercise a decisive, independent role in large-scale land conflict. But I do assert their ability to play an independent role at every level from benign operations to medium scale warfighting, and to make a substantial contribution to the joint campaign beyond that point.

Taken overall, I submit that what I have described merits the description that I used at the start, of a fresh and intellectually stimulating approach to the use of the maritime power. Over the next few weeks and months, I want many more people inside and outside the MoD to become conversant with 'the maritime contribution to joint operations'.

Next week I hang up my seaboots after nearly six years in the Ministry as Vice Chief and latterly as First Sea Lord. Six years that have seen a revolution in our affairs through the Defence Cost Studies and the recent Defence Review.

I leave at a most exciting point – one might almost say a watershed point – at which we have reaffirmed the Royal Navy's joint tradition; a point where we have seen a swing from a continental to an expeditionary strategy; a point at which we now envisage an operational scenario much more complex and much less singular than in the past with a joint, integrated and indivisible battlespace and a point at which maritime forces have a clear and pivotal role.

I wish I was starting all over again.

# Endnotes

1   RAdm Royer M Dick CB CBE DSC**, who as a commodore was Uncle Ned's chief of staff when Cunningham returned to the Mediterranean as Naval Commander Expeditionary Force North Africa and Mediterranean. It was Dick who, echoing the orders of Anson two centuries before, ordered the fleet to annoy and distress the enemy, "by taking, sinking, burning, or otherwise destroying all their ships and vessels" and who had written Cunningham's orders in 1943 for Operation Retribution: "Sink, burn, and destroy. Let nothing pass."

2   Cdre E Hugh Lee, DSC, who as ABC's flag lieutenant had orchestrated the ruse in which he and his admiral had pretended to go ashore to play golf, for the benefit of watching spies, while the fleet prepared to sail from Alexandria for the Battle of Matapan.

3   Cunningham, Andrew, KT GCB OM DSO, *A Sailor's Odyssey: The Autobiography of Admiral Andrew Cunningham,* Foreword by Admiral Sir Jock Slater (Barnsley: Seaforth, 2022). Originally published in 1951 and written with the assistance of Captain Taprell Henry Dorling, a destroyer officer who under the penname of 'Taffrail' wrote several books about the Navy.

4   Warner, Oliver, Admiral of the Fleet Cunningham of Hyndhope (London: John Murray, 1967); Simpson, Michael, The Cunningham Papers: The Mediterranean Fleet, 1939–1942. Vol. 1 (London: Navy Records Society, 1999); Simpson, Michael, The Cunningham Papers: The Triumph of Allied Sea Power 1942–1946. Vol. 2 (London: Navy Records Society, 2006).

5   Winton, John (1998) *The Greatest Admiral since Nelson*, foreword by Jock Slater (London: John Murray).

6   Thomson, Arthur (1909). 'Daniel John Cunningham. Born April 15th, 1850; Died June 23rd, 1909'. *Man* Vol. 9, pp 97–99.

7   Hore, Peter (2018) *Henry Harwood: Hero of the River Plate*, Foreword by Admiral Sir Jock Slater (Barnsley: Seaforth, pp 1–10 'The Stubbington Boys'.

8   Under the command of Captain RC Prothero, she was flagship of Vice-Admiral Sir Robert Harris when he was Commander-in-Chief, Cape of Good Hope Station in South Africa 1898–1900. In 1899 one of HMS *Doris*'s 4.7-inch guns was mounted

on an improvised field carriage during the Second Boer War and was known as *Joe Chamberlain*. Captain Prothero, known as 'Prothero the Bad, was a man of violent temper who terrified his officers and crew alike.

9   Throughout her life, *Kelly*, from commissioning to sinking, was commanded by Mountbatten, as Captain 5th Destroyer Flotilla, until she was lost in action in 1941 during the Battle of Crete. The 1942 film *In Which We Serve* starring Noël Coward and John Mills was based on *Kelly*.

10   Roberts, Andrew (2008). *Masters and Commanders: How Roosevelt, Churchill, Marshall, and Alanbrooke Won the War in the West.* (Allen Lane). The antipathy between Cunningham and Mountbatten was mutual, see: Ziegler, P. (1985) *Mountbatten: The Official Biography* pp 231, 486  (London: Collins).

11   Churchill, Winston. *The Second World War Volume III, 'The Grand Alliance'*, Chapter XVI 'Crete: The Battle. After the Italian armistice in 1943'. Cunningham also gave the world his famous signal: "Be pleased to inform their Lordships that the Italian fleet lies under the guns of the fortress of Malta. God save the King." Churchill p 102.

12   Simpson, Michael (2004) *A Life of Admiral of the Fleet Andrew Cunningham: A Twentieth-Century Naval Leader*, p 209. (Routledge).

13   LtCol J Cunningham, 1882–1968, physician and bacteriologist in the Indian Medical Service.

14   Gen Sir Alan Gordon Cunningham 1887–1983, noted for his victories over Italian forces in the East African Campaign during the Second World War. See: Vincent, D. (2024) *The Forgotten General: Sir Alan Cunningham GCMG, KCB, DSO, MC* (Amberley).

15   Jock made a point each year of visiting Derrick Johnstone and his wife Susie at Ness House on the front at Stromness. Johnstone, a veteran of wartime Arctic convoys, was a staunch socialist who much enjoyed the political chat particularly with the Scottish poet George Mackay Brown, with whom he enjoyed a home brew, and Ian McInnes, the art master and later headmaster of Stromness Academy and 'Orkney's renaissance man'. See: Cooper, N. (2022) 'Ian McInnes – Orkney's Renaissance Man'.

16   See: https://spink.com/lot/5019130 An Outstanding CB DSO OBE group of twelve medals to RAdm WJ Munn sold for £6,500.

17   RAdm RJ Hill (1929–2017). See *Daily Telegraph* obituary 3 May 2017.

18   Adm Sir Frank Hopkins KCB DSO DSC (1910–90).

19   Many years later Jock was disappointed to discover that a vandal had painted out most of the names except that of Prince Charles.

20   Members of the ship's company were the audience for the December 1960 episode of 'The Navy Lark, Johnson's Birthday', and the September 1967 episode, 'Troutbridge's Silver Jubilee', which coincided with *Troubridge*'s own September 1942 launch date. Many years later the BBC ran a series called *The Reunion*, bringing together members of 'The Navy Lark' cast and for which Slater was interviewed.

21   Unlike the Navy sixty years later, when a first command might be a multi-billion pound Type 45 destroyer, and come to a mid-rank commander, perhaps aged in his forties and therefore, arguably, much less likely to take risks than his predecessor in previous generations.

22    Captain RFG 'Ronnie' Laughton (1930–83), a grandson of the historian Sir John Knox Laughton.

23    Captain NJ 'Nick' Barker CBE (1933–97), captain of HMS *Endurance* during the 1982 Falklands War.

24    Lieutenant Commander James Philip de Havilland Saumarez (1937–2023), the last of the generations of the Saumarez clan to command a RN ship – HMS *Gossamer*, formerly named *Miner II*, a controlled mine layer built by Philip and Son at Dartmouth during the Second World War. See *Daily Telegraph* obituary 7 Aug 1923.

25    The author is grateful to Cdr JLL Prichard and Cdre AJC Morrow CVO, term-mates at Dartmouth in 1962, and to Robert Hardman for help about *Britannia*.

26    VAdm Sir Peter Dawnay KCVO CB DSC (1904–1989) Fleet Wireless Officer in the battleship HMS *Duke of York* at the Battle of North Cape, and Flag Officer Royal Yachts 1958–62.

27    Captain DG Roome LVO (1923–2009).

28    Lieutenant FW Pardy MVO (…–1978).

29    Some of the furniture and fittings from the *Victoria and Albert* were transferred to *Britannia* and some other equipment was also second-hand: the evaporators came from the battleship HMS *Queen Elizabeth*, built from 1912–13 and scrapped in 1948; the turbogenerators came from the *Minotaur*-class light cruiser HMS *Tiger*, scrapped on the stocks in 1946; and the emergency generator had been the main engine of the submarine HMS *Vampire*, decommissioned in 1945 and broken up in 1950.

30    'A New Royal Yacht'. *The Times*, 9 October 1951.

31    Hennessy, P (2010) *Secret State – Preparing for the Worst 1945–2010*. (London: Penguin Books).

32    Warrant Officer 'Norrie' Norrell (1933–2021) See *Daily Telegraph* obituary 12 October 2021.

33    LtCol Sir Martin Gilliat GCVO MBE (1913–1993) private secretary to the Queen Mother for 37 years.

34    Sods is supposed to be an abbreviation for 'ship's operatic and dramatic society'.

35    Sir Hugh Byatt KCVO CMG (1927–2011).

36    AF Sir William Staveley GCB (1928–97).

37    VAdm Sir James Weatherall (1936–2018 ) See *Daily Telegraph* obituary 28 March 2018.

38    Cdr JMB Walkey (….–2002)

39    VAdm Sir Robert Gerken KCB CBE (1932–2022). See *Daily Telegraph* obituary 12 January 2023.

40    SurgVAdm AL Revell (1935–2018). See *Daily Telegraph* obituary 6 January 2019.

41    Adm Sir John Treacher (1934–2018) was widely tipped to become First Sea Lord but when he found that the incumbent, Edward Ashmore, had laid other plans, he retired, shortly before the Silver Jubilee Fleet Review at Spithead (which he had planned), avowing to secure the financial security of his family. See *Daily Telegraph* obituary 3 May 2018.

## ENDNOTES

42 Clark, Victor *On the Wings of a Dream* (1960) and *Triumph and Disaster* (1994). See *Daily Telegraph* obituary 13 Jan 2006.

43 There is an apocryphal story that circulated in the Fishery Protection Squadron that one or other commanding officer of a Ton-class ship was admiral of the Scottish fisheries in a line of succession from Admiral Nelson when he was in command of HMS *Albemarle* in 1781. This may be an echo of the fact that there was a Henry Nelson who was admiral of the herring fleet in the late eighteenth century.

44 Mayhew was heir to the cabinet-ranking position of First Lord of the Admiralty, but soon it too would be abolished and replaced by the Parliamentary Under Secretary of State for Defence for the Royal Navy.

45 LtCdr RL Brooke (….–2002)

46 VAdm Sir Charles Mills KCB CBE DSC (1914–2006). See *Daily Telegraph* obituary 14 September 2006.

47 Capt MF Parry (….–2004)

48 RAdm RIT Hogg CB (1932–….), a talented officer who was Flag Officer First Flotilla 1984–86, Chief of Staff to the Commander-in-Chief Fleet 1986–87, but resigned to work in industry. Interview 26 May 2023.

49 VAdm Sir Ian McIntosh KBE CB DSO DSC (1919–2003) Australian-born, torpedoed in 1941 when he took command of a lifeboat with 82 survivors on board, 26 more than the boat was rated for, and navigated 1,500 miles in 23 days to Brazil. See *Daily Telegraph* obituary 4 August 2003.

50 Scene of the Battle of Cocos on 9 November 1914 between the Australian light cruiser HMAS *Sydney* and the German light cruiser *Emden*, which had attacked the cable relay station on Direction Island.

51 Adm Sir Jeremy Black (1932–2015), charismatic gunnery officer who commanded the aircraft carrier *Invincible* during the Falklands War, for whom his devoted ship's company coined the epithet 'There and Back with JJ Black'. See *Daily Telegraph* obituary 1 December 2015.

52 RAdm Sir Ronald Forrest KCVO (1923–2005) was Defence Services Secretary (1972–75).

53 Captain ISS Mackay (1924–93).

54 White's, founded in 1693 and the oldest gentlemen's club in London, considered by many to be the most exclusive. Sir Eric Penn GVCO OBE MC (1916–93) former Grenadier Guards and Comptroller (1964–81), had a reputation for severity and punctiliousness, expecting a 100% from his staff. He was, however, also courteous and diplomatic. Patrick Terence William Span Plunket, 7th Baron Plunket (1923–75) former equerry to HM Queen Elizabeth II and Deputy Master of the Household of the Royal Household (1954–1975).

55 Sir John Wriothesley Russell GCVO CMG (1914–74).

56 Duncan, Andrew (1970) *The Queen's Year: The Reality of Monarchy*.

57   Boothroyd, Betty (1989) 'By Appointment', in *The Punch Book of Utterly British Humour* (London: Grafton Books).

58   Eric Robert Russell Linklater CBE (1899–1974) Scottish poet, fiction writer, military historian, and travel writer: though born in Wales his family came from Orkney and he was educated at Aberdeen Grammar School and the University of Aberdeen, where he was rector from 1945–48.

59   Bernard Marmaduke Fitzalan-Howard, 16th Duke of Norfolk and Earl Marshal KG GCVO GBE TD (1908–75).

60   AVM PG Beer CB CBE LVO (1941–….) equerry to the Queen 1971–74, Commander British Forces Falkland Islands 1991–92, home bursar at Jesus College, Oxford 1997–2006.

61   Sir James Burnet (1928–2012), known as Alastair Burnet, a journalist and broadcaster.

62   McLuskey, James Fraser (1951) *Parachute Padre: Behind German Lines with the SAS, France 1944* (Crawley: Strong Oak).

63   Chapman Pincher, Harry, 'Interview with Admiral Sir Jock Slater', *The Field*, July 1998.

64   LT WDA Hacking email 26 February 2023.

65   RAdm PM Franklyn CB MVO (1946–….) email 23 October 2023.

66   AF Sir Edward Ashmore GCB DSC (1919–2016). See Daily Telegraph obituary 2 August 2002.

67   VAdm Sir Thomas Baird KCB (1924–….).

68   However, in Gibraltar when Miller preparing to run an exercise in the Mediterranean from the carrier HMS *Ark Royal*, her captain, Desmond Cassidi, was obliged to place Miller 'sick' and that was the tragic end of his career. Some years later, while chief executive of the Missions to Seamen at its AGM, he dropped dead in front of Princess Anne.

69   *The Cod War: Naval Operations off Iceland in Support of the British Fishing Industry (1958–76)* Vol BR1736(57) (1990). London: HMSO.

70   Capt MJF Rawlinson email 12 October 2024.

71   Cdr BA Raymond.

72   Cdr RD Sanderson email 14 September 2024.

73   Capt JE Dykes email 25 January 2023.

74   Ministers and Departments: England. The Civil Service Yearbook. London, England: HM Stationery Office. 1974, p 110.

75   Originally Their Lords Commissioners of the Admiralty (sometimes referred to as 'TL') had sat around the table in the Admiralty board room, with its Grinley Gibbons carvings, its wind vane, and its pull-down charts of the world's oceans, to hear letters read to them from admirals and captains around the globe, to reach a consensus, and to issue orders by letter to individual ships often in distant seas.

76   RAdm Gwynedd 'Gwyn' Idris Pritchard, (1924–2012).

77    VAdm Sir John Cox, KCB (1928–2006): born in Peking, he first went to sea as a boy in a small rowboat, when he warned the British fleet of the seizure of British embassy property by pirates. This resulted in him receiving two reprimands for putting to sea without telling anyone where he was going, one from the Commander-in-Chief, China Station, the other from his mother.

78    Staveley did indeed briefly become FOF2 in October 1976, but in March 1977 he was relieved by RAdm Martin 'Whiskey' Wemyss and Staveley was translated to become FOCAS.

79    Cdr PJ Mosse email and attachments 4 March 2024.

80    Ibid.

81    FOST letter 3003/30/77.A of 8 July 1977.

82    Cdr RD Hunter email 20 November 2024.

83    Vincent (2024) op. cit.

84    Adm Sir Richard Fitch KCB (1929–1994).

85    VAdm Sir John Webster KCB (1932–2020) also landscapist and marine artist. See *Daily Telegraph* obituary 21 Oct 2020.

86    The Battle of Taranto: on the night of 11/12 November 1940, Swordfish torpedo-bombers of the Fleet Air Arm launched from the carrier *Illustrious* conducted the first airborne ship-to-ship naval attack in history.

87    Alex Marsh email 2 April 2024 and attached note.

88    Leach, H. (1993) *Endure no Makeshifts: Some Naval Recollections* (Leo Cooper).

89    Adm Sir David Hallifax KCB KCVO KBE (1927–92).

90    Other trials kit was a laser gun intended to blind enemy pilots, but this was never used.

91    RAdm JG Tolhurst CB (194–-….) email 26 September 2023.

92    Adm Sir John Brigstocke KCB (1945–2020). See Hore, Peter (2024) *Brigstocke, Sir John Richard (1945–2020), naval officer, ombudsman, and public servant.* Oxford Dictionary of National Biography.

93    Tolhurst op. cit.

94    Cdr TGH Gedge AFC email 26 April 2024.

95    Capt EM Hackett interview 17 October 2023.

96    Adm Sir Derek Reffell KCB (1928–2025).

97    Tolhurst op. cit.

98    *The Guardian*, '"I returned a changed man": Prince Andrew deletes Falklands war post', 2 April 2022.

99    VAdm Sir Paul Haddacks KCB (1946–….) email 18 April 2024.

100   Cdr Beresford 'Berry' V C Reeves, LVO (1945–2021), a brilliant navigator.

101   Capt David B N Mellis DSC (1915–2006) while navigator of HMS *Malcolm* in 1940 during the Dunkirk evacuations, Mellish rallied troops to the harbour by playing his bagpipes from *Malcolm*'s bridge: in retirement he would greet ships passing through

the Sound of Mull by playing from the ramparts of Duart castle where he was the Comptroller. See: Mellis, D.B.N. (2002) *Mostly from the Bridge*. Oban: Oban Print Shop.

102  LtCdr I Watson.

103  Admiral James Aloysius "Ace" Lyons (1927–2018)

104  Prime Minister Margaret Thatcher laid the keel of the first boat, HMS *Vanguard*, on 3 September 1986.

105  Sir Richard Mottram GCB (1946–….). In 1985 Mottram was a witness for the prosecution in the trial of Clive Ponting, under the Official Secrets Act, for passing information to Labour MP Tam Dalyell about the sinking of the Belgrano during the Falklands War. When asked whether answers to parliamentary questions should be truthful and not deliberately ambiguous or misleading, there was a silence before Mottram replied: "In highly charged political matters, one person's ambiguity may be another person's truth." Mottram was thought to be particularly antipathetic towards the Navy: popular rumour said that while an undergraduate at Keele a midshipman had stolen his girlfriend.

106  Operation CORPORATE 1982 – the carriage of nuclear weapons by the Task Group assembled for the Falklands campaign (PDF). CBRN Policy (Report). United Kingdom Ministry of Defence. Archived from the original (PDF) on 26 October 2012. All were relegated to theatre or tactical use and the presence of some of these warheads in ships in the South Atlantic during the Falklands War had been a potential source of embarrassment.

107  TNA DEFE 23/322 Future theatre nuclear weapons for the Royal Navy. Former file reference 2NDPUS/ATOMIC/2 PART 2.

108  Reagan, R. (1984) *Address to the Nation and Other Countries on United States–Soviet Relations, Ronald Reagan*. Available at: https://www.reaganlibrary.gov/archives/major-speeches-1964-1989/major-presidential-speeches-first-term-1981-1984

109  The Honourable Franklin C Miller (2012) The Scowcroft Group Independent Consultant. Available at: https://www.navyhistory.org/wp-content/uploads/2011/04/Miller-bio.pdf

110  The Chevaline project survived in secrecy through the administrations of Prime Ministers Harold Wilson (twice), Edward Heath, and James Callaghan until, in 1980, Margaret Thatcher thought that she could no longer hide the £1bn overspend.

111  Mackby, J. and Cornish, P. (2008) 'US–UK Nuclear Cooperation After 50 Years', *Center for Strategic & International Studies*.

112  *Reagan and Gorbachev: The Reykjavik Summit* (2018) *Atom Heritage Foundation*. Available at: https://ahf.nuclearmuseum.org/ahf/history/reagan-and-gorbachev-reykjavik-summit/

113  'NATO 49th Nuclear Planning Group Communique 22 October 1986' (1986). Available at: https://archives.nato.int/uploads/r/null/1/4/140970/PRESS_RELEASE_M_NPG_2_86_32_ENG.pdf

114   Sir Michael Pakenham, Head of Arms Control and Disarmament Department at the FCO, 1983–87. See: Kandiah, Michael D, and Gillian Staerch, editors. 'The British Response to SDI'. Centre for Contemporary History Oral History Programme, London, 2005.

115   Cdre A Menzies, interview 21 Nov 2023.

116   RAdm King became Naval Secretary in 1987: when he was shown his line on the flag plot sending him to Naples and was told by the then First Sa Lord, "that was that just in case he thought otherwise". He duly went to Italy in 1988, was promoted to vice admiral, made KBE and retired in 1991. By contrast, when RAdm Clare took up a similar appointment, as Director of Operational Management in the new Regional Command Allied Forces North Europe (AFNORTH) in Brunssum, Holland, also known as the 'Coal Mine', he found there were "no levers to pull" and resigned to become a museum director without waiting for any promotion or a knighthood. This may have been a miscalculation because his successor and next after Clare on the voting list for promotion to flag rank, RAdm Stanhope, made a good fist of this new NATO appointment, enjoyed rapid progress up the flag list, and became First Sea Lord. Another consequence was that the third officer on the voting list, the submariner RAdm McClement, became ACNS even though he had very little experience of the workings of the MoD. Menzies op. cit.

117   Capt MC Gordon Lennox. See *Daily Telegraph* obituary 15 Feb 2025.

118   Cdr SC Fraser email 24 May 2023.

119   The British Nore Command was abolished in 1961 and the responsibilities and functions transferred to the Flag Officer, Scotland in 1961. Commander Northern Subarea was subordinate through CINCEASTLANT to SACLANT.

120   The earliest report of this letter, with embellishments, is found Tucker, Jedediah Stephens. 'Article X Naval Biography: Memoirs of Admiral the Early of St Vincent'. *Monthly Review*, 1844, p 71. The next version, with a slightly different spin occurs in Mahan, Alfred T. 'Admiral the Earl of St. Vincent'. *The Atlantic*, March 1893.

121   Capt JA Roberts MBE.

122   Cdre CJ Childs.

123   Cdre AW Netherclift OBE.

124   VAdm Sir Toby Frere KBE (1938 2000). See Daily Telegraph obituary 9 April 2020.

125   Alan Kenneth Mackenzie Clark (1928–99) Conservative MP, author, diarist, and military historian, including *The Donkeys* (1961), which inspired the musical satire *Oh, What a Lovely War!* In 1989 Clark was Minister of Defence Procurement and must have been a nightmare to the Defence Secretary, Tom King, as it was known that he had a private line to Prime Minister Margaret Thatcher.

126   Stephen, G.M. (1991) *The Fighting Admirals: British Admirals of the Second World War* (Leo Cooper). Even though cued by Cunningham's former flag lieutenant, Hugh Lee, who sent Jock a copy of his vitriolic letter to Stephen, Jock wisely forbore to join in any attack. Stephen finished his teaching career as High Master of St Paul's School, London. His book, and his judgement, which was so out of kilter with others, is largely forgotten.

127 Croft, Dorman, Rees and Uttley, Britain and Defence 1945–2000, 2001 A brief guide to previous British defence reviews.

128 Slater, JCK, *Fleet Support Newsletter* no 1, Jun 1990.

129 To name but a few: NMS = New Management Strategy, MONITOR = an asset management study, ILS Integrated Logistics Support, OASIS = Onboard Automated Stores Information System, LFA = a consultancy looking at the Logistics Functional Area, AFSUP90 = a review of Afloat Support, FEC = Fleet Effectiveness Committee, NLSC = Naval Logistic Support Concept.

130 Committee of Public Accounts (1990) *Vol 42, Ministry of Defence: Fleet Maintenance.* London: HMSO.

131 Slater, JCK, *Fleet Support Newsletter* no 2, December 1990.

132 Bond, Peter, *The Third Century 1904–2004: 300 Years of British Gibraltar, 1704–2004.*

133 Laughton Mathews, Vera, *Blue Tapestry*, Hollis & Carter, 1949. See also: Hore, P. (2021) *Bletchley Park's Secret Source: Churchill's Wrens and the Y Service in World War II* (London: Greenhill Books).

134 Sherit, K. (2020) *Women on the Front Line: British Servicewomen's Path to Combat* (Amberley). In the late 1980s women began to receive training in small arms and were allowed to carry weapons for guarding and self-defence purposes. See also: Sherit, K. (2013) The integration of women into the Royal Navy and the Royal Air Force, Post-World War II to the mid-1990s, thesis. King's College London (University of London).

135 The legal changes were the Equal Pay Act (1970), the Employment Protection Act (1975), and the Sex Discrimination Act (1975).

136 Winton, John (1984) *The Good Ship Venus* (Michael Joseph). John Winton was the pen name of LtCdr John Pratt (1931–2001), an engineer officer who served in the Korean War and the Suez Crisis. While still serving he wrote the comic novel *We Joined the Navy* (1959), introducing the character of the 'Artful Bodger'. A dozen other novels and more than a score of popular histories including a biography of 'ABC' Cunningham (1998) followed. Winton was naval obituarist at the *Daily Telegraph* for fourteen years until his death.

137 Adm Sir Michael Livesay KCB (1936–2003), Director of Naval Warfare during the Falklands War when he developed rules of engagement, Flag Officer Sea Training in 1984, Assistant Chief of the Naval Staff in 1986, Flag Officer Scotland and Northern Ireland in 1989, and Second Sea Lord in 1991–92.

138 Sherit op. cit.

139 Admiral Alan West, Baron West of Spithead, GCB, DSC, PC (1948–….) First Sea Lord and Chief of the Naval Staff 2002–06 and Parliamentary Under Secretary of State at the Home Office with responsibility for security and a security advisor to Prime Minister Gordon Brown 2007–10. Interview 14 December 2021 and emails 17 December 2021.

140 Denise St Aubyn Hubbard (1924–2016) Japanese translator at Bletchley Park, represented Britain at high diving in the 1948 Olympics, was the only female skipper in the Royal Naval Auxiliary Service for eight years, and in 1988, aged 64, became the oldest woman to sail single-handed across the Atlantic. See book *In at the Deep End* (1993). See *Daily Telegraph* obituary 12 February 2016.

141   The five non-combatants were the survey ships HMS *Hecla* and HMS *Roebuck*; the offshore patrol vessel HMS *Shetland*; the seabed operations vessel HMS *Challenger*; and the frigate HMS *Juno*, then used as a day-running navigation training ship.

142   Sherit op. cit.

143   Archibald Gavin Hamilton, Baron Hamilton of Epsom, (1941–….) Parliamentary Private Secretary to Prime Minister Margaret Thatcher 1987–88 and Minister of State for the Armed Forces 1988–93.

144   Rear-Admiral Roy AG Clare (1950–….) emails 1 August 2024 et seq.

145   NMRN Oral History Collection: Lord Hamilton of Epsom interviewed by Katy Elliott, 4 July 2006, accession number 2006.65, track 3 and track 6. Hamilton was similarly unimpressed by the Army's proposals in a paper of November 1988 called Manning and Recruitment in the Lean Years of the Nineties i.e. MARILYN, which made limited proposals for the wider employment of the Women Royal Army Corps.

146   Wilkinson, N. (2020) *Life on the Boundary* (Exeter: Short Run Press).

147   Wilkinson op. cit.

148   Adm Sir Brian Brown (1934–2020) was promoted to rear-admiral and appointed Director-General Naval Personnel Services in 1986, retitled Director-General Naval Manpower and Training later that year, promoted to vice-admiral in 1988, and was Second Sea Lord and Chief of Naval Personnel 1988–91. Enjoyed an early career as a helicopter pilot and was only the second supply officer to reach 4-star rank.

149   In the group ships were also included "one or two T22 frigates … [which] would increase the early availability of a significant number of billets in the surface fleet for WRNS". Questions about women as divers and aircrew in submarines and in RFAs were raised and discussed inconclusively.

150   VAdm PA Dunt CB (1947–2020) email 23 August 2017. See *Daily Telegraph* obituary 5 November 2020. An engineer, Captain JA Marshall MVO, was appointed to lead WSSIT. By May 1991 WSSIT handed its responsibility for integration to DWRNS, Chief Officer/ Commander Rosie Wilson.

151   AF Sir Ben Bathurst GCB (1936–2025). Bathurst, B.D. and Tyrie, N. (2004) 'Bathurst, David Benjamin (Oral history)', *Imperial War Museum*. Available at: https://www.iwm. org.uk/collections/item/object/80024679. See Daily Telegraph obituary 13 October 2025.

152   Captain Pippa Duncan became the Chief Naval Officer for Woman in 1997.

153   Later, the incorporation of senior female officers onto the captains' plot allowed the better management of their careers and prospects, and would in 2004 allow the gifted Carolyn Stait, who had started her naval career as a Third Officer, WRNS to become a Commodore, RN (OF6) and to command HMS *Neptune*, the Clyde submarine base. When First Sea Lord Oswald was asked how long it would take before there was the 'First Sea Lady' he replied that it had taken him 40 odd years; by contrast, RAdm Terry, who became the Navy's first female admiral in 2022, was commissioned as a lieutenant in 1997.

154     Behind the scenes there was a silly spat about houses. On moving down from London to Portsmouth, Robin Ross, as CGRM, would become the senior 3-star officer in the area and expected to live in 9 The Parade, which after Admiralty House was the second grandest residence in the dockyard, where the Admiral Superintendent had lived. Jock supported this move but some senior naval officers chose to be upset, particularly when the house was renamed Mountbatten House. As another Royal Marines officer remarked: "There were lots of issues to deal with and this need not have been one of them!"

155     London Gazette 6 April 2001: "The Queen has been graciously pleased to approve the following award in recognition of gallant and distinguished services during operations in Sierra Leone during the period 2nd to 12th May 2000: Queen's Gallantry Medal: Major Philip James Conyers Ashby, Royal Marines."

156     VAdm Sir Roy Newman KCB (1936–….) interview 22 March 2023.

157     Haddacks op. cit.

158     RAdm TM Karsten email 12 July 2023.

159     LtCdr MS McBain MBE, who was featured in an MoD press release that read: "Royal Navy officer rises up the Pink List: a Royal Navy officer has been voted the 51st most influential figure in the UK gay and lesbian community, eclipsing such household figures as Lord Mandelson and Gok Wan."

160     ACM Sir Patrick Hine GCB GBE (1932–….) Joint Commander British Forces Gulf War (1991).

161     AM Sir Ian David Macfadyen KCVO CB OB (1942–….) Chief of Staff, Headquarters British Forces Middle East and later Commander of British Forces 1990–91.

162     Cdre CJS Craig CB DSC. See: Craig, C. (1995) *Call for Fire: Sea Combat in the Falklands and the Gulf War*. (London: John Murray).

163     Capt PCB Canter CBE (….–2006) commanded HMS *Active* in the Falklands War.

164     MRAF Sir Peter Harding GCB (1933–2021) Chief of Defence Staff 1992–94.

165     Their titles varied: First Naval Lord until 1904, First Sea Lord and Chief of Naval Staff from 1917, Chief of the Imperial General Staff 1909–1964.

166     Previously, Dickson had been Chief of the Air Staff (1953–56) and was the second former naval officer to hold the appointment. The first was Air Vice Marshal Sir Frederick Sykes, CAS in 1918–19.

167     Hill, R. (2000) *Lewin of Greenwich: The Authorised Biography of Admiral of the Fleet Lord Lewin* (London: Cassell).

168     Gen Sir John Waters GCB CBE (1935–2025). See *Daily Telegraph* obituary 4 March 2025 "Waters could be quite fierce. He had no time for bluffers or shirkers …"

169     Sir Malcolm Rifkind KCMG (1946–….). Zoom call and email 4 March 2024.

170     Gen Sir Richard Shirreff KCB CBE (1955–….). Telephone interview 23 June 2022. See also: Guthrie, Charles (2022), *Peace, War and Whitehall* p 196 (Oxford: Osprey Publishing).

171     Harding. See *Daily Telegraph* obituary 22 August 2021 and *The Times* obituary 22 August 2021.

## ENDNOTES

172  Private information.

173  Sir Antony Buck (1928–2003) Tory MP and Under Secretary for the Navy 1982–84. See *Daily Telegraph* obituary 11 October 2003.

174  Sokolow, B. and Crofts, A. (1996) *The Making of a Modern Mistress* (London: Smith Gryphon).

175  The author heard about this while working in the MoD and others must have known too.

176  Esnal, M. 'Qué fue de Bienvenida Pérez, la mujer que "estafó" a un jefe del Ejército', *El Español*, 19 May 2019.

177  *The Times*, 'Defence Chief Resigns Over Affair with Wife of Ex-Minister', 15 March 1994

178  Macintyre, D. 'RAF chief apologises to ministers: Speech on cuts "was not intended as a personal slur". Donald Macintyre reports', *The Independent*, 10 November 1993.

179  K Rose (1924–2014). Rose, Kenneth. *Who Loses, Who Wins: The Journals of Kenneth Rose: Volume Two 1979–2014* (Journals of Kenneth Rose 2) (Orion), edited by D.R. Thorpe. Two volumes were published in 2018 and 2019. A review in The Spectator by Philip Ziegler said: "He was, of course, a snob — nobody could write a social column in the Sunday Telegraph for more than 50 years without some snobbish instincts — but he was an intelligent one, singularly well informed, and capable from time to time of administering a sharp bite to the noble hands that fed him his material." See Daily Telegraph obituary 29 January 2014.

180  Rifkind op. cit.

181  AM Sir John Walker (1936–2025) See *Daily Telegraph* obituary 13 February 2025. 'Defence intelligence chief who teamed up with former Thatcher adviser David Hart to deliver a bombshell review of RAF spending, estimated to save up to £3 billion'.

182  ACM Sir Michael Graydon GCB CBE (1938–….) telephone interview 17 July 2023. See also Graydon, Michael James oral history at IWM. https://www.iwm.org.uk/collections/item/object/80024680

183  Grant, E. (1995) 'The Naval Dental Services – Present, past and future', *Journal of the Royal Naval Medical Service*, 81.

184  Admiral Jacques Lanxade (1934–….), former French Navy chief, co-author of a proposed reform of NATO, chief of staff to President Mitterand 1989–91, chief of defence of the French armed forces 1991–95.

185  RAdm S Moore CB (1946–….) emails 15 November 2021 et seq.

186  Admiral Harold 'Betty' Raynsford Stark USN (1880–1972),Chief of Naval Operations 1939–42 and Commander, US Naval Forces, Europe (COMNAVEUR) 1942–45.

187  Bergman Rosamond, A. (2000). *BALTBAT: The emergence of a common defence dimension to Nordic co-operation* (pp 1–27). Copenhagen Peace Research Institute (COPRI).

188  VAdm Sir Jeremy Blackham, KCB (1943–….) commanded HMShips *Beachampton*, *Ashanti*, *Nottingham* and *Ark Royal*. Director of the Royal Navy Staff College, Director of Naval Plans, Chief of Staff to CNH, Director-General of Naval Personnel Strategy, Assistant Chief of the Naval Staff, Deputy Commander-in-Chief Fleet and Deputy Chief of the Defence Staff (Equipment Capability) 1999–2002. Editor of *The Naval Review* 2003–….

189  Commodore PJ Tribe (1944-….)

190  Commodore AJG Miller CBE (1952-….) who survived the sinking of HMS *Coventry* during the Falklands War..

191  Keith Michael Patrick O'Brien (1938–2018) Archbishop of St Andrews and Edinburgh 1985–2013, Cardinal in 2003: though he called homosexuality "moral degradation" he resigned in 2015 after allegations that he had engaged in inappropriate and predatory sexual conduct with priests and seminarians under his jurisdiction.

192  The Channel Committee consisted of the chiefs of naval staff of Belgium, the Netherlands, and the United Kingdom and served as an advisory and consultative body to the Commander-in-Chief, Channel.

193  Commander LSG Hulme email 22 April 2025 et seq.

194  TNA ADM 186/66 Naval War Manual (1925) formerly CB 973. See also ADM 1/20470 Revision of Naval War Manual 1946–1948, and ADM 234/590 Naval War Manual (1961 reprint).

195  Corbett, J.S. (1905) *Fighting instructions: 1530–1813: with elucidations from contemporary authorities Vol 29* (London: Navy Records Society).

196  Corbett, J.S. (1908) *Signals and instructions 1776–1794: with addenda to vol. 29 Vol 35* (London: Navy Records Society).

197  Corbett, J.S. (1911) *Some Principles of Maritime Strategy* (London: Longmans, Green).

198  Armstrong, Benjamin 'BJ', 'Mahan Versus Corbett in Width, Depth, and Context', *Military Strategy Magazine*, Volume 7, Issue 4, winter 2022, pp 16–21.

199  For a full discussion of this see Corbett, J.S. (1988) *Some Principles of Maritime Strategy Vol Classics of Sea Power*. Edited by E. Grove (Annapolis: US Naval Institute Press).

200  Roskill, S. (1968) *Naval Policy between the Wars: 1 The Period of Anglo-American Antagonism 1919–1929* (2 vols), pp 535–37 (London: Collins).

201  TNA ADM 239/261 Fighting Instructions (1939) formerly CB 04027(39). See HMS Hood Association-Battle Cruiser Hood: References & Research materials- ADM 239/261- (C.B.04027) the fighting instructions (1939). Available at https://www. hmshood.org.uk/reference/official/adm239/adm239-261_Intro.html

202  Mäder, M. (2004) *In Pursuit of Conceptual Excellence: The Evolution of British Military-Strategic Doctrine in The Post-Cold War Era, 1989–2002* (Bern/Lausanne: Peter Lang Publishing). Brigadier General Markus Mäder visiting fellow at the Centre for Defence Studies at King's College London 2001–03.

203  Design for Military Operations – The British Military Doctrine (Army Code 71451). Prepared under the Direction of the Chief of the General Staff. London: HMSO, 1989;

Design for Military Operations – The British Military Doctrine (Army Code 71451). Prepared under the Direction of the Chief of the General Staff. Upavon: DGD&D, 2nd Edition, 1996. URL http://www.army.mod.uk/linked_files/bmd.pdf

204 Air Power Doctrine (AP 3000). Prepared under the Direction of the Chief of the Air Staff. London: Royal Air Force, 1991.

205 Mäder op. cit.

206 Vice Admiral John McAnally, CB, LVO (1945–….).

207 Adm Sir Jock Slater (1993), 'A fleet for the 90s', *RUSI Journal*, 138:1.

208 McAnally email 21 December 2024.

209 No minutes of this seminar have been identified.

210 See Mäder op.cit, also Codner, M. (2025) 'Strategy, Doctrine, Policy and Concepts for Force Development', in *Maritime Strategy for Medium Powers in the 21st Century*. Forthcoming.

211 Foreword by Admiral Sir Jock Slater in *The Fundamentals of British Maritime Doctrine* (BR 1806), 1st Ed.

212 There were four Heads of Defence Studies (Royal Navy), Captain GASC Wilson 1987–92, Captain CLW Page 1992–96, Captain PG Hore 1997–2000, and Captain SC Jermy 2000– until the post was disestablished. Each was given a wide remit to liaise between the defence, academic, and NGO communities, to help develop naval strategy and concepts, and to promote the 'naval case'.

213 Codner, M. (2025) 'Strategy, Doctrine, Policy and Concepts for Force Development', in *Maritime Strategy for Medium Powers in the 21st Century*. Forthcoming.

214 Churchill and Beatty had first met in their twenties, when Beatty was commanding a river gunboat, *Fateh*, on the Nile and Churchill was an officer in Beatty's father's old regiment, the 4tth Hussars. During the Anglo-Egyptian conquest of Sudan, Beatty had ascended the cataracts of the Nile in a gunboat, equipped with a case of champagne, and it was with this nectar that the two men sealed their friendship during the Fashoda Crisis of 1898. Churchill and Beatty were both touching their forties when Beatty entered Churchill's room in the Admiralty and after Churchill exclaimed, "You seem very young to be an admiral," Beatty quipped, "And you seem very young to be First Lord."

215 Vice Admiral Sir Fabian Malbon, KBE (1946–2026).

216 NAVSEC 6/4/3 of 12 Oct 1982.

217 AF Sir Michael Pollock GCB LVO DSC (1916–2006), gunnery officer of the heavy cruiser HMS *Norfolk*, was awarded the DSC during the Battle of the North Cape on Boxing Day 1943 against the German battleship *Scharnhorst*.

218 RAdm AJ 'Jock' Miller (1926–86), see footnote 68.

219 Adm Sir 'Jim' Eberle, GCB (1927–2018) Commander-in-Chief Fleet (1979–81), Commander-in-Chief Naval Home Command (1981–82), and later Director of the Royal Institute for International Affairs. See *Daily Telegraph* obituary 20 May 2018.

220 Adm Sir Michael Layard KCB CBE (1936–….) Second Sea Lord 1992–95.

221 *A Strategy for the Future Officer Corps of the Royal Navy & the Royal Marines*, Officers Study Group Report D/OSG/5/l/2 dated 31 March 1993. VAdm Sir Michael Layard chaired the study and the senior officers who assisted were JV Burke esq, Capt AW Netherclift OBE and Capt RC Moore.

222 Until 1958 there had been commodores first and second class, the former dressing as rear-admirals and the latter as wearing a single broad stripe with a curl above it.

223 Cdre B Burns CBE, Naval Assistant to the Naval Sectary 1992–2001. Jock was his third First Sea Lord. Interviews 3 January and 5 December 2023.

224 Sullivan, F. (1976) 'The Naval Schoolmaster during the Eighteenth Century and the Early Nineteenth Century', *Mariner's Mirror*, 92(4), pp 311–326. See also: Nixon, J. and Rose, M. (2019) 'The Instructor Officer Specialisation of the Royal Navy and its Trainees', Royal Navy Instructor Officers' Association.

225 LtGen Sir Robert Fulton KBE KStJ (1948–….) Commandant General Royal Marines 1998–2001.

226 LtGen Sir Henry Beverley KCB OBE (1935–….) Commandant General Royal Marines 1990–94 email 3 January 2024. MajGen DAS Pennefather CB OBE (1945–….) Commandant General Royal Marines emails 7 January 2024 and attachment et seq. LtCol GA Gelder (….–….) email 10 January 2024 and attachment. Jock's revolution would lead in 2025 to the appointment of General Sir Gwyn Jenkins as the first Royal Marines officer to be First Sea Lord and Chief of Naval Staff.

227 In August 1996 White was following up a telephone call from Jock with what he called "a non-letter after a non-conversation". He and Jock thought then that Jock might relieve Inge as CDS in the spring of 1997.

228 It would be unfortunate that the brainy Abbott and the wily Guthrie did not make a good team.

229 Menzies op. cit.

230 Hore (2018) op. cit. p 140.

231 Brigstocke remained bitter and put his feelings in writing to the First Sea Lord in December 1997, and, dissatisfied, complained from retirement. As late as the summer of 2000 Jock was obliged to comment on a formal representation by Brigstocke.

232 Lustig-Prean, D. (1999) 'People Are Discharged for One Private Aspect of their Private Lives, not for any Misconduct', *RUSI Journal*, 144(3), pp 90–92.

233 Lustig-Prean email 30 July 2024.

234 Sherit, K. (2013) The integration of women into the Royal Navy and the Royal Air Force, Post-World War II to the mid 1990s, thesis. King's College London (University of London).

235 West email 1 August 2024.

236 Terrill, Christopher (1995) *HMS Brilliant: In a Ship's Company.* (London: BBC Books).

237 *Daily Mail* 3 November 1995.

238 *Sunday Telegraph* 31 December 1995.

239  ACM Sir Richard Johns GCB KCVO CBE (1939–….) interview 8 August 2023.

240  Parker, P. (2024) *Some Men in London: Queer Life, 1960–1967*. (London: Penguin Books).

241  FM Charles Guthrie, Baron Guthrie of Craigiebank GCB GCVO OBE (1938–2025) interview 14 December 2023.

242  Nicholas Soames Baron Soames of Fletching, interview 14 November 2023.

243  RAdm S Moore email 15 November 2021 et seq.

244  Adm Sir Nigel Essenhigh emails 31 May 2024 et seq.

245  Bathurst op. cit.

246  Rifkind op. cit. Rifkind became Foreign Secretary in July 1995: the appointment of White to Gibraltar was an interim appointment and part of a wider FCO plot to place a professional diplomat as governor.

247  Bett, M. (1995) 'Independent Review of the Armed Forces' Manpower, Career, and Remuneration Structures: Managing People in Tomorrow's Armed Forces', HM Stationery Office. Conducted by Sir Michael Bett into the services' pay. Etc. and which made significant recommendations regarding rank structures, pay, pensions, housing, and broader conditions of service within the military.

248  *Sunday Times* 29 January 1995 Profile 'Steering a steady course to the top'.

249  Soames op. cit. Earl Howe Zoom call 10 November 2022.

250  Rose op. cit.

251  Adm Sir Mark Stanhope email 26 August 2022. There was "No reference to loss of credibility due carrier arguments in the MoD at the time etc!"

252  The Anchorites is an informal dining club that has met since 1919 for five or six dinners a year, with a maritime guest speaker: the dinners offer a networking opportunity for members and their guests.

253  Presumably a reference to proposed sale of Admiralty Arch, a small part of which was the official residence the First Sea Lord. Jock's chances of resisting this proposal were spoiled when Hill-Norton, entered the row over the disposal of the MoD's historic buildings and called the Secretary of State, Portillo, "a little creep". Jock and Portillo exchanged good natured, hand-written letters, Jock hastening to distance himself from Hill-Norton and Portillo replying, "it was very kind of you to write such a generous note, I appreciate it very much."

254  PREM 19/5949 Records of the Prime Minister's Office: Correspondence and Papers, 1979–1997 Meetings with the Chiefs of Staff, and other papers in the author's collection.

255  Rose op. cit.

256  Johnstone-Bryden R. (2003) *The Royal Yacht Britannia: The Official History*. (London: Conway Maritime).

257  Effingham, Earl of. "HMY 'Britannia.'" *HMY "Britannia" (Hansard, 10 December 1996)*, 1996, api.parliament.uk/historic-hansard/lords/1996/dec/10/hmy-britannia. Effingham also reminded the House of Lords of *Britannia*'s singular action evacuating about 1,000 people from Aden in 1986. Instead of the 6,000-tons *Britannia*, the 16,000-

tons SS *Uganda* was taken up from trade and converted to a hospital ship, and the 2,800-tons hydrographic survey ships HMSs *Hecla*, *Herald*, and *Hydra* were converted for use as ambulance ships.

258 Johnstone-Bryden op. cit.

259 Johnstone-Bryden op. cit.

260 Hamilton, Archie. 'Royal Yacht Britannia'. *Royal Yacht Britannia (Hansard, 1 February 1993)*, 1993, api.parliament.uk/historic-hansard/written-answers/1993/feb/01/royal-yacht-britannia

261 PREM 13/2355 HM The Queen's suggestion that the use of the royal yacht should be discussed in connection with the country's economic difficulties 1968 Jan 01–1968 Sep 30.

262 Johnstone-Bryden op. cit.

263 PREM 16/267355 Suggestion that the royal yacht be taken out of service as part of implementation of Defence Review proposals 1974 Nov 19 – 1974 Dec 03, and Hampshire, E. (2024) *The Royal Navy in the Cold War Years 1996–90*, pp 371–2, 377, 392, 426, 428 (Barnsley: Seaforth Publishing).

264 *Herald of Free Enterprise* was a roll-on/roll-off ferry that capsized as she was leaving Zeebrugge on the night of 6 March 1987, killing 193 passengers and crew.

265 'Gen. Schwarzkopf, Sir, Is Knighted by Queen'. *Los Angeles Times*, 21 May 1991 www.latimes.com/archives/la-xpm-1991-05-21-mn-2419-story.html. Presumably when HM Queen visited Tampa, Fl in *Britannia*

266 DEFE 69/1784 Royal Yacht Britannia Project 96: SR(S) [Staff Requirement (Sea)] 7089 the replacement Royal Yacht; use as a hospital ship; 1991/92 refit discussions 1990 Aug 29 – 1991 Sept 9.

267 DEFE 69/1782 Royal Yacht Britannia concept design study: SR(S) (Staff Requirement (Sea)) 7089 the replacement Royal Yacht; 1991/92 refit project initiation submission; Royal Yacht as a Defence Support Agency status concept; Royal Yacht Programming.

268 DEFE 69/1782 Royal Yacht Britannia concept design study: SR(S) (Staff Requirement (Sea)) 7089 the replacement Royal Yacht; 1991/92 refit project initiation submission; Royal Yacht as a Defence Support Agency status concept; Royal Yacht Programming.

269 Bathurst op.cit, and email 5 January 2025 et seq.

270 Evans, Michael, 'Britannia to Be Sold or Scrapped', *The Times*, 24 June 1994.

271 Maldwin Drummond OBE (1932–2017) orchestrated a quixotic project, known as Future Ship Project 21, for a new national flagship which could be used as a royal yacht or for trade missions and sail training, successfully obtaining promises of several millions of pounds for the project. See PREM-19-6241-2 f 50 Maldwin Drummond to Cabinet Secretary Sir Robin Butler 1 February 1996. See also *Daily Telegraph* obituary 10 April 2017.

272 Evans, Michael, 'Queen May Share New Britannia', *The Times*, 2 October 1995.

273 Michael Evans won the Desmond Wettern Media Award (now called The Desmond Wettern Award for Best Journalism) in 1997 after a voting lobby strongly supported

within the Royal Navy.


274    PREM-19-6241-2 f 105 Records of the Prime Minister's Office.

275    PREM-19-6241-2 ff 76-104 Cabinet Office to SoS for Defence 12 Dec 1995.

276    PREM-19-6241-2 ff 55-6.

277    Ibid. f 36.

278    Ashbourne, Lord. "HMY 'Britannia'". *HMY "Britannia" (Hansard, 10 December 1996)*, 1996, api.parliament.uk/historic-hansard/lords/1996/dec/10/hmy-britannia

279    PREM-19-6241-2 f 38 Draft Statement on a Replacement Royal Yacht Q&A Material and PREM-19-6241-2 f 42 ibid.

280    PREM-19-6241-2 pp 25–6.

281    PREM-19-6241-2 f 24 12 March 1996.

282    PREM-19-6241-1 see for example ff 105, 99.

283    PREM-19-6241-1 ff 63-71 and PREM-19-6241-1 ff 72-3 11 December 1996.

284    PREM-19-6241-1 f 38 Cabinet Secretary to Prime Minster 20 January 1997.

285    PREM-19-6241-1 ff 27-9.

286    Major, John Roy (2000) *John Major: The Autobiography*, pp 635–36 (HarperCollins).

287    PREM-19-6241-1 ff 27-9 Alex Allan PS/PM to Mark Gibson PS/Deputy Prime Minister 21 Jan 97 and PREM-19-6241-1 ff 55-6 PS/PM to PS/DPM 19 Dec 95 and f 23 Margaret Aldred/PS MoD to PPS/PM 22 January 1997. Portillo Zoom call.

288    RAdm AJ Rix CB (1956–....) interview 13 December 2022.

289    PREM-19-6241-2 f 13 Government Chief Whip to Prime Minister 16 February 1996. See also Purves, Libby, 'Is This the New Britannia?' *The Times*, 3 February 1996, and PREM-19-6241-1 ff 64-5 Defence Secretary Michael Portillo to Prime Minster 19 December 1996.

290    Portillo, Michael. 'Statement on the Royal Yacht'. *House of Commons – Hansard – UK Parliament*, 22 Jan. 1997, hansard.parliament.uk/Commons/1997-01-22

291    USNIP March 1996.

292    Slater, J. (1996) 'The Commanders Respond', US Naval Institute Proceedings, 122(3).

293    Project Horizon was the Anglo-French Future Frigate or AFFF, briefly became the France-UK-Italian frigate or FUKIT before the tri-national project was dissolved. Steel for the first Type 45, HMS *Daring*, was not cut until 2003.

294    Two assault ships HMS *Albion* and *Bulwark* were ordered on 18 July 1996.

295    Slater, J. (1997) 'The Commanders Respond', *US Naval Institute Proceedings*, 123(3).

296    Gordon, A. (1986) *The Rules of the Game: Jutland and British Naval Command* (London: John Murray).

297    Barker, N. (1997) *Beyond Endurance: An Epic of Whitehall and the South Atlantic Conflict*. (Barnsley: Pen & Sword).

298    Greenwich had been the Navy's university since 1893, was home to the school of naval architecture, the war college, the staff college, and, since 1959, Jason, a small nuclear

reactor. Distinguished professors of mathematics, mechanics, physics, and history had included Bernard Haigh, John Knox Laughton, Bryan Ranft, and Geoff Till.

299  Pocock, T. (1996) *A Thirst for Glory: The Life of Admiral Sir Sidney Smith* (London: Aurum), and Rodger, N.A.M. (1997) *The Safeguard of the Sea: A Naval History of Britain, 660–1649* (London: Harper Collins).

300  Guy Hudson's education at Oxford had been interrupted in 1940 when he was commissioned into the RNVR and served in motor torpedo boats in the Mediterranean and the Channel, and was awarded a DSC for operations during the Normandy landings. Hudson did not return to Oxford but became a solicitor and died in Devon in 1995, leaving a generous bequest to further the education of officers of the Royal Navy and Royal Marines at the university.

301  Hardman, Robert (2011) *Our Queen* (London: Hutchinson).

302  Cook, Margaret (1999) *A Slight and Delicate Creature: The Memoirs of Margaret Cook*, p260 (Weidenfeld & Nicolson).

303  Campbell, Alastair, and Richard Stott (2007) *The Blair Years: Extracts from the Alastair Campbell Diaries*. p 218 (Hutchinson). Campbell wrote: "I knew he would."

304  Morrow, interview 14 January 2025.

305  Pierce, Andrew, 'Royal Talks That Salvaged Britannia', *The Times*, 4 August 1997.

306  Watkins, Emma, 'Last Post for Captain's Brass Trumpet', *The Times*, 4 August 1997.

307  Mandelson, Peter, 'Britannia Saved from the Scrapyard', *BBC News* 1997 www.bbc. co.uk/news/special/politics97/news/08/0803/yacht.shtml

308  Bevins, Anthony, 'Brown Confirms End for Royal Yacht', *The Independent*, 28 September 1997.

309  Clarke, Kenneth (2017) *Kind of Blue: A Political Memoir*, pp 322–23 (Pan Books).

310  Prichard, John. *1997 Future Royal Yacht Design Brochure*. AD/BIS/RY(F)/ 1 7/3, 1997.

311  Irving Thomas Stuttaford, OBE (1931–2018), Conservative MP 1970–74, medical correspondent of *The Times* 1981–2009, columnist of *The Oldie* 1994–2018; parodied in *Private Eye* as 'Dr Thomas Utterfraud".

312  On 17 February *Invincible* was able to declare a step change in capability of joint UK maritime air power: two GR7s started flying with thermal imaging airborne laser designation (TIALD) pods enabling them to attack targets in Iraq without land-based or US Navy laser designation.

313  *Invincible* letter 226/03 of 16 March 1998.

314  Earlier versions of the RAF's Harrier were built by Hawker Siddeley. Another aircraft in the Harrier family was the McDonnell Douglas (now Boeing) Harrier AV-8 operated by the United States Marine Corps (USMC), the Italian, Spanish, and Thai navies. The only overseas sale of the FA2 was to India.

315  Cunningham, A. and Slater, J. (2022) *A Sailor's Odyssey: The Autobiography of Admiral of the Fleet Viscount Cunningham of Hyndhope*, pp 317, 406–7 (Seaforth). For a fuller discussion of this issue see Hore, P. (2018) *Henry Harwood: Hero of the River Plate*, PP 144–46 (Barnsley: Seaforth).

316   Johns op. cit.

317   Adm Sir James Burnell-Nugent KCB CBE (1949–….). Burnell-Nugent, J. (1998) HMS *Invincible* and operation Bolton – A modern capability for a modern crisis. *RUSI Journal*, 143(4), 19–26. https://doi.org/10.1080/03071849808446282

318   AM Sir Timothy Jenner KCB (1945–….) Zoom call 28 September 2021.

319   Admiral Jay Johnson USN email 24 February 2023 et seq. In the sidelines, Johnson expressed American misgivings about there being a French naval cell at Northwood, and Jock reassured him that its purpose was to deconflict submarine activities and that was all. So, Johnson was surprised that the captain of the nuclear deterrent boat HMS *Victorious* was a Commander Didier Lombard. Jock hastened to reassure Johnson that Lombard was as English as they came.

320   NAVB/P97(9) *The Contribution of Maritime Forces to Joint Operations and their Wider Utility* see D/CNS 100/05 of 8 January 1998.

321   In 2006 the RAF would take No 3 Group headquarters as a savings measure and merge its functions into RAF No 2 Group.

322   Hastings email 4 May 2021 et seq.

323   Childs, N. (2014) *Britain's Future Navy* (Barnsley: Pen & Sword Maritime).

324   In a message to the Royal Navy, West would say "We must continue the shift in emphasis away from measuring strength in terms of hull numbers and towards the delivery of military effects… I am confident that these changes will leave the Navy better organised and equipped to face the challenges of the future."

325   *The Independent* 10 April 1998.

326   BBC Thursday, 9 April, 1998, 16:02 GMT 17:02 UK.

327   Jock proudly noted that Orcadian John Elphinstone was another of the British officers lent to the Empress Catherine II to reform the Russian navy.

328   Annie's personal interpreter was Karen Pearce.

329   Robert Avery email 24 January 2025. See: Fields, David, and Robert Avery (2025) *The Royal and Russian Navies: Cooperation, Competition and Confrontation* (Manchester University). Also, Grove, Eric, 'The Inside Story of FRUKUS', *Warships International Fleet Review*, 2010. See Daily Telegraph obituary 4 September 2025.

330   For which Jock had provided a foreword.

331   Cdre BAL Goldman email 1 September 2023 et seq.

332   Rydeman, J. (2013) *The Divine Sea: Navigational Recollections from Lee County Jail* . Jack Rydeman is the pseudonym of LtCdr Peter F Payne.

333   Prosopagnosia is the medical term for face blindness: Jock belonged to that small proportion of the population <1% who are super-recognisers who can memorise and recall faces, often having seen them only once.

334   Slater, J., Harrold, J., and Pearce, M. (2016) 'Dartmouth Oral History Project', *Britannia Museum*.

335   Michael Vlasto email 21 April 2025.

336   Max Hastings email 24 September 2021.

# Bibliography


Baker, R. (1977) *Dry Ginger: The Biography of Admiral of the Fleet Sir Michael Le Fanu* (W H Allen).

Barker, N. (1997) *Beyond Endurance: An Epic of Whitehall and the South Atlantic Conflict*. (Barnsley: Pen & Sword).

Bower, T. (2016) *Broken Vows: Tony Blair, the Tragedy of Power* (London: Faber & Faber).

Brooke-Holland, L., Mills, C., and Walker, N. (2023) *A Brief Guide to previous British Defence Reviews*. Available at: https://researchbriefings.files.parliament.uk/documents/CBP-7313/CBP-7313.pdf

Campbell, A. and Stott, R. (2007) *The Blair Years: Extracts from the Alastair Campbell Diaries* (London: Hutchinson).

Childs, N. (2009) *Age of Invincible: The Ship that Defined the Modern Royal Navy*. (Barnsley: Pen & Sword Maritime).

Childs, N. (2014) *Britain's Future Navy* (Barnsley: Pen & Sword Maritime).

Clarke, K. (2017) *Kind of blue: A political memoir* (Pan Books).

Cook, M. (1999) *A Slight and Delicate Creature: The Memoirs of Margaret Cook* (Weidenfeld & Nicolson).

Cooper, N. (2022) 'Ian McInnes - Orkney's Renaissance Man'.

Cunningham, A. and Slater, J. (2022) *A Sailor's Odyssey: The Autobiography of Admiral of the Fleet Viscount Cunningham of Hyndhope* (Seaforth).

Dutton, J. (2000) 'The Royal Marines Today', *RUSI Journal*, 145(4), pp 21–24. doi:10.1080/03071840008446547

Fields, David, and Avery, Robert (2025), *The Royal and Russian Navies: Cooperation, Competition and Confrontation: Cooperation, Competition and Confrontation* (Manchester University)

Gordon, A. (1986) *The Rules of the Game: Jutland and British Naval Command* (London: John Murray).

Graham, A. and Grove, E. (2011) *HMS Ark Royal: Zeal Does Not Rest 1981-2011* (Maritime Books).

Grant, A. (2024) *Sex, Spies and Sandal: The John Vassall Affair* (London: Biteback Publishing).

Grove, E. (ed.) (1997) *The Battle and the Breeze: The Naval Reminiscences of Admiral of the Fleet Sir Edward Ashmore* (RN Museum Publications).

Guthrie, C. (2021) *Peace, War and Whitehall* (Oxford: Osprey Publishing).

Hampshire, E. (2024) *The Royal Navy in the Cold War Years 1996-90* (Barnsley: Seaforth Publishing).

Hardman, R. (2011) *Our Queen* (Hutchinson).

Hardman, R. (2023) *Queen of our Times: The Life of Elizabeth II* (Pan Books).

Heathcote, T.A. (2012) *The British Field Marshals 1736-1997: A Biographical Dictionary*. (Barnsley: Pen & Sword Military).

Hennessy, P. (2010) *Secret State - Preparing for the Worst 1945–2010* (London: Penguin Books).

Hill, R. (2000) *Lewin of Greenwich: The Authorised Biography of Admiral of the Fleet Lord Lewin* (London: Cassell).

Hore, P. (2018) *Henry Harwood: Hero of the River Plate* (Barnsley: Seaforth).

Jackson, B. and Bramall, D. (1992) *The Chiefs: The Story of the United Kingdom Chiefs of Staff*. Brassey's.

John, R. (1987) *Caspar John* (Collins).

Johns, R.S. and Johns, R.S. (2018) *Bolts from the Blue: From Cold War Warrior to Chief of the Air Staff* (Grub Street).

Johnstone-Bryden, R. (2003) *The Royal Yacht Britannia: The Official History.* (London: Conway Maritime).

Johnstone-Bryden, R. (2015) *HMS Illustrious (V) 1982–2014: The Royal Navy's Longest Serving Aircraft Carrier* (Royal Navy Commissioning Books).

Kandiah, M.D. and Staerch, G. (eds.) (2005) 'The British Response to SDI'. Centre for Contemporary History Oral History Programme.

Kerr, J. (2017) *A Memoire* (self-published).

Leach, H. (1993) *Endure no Makeshifts: Some Naval Recollections* (Leo Cooper).

Lustig-Prean, D. (1999) 'People Are Discharged for One Private Aspect of their Private Lives, not for any Misconduct', *RUSI Journal*, 144(3), pp 90–92. doi:10.1080/03071849908446410

Mahan, A.T. (1893) 'Admiral the Earl of St. Vincent', *The Atlantic*, March.

Major, J.R. (2000) *John Major: The Autobiography* (Harper Collins).

Middleton, P. (2010) *Admiral Clanky Entertains* (Matador).

Ministry of Defence, C.P. (2012) 'Operation CORPORATE 1982 The carriage of nuclear weapons by the Task Group assembled for the Falklands campaign'.

Natzio, G. (1995) 'Homosexuality – can the Armed Services Survive It?', *RUSI Journal*,

140(6), pp 39–46. doi:10.1080/03071849508445971

Parker, P. (2024) *Some Men in London: Queer Life, 1960–1967* (London: Penguin Books).

Prichard, J. (1997) *1997 Future Royal Yacht Design Brochure*. AD/BIS/RY(F)/17/3.

Richards, G.S.D. (2014) *Taking Command: The Autobiography* (Headline).

Rifkind, M. (2016) *Power and Pragmatism: The Memoirs of Malcom Rifkind* (London: Biteback Publishing).

Roberts, A. (2008) *Masters and Commanders: How Roosevelt, Churchill, Marshall, and Alanbrooke Won the War in the West* (London: Allen Lane).

Rose, K. (2019) *Who Loses, Who Wins: The Journals of Kenneth Rose: Volume 2 1979–2014*. Edited by D.R. Thorpe (Orion Publishing Group).

Rydeman, J. (2013) *The Divine Sea: Navigational Recollections from Lee County Jail*. Jack Rydeman. Pseudonym of Peter Payne.

Sherit, Kathleen (2020) *Women on the Front Line: British Servicewomen's Path to Combat* (Gloucestershire: Amberley)

Sherit, Kathleen. (2013) *The Integration of Women into the Royal Navy and the Royal Air Force, Post-World War II to the Mid 1990s*. thesis. King's College London (University of London).

Simpson, M. (1999) *The Cunningham Papers: The Mediterranean Fleet, 1939–1942 Vol 1* (Ashgate).

Simpson, M. (2004) *A Life of Admiral of the Fleet Andrew Cunningham: A Twentieth-century Naval Leader* (Routledge).

Simpson, M. (2006) *The Cunningham Papers: The Triumph of Allied Sea Power 1942–1946 Vol 2* (Ashgate).

Slater, J. (1993) 'A Fleet for the 90s', *RUSI Journal*, 138(1), pp 8–20. doi:10.1080/03071849308445672

Slater, J. (1998) 'The Maritime Contribution to Joint Operations', *RUSI Journal*, 143(6), pp 20–24. doi:10.1080/03071849808446322.

Sokolow, B. and Crofts, A. (1996) *Bienvenida: The Making of a Modern Mistress* (London: Smith Gryphon).

Stocker, J. (2004) *Britain and Ballistic Missile Defence, 1942-2002* (London: Frank Cass).

Thompson, J. (2000) 'The Royal Marines and Amphibious Operations in the 20th Century', *RUSI Journal*, 145(4), pp 15–20.

Tucker, J.S. (1844) 'Article X Naval Biography: Memoirs of Admiral the Early of St Vincent', *Monthly Review*, p 71.

Vincent, D. (2024) *The Forgotten General: Sir Alan Cunningham GCMG, KCB, DSO, MC* (Amberley Publishing).

Warner, O. (1967) *Admiral of the Fleet Cunningham of Hyndhope: The Battle for the Mediterranean* (John Murray).

Watkins, E. (1997) 'Last Post for Captain's Brass Trumpet', *The Times*, 4 August.

Watson, B. (2005) *Commander-in-Chief: A Celebration of the Life of the Admiral of the Fleet Lord Fieldhouse of Gosport*. Royal Navy Submarine Museum.

Winton, J. (1998) *Cunningham: The Greatest Admiral since Nelson* (John Murray).

Ziegler, P. (1985) *Mountbatten: The Official Biography* (London: Collins).


# Index of principal people, ships and selected subjects in the text

# INDEX OF PRINCIPAL PEOPLE, SHIPS AND SELECTED SUBJECTS IN THE TEXT

# Timeline

| Year | Rank | Appointment | Event/where |
|---|---|---|---|
| 1956 | **Cadet &** | BRNC, Dartmouth | Sword of honour, |
| 1957 | **Midshipman** | | Queen's telescope |
| 1958 | | | |
| 1959 | **Sub-Lieutenant** | HMS *Troubridge* | West Indies |
| 1960 | **Lieutenant** | HMS *Yaxham* | Portland trials ship |
| 1961 | | HMY *Britannia* | Season officer |
| 1962 | | HMS *Cassandra* | Far East |
| 1963 | | Royal Naval College, Greenwich | Lieutenant's Course |
| 1964 | | | |
| 1965 | | HMS *Soberton* | First Lieutenant/In command |
| 1966 | | HMS *Dryad* | Long Navigation Course |
| 1967 | | HMS *Victorious* | Far East |
| 1968 | | HMS *Scarborough* | Dartmouth Training Squadron |
| 1969 | **Lieutenant-Commander** | Equerry to HM the Queen | MVO (later LVO) |
| 1970 | | | |
| 1971 | | | |
| 1972 | **Commander** | HMS *Jupiter* | In command, Second Cod War |
| 1973 | | | |
| 1974 | | Directorate of Naval Operations & Trade | Third Cod War |
| 1975 | | | |

| Year | Rank | Appointment | Notes |
|---|---|---|---|
| 1976 | **Captain** | HMS *Kent* | In command |
| 1977 | | | |
| 1978 | | Royal College of Defence Studies | |
| 1979 | | Directorate of Naval Warfare | Prime Minister Margaret Thatcher |
| 1980 | | | Armilla Patrol begins |
| 1981 | | HMS *Illustrious* | In command, John Nott Review |
| 1982 | | | Falklands War |
| 1983 | | | |
| 1984 | | HMS *Dryad*/SMOPS | In command |
| 1985 | **Rear-Admiral** | Assistant Chief of Defence Staff (Policy & Nuclear) | |
| 1986 | | | |
| 1987 | **Vice-Admiral** | Flag Officer Scotland & Northern Ireland | COMNORLANT, COMNORECHAN NBC Rosyth |
| 1988 | | | KCB |
| 1989 | | Chief of Fleet Support | First Gulf War, |
| 1990 | | | Options for Change |
| 1991 | **Admiral** | Commander in Chief Fleet | CINCHAN, CINCEASTLANT Prime Minister John Major Bosnian War |
| 1992 | | | |
| 1993 | | Vice Chief of Defence Staff | Defence Costs Study/ |
| 1994 | | | Front Line First Bett Review |
| 1995 | | | GCB |
| | | First Sea Lord | Prime Minister Tony Blair Strategic Defence Review |
| 1996 | | | |
| 1997 | | | |
| 1998 | | | |
| 1999 | | Remains on the Active List | |

Main Appointments thereafter: non-executive director of Vosper Thorneycroft and Lockheed Martin (UK), Elder Brother Trinity House, Prime Warden Shipwrights Company, Chairman of the Imperial War Museum, Chairman of the RNLI, Deputy Lieutenant of Hampshire.